Isaac the Syrian's *Spiritual Works*

Texts from Christian Late Antiquity

45

Series Editor

George Anton Kiraz

TeCLA (Texts from Christian Late Antiquity) is a series presenting ancient Christian texts both in their original languages and with accompanying contemporary English translations.

Isaac the Syrian's *Spiritual Works*

Edited and Translated by
Mary T. Hansbury

gorgias press
2016

Gorgias Press LLC, 954 River Road, Piscataway, NJ, 08854, USA

www.gorgiaspress.com

Copyright © 2016 by Gorgias Press LLC

All rights reserved under International and Pan-American Copyright Conventions. No part of this publication may be reproduced, stored in a retrieval system or transmitted in any form or by any means, electronic, mechanical, photocopying, recording, scanning or otherwise without the prior written permission of Gorgias Press LLC.

2016

ISBN 978-1-4632-0593-5   ISSN 1935-6846

Library of Congress Cataloging-in-Publication Data

Names: Isaac, Bishop of Nineveh, active 7th
century, author. | Hansbury,
  Mary, editor, translator. | Isaac, Bishop of
Nineveh, active 7th century.
  Works. Selections. | Isaac, Bishop of Nineveh,
active 7th century. Works.
  Selections. English.
Title: Isaac the Syrian's spiritual works
       / edited and
  translated by Mary Hansbury.
Description: Piscataway, NJ : Gorgias Press, 2016.
| Series: Texts from late
  Christian antiquity, ISSN 1935-6846 ; 45 | In
English and Syriac; with
  English text translated from Syriac. | Includes
bibliographical references.
Identifiers: LCCN 2016027996 | ISBN 9781463205935
Subjects: LCSH: Spiritual life. | Prayer.
Classification: LCC BR65.I652 E6 2016 | DDC
248.8/9--dc23
LC record available at
https://lccn.loc.gov/2016027996

Printed in the United States of America

TABLE OF CONTENTS

Table of Contents v
Isaac the Syrian: *The Third Part* 1
    Preface 1
    Context 2
    Sub-text 2
    Outline 4
    Text and Translation – Isaac the Syrian: *The Third Part* 8
        Chapter I 8
        Chapter II 26
        Chapter III 32
        Chapter IV 58
        Chapter V 78
        Chapter VI 92
        Chapter VII 130
        Chapter VIII 162
        Chapter IX 178
        Chapter X 200
        Chapter XI 236
        Chapter XII 260
        Chapter XIII 292
        Chapter XVI 312
    Biblical References 316
    Some Key Concepts 322
    Abbreviations 324
    Bibliography of Works Cited 325
        Ancient Authors and Translations 325
        Modern Works 331

Two Discourses of the *Fifth Part* of Isaac the Syrian's Writings...339
    Introduction 339
    Conclusion..345
    Bibliography 347
    Text and Translation – From the *Fifth Part* of Mar
        Isaac, bishop of Nineveh..350

ISAAC THE SYRIAN: *THE THIRD PART*

PREFACE

Little is known of Isaac's life. Only two brief references give details.[1]

Both agree that Isaac was a native of Beth Qaṭraye. It is then noted that he became a monk and teacher near his home. Catholicos Giwargis consecrated him as bishop of Nineveh (*ca.* 676). Soon Isaac asked to resign and he lived as a solitary in Beth Huzaye, in the mountains of Khuzistan. He studied Scripture so much that he became blind and had to dictate his writings, which explains certain difficulties of his style. He died at an advanced age and was buried at Rabban Shabur.

This translation of Isaac III is based on one recent manuscript conserved in Tehran, Issayi Collection, ms 5. Of the 133 folios, 111 are by Isaac, or 17 texts. Of these 14 had not previously been known: 1–13, 16. Two others may be found in Is.I: 14 and 15 appearing as 22 and 40. And 17 corresponds to 25 in Is.II. These three chapters have not been included in this translation.[2]

As to the content of Is.III, it seems more concentrated. Concepts already found in Is.I and Is.II are found here. But rather than expansion, there is clarification of important themes already found in Is.I and Is.II. As noted by Chialà, the first theme here is prayer and intimacy with God in 1–IV, VIII–IX, and XVI. Whereas God's infinite love for creation is found in V–VI and IX. In VII

---

[1] J.B. Chabot, "Le Livre de la chasteté, composé par Jésusdenah, Evêque de Basrah," in *Mélanges d'Archéologie et d'histoire* 16 (1986), 277–78; I.E. Rahmani, *Studia Syriaca* (Lebanon: Charfet Seminary, 1904), p.33.

[2] For a more detailed analysis of the manuscript see S. Chialà *CSCO* 246, VIII–XXIII. And see S. Brock *CSCO* 224, XXXI–XXXII.

and X there are texts of prayers. In XII and XIII are letters sent to solitaries in difficulty.

CONTEXT

According to Paolo Bettiolo, the major influences on Isaac are Theodore of Mopsuestia, Evagrius and John the Solitary. In addition to the many citations of Theodore, Bettiolo notes how much of Isaac's structure derives from Theodore, including: two worlds, this world and the world to come; the first as pedagogy of the second, and the world as school; angelology; human mortality and salvation history; even Isaac's Christological terminology, though more evangelical in tone than Theodore.[3]

As to Evagrius, Bettiolo sees in addition to the numerous direct quotations of Evagrius, his role as guide in the discernment of experiences of contemplation and as master of pure prayer.

Finally there is the influence of John the Solitary in Isaac, seen in the development of the three stages of the life of the soul as well as a sense of "new world" and all that it implies. And hope is fundamental to John the Solitary's eschatology, a gift from God transcending human initiation, based on the resurrection of Christ and the grace of baptism. It has been said that John the Solitary derives this from Theodore of Mopsuestia.[4]

SUB-TEXT

But perhaps the most striking influence on Isaac, at least in this manuscript, is Scripture. It is reading (*qeryanâ*) which generates continual prayer (IX.12) and of course it is the reading of Scripture which is intended. Reading is for prayer (IX.3). Reading is meditation and prayer (IX.11). Prayer without reading is weak (IX.15). In addition there are very many citations and allusions to Scripture in this manuscript making it seem almost like a sub-text.

Writing about Dadisho‘, a contemporary of Isaac who also originated from Beth Qaṭraye and later lived in the same monastery

---

[3] P. Bettiolo, *Isacco di Ninive, Discorsi Spirituali e altri opusculi* (Bose: Edizioni Qiqajon, 1989), 35–39.

[4] J.-M. Lera, "Theodore de Mopsuestia," *DSpir* XV (1991), 385–400.

of Rabban Shabur as did Isaac, Bettiolo examines the anthropological dimension of *qeryanâ* and how it leads to purity of heart and to the vision of the spiritual meaning hidden in Scripture and in nature. Bettiolo alludes to Evagrian influence as he sketches this itinerary in Dadishoʿ, of how one is led by *qeryana* to personal integrity and to the light of the Trinity.[5]

As mentioned there is Evagrian influence in Isaac. And according to Columba Stewart, exegesis was everything for Evagrius. "It was not about finding suitable garnish for his theological speculations or merely an aspect of monastic pedagogy. It was a mode of being, a keying himself into texts recited by heart day in and day out. He wrote that monastic life means 'knocking on the doors of Scripture with the hands of the virtues'." (*Thoughts* 43)[6]

Finally, John the Solitary drew his inspiration entirely from Scripture. I. Hausherr who has written extensively about him says it was a major influence on him and Hausherr had found only one non-Biblical reference in all of John the Solitary's writings: Ignatius of Antioch.[7]

Some recent scholarship has looked at the influence of Evagrius on Isaac in trying to track key concepts like pure prayer.[8] In conclusion, it reflects on how the shift from a Neoplatonic Evagrian approach to what one finds in Isaac might have occurred. I think the shift occurs through Scripture in that while Evagrius is notable for his use of Scripture, Isaac surpasses him.

So I have included with the kind agreement of Sabino Chialà, all the citations and allusions to Scripture, for this reason. Also included are many notes from the *CSCO*. These help to offset ques-

---

[5] P. Bettiolo, "Esegesi e purezza di cuore. La testimonianza di Dadišoʼ Qatraya (VII sec.), nestoriano e solitario," *ASE* 3 (11986), 201–13.

[6] C. Stewart, "Imageless Prayer in Evagrius Ponticus," *JECS* 9 (2001), 199–201.

[7] It is quite possible that some references to other authors had been deleted from his work in an effort to sanitize his writings of "heretical influences."

[8] See B. Bitton-Ashkelony, "The Limit of the Mind (ΝΟΥΣ): Pure Prayer according to Evagrius Ponticus and Isaac of Nineveh," *ZAC* 15 (2011), 291–321.

tions of authorship of Isaac III, since they demonstrate so many connections to Isaac I and Isaac II, as well as giving insight into the text. Only references that I could access personally are included. One could consult the *CSCO* text and profit from many more references.[9]

Great gratitude is also due for the scholarship of Paolo Bettiolo, Sebastian Brock and André Louff – how helpful this has been.[10]

To conclude with a quote from Isaac:

> We should consider the labor of reading Scripture to be something extremely elevated, whose importance cannot be exaggerated. For it serves as the gate by which the intellect enters into the divine mysteries and takes strength for attaining luminosity in prayer: it bathes with enjoyment as it wanders over the acts of God's dispensation which have taken place for the benefit of humanity – acts which make us stand continually in wonder, and from which meditation too takes strength, this being the first-fruits of this mode of life about which we are talking: from these acts prayer is illumined and strengthened. (Is.II XXI.13)

OUTLINE

I	*Discourse on the solitary life and on the figure of the future realities which are depicted in it by those who hold to it truly; and on the comparison <found> there with the way of life after the resurrection.*	p. 8
II	*Concerning the order of the body when we are alone, and concerning the modesty of the exterior parts of the body.*	p. 26
III	*Of the same Mar Isaac. On prayer: how it binds our*	p. 32

---

[9] S. Chialà, *Isacco di Ninive. Terza Collezione* CSCO 246–247 (Louvain: Peeters, 2011).

[10] For the use of the Syriac text, thanks are due to CSCO (Peeters), and to Andrea Schmidt (Louvain) for her assistance in negotiating the process.

	mind to God and causes it to cleave to the meditation in it; and how by means of the excellent stirrings which are in it the mind is strong against the love for this world from which <come> the passions.	
IV	*Of the same Mar Isaac. Second discourse on prayer: what is the exact prayer which happens according to the perfection of the mind.*	p. 58
V	*Of the same Mar Isaac. On the creation and on God.*	p. 78
VI	*Of the same Mar Isaac. The purpose of exhortation in agreement with the foregoing <account>: concerning the sweetness of divine judgment and the intention of His providence.*	p. 92
VII	*By the same Mar Isaac. Prayer impelled by the insights of the things which were said. For there is in <prayer> a great signification, from time to time at prayer one turns to contemplate it, then again turns back to prayer. And in the noble passion of the mind, one offers amazing stirrings for the sake of all these great things which are ours.*	p. 130
VIII	*Again of the same Mar Isaac. On how the saints are set apart and sanctified by the inhabiting of the Holy Spirit.*	p. 162
IX	*Of the same Mar Isaac. A synthesis of all kinds of labor concerning the part of the mind: what power and action belong to each one of them.*	p. 178
X	*Converse of prayer of the solitaries, composed with metrical speech and according to the limits of insight. Words which seize the heart and restrain from the distraction of earthly things. <Words> composed for the consolation of solitaries with which they converse at night, after the time of the office, that their body might be relieved of sleep.*	p. 200
XI	*Again of the same Mar Isaac. Concerning that: "you have been raised with Christ," as said by the divine*	p. 236

	Apostle; and concerning this divine sacrifice which the holy Church accomplishes for the living and the dead for the sake of the hope of what is to come: what is effected by this sacrifice and in a special way for a believing lay person because of the firmness of his hope.	
XII	*Again, a letter of exhortation by Mar Isaac concerning <how>solitary life can be affected <when lived> in the midst of others, which was sent to a monk who desired to be assured about this. The monk had written him concerning his thoughts, asking if there was in them any blame from God. <Isaac> exhorts to surrender oneself to the afflictions of this life, with a prompt intelligence which examines God's hidden reasons.*	p. 260
XIII	*Again, a letter on the abodes in which holy men enter by the stirrings existing in the mind, in the journey on the way to the house of God.*	p. 292
XVI	*Of the same.*	p. 312

Text and Translation –
Isaac the Syrian: *The Third Part*

Chapter I

Discourse on the solitary life and on the figure of the future realities which are depicted in it by those who hold to it truly; and on the comparison <found> there with the way of life after the resurrection.[1]

1   The life of solitaries[2] is higher than this world for their way of life is similar to that of the world to come;[3] namely they do not take wife or husband. Instead of this, face to face, they experience intimacy with God. By means of the true icon of the world beyond, they are always united to God in prayer. For prayer more than any other thing, draws the mind to fellowship with God and makes it shine in its ways.

---

[1] Way of life after the resurrection (*dubbârâ d-bâtar qyâmtâ*): Is.I 254; Is. II VIII.6; Is.III VI.54. See also John Sol. *Soul* 11, 56, 85–87, 89 and his *Letter on the Mystery of the New Life*, Rignell (1941) 3,10.

[2] Solitary (*îhîdâyâ*) or single one describes a solitary monk as opposed to one living in community. But the term goes beyond celibacy or eremitical life to indicate a unity within the solitary and his unity with God. In the N.T. *îhîdâyâ* is the Only Begotten Jesus Christ (Jn.1:14,18; 3:16,18; 1 Jn.4:9). And Aphrahat says of Christ: "the Only Begotten (*îhîdâyâ*) Who is from the bosom of his Father shall cause all solitaries (*îhîdâyê*) to rejoice," Demonstrations, 6:6. On the term in Aphrahat, see Koltun-Fromm, "Yokes of the Holy-Ones." Koonammakkal, "Ephrem's Ideas on Singleness." And see Griffith, "'Singles' in God's service."

[3] World to come (*'âlmâ da-'tîd*): Heb.2:5; 6:5. See Is.II V.15; XI.13; XIII.2; XXIX.11; XXXVI.1; XXXIX.8,21; XL.14. Found often in Is.I and in the *Keph.* See John Sol. *Soul* 9, 16, 89; see also Evag. Cent. II.26,73; III.65.

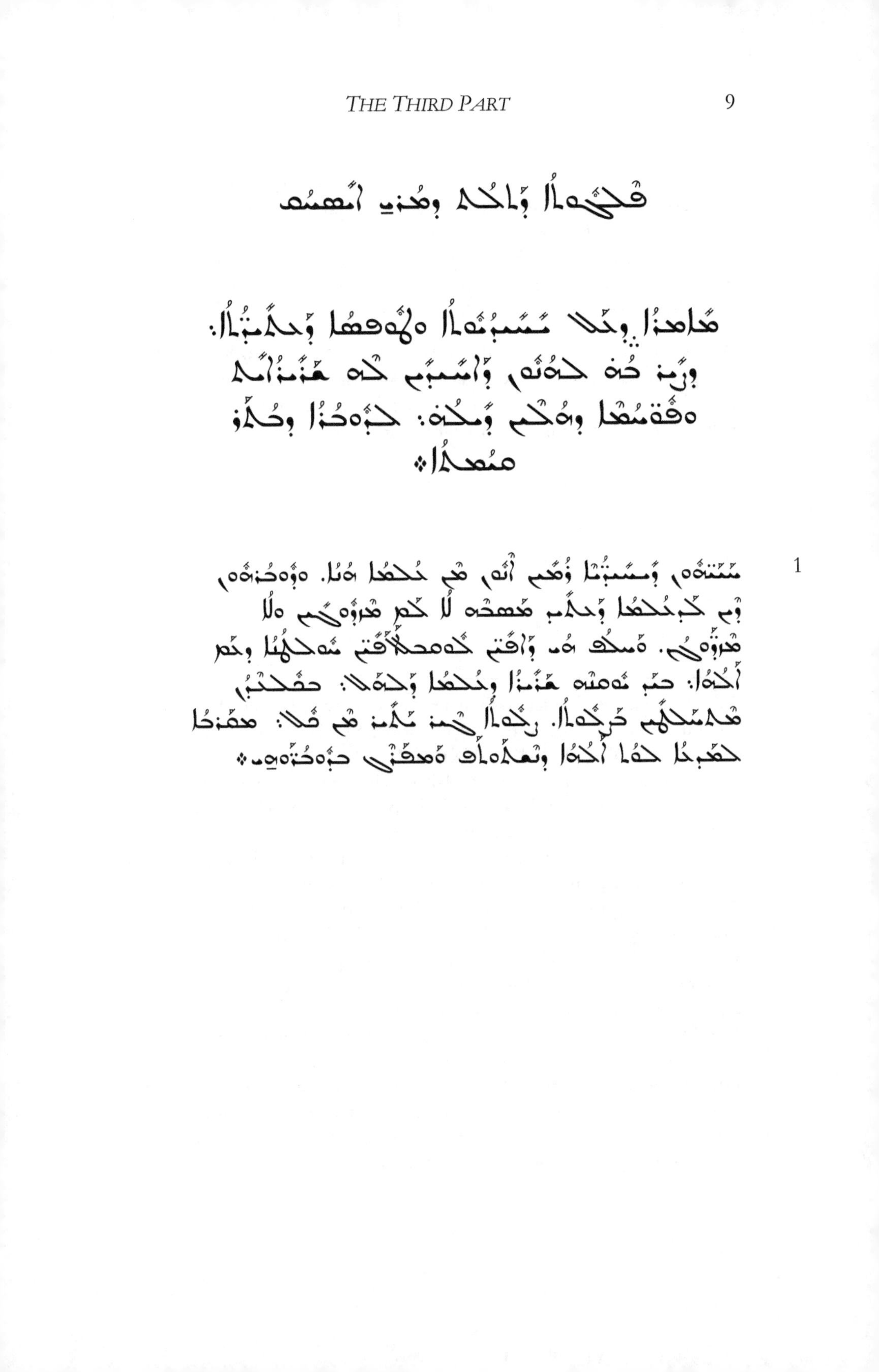

2   I also think that at the time of prayer our requests are usually granted us by those of former times, so that we might take refuge in the prayers of these excellent ones. Because of their uprightness and their good ways, which especially bring them to mind, also our prayer is purified from laxity or laziness or the distraction of thoughts, by their zeal[4] for what is excellent.

3   And even God, Lord of all,[5] how many times He condescends to our petitions because of this, so that we might be ever more ardent to imitate what is in them and so as to magnify in our eyes that excellent order which is so honorable for Him.

---

[4] Zeal (*tnânâ*): understood in a positive sense in Is.I 392–95. Whereas John the Solitary looks at the negative side, *Soul* 21–22. Is.II has both dimensions: IX.T; XVII.1–4; 9,10; XIX.I; XXI.10; XXXIX.19.

[5] Lord of all (*mârê-kul*): de Halleux cites this as a trace of the early Syriac creed in John Sol., see de Halleux, "Le Milieu Historique," 299–305; see also Connolly, "Early Syriac Creed." Connolly points to *mârê-kul* in Aphrahat and in the *Acts of Thomas* in his attempt to shed light on the Syriac Creed "before it came under the influence of the Nicene and post Nicene definitions." See Aphrahat I.19, II.19; Ephrem, *Hymns on Faith* (21 times), *Homily on Our Lord* VII; *Book of Steps* V,15, IX.1, XXI.7. An alternate translation of *mârê-kul* in Syriac literature is "Lord of the universe." This term as *ribbono shel ʿolam* is often found in the Jewish liturgy and in rabbinic literature. See the *Minor Tractates of the Talmud* 21, 40, 48 50, 98, 548. In *Midrash Tehillim* (a compilation containing material from as early as the 3rd cent. and according to Buber edited in the Talmudic period in Palestine), practically every psalm's commentary includes the invocation. See Buber, *Midrash Tehillim*. See also Braude, *Midrash on Psalms*. In the Jewish Prayer book, in the morning service, "King of the universe (*melekh ha ʿolam*) occurs 27 times. See also 2 Maccabees 7:9.

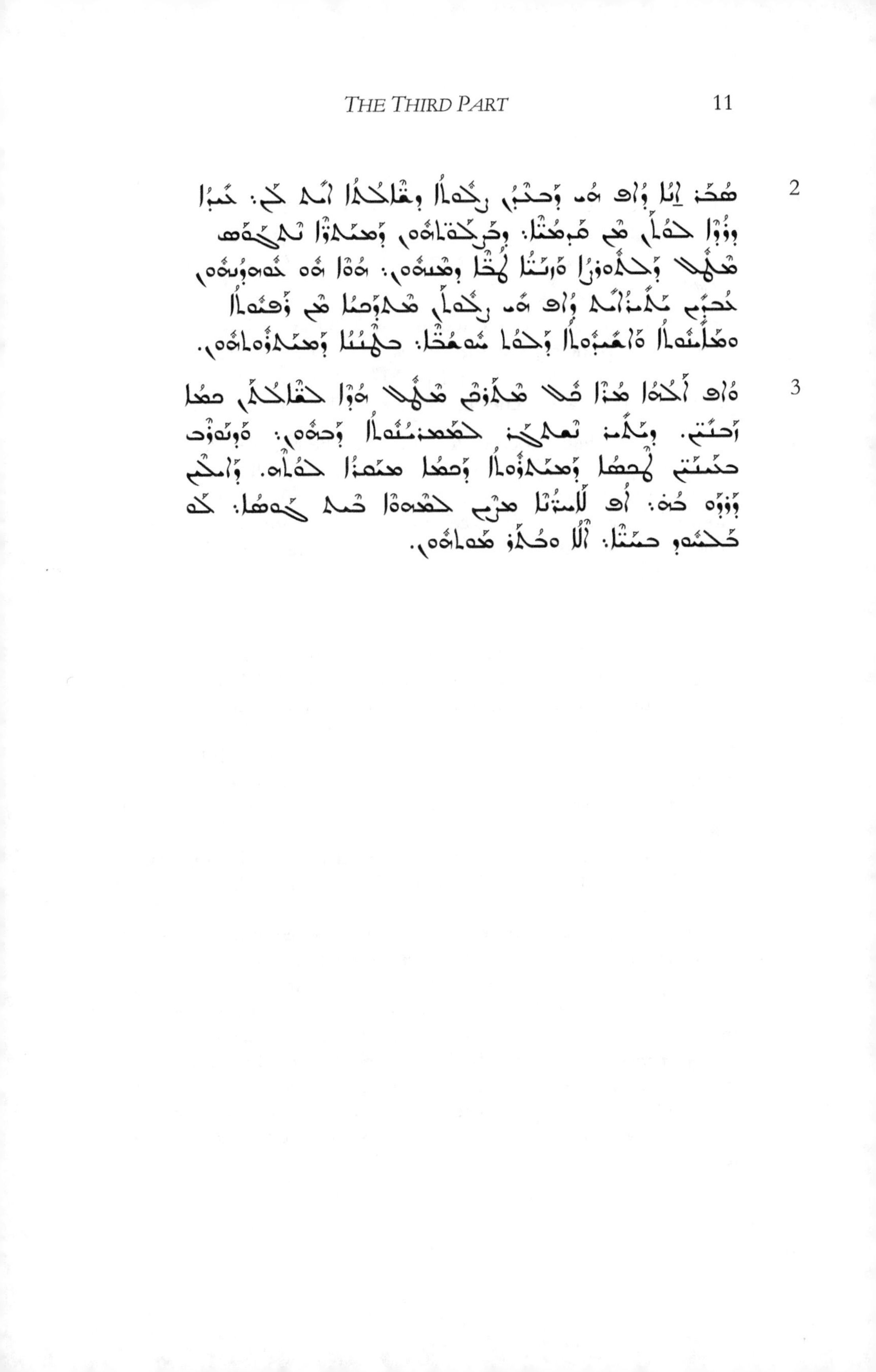

4   I say this according to the intention of the Scriptures. Because <God> does everything according to the intention ordained by Him, magnifying also His saints in this; as it is written: *I will overshadow this city, I will save it for my own sake and for the sake of my servant David.* [6]

5   These are the ways of converse <with God>.[7] Two of these concern the principles of the labors of the heart in stillness.[8] By these the mind is fortified and purified; it drives away sloth and yearns to remain at all times in converse with what is virtuous.

6   The <mind>, then, proceeds to set on fire the remembrance of the world which rules it but to be inflamed continually with the remembrance of good things. Thus it arrives at the limpidity[9] of the labor of the mind. Of this excellent labor, there are two other principles which remain of the signs from above: the principle toil and the excellent reflection.

---

[6] 2 Kgs.19:34; Is 37:35; cf. 2 Kgs.20:6. On "overshadow" see Brock, "Maggnânûtâ." For a slightly revised version, see Is.II XVI. See also Is.I 390–92. For a helpful survey, see Brock "From Annunciation to Pentecost." And see his "Passover, Annunciation and Epiclesis."

[7] Converse <with God> (‘*enyânâ d-alâhâ*): Sahdona I 111; Is. *Keph.* II 45; Is.I 548. In 7th cent. East Syrian writers ‘*enyânâ d-‘am alâhâ* is also found, see Shubhalmaran 1.IV.3. For other forms and examples, see Is.II XXX.1.

[8] Stillness (*šelyâ*): Sahdona (I 107) says that in the life of stillness (*šelyâ*) the "way of life after the resurrection" (*dubbârâ d-bâtar qyâmtâ*) is anticipated.

[9] Limpidity (*šapyûtâ*) or transparency of soul opens one to revelation and entry to the New World. There are two references to it in biblical writings: 4 Esdras 6:32 and Apoc. Baruch 66.1. In the 4th cent. the term occurs several times in Ephrem. In his *Hymns on the Nativity* 3.8, he refers the term to Christ. In the works of John Sol. one finds very frequent usage of *šapyûtâ*, see Lavenant, *Dialogues et Traités*. In the Introd. Lavenant notes a passage in John's writings where Christ is referred to as the model of limpidity. The term also occurs frequently in Isaac (see esp. Is.II VIII.15) as well as in Joseph Hazzaya. See Bunge, "Le 'lieu de la limpidité'."

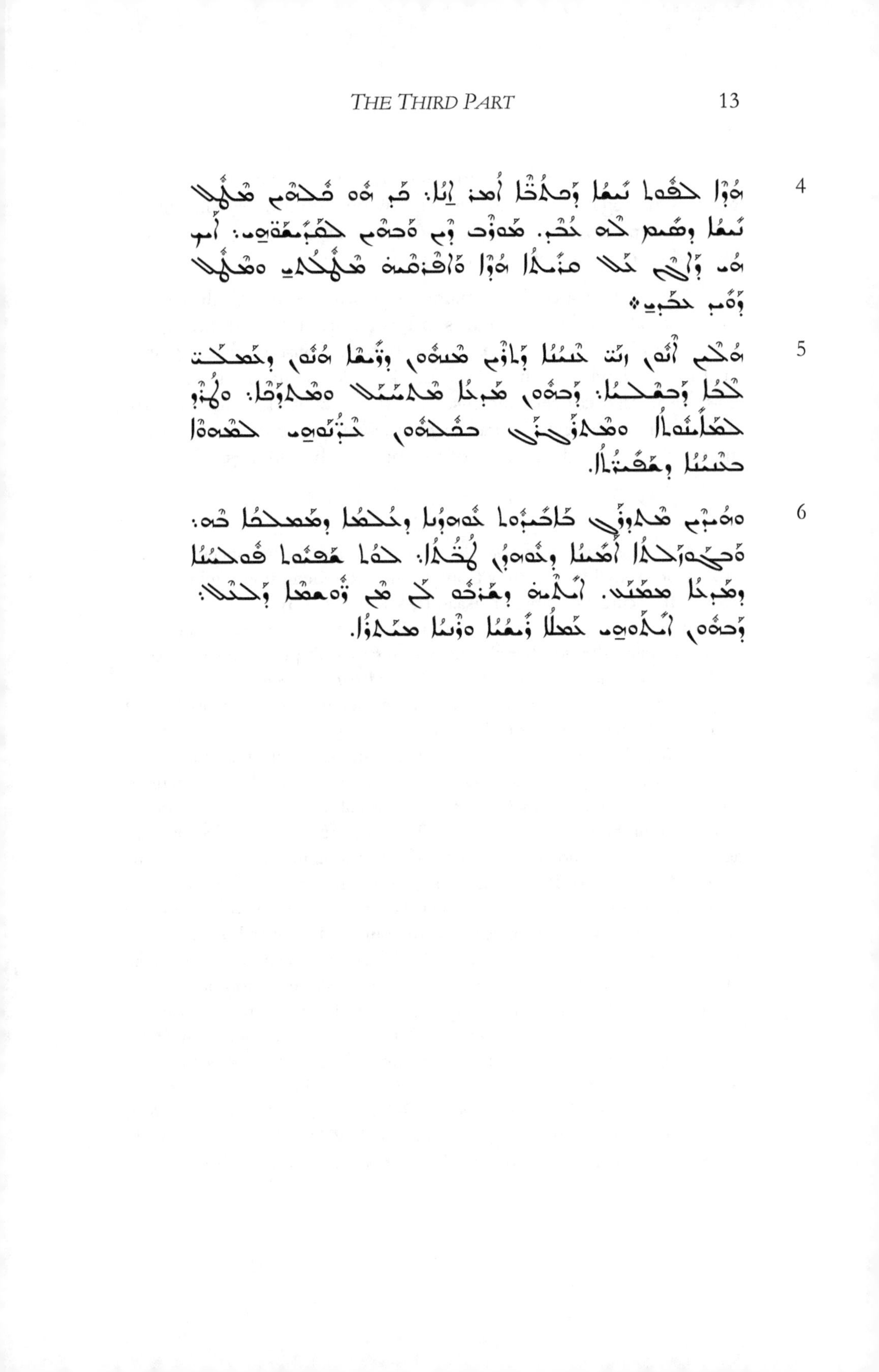

7   The first of the principles corresponds to inquiring into created realities and again marveling at the Divine Economy[10] <in our regard>, for mercy, or for our human nature at the end. On the other hand, the next principle is reflection.

8   Excellent is that one who remains alone with God: this draws him to continual wonder[11] at what is in His nature. His own intelligence is lifted up because from this time it becomes wise concerning spiritual things, having both an excellent knowledge and faith <in the> mysteries. Also concern increases for the new world[12] and care for future things, earnest meditation on these things and continual migration,[13] which is the journey of the mind to these things.

---

[10] Divine Economy (*mdabbrânûṯâ*) gr. *oikonomia*: it concerns divine providence for all of humanity from creation to redemption until the New World. It occurs frequently in Isaac II, see Index (*CSCO*). Already in the 5th cent. one sees the concept defined by Philoxenus of Mabbug, concerning episcopal administration but also his vision of God's providential workings for human salvation. See Michelson, "*Practice Leads to Theory*." Finally, see the analysis by Becker of Divine Pedagogy, including specific remarks about Isaac, see Becker, *Fear of God*, 22–40; 184–88.

[11] Wonder (*tehrâ*): ecstasy begins with astonishment or wonder (*tehrâ*) and may lead to helpless amazement or stupor (*temhâ*). *Tehrâ* sometimes indicates movement and *temhâ* the point of arrival where the spirit is without movement in the fulfillment of desire. The roots of wonder lie deep in Syriac tradition. Isaac quotes Theod. of Mop. that *tehrâ* in God is the "unique science," see Is.I 304. Ephrem is constantly amazed in wonder at the Incarnation and at the Eucharist, but also at the created world as both Scripture and the natural world are revelatory. In John of Dalyatha both *tehrâ* and *temhâ* occur frequently, (see the *Letters*), his use being even more symbolic than that of Ephrem, but they both see wonder as a revelation of the New World. See my " 'Insight without Sight'," and see Louf, "Temha-stupore."

[12] New world (*'alma ḥadtâ*): N.T. Mt.19:28; Odes of Solomon 33:12; Aphrahat, *Demonstrations* 12:2; Theod. of Mop. *WS* V 119; *Book of Steps* X.6, XV.4, IX.40, XXV.3, XXX.3; it occurs frequently in John Sol.: two discourses are dedicated to it. See Jacob of Serug, Bedjan (1906) Hom. 54.612; Bedjan (1902) Hom. 9.815. See also Is.II V.5; VII.2; VIII.4, 5,7; XIV.39; XV.8; XVI.6; XX.6; XXXVIII title. Found frequently in Isaac *Keph*.

_____

[13] Migration (šunāyâ): indicates the movement from earthly realities to the life in God. See Is.I 2: "No one is able to come near to God save only he who is far from the world. For I do not call separation the departure (šunāyâ) from the body, but from bodily things." In Evagrius there are four types of migration, the last being "with the Trinity," Cent. II.4.

9   Mysteries are revealed, worlds are transfigured in the mind and thoughts are altered within the flesh, <such that> it no longer seems like flesh. The mind changes abodes and is brought from one to another, not of its own will. In its course, however, it remains gathered and united to the Divine Essence; and the intellect[14] at the end of its course, turns to the first cause and origin. Thus the nature of rational beings observes the sublime order of God's love, by consideration of the <Divine Essence>.

10 All of this <occurs for the sake of rational beings even without persuading <God> by good intention. Nor will there be those who are heirs or who are made heirs,[15] for all will be gathered as one and remain quiet to marvel at a love as great as this. They will also be stirred up! For even one's way of life improves with this, since it is more diligent.

---

[14] Intellect (*hawnâ*): here "at the end of its course" may refer, according to Brock, to "the ladder of the intellect of which blessed Evagrius spoke, and the being raised up above all ordinary vision...", see Is.II XXXV.7. And see Evag. Cent. IV.43.

[15] Cf. Is.I 201; *Keph.* III 57, indicating that this happens without human mediation but by revelation.

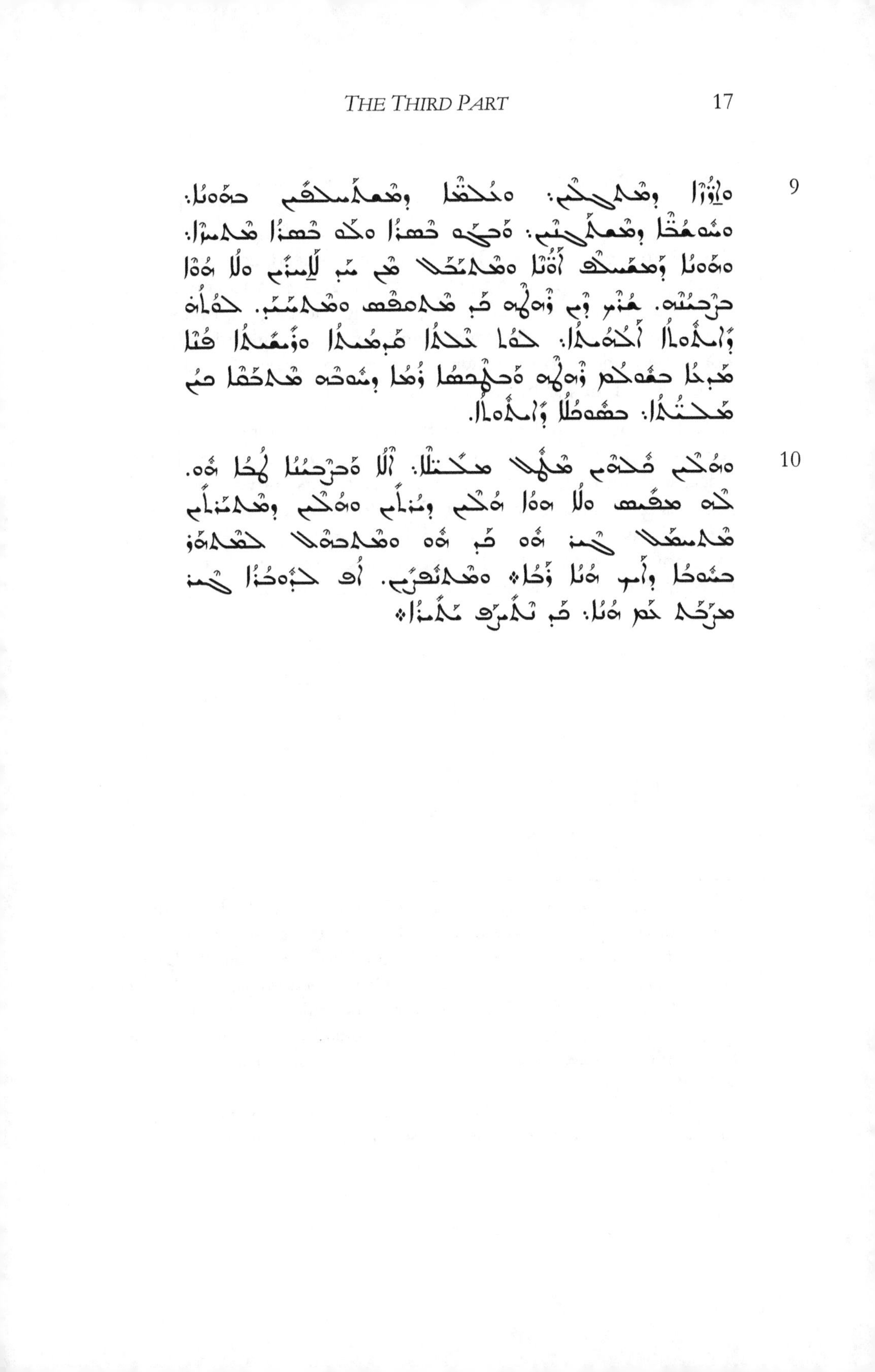

11 \<Because of\> converse \<with God\> and not working with any of the realities here below, the \<solitaries\> observe, as with the eyes of the soul,[16] that future way of life. They conform the things of this life to the life beyond. Because of this, indeed, converse ceases there and one is united to the One who is above word and silence. In this also they are careful now, causing the tongue, minister of the word, to cease \<speaking\>; and commanding with authority not to be anxious to speak without necessity, except for stirrings[17] in prayer and the psalms, to help bind the mind.

12 If, indeed, one would persist in these elevated realities, prayer and psalms, and remain according to the order of a life in perfect silence, without trials but being with those things above – previously one was completely incapable of this. Now one may in fact care for the body as a vessel of service for the Creator, purifying it with care, not as a terrestrial reality which serves the earth, but as a vessel of holiness which is ready to be raised to heaven.[18]

---

[16] Eyes of the soul (*'aynê d-nafšâ*): cf. Eph.1:17, see Is. I 391 for his comment on Ephesians where "eyes of the heart" is used. Both reflect terms of spiritual sensitivity as opposed to bodily perception. Beulay discusses this spiritual awareness which goes beyond knowledge, see his *Lumière*, 64–83. See John Sol. *Soul* 2, 4–6 for his definition of the soul.

[17] Stirrings (*zaw'ê*): in pure prayer one's mind can be full of stirrings but in spiritual prayer there is only wonder (*temhâ*). See Is.I 170. On this see: Alfeyev, *Spiritual World*, 218–23.

[18] Isaac seems to suggest that contemplation purifies, making it possible for one to live on earth as a vessel of service in anticipation of the kingdom.

THE THIRD PART

13 On account of that kingdom which they will personally delight in beyond, even now in this life they delight <in it> by the earnest desire of their heart. They imagine <it> as in the mysteries, and become transformed in its image by the grace of the Spirit. For even when the reality is remote, with earnest desire one is able to share in it, as it were, mentally. It makes the soul as if insane with joy, freeing it entirely in the mind's flight to make it a sharer[19] with that One who is above all, while nothing at all is mingled with the mind.

14 By stillness of the body and ceasing from this world, solitaries imagine the true stillness and the withdrawal from nature which will occur at the end of the corporeal world. By means of the mind, <the solitaries> are united with the world of the spirit. By means of meditation,[20] they are involved in the expanse above. Thus, symbolically they remain continually in the future reality.

---

[19] Share (*šautâputâ*): occurs in John Sol. with the sense as found in Theodore of Mopsuestia who chose not to discuss divinization but rather *sharing* in the divine nature through grace. For a listing of the occurrences of *šautâputâ* in Theodore see Abramowski, "Theology of Theodore," 13–17. For some of the Christological aspects of *šautâputâ* in John Sol. and in Philoxenus, see de Halleux, "La Christologie."

[20] Meditation (*hergâ*): Alfeyev gives the definition for Isaac. "Meditation on God presupposes remembrance of the whole economy of God concerning humanity, beginning with the creation of man, including the Incarnation and finishing with the life of the age to come." See *Spiritual World*, 208–16. John of Dalyatha continues this very objective approach to *hergâ*. He dedicates a homily to the *Meditation on the Economy of Our Lord* (Hom.24): meditating on the life of Christ, seeing by thought (*re'yânâ*) what the disciples saw with the senses. By this meditation one purifies the heart which (like a mirror) reflects the rays of His glory. See Beulay, *L'Enseignement*, 118–22.

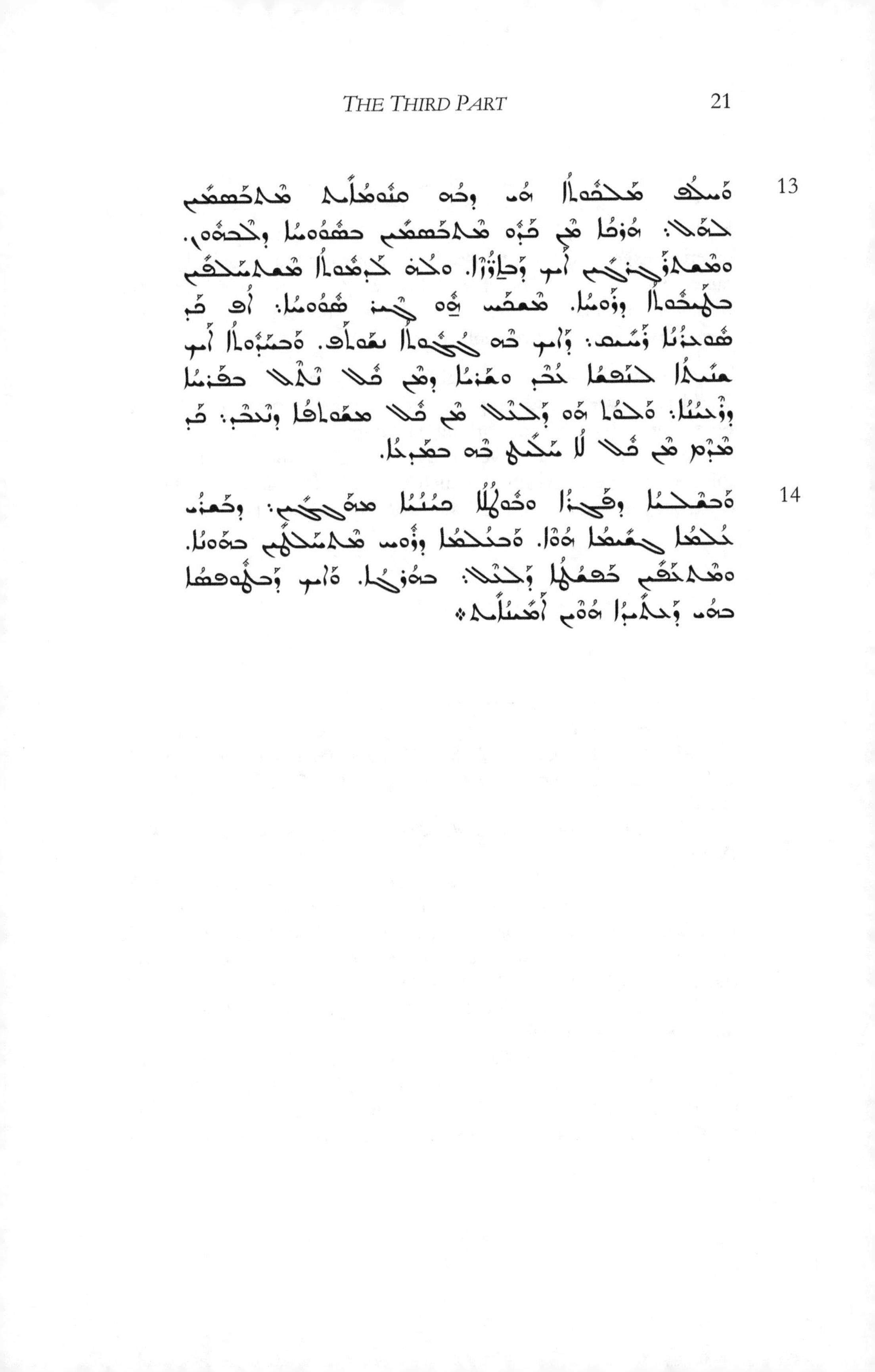

15   O our brother, as a weary merchant,[21] more than anything else let us be earnest about the way of life of the mind.[22] If then God and his love, which is above every course of life might only be found by exterior exercises, the philosophers more than us would have attained to His love. Therefore while we forcefully administer the things of the body, let us ask God with suitable zeal for what is necessary, on account of such things.

16   There is nothing which is capable of removing the mind from the world as converse with hope;[23] nothing which unites with God as beseeching His wisdom; nothing which grants the sublimity of love as the discovery of His love for us. There is nothing which lifts the mind in wonder, beyond all which is visible, to abide with Him far off from the worlds, as searching[24] the mysteries of His nature.

---

[21] Merchant: Isaac encourages being a prudent merchant and avoiding laxity, see Is.I 179, 325, 467, 565. He also speaks of dealing prudently with spiritual merchandise (*tēgurtâ*): Is.I 9, 96, 177, 216, 297, 355, 408; Is. II XIV.7.

[22] Way of life of the mind (*dubbârâ d- re‘yânâ*): see Is.I 304, 411; *Keph.* IV 15, 47.

[23] Converse with hope (*‘enyânâ d-sabrâ*): for some of his reflections on hope, see Is. I 291, 454, 511, 543; *Keph.* III 28–29. John Sol.'s vision of hope is evident in Isaac: it is creative and unique in early Syriac literature, based on Scripture and sacramental anthropology; he returns to it constantly in *Soul* 11, 21, 57, 67, 71–73, 89. And see Lavenant, *Dialogues* 47, 48, 51, 52, 163. Lera says John derives *sabrâ* from Theodore of Mopsuestia, see Lera "Theodore de Mopsueste."

[24] Searching (*‘ûqabâ*): here to search is seen in a positive way. Normally the Syriac tradition, for example Ephrem struggling against Arianism, rejects searching and investigating matters of faith, that only wonder (*tehrâ*) and admiration can lead to knowledge of God, i.e. through revelation.

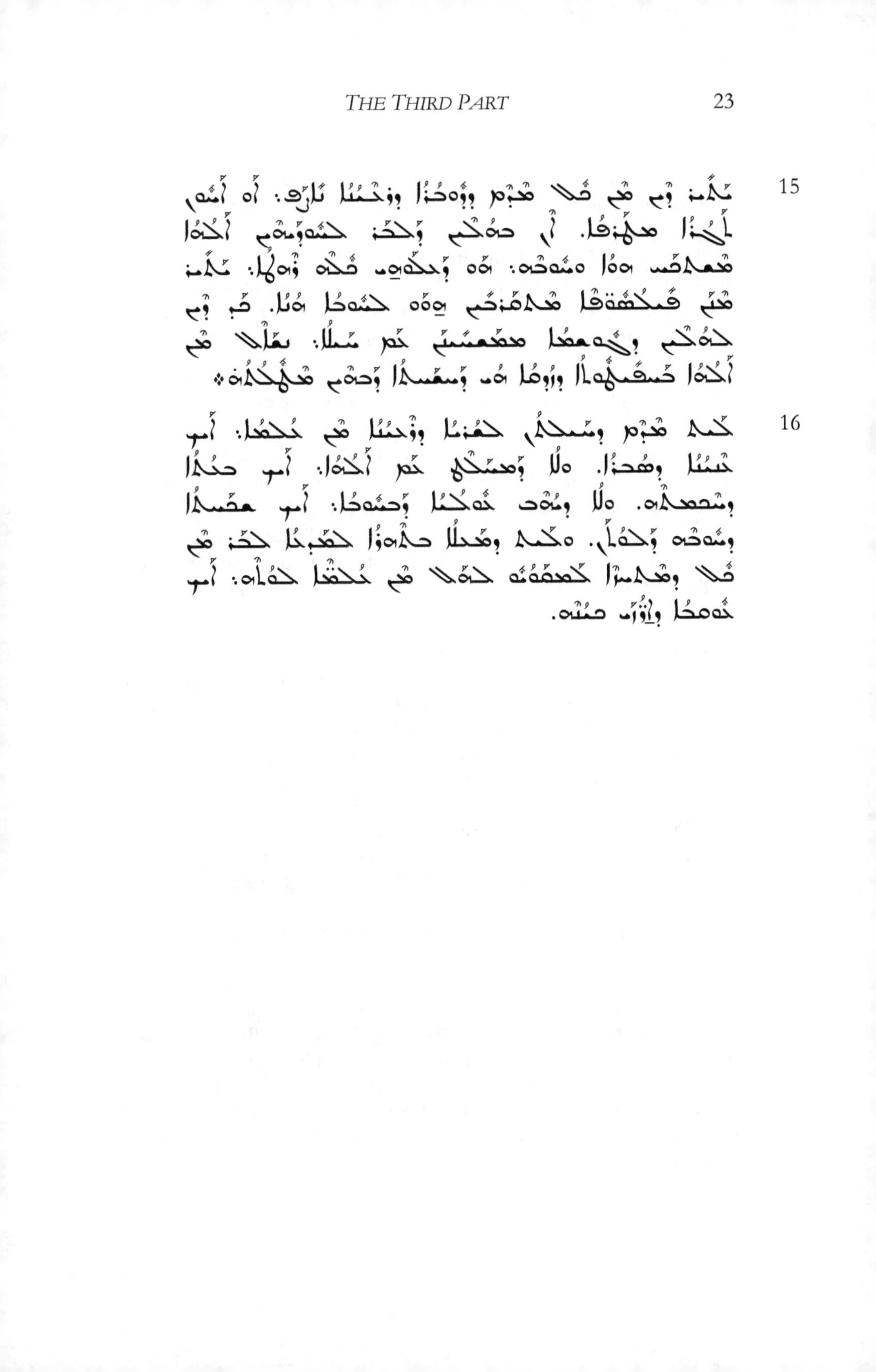

17 The nature of the Essence is invisible but can be known by means of His mysteries. That is to say, those mysteries which <God> wills that they be made known. And they are known by means of meditating on the structure of the universe.[25] <This occurs> especially by continual consideration of God's Economy in its various revelations, given indeed to inform the diligent mind which inquires faithfully and searches these things assiduously.

18 This is praiseworthy meditation and pure converse with God. This is what excellent reflection sows in the soul and <the soul> finds there pure wisdom. This is the glorious life of solitaries, dwelling completely alone and choosing a place far from the world: that marvelous place which manifests the mystery of the resurrection, indicating the existence which will be known in heaven and the life with God. Indeed <the solitaries> are mystically dead and mystically alive and they are raised up mystically while the body is on the earth. The Spirit acts by means of the mind and accomplishes all of this.

---

[25] Meditating on the structure of the universe: even if not directly intended by Isaac here, one may see the revelatory aspect of creation mentioned in Rom.1.20. And elsewhere Isaac does say:
> The first book given by God to the rational beings,
> is the nature of created beings. Written things have
> been added only after aberration. (Is.I 61)
> Ephrem said Nature and Scripture are witnesses to God:
> In his book Moses described the creation of the natural world,
> so that both the natural world and His book might testify to the Creator:
> the natural world, through humanity's use of it, the book,
> through his reading of it.
>   (*Hymns on Paradise* 5.2)

Bou Mansour elaborates on the rich symbolic interplay between the two in Ephrem, see his *Pensée symbolique*, 121–29. See also Brock, "Humanity and the Natural World," and his "World and Sacrament." John Sol. *Soul* 4, has *wisdom of nature* and *wisdom of the Scriptures*. For nature (*kyanâ*) and its revelatory aspects in Jacob of Serug, see Bou Mansour, *Théologie*, 442–47. Evagrius cautions however that God's nature is never seen in creation, only the *mdabbrânûtâ* of his wisdom, Cent.V.51.

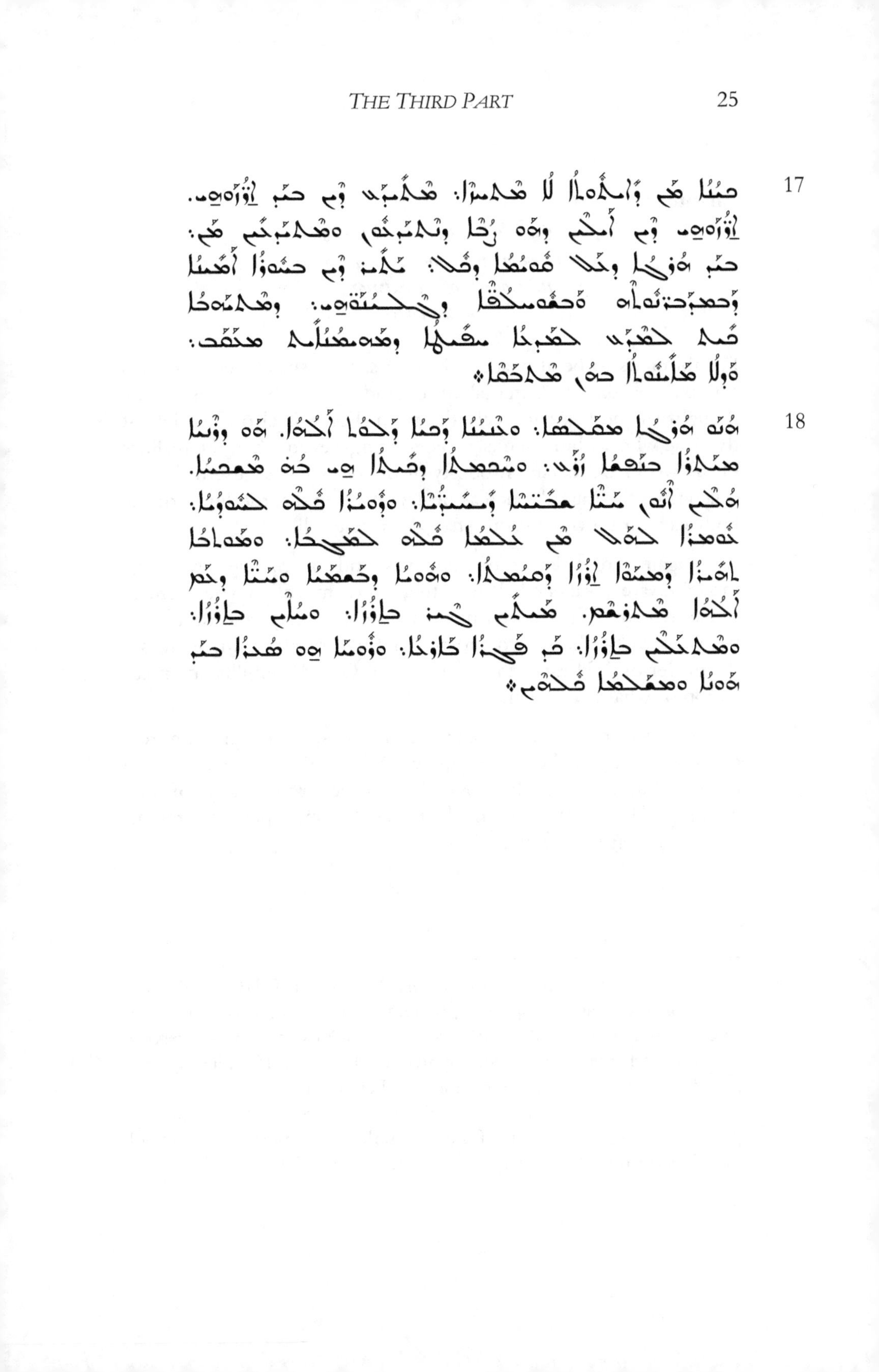

Chapter II

*Concerning the order of the body
when we are alone, and concerning
the modesty of the exterior parts
of the body.*

1. For thoughts to be at peace, it is necessary to show great care also for exterior things. External order, indeed, is able to move the thought of the heart in every direction. For it is also a teacher of that one who within <tends> to evil things, even when the realities of the world are distant. Modesty of the body is very useful for excellence of the mind,[1] whereas neglect or even disorderliness of the body can stir up very vicious struggles in the cell.

2. And again, from laxity of the eyes and of the senses, many thoughts are awakened. When they were mortified you were at peace in your affairs. Even now many habits may take root from the ways of the body and prostrations before Him: this increases the prayer of the heart and passion[2] <for God>, humility and meditation of what is excellent.

3. As to ways of converse with excellent realities, these are: to impress one's soul with the beauty of the way of life of the saints, so as to be stirred up by it; to adorn oneself with the virtuous ways of their manner of life so that one might receive in one's person a resemblance of their way of life.

---

[1] Excellence of the mind (*myattrûtâ d-re'yânâ*): in Is.III XIII.4, Isaac speaks of three stages of spiritual progress — way of life, fervor and excellence of the mind. See also Is.II XXXIV.3; XXXIX.15. For an overview of various schemata for the development of the spiritual life, including as found in Isaac, see Brock, "Some Paths to Perfection."

[2] Passion (*ḥaššâ*): in Isaac though there are roots in Evagrius, the positive and negative aspects of the term reflect the influence of John Sol. as well. See Brock, "Discerning the Evagrian," 65–6; 70–1.

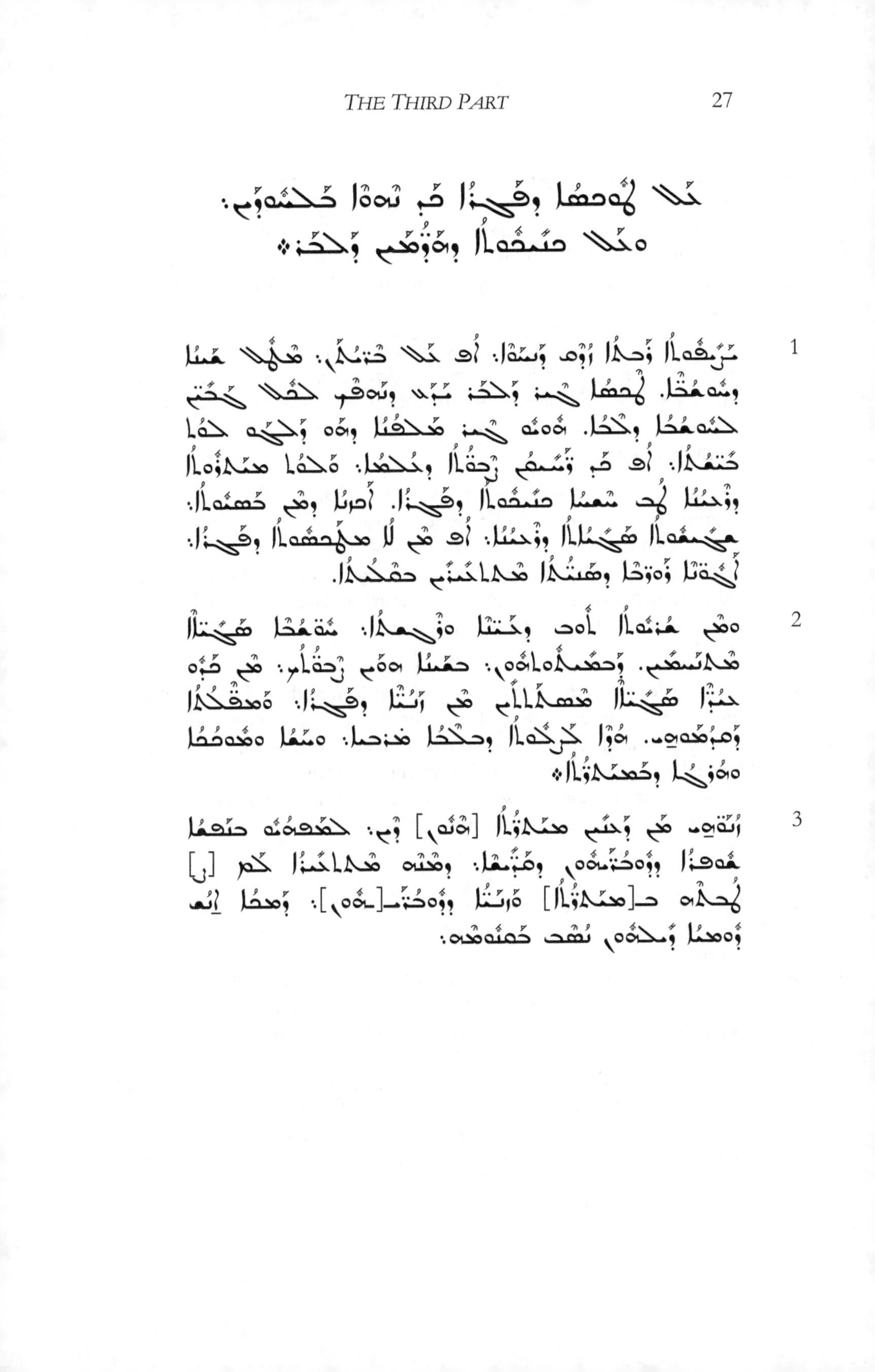

4   That is: patience, joy in afflictions, quietness of ways, perseverance in solitude, modesty of the parts of the body, contempt for bodily desire, incessant solicitude for holiness – while not reckoning that one has arrived. From this <one learns> to control involuntary zeal in the soul which arises as a manifestation of the pride lying in wait within.

5   Observing such things as the ways mentioned in the stories of all the saints, as in a mirror,[3] one receives a model and effortlessly moves along the way in the remembrance of the patience and the beauty <of the saints>: those whose resemblance truly fills the soul with great joy.

6   Again, by the victories of the saints, the soul <of the solitary> wandering from the world receives consolation in the battles which seize it and obtains contempt of conscience and a humble heart. Adorning oneself with excellent ways, from this time <the solitary is without> doubts or fear[4] and understands only the fatherhood <of God> and his sonship: there is nothing else between him and God.

7   This order of perfection requires the aim of solitary life in stillness and labour alone in the cell. It <requires> a humbled body and a renewed mind; senses weakened and an elevated understanding; enfeebled parts of the body but thoughts shining in their splendor. Also required is a mind which soars and is lifted up to God in contemplation[5] of Him and a mind withdrawn from the world while its thought wanders in God.

---

[3] Cf. 1 Cor.13:12; 2 Cor.3:18. See Brock, "Imagery of the Spiritual Mirror."

[4] On the levels of fear, see Is.I 430: "He who is bodily, fears as an animal fears being slaughtered; he who is rational, fears the judgment of God; he who has become a son is adorned by love and not taught by the rod of fear." See also *Keph.* I 11, 17.

[5] Contemplation (*te'ōryā*): found frequently in Isaac. See Brock, "Some Uses of the Term *theoria*." See Is.I 17: "Let excellence be reckoned by you as the body, contemplation as the soul. The two form one complete spiritual person, composed of sensible and intelligible parts." And

---

see Is.I 128 where Brock notes (Is.II VII.1) that Isaac provides a definition of *theoria*: ʿammîqût ḥzâtâ napsânâytâ, "profundity of the soul's vision."

8   Such a one is involved with the flesh but his thought does not dwell with it. And though he is agitated by this, he is completely occupied by the things which abide and which are much greater than him. <His> body is worn and troubled but the heart has exulted with joy, unwittingly, as it is said: *the heart is not lifted up.*[6]

9   O Christ, <You> who enrich all, confirm Your hope in my soul and bring me out of darkness to the knowledge of Your light because I praise You with the praises of the heart, not only with the mouth.

---

[6] Ps.131:1.

8 ܘܟܕ ܗܐ ܡܬܕܐܝܢ ܚܘܒܝ ܘܡܚܩܬܗ ܘܪܚܝܟ ܡܢܗ ܡܟܠܬܝ܀
ܚܢܢܐ ܕܟܕ ܟܘܡܥܐ ܟܡ ܕܐܝܬܘܗܝ ܘܐܢܐ ܕܘܪ ܚܢܒܪܘܬܐ.
ܒܠܚܘܕ ܒܪܚܡܝܟ ܟܕܝܢ ܠܐ ܡܬܕܐܝܢ ܟܠܚܕ܀

9 ܗܘܚܢܝ ܩܢܘ ܕܢܩܥܝܢ. ܡܩܡܝܢܐ ܡܕܠܐܙ ܩܠܐ: ܘܐܩܦܢܝܢ ܓܢ ܫܩܘܕܐ ܓܒܪܕܐ ܕܒܐܘܦܢܝ. ܘܐܢܗܘܢܝ ܐܚܕܢܬܐ ܕܟܟܐ. ܘܠܐ ܗܘܐ ܕܩܘܡܐ ܚܟܫܘܝ܀

Chapter III

Of the same Mar Isaac. On prayer: how it binds our mind to God and causes it to cleave to the meditation in it; and how by means of the excellent stirrings which are in it the mind is strong against the love for this world from which <come> the passions.

1. There is no way of life which is able to withdraw the mind from this world and preserve it from stumbling as meditation about God. This work is difficult but amazing, also easy and sweet. You, my beloved, love to remain in continual meditation[1] on God because it is a door against all corruptible thoughts. Begin with a great number of prayers: continual prayers are a constant meditation on God.

2. That we might be persevering in prayers, this prayer must stir up the heart to increasing meditation about God. Then it makes the mind heavenly, by means of excellent stirrings which are according to divine instruction, through the words of prayer which adhere to the fear of God.

3. By that which our Lord already taught in the commandments which precede prayer, <we are told> how the life of Christians must be and what one ought to ask in prayer.[2] It is known, indeed, that the one who acts according to these ways, has learned by divine instruction and is diligent to present the requests in prayer to God, that they might become realities. One feels that such thoughts at the moment of prayer arise in him because of these ways. Since it must needs be that as we wish our way of life to be, so must be also our prayer.[3]

---

[1] Continual meditation on God (*hergâ ammînâ db-alâhâ*): see Is.II X.16, XVIII.3, XX.27, XXIX.9; *Keph.* I 77, IV 47. For *hergâ ammînâ* on scripture see Is.I 125; 379.

[2] Mt.5:17–6:8.

[3] On how prayer relates to way of life, see Is.I 34: "Prayer accords strictly with behavior." In Is.II XIV.37 commenting on the Our Father, Isaac says: "So our prayer should be inspired by its sense, and we should set our lives aright in strict accordance with it...". See similarly Theodore of Mopsuestia, *Homélies* XI 1, 3 and Mark the Monk, *Justified by works* 153.

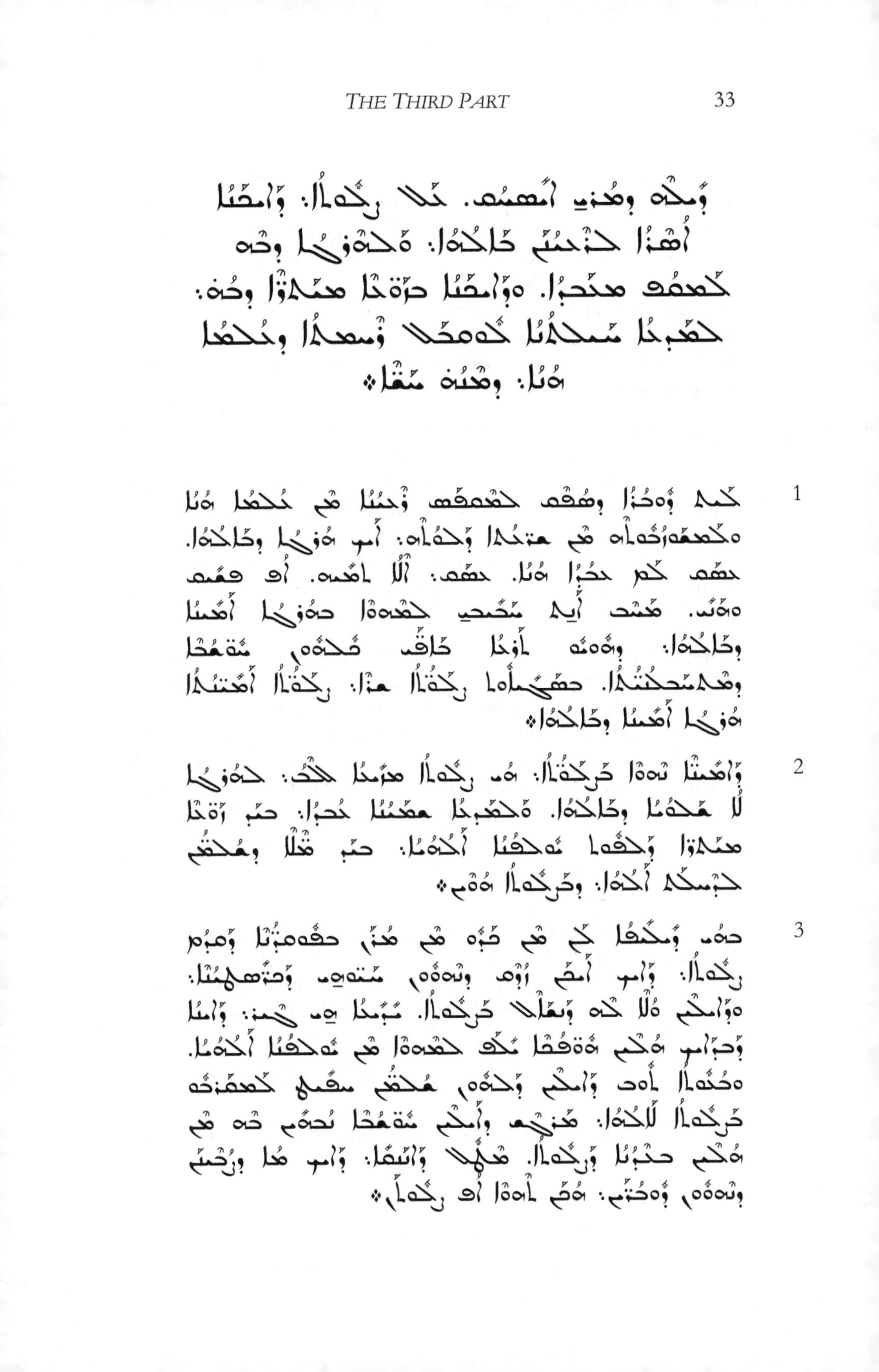

4   And lest there be in them anything alien to perfection, those who are brought up according to divine instruction for the life of perfection, have been taught by our Lord not to babble like the pagans, but to present to God wise requests seasoned with heavenly hope.[4] <Our Lord> has shown them the providence of God[5] on their account, and that their mind <ought> not be occupied with worldly and temporal realities. But they must acquire a fine mind for the things which are becoming of those who await familiarity <with God>.[6]

5   Also, not even these realities does God give to them because of their prayer, since He has no need of prayer who at Creation had no need of the supplication of creatures;[7] how then more excellent is Creation than the gifts after it! But <this prayer is necessary> that they might have the fullness of meditation on the invisible realities, and that their mind because of the form of the prayer may be full of these realities, and that they might already perceive what is the hope of things to come.

6   What then of this? That while they remain in this wonderful reflection, discerning each one of the petitions made to God with diligence, rightly henceforward they earnestly desire to proceed in the way of life fit for that good and glory to which they are summoned. And by means of these realities, they remain continually where they are elevated from this world, in familiarity[8] and affinity with God and in the study and knowledge of His mysteries.

---

[4] Cf. Mt.6:7; Col.4:6.

[5] Providence of God (*bṭîlûtâ*): occurs frequently in Isaac. See Is.I 65, 103, 262, 304, 337, 422, 489–90, 498; Is.II VIII.26; XVII. 6, 8; *Keph.* I 51, II 73, 102. See also Evag. Cent.VI. 43, 59, 75. And for divine providence (*bṭîlûtâ alâhâyâ*) see Evag. Muyldermans, "La Foi de Mar Évagre," pp.167–69.

[6] Cf. Mt.6:25–34.

[7] On "…no need of the supplication of creatures…," see Evag. *Letter to Melania*, 56 (Vitestam p.22).

[8] Familiarity (*bayâtyûtâ*): see Is.III IV 19; *Keph.*IV 55; John Sol. *Soul* 86.

THE THIRD PART

7 Therefore, if as the blessed Interpreter said, "every prayer whatever it be, is instruction for life,"⁹ since for every form of prayer, offered in earnest by an intelligent person according to the order of divine instruction, the mind prepares a certain meaning by which it is released from the flesh. By this reflection it becomes bound to those realities which instruct for life,¹⁰ and that imprint <on the present> the memory of the immortal manner of life and what is beyond life.

8 So the elements in the form of prayer were arranged by our Lord, whose instruction is elevated and very succinct: excellent knowledge about the incorruptible life and of the Spirit. Because of this, every time we pray a thousand insights arise in our mind: from where we are in nature, that is, from the earth; from what we are and by means of whom and with which lineage we are related; with what mysteries we share in; where we are prepared to be led; what manner of life this mystery depicts; in what way, in figure, have we already now learned wisdom regarding the <future> hope. And because by means of the mind, we alone have fellowship and are brought near to the realities of the <future> life and the amazing ways suitable to it, the realities strengthen, indeed, the <mind> according to the mystery here below.

---

⁹ See Theod. of Mop. *Homélies* XI 1, as reflected also in Is.II XIV.36.
¹⁰ Cf. Titus 2:12.

THE THIRD PART

9   Prayer, therefore, according to perfection – of those who as it were have preferred a life such as this, have eagerly desired heaven and have taken on the perfect commandments[11] – commenting, that is: *Do not be preoccupied for your bodies of what we will eat or what we will drink or with what we will be clothed;*[12] and also: *The Father knows that also for you these things are necessary,* before they are made known in confident prayer.[13] And because they have been raised above all earthly realities, in the perfection of the mind, Our Lord gave a commandment: *Seek only the kingdom of God and His righteousness.*[14]

10 Prayer such as this, in the manner of the perfect life and which takes pains to be in accord with the reading <of Scripture>, becomes uprightness of the mind, admonition for excellent ways, freedom regarding realities which elevate, meditation of the Spirit,[15] remembrance of heavenly realities and reflection on hidden realities. Because all of these ways of thinking are enclosed, succinctly, in prayer which instructs concerning the future perfection.

11 So this prayer rightly strengthens the mind of those who dare to conduct themselves on earth, in the perfect way of life of the mystery of future behavior. "Continual prayer clothes the mind with strength," says blessed Basil;[16] that <prayer> which is from the love of this reading of the Gospel. But which mind? It is clear that this concerns those who are eager for heavenly life, who have become strong by the reading of the Gospel. They have despised earth, have longed for heaven and have depicted before their eyes the future perfection.

---

[11] Perfect commandments (*paqdânê gmîrê*): *Book of Steps* VII.1, XI.1, XIX.5, XXX.2; see Brock, "Some Paths to Perfection."

[12] Mt.6:31.

[13] Mt. 6:32; Mt.6:8.

[14] Mt.6.33.

[15] Meditation of the spirit (*hergâ d-ruḥ*) compare with *hergâ rûḥânâ*, Is.III IX.9.

[16] Based on careful analysis of the research of de Halleux, Brock and Bettiolo, Chialà attributes authorship here to John Sol. See Bettiolo, "Sulla preghiera," pp. 76–77.

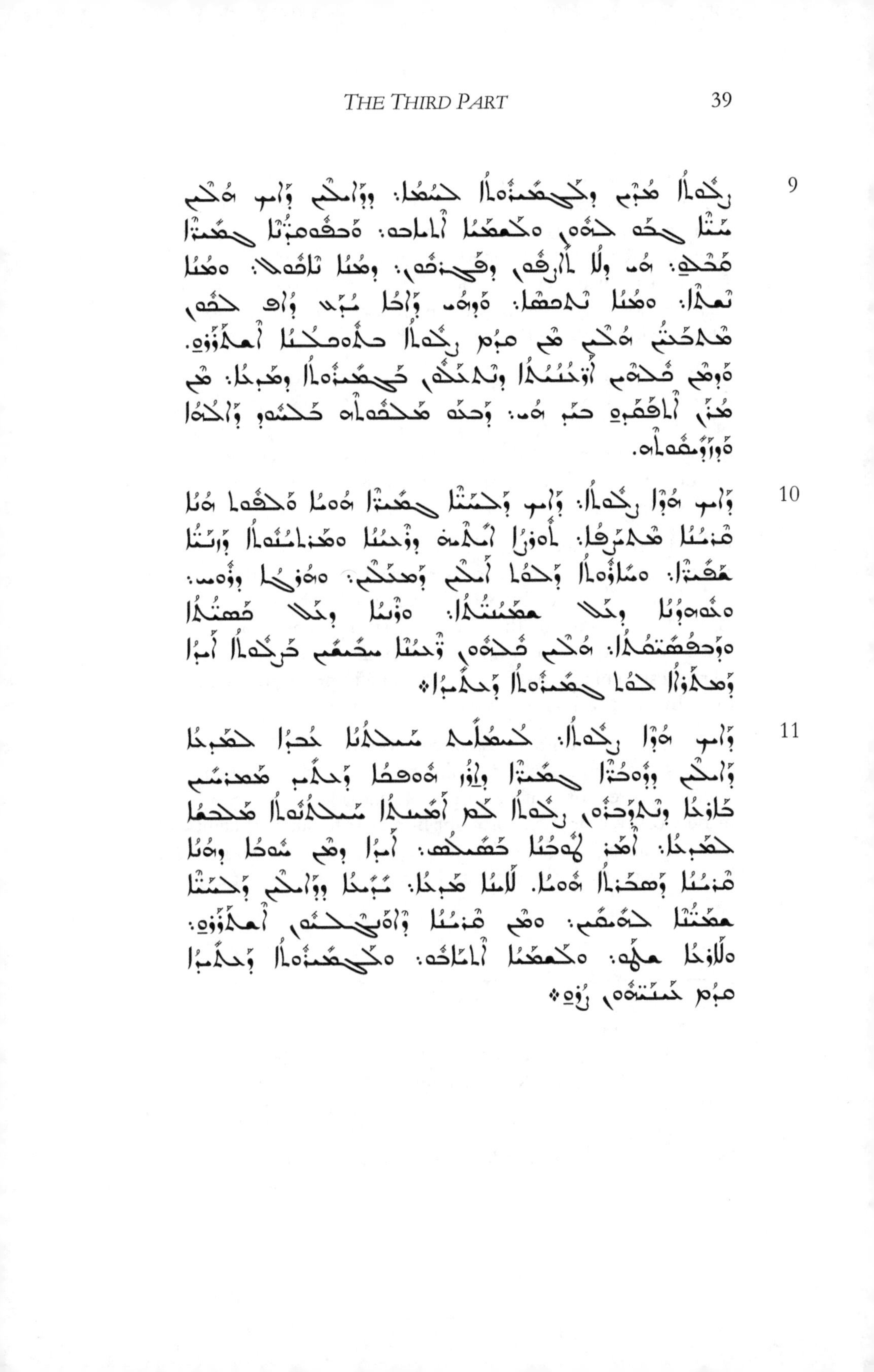

12 It is clear that from this prayer and meditation of those who engage in it in an excellent way, they obtain encouragement and strength in their minds, because hope inflames their ways of thinking. From here they receive the strength to grasp firmly whatever they possess, and to gladly endure the evils on earth, such as to consider them as nothing at all in comparison with the future good things which were promised them.

13 Soon after, these things will be made ready for them, but even now from time to time, *they become transformed into <his> image in the mirror of their own thought, by means of the grace of the Spirit.*[17] According to the ardent desire of the will, this force suitably clothes the mind, by means of perfect prayer which shows the way to this ascent, beyond the world.

14 Immediately, indeed, at the remembrance of those heavenly realities that are attended to as requests in prayer, the soul which had already despised this world, expands by means of the love of God. And because of this there are struggles against <the soul>, while the mind rests in hope, strengthened by means of the elevated requests which it has learned to make in prayer, persuaded about them by our Lord who said: *Our Father who art in heaven.*[18]

15 O compassion and greatness of the goodness of God, to which He elevates created nature! But it also calls to mind the holiness of that divine Nature[19] of which, by grace, that one who is son has been made worthy. For it has brought him near to such a height of holiness – granting insight – that the Nature, to which belongs the holiness, has given to the creature by grace what does not belong to it by nature.

---

[17] Cf. 2 Cor. 3:18.

[18] Mt. 6:9.

[19] Divine Nature (*kyânâ alâhâyâ*): see Is.I 570; Is.II VIII.4,6; X.25; XI.35; XIV.42; XVIII.3; XXXVIII, title,4; XXXIX.22; XL,title; *Keph.* I 22; II 19, 44. Brock suggests derivation from Theodore of Mopsuestia *Homélies* I 16–17, V 1, 3–4. See also Vadakkel, *Anaphora of Mar Theodore*, pp. 54, 58, 70. See Evag. *Letter to Melania*, 28 (Casiday; Frankenberg, p.618).

THE THIRD PART

16   To this <holiness>, it is fitting that the way of life of living beings on earth be in accord, as <God> said to Moses: *You shall be holy, because I am holy.*[20] If holiness is becoming to servants because of the word of God to them, how much more, then, to the sons[21] <for whom> the reflection of prayer makes the mind ascend to insights such as these, and to an elevated meditation such as this. This <occurs> by means of the kinds of requests which conform the force of the verses of <prayer> to divine instruction.

17   So it is for the rest of the verses <of the "Our father">.[22] In them, other insights are in motion, showing us it is good that one of noble birth who is ready to return to the Kingdom, have no corruptible realities of here below. As the mind remains close to <God> it is bound by His love; and it is right that the sons of God consider it shameful that their thinking persist on earth and in what is theirs.

18   For this we ask help in deference to His will, as we ought to do: that His grace which is called Kingdom,[23] be inclined to us and in the apperception of it we forget earth, remaining mysteriously in those <heavenly> realities, by a transmigration which in the mind teaches us about the two <worlds>. From within this, there is the force by which we are transformed, and by means of which we abide in the excellent realities; although being on earth we show the manner of life which is in heaven.

---

[20] Lv. 19:2.

[21] See the comments of Theodore of Mopsuestia on this distinction between servants and sons – citing Gal. 4:24–25, Eph.2:13, Rom.8:15 – in his "Commentary on the Our Father," *Homélies* XI 7–8.

[22] See Pasquet, "Le Notre Père."

[23] Mt.6:10.

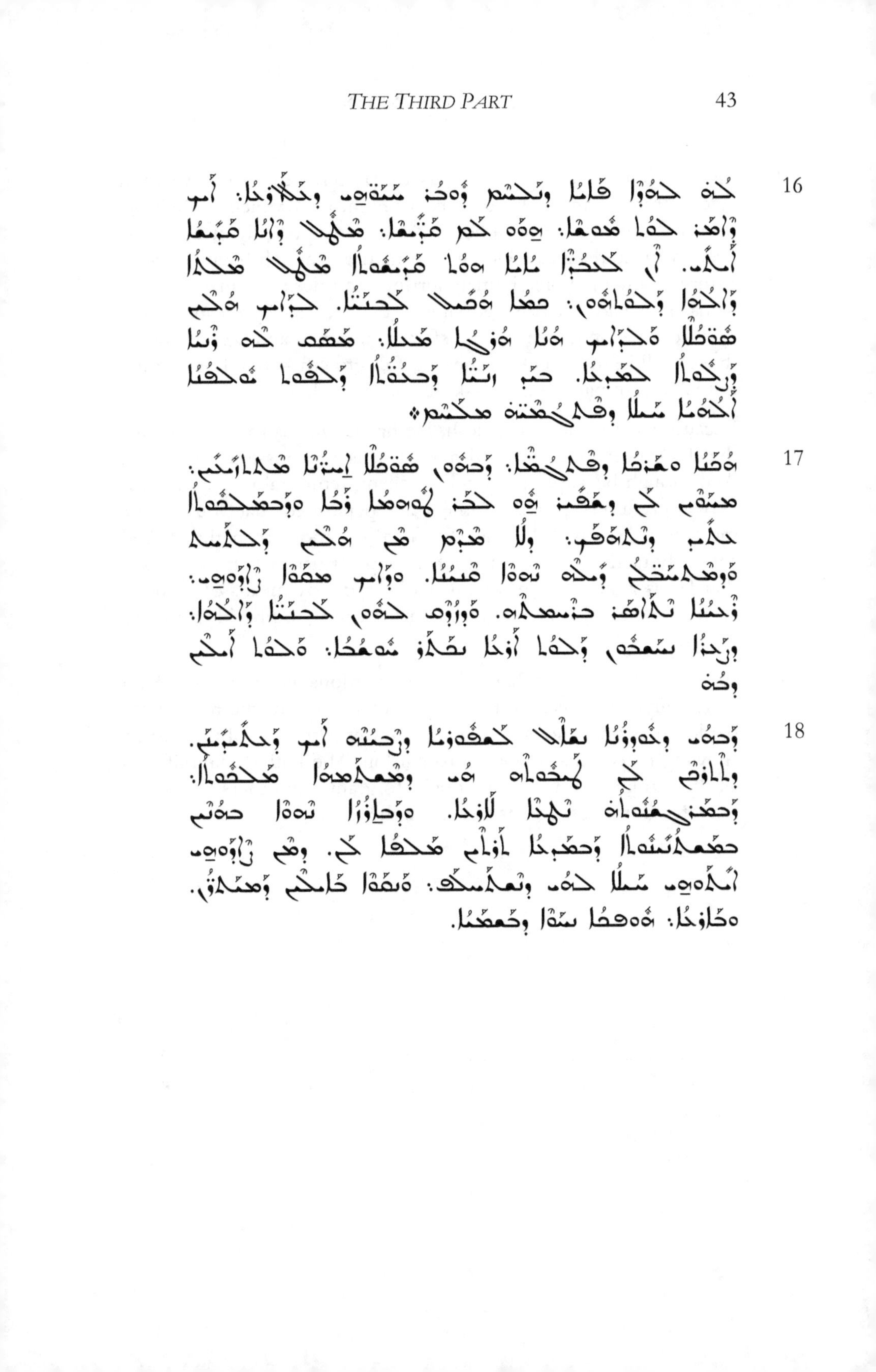

19 May we obtain encouragement as we perceive that we have been given strength and help, a force from heaven which is invisibly near, continually, and it upholds <us>. Unexpectedly, it brings us near to those realities which lift up nature. Though having a weak nature, many opinions, human stirrings and desires remain foreign to us. If it had not been possible – that is, that by means of the force of the Spirit we be transferred at times and we remain in those realities even before there is full growth – our Lord would not have commanded us to ask this of the Father.

20 Because we are still in the flesh, He has taught us to ask today for the thing needed, as now without it, it is not possible <to live>. And though because of what is excellent, temporal realities appear very superfluous, just the same I am persuaded that your nature must ask. Ask then, but not for anything more than this.[24] And again about this *give us*,[25] it teaches to put trust in Him, signifying that He is anxious even for our base needs. By means of requests such as these, <God> humbles Himself caring to provide for these things.

21 We learn again from here that He pardons what we ask Him concerning sins. Because He teaches us to present the request for pardon,[26] as one who is persuaded that this is the will of the Father, showing indeed that He loves to pardon. The Father Himself says all these things; and that one ought to grant <to others> what we ask <for ourselves>, so as to receive the same.

---

[24] Theodore of Mopsuestia confirms this, quoting 1 Tim.6:6–8, see *Homélies* XI 14.

[25] Mt.6:11.

[26] Mt.6:12.

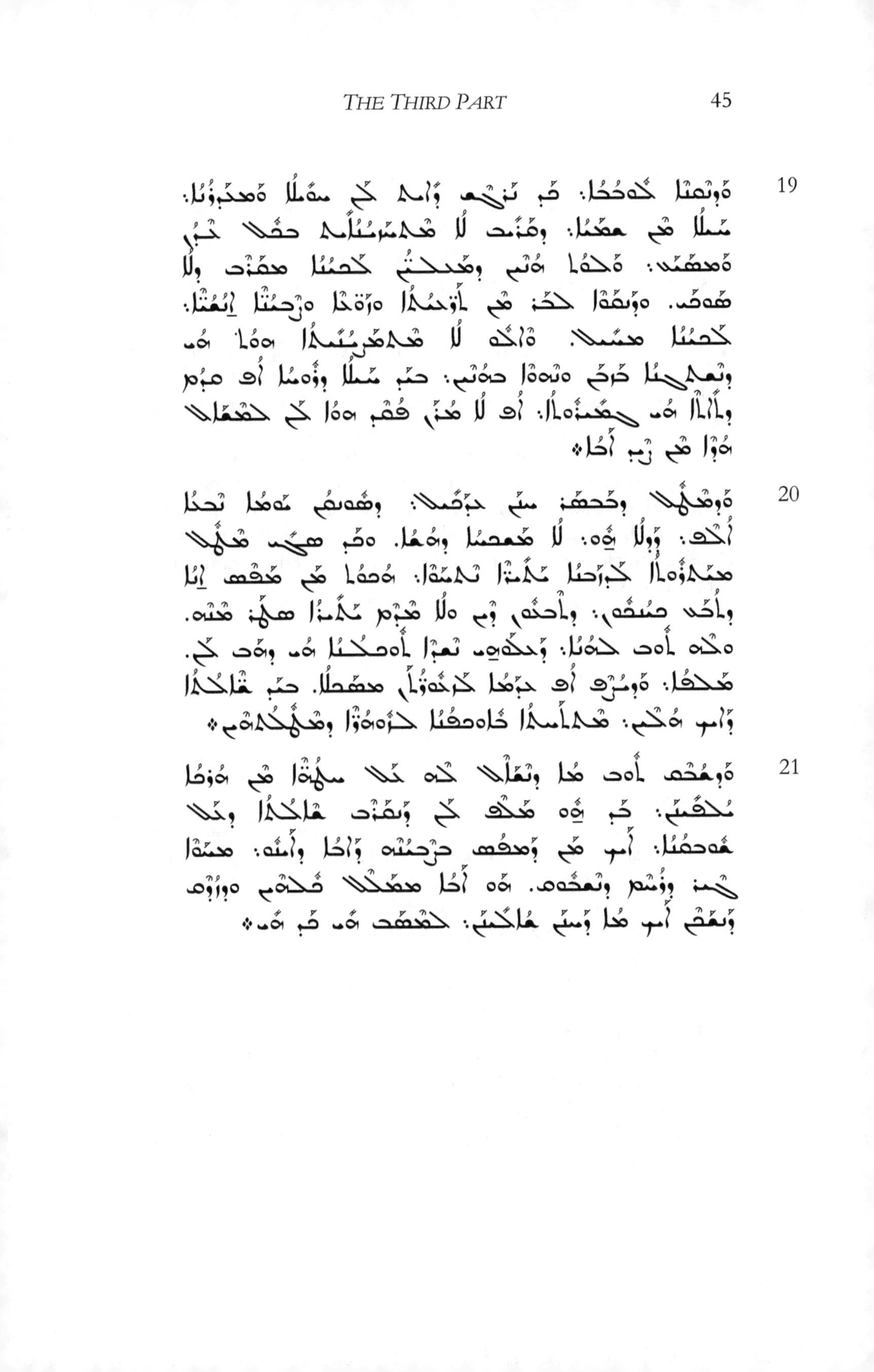

22 But as we must fight unexpected temptations, and <even> other than this²⁷ – stirrings of the flesh whether those afflicting it from without or by a heavenly sign²⁸ – we need to be preserved in the midst of all these adversities. Then, being necessary that we ask for this, from the same *sedra*²⁹ we find what may make us wise <about it>.

23 So may we find refuge in the One from whom is salvation for all who breathe in the flesh and for what, beyond the flesh, is impelled by life.³⁰ Because He governs all and without Him nothing is possible – He whose glory is from His Nature, and His Kingdom is above all, and His power holds all the frontiers – He had willed that by <using> the form of prayer with which we attend to these realities that concern Him, the remembrance of Him may be with us always. Because by these realities, we have access to the sublime cloud of thick darkness of the knowledge of Him³¹ and His love for humanity.

---

[27] Mt.6:13.

[28] Temptations may come from nature, demons and other persons. And some are permitted by God "by a heavenly sign (*remzâ*)": provoked by God – Is.I 298–303, 531; or permitted by Him – Is.I 278–79, 415–16. One is even allowed to pray not to be tempted: Is.I 36–37. And in Is.II XVIII.1: "The soul receives limpidity (*šapyûtâ*) after experiences (consisting) in struggles."

[29] Formula of prayer (*sedrâ*): here indicates the Our Father.

[30] This is a possible reference to the dead. On the quality of life after death, see Is.III XI.6.

[31] Cloud of thick darkness of the knowledge of Him (ʿ*arpellâ d-îdaʿteh*): cf. Is.I 193, 217, 517; Is.II V.1; VII.1; IX.11; X.17, 24; *Keph.* I 36, 51, 52; II 73, 102. Though the term occurs in Gregory of Nyssa, see Beulay, *Lumière*, 138–44, Brock suggests that the influence here is more likely Ps. Dionysius, e.g. *Mystical Theology* I.3, II.

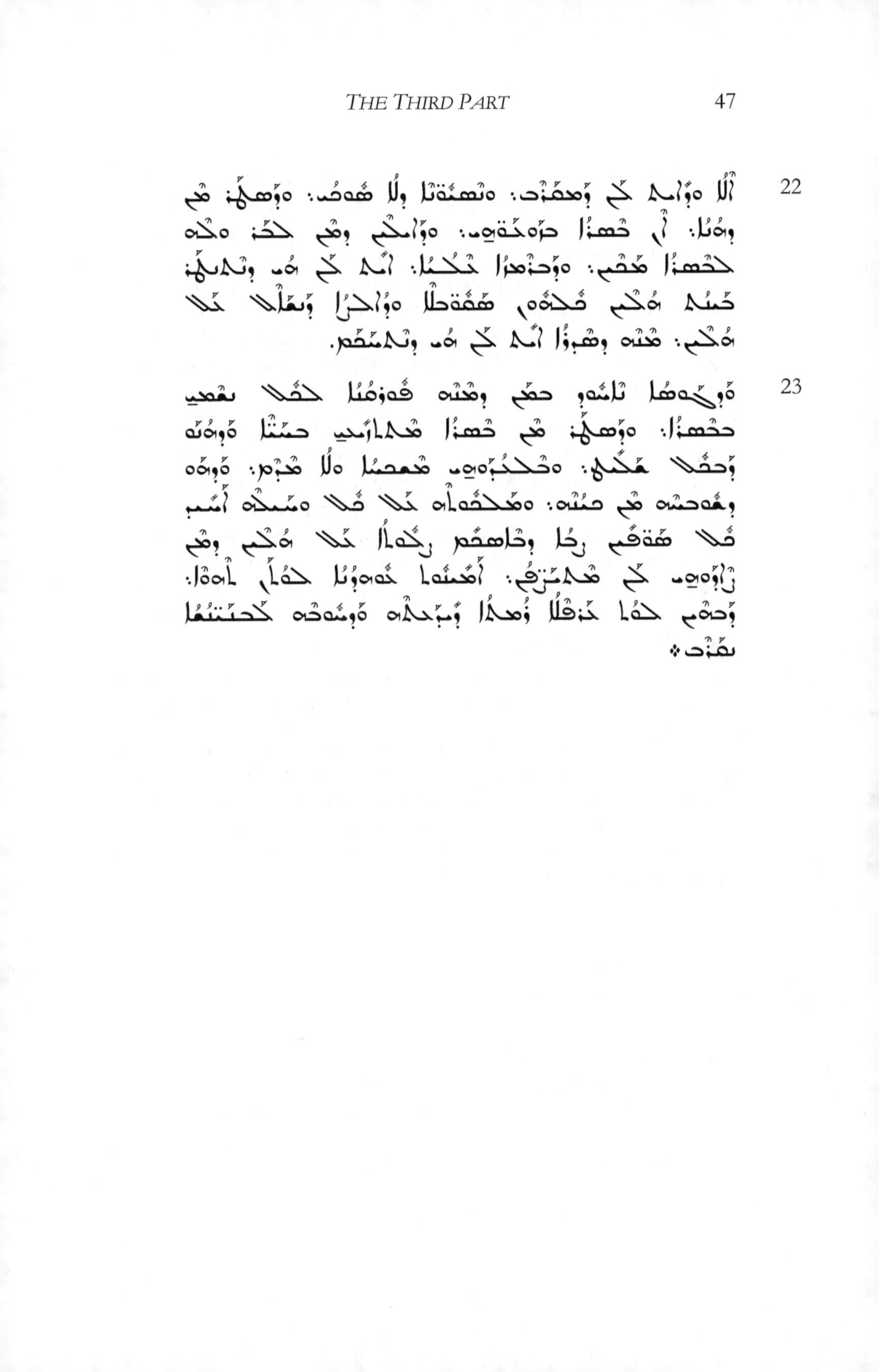

24 Well said by blessed Mark the Solitary: "The one who prays with insight, endures whatever happens to him."[32] The form of prayer in fact, is such that by various and marvelous insights, it strengthens our mind and prepares it lest it become a receptacle of passions, as Evagrius said. For it happens necessarily, that whoever prays with discernment, prepares that excellent word of prayer, full of insights for the struggle against the flesh. Thus it inflames him with love for future realities; <love> which the knowledge of those realities stirs in the one who prays.

25 When, indeed, on account of this he is ready to resist nature and to separate from what is our own and <to separate> the mind from the flesh, he must ask for great strength to endure those realities which after this are set in motion. But the insights which are from the prayer and the gifts in it, by means of hope, make such difficulty appear as nothing in the eyes of <the one who prays>, even when it is something very hard. When he beheld this, the blessed Evagrius said: "Prayer makes the mind strong and prepares it lest it become a receptacle of passions."[33]

26 Also, indeed, Mark indicated the difficult struggles which are stirred up after the insights of prayer and the intelligence which is in it.[34]

27 These insights, while they prepare us by means of the consideration of future realities to be moved outside of the flesh – <while remaining> on earth – they may charge us at the same time to endure the tempests which necessarily are stirred up. Such temptations whether from nature, from demons, or from persons, arise against the one who loves to walk in this way.

---

[32] Mark the Monk, *On the Spiritual Law* 115.
[33] See Evag. *Praktikos*, 49 (Bamberger); cf. Evag. *Gnostique*, 49 (Guillaumont).
[34] Mark the Monk, *Justified by Works* 81.

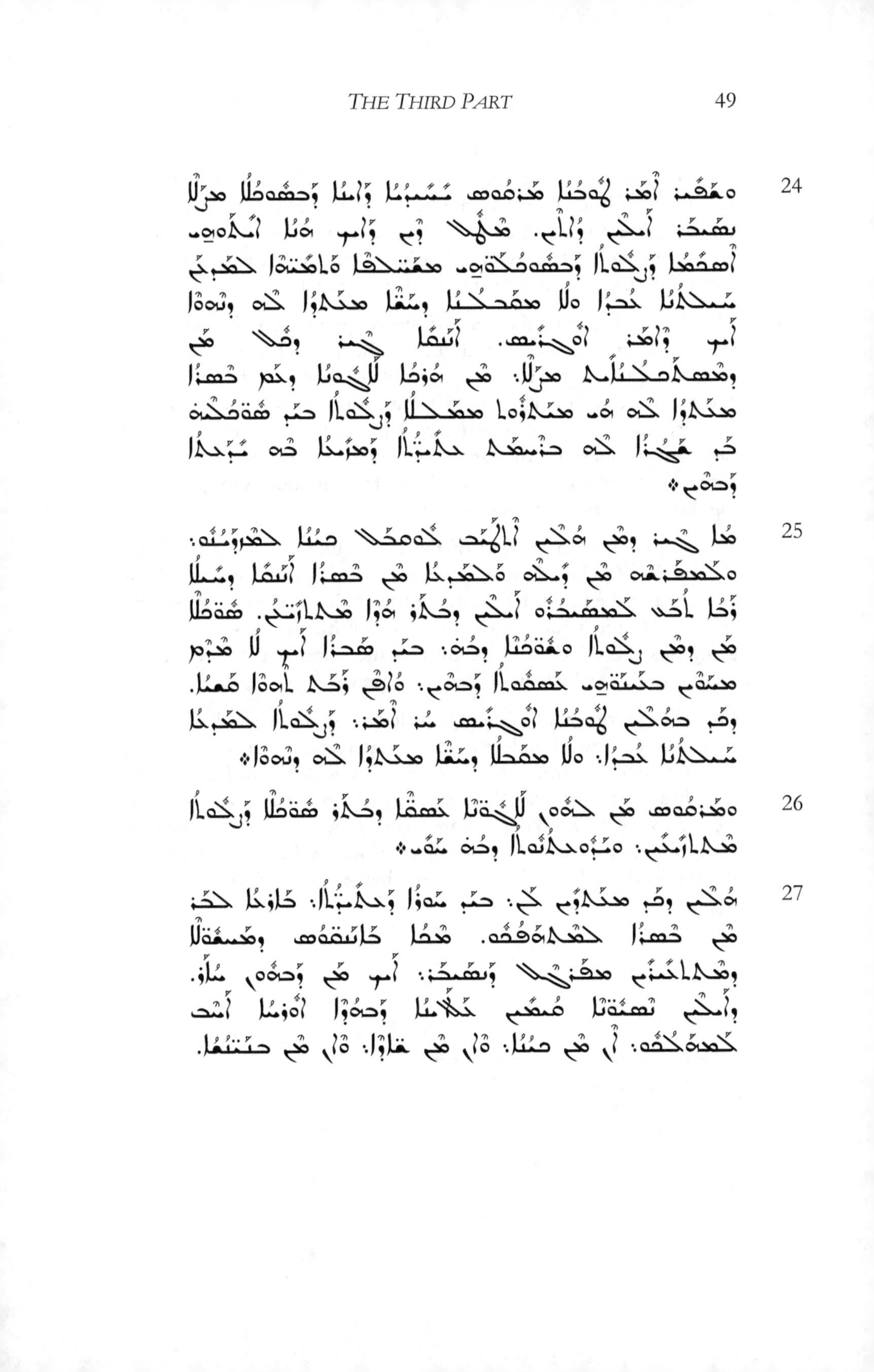

28 Evagrius, indeed <said>: "the mind which remains in the sweetness of hope increases the help that comes from prayer"; not only because it is capable of showing how all struggles are as nothing – easy and not difficult – but also because it treats with contempt the flesh which is the cause of the struggle.

29 This is, my beloved, the way of life of prayer; this is our divine meditation in <prayer>; and this is the perfect labor! Whoever wishes to prepare for the divine ascent by means of the mind, seek a solitary habitation abstaining from worldly care: this generates serenity and stillness of the heart. By means of continual rest in God and stillness of thoughts, the mind may observe the whole form of prayer and receive knowledge from it about God by entering the mysteries <contained> in the verses.

30 Prayer, therefore, by means of the meditation <involved>, draws the mind to God at all times. By means of its variety, it strengthens and purifies the mind. By means of the study <included>, it sanctifies it. This meditation is the origin of all meditations, and necessarily ties the mind to God. By this the mind is illumined about hidden realities which are within <the prayer>.

31 From these, one may obtain knowledge of the exalted things of God. Henceforward, indeed, it may be perceived that we are *sons of the Father who is in heaven, heirs of God and fellow heirs with Jesus Christ.*[35] One has the trust to say: *I am ready not only to be imprisoned, but to die for the name of our Lord Jesus Christ;*[36] and: *I am crucified to the world and the world is crucified to me;*[37] and <again>: *Who will separate me from the love of Christ? Peril, nakedness,* poverty, shame, infirmity, death?[38]

---

[35] Cf. Mt.5:45; Rom. 8:17.
[36] Acts 21:13.
[37] Gal. 6:14.
[38] Rom. 8:35 (Peshitta).

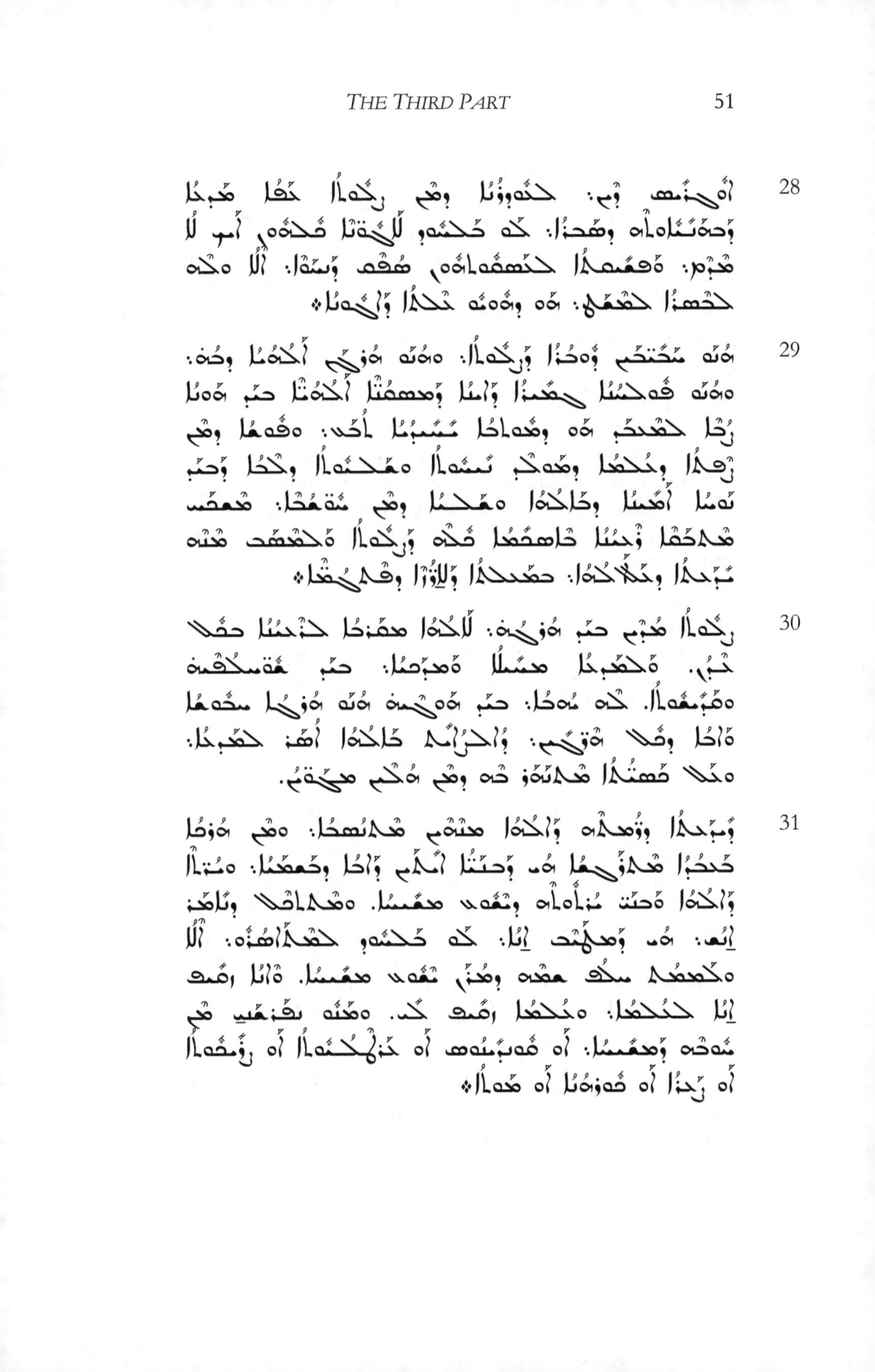

32   The holy Nature of Christ is therefore worthy of all praise! By His Economy, He has lifted us up from looking on earthly realities and directs the mind to the divine ascent which is above the world. By means of converse in prayer,[39] He has brought us near to the vision of the heavenly Kingdom and continual meditation of what is in it – to where we prepare to offer to the Father, by means of <Christ>, continual adoration of the Spirit.

33   This <adoration> which cannot be limited, not by the body, not by a place, not by the highest <heavenly> spheres, <occurs> in the mind by its stirrings. It is infinite and uninterrupted *stupor*[40] on account of God. <It happens> in that place without corporeal realities, by that way of life more exalted than the order of prayer. *Wonder* is its minister, and instead of faith providing the wings for prayer, there is the true vision[41] of that in which consists our Kingdom and our glory.

34   Here there is no more need that God reveal Himself, nor need for liturgies or the praise of creatures. Henceforth it is clear to us that, truly for our sake He manifested all these things; and for us He submitted to all of this, and also shows to have need of human praise[42] and of the holiness of spiritual beings.[43]

---

[39] Converse of prayer (*ʿenyânâ da-ṣlôtâ*): see Is.II IV.1; V, title; *Keph.* IV 91. See John Sol. *Soul* 1; Philoxenus 319; Shemʿon d-Tabuteh (Mingana) *WS* VII, pages 51–53, 299b, 309ab, 310a.

[40] Stupor (*tembâ*) together with wonder (*tehrâ*): in their relation to prayer and the reading (*qeryânâ*) of Scripture in Isaac, they go beyond normal human perception of God. See Louf, "*Temha-stupore.*" And see my "Insight without Sight." *Keph.* IV 95 includes a definition of *tembâ* by Theodore of Mopsuestia in the context of Gen.15:12 and Gen. 2:21.

[41] True vision (*hezwâ šarrîrâ*): Is.I 183; Is.II X.17, XIV.30; John Sol. *Soul* 61; Gregory of Cyprus 102.

[42] On praise due to God, elsewhere in the tradition, praise and thanksgiving are integral to St. Ephrem's thinking. He says the lack of it caused Adam to fall since "he ate fruit and did not give praise." See Memra III.6 in Hansbury, *Hymns of St. Ephrem.* A similar reflection occurs in Ephrem's *Commentary on the Diatessaron* 19.4.

… 32

… 33

… 34

---

[43] According to Chialà, intended here is the "Holy, holy, holy" of the seraphim, Is.6.3. See Vergani, "Isaia 6," 179–92 where he examines the rapport between human nature and the uncreated angelic world according to John Sol. And see the *Letter to Hesychius* 66 which instructs to begin personal prayer with the cry of the seraphim: "Holy, holy, holy, Lord almighty, with whose glory both heaven and earth are filled."

35   In the life beyond, indeed, we will receive the whole truth concerning God the creator – not about His Nature but about the order of His majesty, and of His divine glory and His great love for us. There, all the veils and titles and forms of the Economy, will be taken away from before the mind;[44] there, we will no longer receive His gifts in the name of our petition, nor the grace of knowledge in a measured way. In the life beyond, indeed, God will truly show that even in the requests made here below, He does not give what we request because of our petition, but He has made the petition an intermediary. For He has clothed it in the form of words, bringing the mind to wander[45] in the Essence of God and in the knowledge of His care for us.

36   When, then, we receive what the order of prayer at no time could obtain, and for which the mind had not imagined requests – because this had not arisen in the human heart,[46] and so that rational beings might receive what their nature did not know to request – then we perceive that God, in this life and in the life beyond, gives by reason of His love, even making the cause <of the gift> depend on us. And because of His great grace He ascribes His gift to the goodness of our prayer and that of our way of life.

37   O mankind who have received such a Lord! O sweetness and goodness without measure! For when we receive the knowledge of all of this, then we will learn the true fatherhood <of God>, and His love and His goodness everlasting, and that God had no need of the world, nor creation, nor the structure of the future <world>, nor the Kingdom of heaven: He whose Nature are the Kingdom, gladness and light!

---

[44] See *Keph.* III 1; see also Evag. *Letter to Melania*, 22–25 (Casiday; Frankenberg, pp. 616–18): "...names and numbers of rational creation and its Creator will pass away...".

[45] Wander (*pehyâ*).

[46] 1 Cor.2:9.

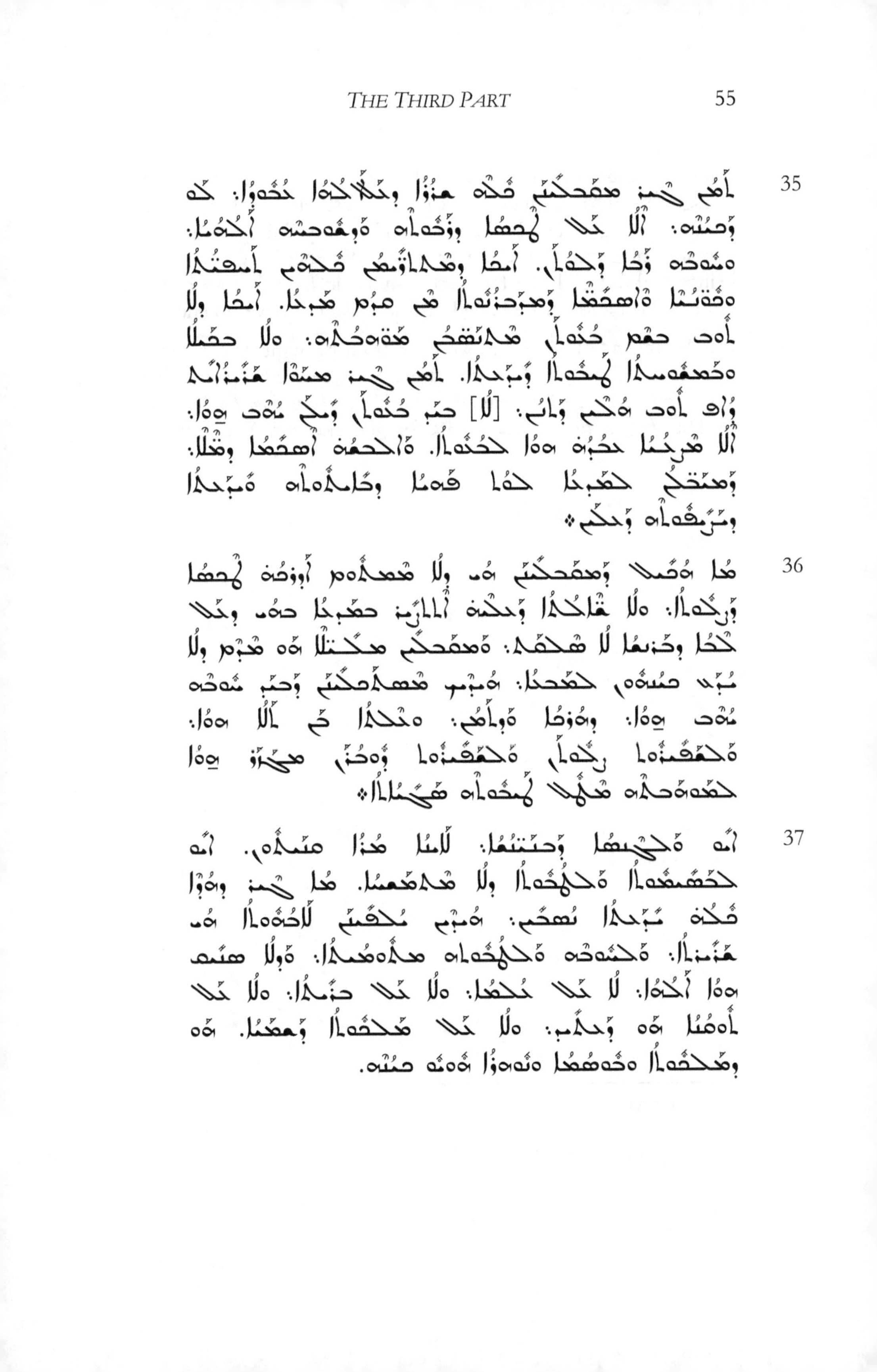

38 But it is because of His goodness that He does these things and has brought us into existence! Because of us, He created all these things: as to give us His Kingdom, His glory, His greatness, His magnificence and all the power of His Essence; and to make us beings without end like Him and clothed in light, whose lives are not cut short and whose Kingdom and existence have no end.

39 It is by means of Him that we have been brought near to all this knowledge; although of mortal nature, we are called *sons of the Father who is in heaven*[47] and we have known Him *who is from the beginning*.[48] To Him *be glory through Jesus Christ*, forever and ever. Amen, amen.[49]

---

[47] Cf. Mt.5:45.
[48] Cf. 1 Jn.2:13.
[49] Cf. Rm.16:27.

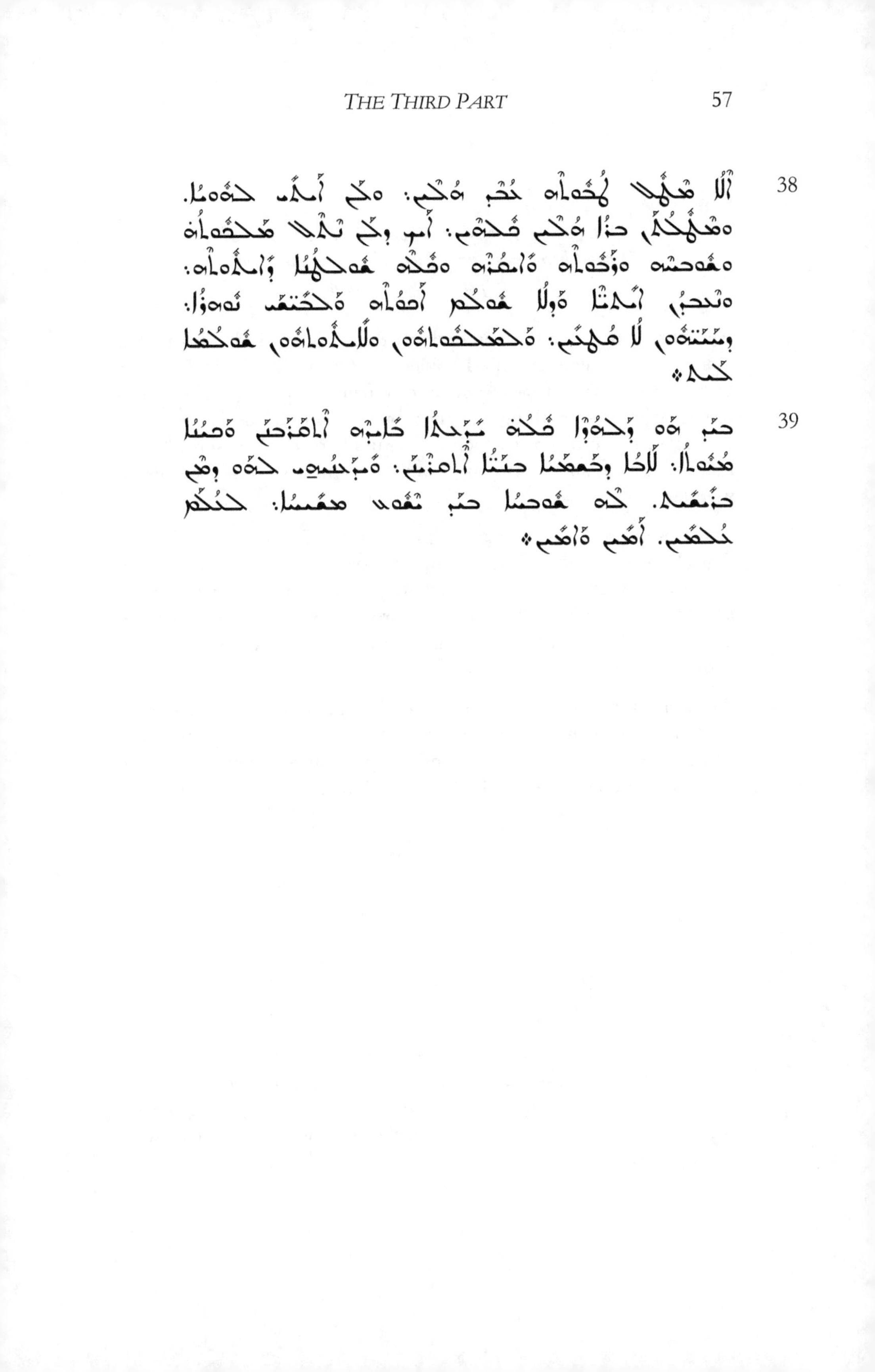

Chapter IV

*Of the same Mar Isaac. Second discourse on prayer:
what is the exact prayer which happens according
to the perfection of the mind.*

1. Authentic prayer[1] is the perception of what is in God. This is that <prayer> in which the mind abides not by means of petitions but by the perfection of love; and one remains in prayer before God not to ask for something or other, but to behold His Essence. So that from those realities which are naturally of the <Essence> one may observe it, at the time of prayer, as by the vision of the eyes, in wonder.

2. There are, indeed, three natural properties which are essentially of that glorious Essence. They <cannot grow> beyond what they are because they are perfect; nor can they be diminished or impoverished by accidental causes.[2] These <properties> are actually known by the mind, which is accustomed to marvel at the stirrings concerning the Essence.

3. As often as the mind seeks to look on what is hidden but falls short of it because of its being concealed <the mind> may, with these <properties> observe as in wonder that Nature which cannot be comprehended naturally, whether by vision, intellect or thought.

---

[1] Authentic prayer (*slôtâ ḥattîtâ*): Is.I 440, 475; *Keph*. IV 69.

[2] God's unchanging Nature: "God's properties are not liable to variations as those of mortals," Is.I 341 (includes a quote from Theodore of Mopsuestia).

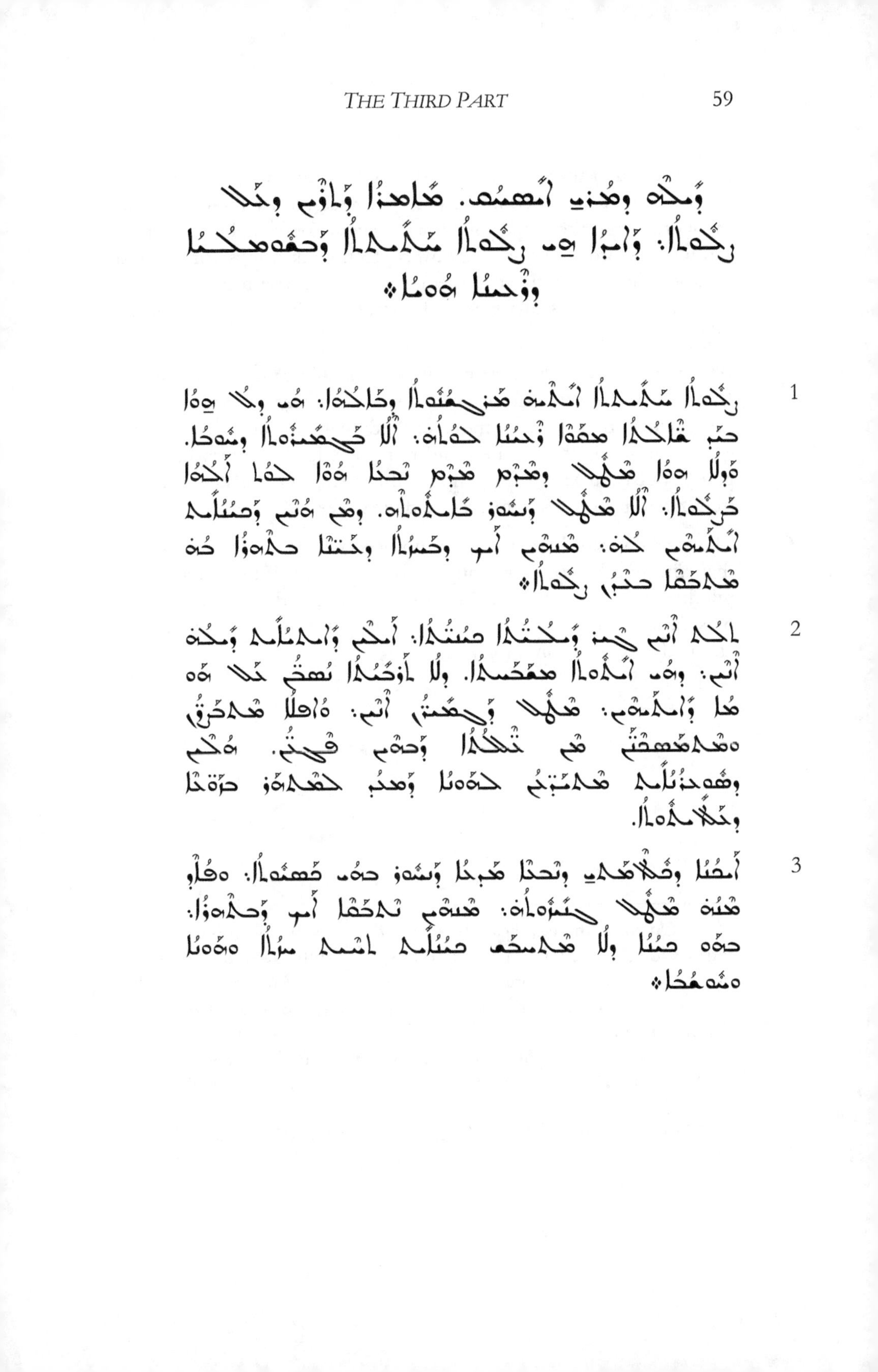

4   I say, then, that there are three indications proper to God's Nature: goodness, love and wisdom.³ By his goodness, indeed, God created the world.⁴ He, then, had love for it <even> before He created it,⁵ setting it in order in His wisdom, perfecting all things for aid and delight, whether for those present realities or those future ones; so that by these things His true and unswerving love for <creation> might be known.

5   But whoever from these properties continually observes the divine Essence, his prayer becomes unlimited and never ceasing. Because the perfection of love is more exalted than prayer stirred by requests. However, when the mind remains with God without dissipation but by reason of a petition, this <shows> weakness of the mind, that it does not yet perceive divine love.

6   The perfection of love, then, has no need to ask for anything other than the mind's contemplating God, insatiably. When indeed the mind enters into love and divine knowledge, it does not desire to present a petition for something or other, not even for <what is> elevated and very honorable.

---

³ On these three indications of the divine Nature – goodness, love and wisdom, see Is.III VII.41: goodness, love and power for good. See also Evag. Cent. II.1: goodness, power and wisdom. And for an extended reflection on love, power and wisdom, see Evag. *Letter to Melania*, 4–12 (Casiday; Frankenberg, p.612).

⁴ Repetition here of creation as an act of goodness and love: see Keph. III 70, with quote from Theodore of Mop.; Is.II X.19, XVIII.18, XXXVIII.1–2,5.

⁵ On creation as a revelation of His love, see Is.III V.14 and *Keph*. IV 78–79.

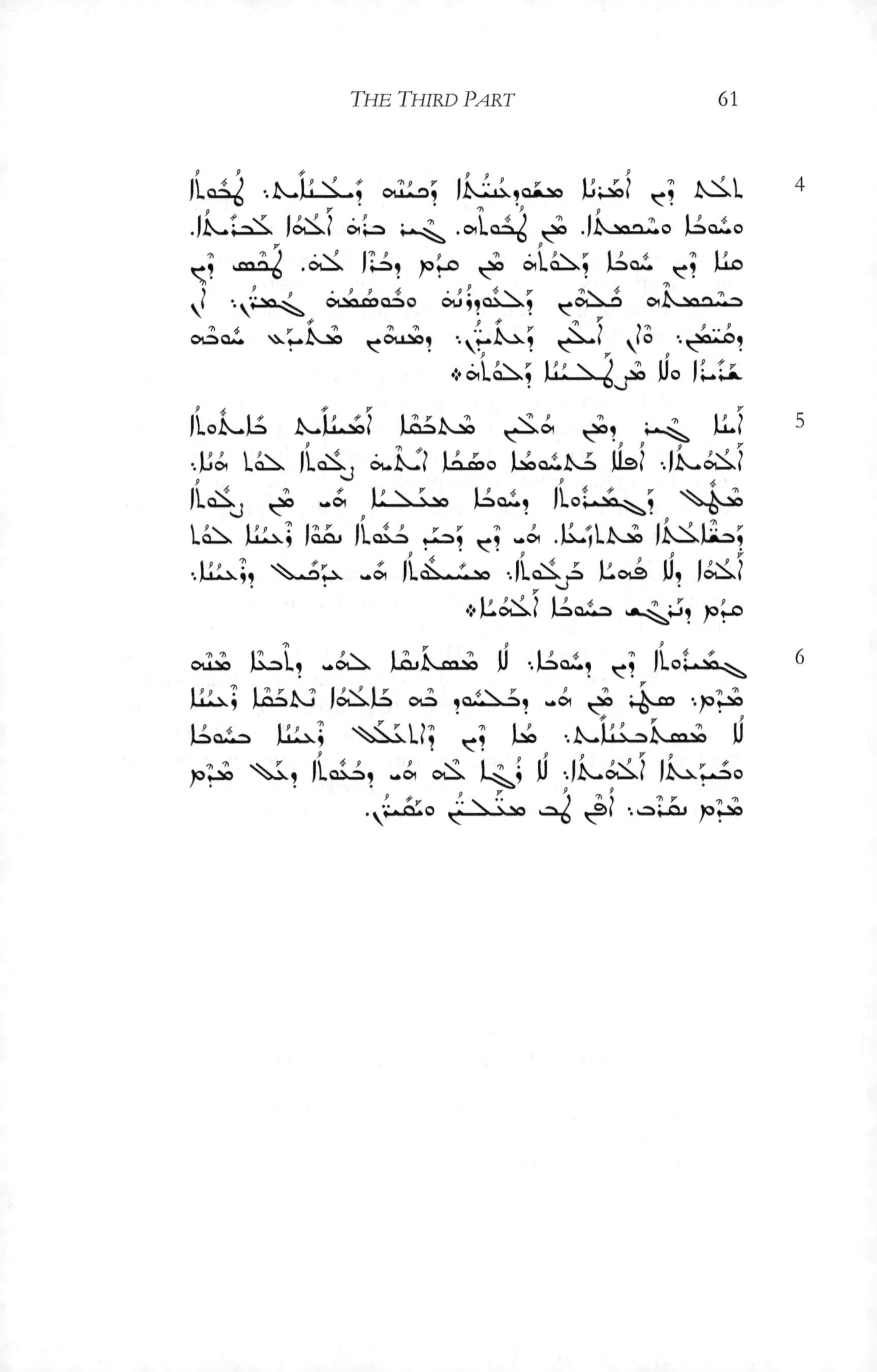

7   Beholding the greatness of God from the fervent love[6] of His mysteries – and receiving this perception – is more excellent than to wander in the realities outside of <God> which are not of His Nature. Prayer, then, of petitions and requests is an array of stirrings and prayers for contingencies, while the gift of love in prayer is the silence of the spirit.[7] For when the mind is united to God, it desists from petition and prayer.

8   If one desists from prayer by his will while his mind is not attracted, by means of a strong sense of wonder, to one of the divine insights,[8] dissipation will rule him and he will be filled with idle memories. But until one reaches these heights in prayer, it is not right to cease from persistent requests. For by means of constant petition, one may be brought near to those great realities of which we spoke.

9   What, indeed, is greater than the prayer which our Savior committed to His church? And this is entirely of petitions and requests! Is it like this because God has need of these? Or because one by one, we must remind Him of them by name? It is known, indeed, that God has no need of this: "Do for me such and such," as if because of this He would know to give the things He ought to give; or as if He would forget or neglect to give them, when we do not pray for each of the things by name. This opinion is an infantile reflection, not of those who have the intelligence of a <mature> mind, nor who have elevated knowledge about God, Creator of all.

---

[6] Fervent love (*ḥubbâ ḥammîmâ*): Is.II XVIII.5; Sahdona II 52, III 93, IV 52.

[7] Silence of the spirit (*šetqâ d-ruḥâ*): Is. II XV.11; cf. John Sol., Bettiolo, "Sulla preghiera,"5, p. 81.

[8] Divine insights (*sukkâlê alâhâyê*): cf. Is. II IX.11.

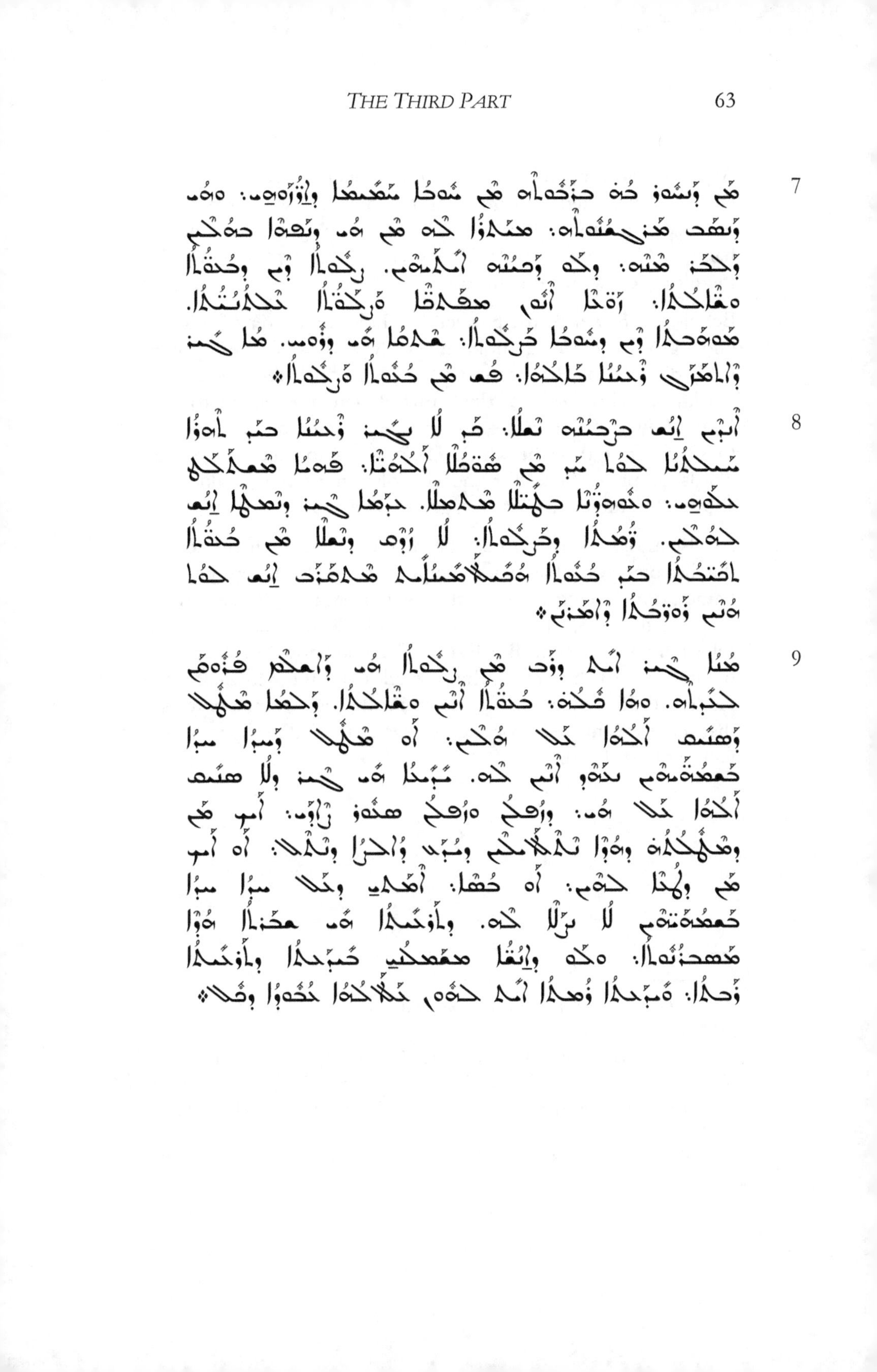

10 Also Macarius, marvelous among the saints, clothed with the Spirit, when he was asked how one ought to pray and why, he said: "It is not necessary to multiply speech, but in prayer to extend one's hand to God and say: 'As You wish and as it pleases You!' He, therefore, knows what helps us."[9]

11 Behold the prayer of the perfect![10] Behold the prayer of those who know God, *as He is*![11] Behold the believer whose faith is strong! As to God's care for His creature, it is truly not because our Lord does not know <about such as this> that He taught explicitly to pray to God: "Give us such and such," but because of our weakness, and to sustain our thought which He gave us to take delight in the words of prayer, and for the consolation of our weakness; but above all to direct us to Him.

12 As also those words at the time of the Passion: when because of the disciples, Jesus had made the prayer; and also the request to the Father, announcing to them that it was because of them that He was making <it>,[12] letting be heard with clear sounds those words full of encouragement. But Jesus also made known to the disciples, by the form of the prayer, the mysteries and the knowledge of the hidden realities, while being clear that those were not prayers and that there was no need for such words to the Father by that human nature of our Lord.

---

[9] *The Sayings of the Desert Fathers*, Macarius the Great #19: Ward, *The Alphabetical Collection*.

[10] Perfect (*gmîrê*): Is.I 250, 271, 495, 568, 578; Is.II VII.3, XIV.27; *Keph.* I 59, II 39, III 46, 89. See *Book of Steps*, XIV; also circulates as Evagrian, see Muyldermans, "Les justes et les parfaits," pp. 143–46.

[11] Cf. 1 John 3:2.

[12] Cf. John 11:42.

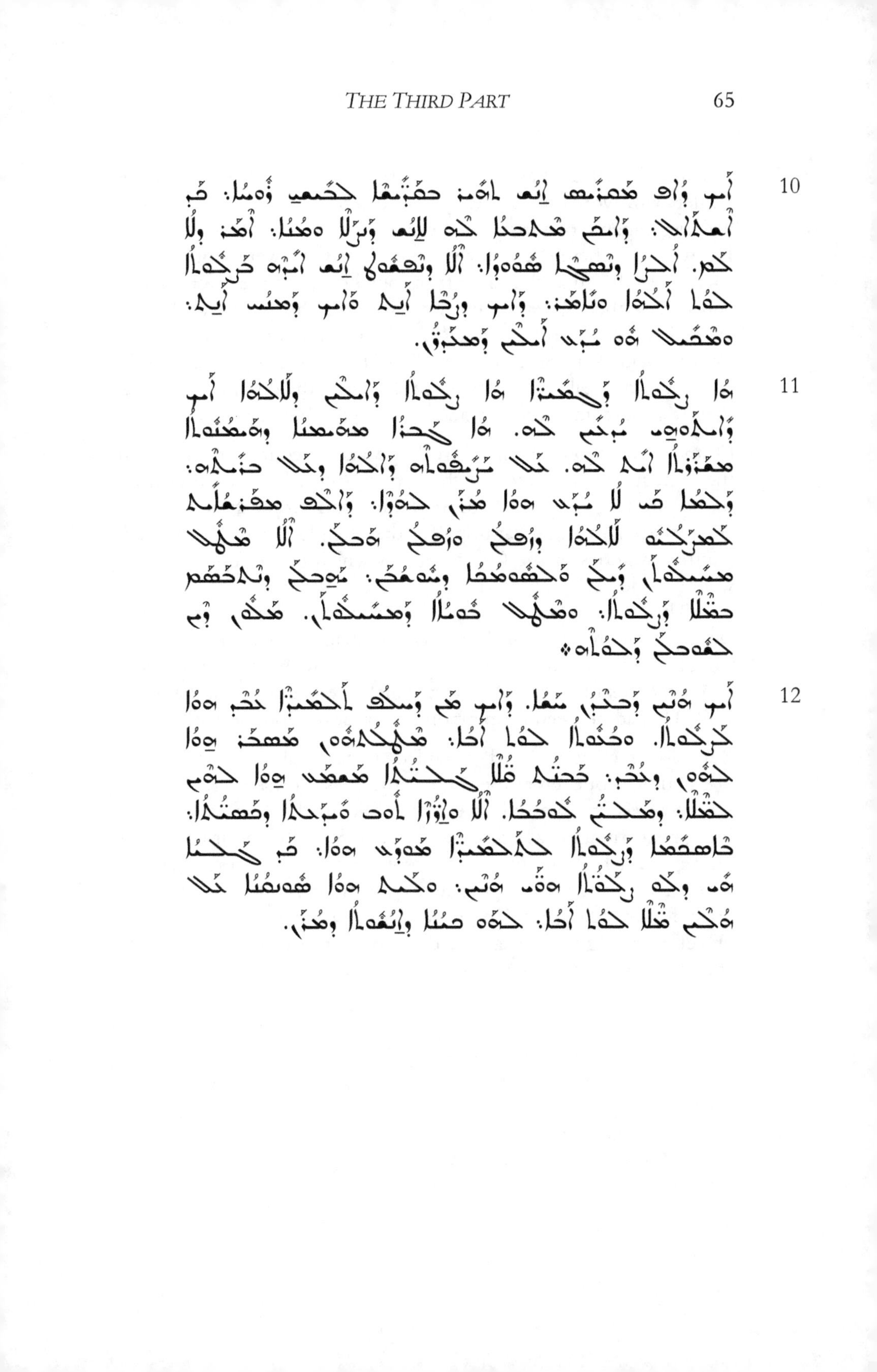

13   And this because what He seemed to want to persuade God the Father with words, was <really> according to His will. Since His will was capable of satisfying the prayer immediately for whatever He wished. Therefore, as we have said, they were not prayers which were heard at that time from our Lord, but they were words concerning the mysteries that by means of the Apostles He had wanted to make known to us. As it was the fulfillment of His Economy in that night, it seemed to Him that it was the time in which those <realities> were to be shown to the disciples, being as there was in them a teaching and a prophecy about future realities.

14   From these <words>, then, are hope and encouragement for all the human race, but how much more for those who are preparing to be brought near to faith in Him. And from these <words come> strength and great hope for the disciples. From them, then, are the mysteries of the future realities which in the future world[13] will be made perfect, indeed.

This is for the instruction of the <disciples> and for the whole world which our Lord was showing, while clothing His words with the form of prayer. From these <words> we also know about the greatness and the glory which He had with the Father,[14] while He had no need for petition or prayer to God the Father.

15   But all which our Lord attended to and showed is full of instruction. Not even at the time of the Passion was there need for a request, as the blessed Interpreter said in the Commentary on John, concerning what was said by our Lord in that hour by way of prayer. Namely: "The one who encounters this Scripture ought to know that here there is a prophecy concerning future realities to be done for the disciples. These are words spoken in the form of prayer. One ought not examine their forms nor their different varieties and not even the aspect of prayer spoken in it."[15]

---

[13] Cf. Heb. 2:5; 6:5. Future world (ʿâlmâ da-ʿtîd): see *world to come*, Is.III I.1.

[14] Cf. John 17:5.

[15] Theodore of Mopsuestia, C.John VI 17,19 (Vosté p.319).

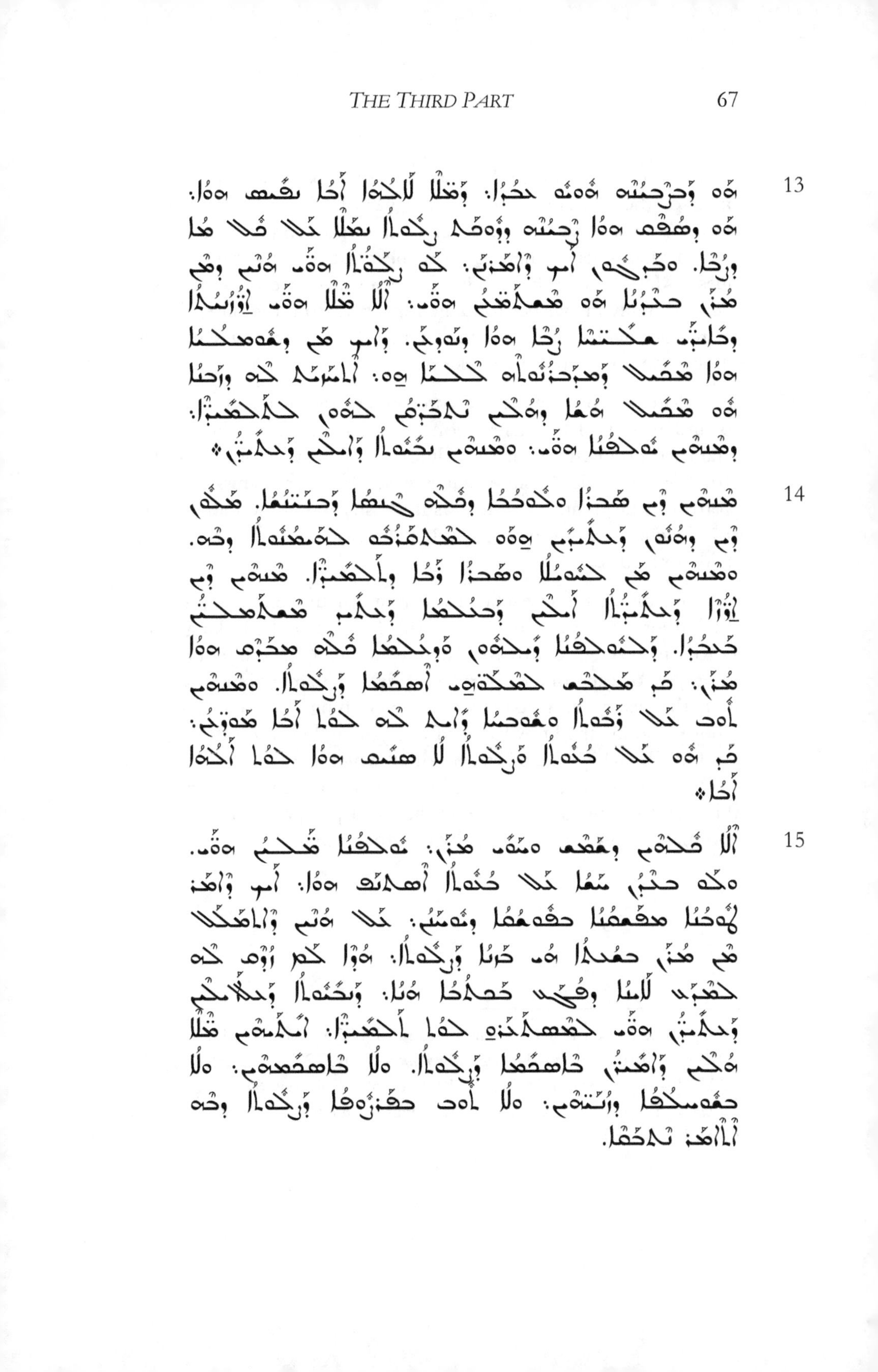

16 And a little before this in the *sedra* where he speaks about the whole order of the words of our Savior, giver of life, the <Interpreter> says: "This is clearly the force which the commentary makes known: that <here> there is no request but only the form of a request. <Jesus> says the words of the prayer in the form of a parable; and if anyone wishes to judge it simply, from the outer form as heard, one will find that many of the <words>, it was not even opportune for them to be spoken."[16]

17 Therefore, as how the blessed Interpreter indicates, it is also for us to understand all the instruction of our Lord: from this we may attain to the intention of the admonition and the form of the instruction. With it, <Jesus> makes wise by the transmission of the words of prayer; and in it, it is as if <Jesus> asks the Father, <and so> teaches the mysteries, spiritual knowledge,[17] and concerning hidden realities.

18 Here in this way, He teaches us to pray for this or that and to ask the Father for these things – as if this knowledge be lacking to our Lord – to show us clearly that there is no need that we remind God in prayer for each one of our necessities, by name; He knows what is in the heart[18] and takes care of everything. But our Savior, to whom belongs the knowledge of everything, because of the loving kindness by which He takes care of all which concerns us, for what is useful for us and for what is for our instruction – He acted in this way to transmit to us the tradition of prayer in a distinct way, and make known the requests by their names.

---

[16] Theodore of Mopsuestia, C.John VI 16,33 (Vosté p.306).

[17] Spiritual knowledge (*îdaʻtâ ruḥânâytâ*): Is.I 217, 318–20, 377, 473, 522, 526–27; Keph. II 75,77; III 49. See John Sol. *Soul* 64–65; Lavenant, *Dialogues* II, p.16 and XI, p.133. Cf. Evag. *Gnostique*, 47 (Bamberger) and Cent. II. 14,20; III 15.

[18] Cf. 1 Kings 8:39; Acts 1:24; 15:8.

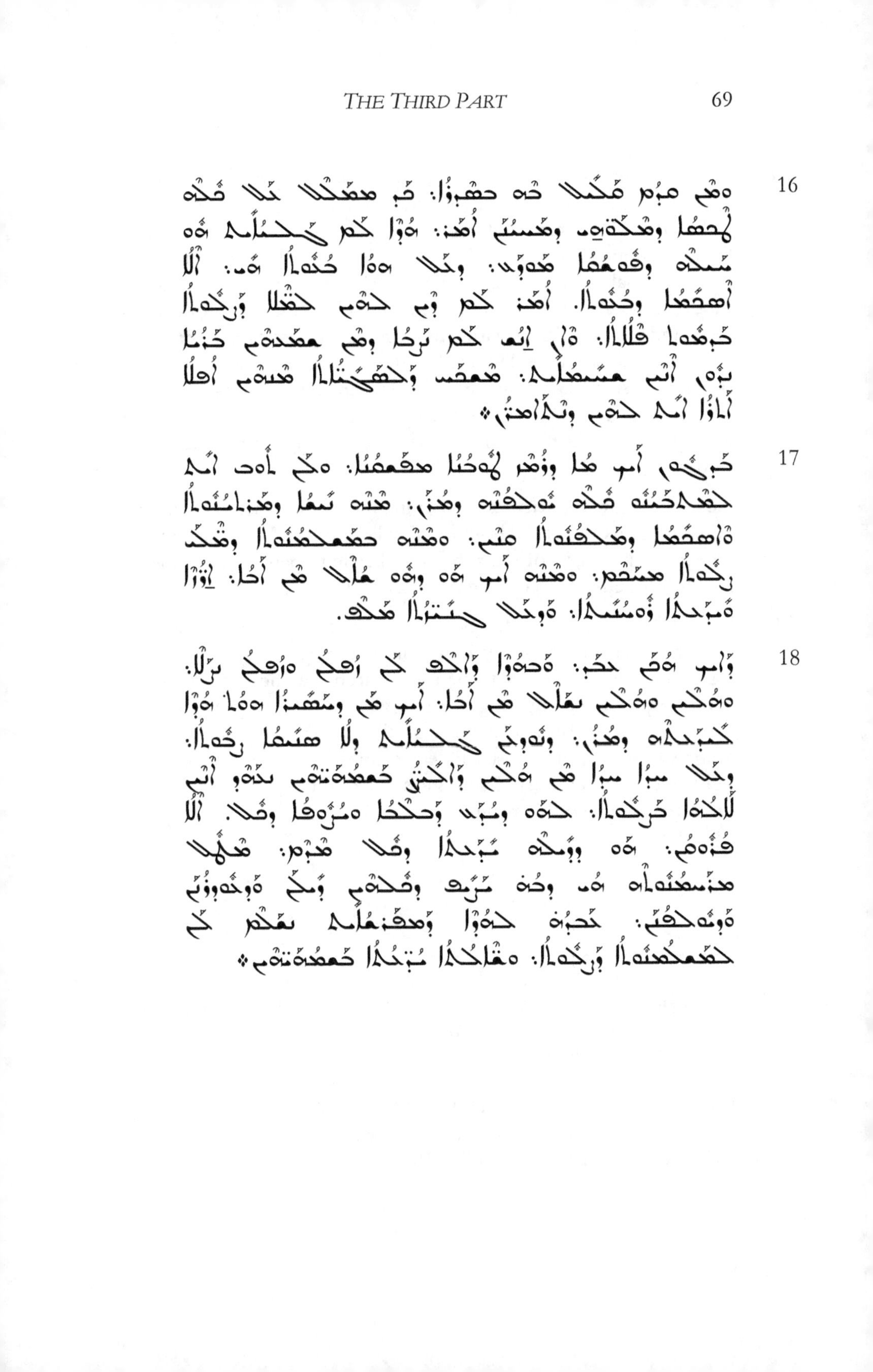

19   But why like this? So that by continual meditation on these <words>, the mind might ascend from earthly realities and by means of the mysteries which are in the words, attain to the sublimity of hope. Because in them there is <what leads> to the correction of habits and instruction about the realities of the mysteries, of the way of life, of understanding and meditation concerning God and on familiarity with Him which, by means of Christ, we have already obtained. The explanation of these things was shown briefly but sufficiently by us, as I think, in the previous discourse. Whoever accurately accesses the doctrine in these portions, I believe that one will not <miss> the excellent taste reserved in that reading.

20   Now then, of the themes determined for this discourse, it only remains for us to speak about the recollected mind.[19] By insight, we ascend to the origin of the subject and laying open the sense, let us gather it together into one, luminously and briefly.

21   When, therefore, one receives the gift of the Spirit,[20] while being in wonder regarding those realities which are taught by means of insight, the mind consents to be more careful at the time of prayer about requests for anything. Indeed, all one's desire grows dim by means of revelation and instead of all that, the knowledge of the Spirit[21] fills one with those hidden realities by the revelation of insight.[22] Then one desists from one's will and only is at rest looking on those imperceptible realities.

---

[19] Recollected mind (*re'yânâ knnîšâ*):Is.I 446; Is.II VII.3; XIV.10; XV.5,6,9; XXI.8; *Keph.* IV 49, 56, 63, 72, 92–93. And see John Sol. *Soul* 14; Bettiolo, "Sulla preghiera," p.76.

[20] Cf. Acts 2:38; 10:45.

[21] Knowledge of the Spirit (*îda'tâ d-ruḥ*): Is.I 30, 221, 337, 475 527; Is.II XII title; XVIII.16; XXXIX.18; *Keph.* II 75, 85.

[22] Revelation of insights (*gelyânâ d-sukkâlê*): revelation by means of understanding, Is.I 162, 352; Is.II VIII.7, 25.

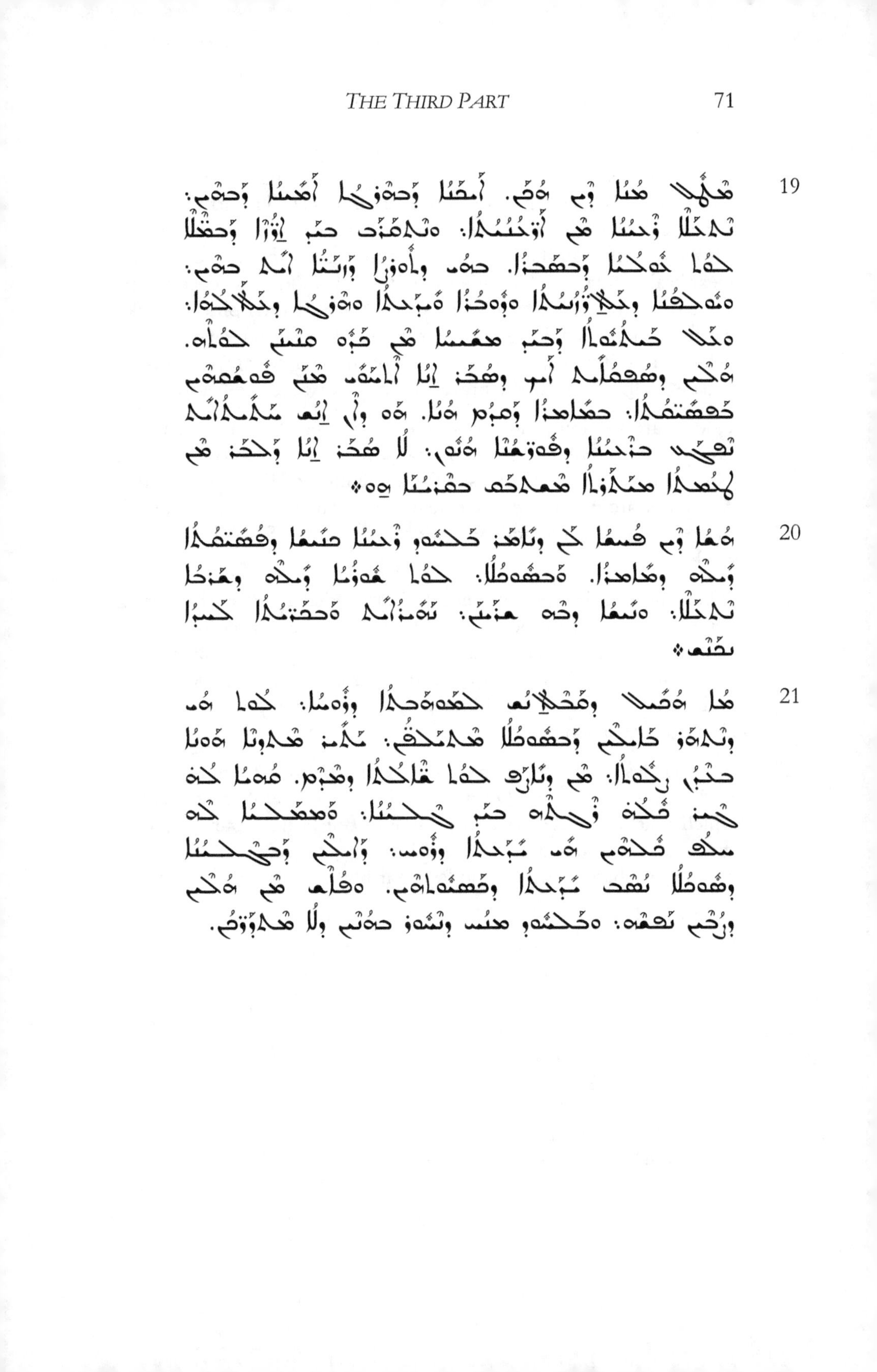

22 This is his prayer: only to marvel at God, according to the order of the spiritual beings who are in heaven and according to that <order> of the future world.[23] In that this gift of the Spirit,[24] continually shows him ineffable realities by means of insight, and in an inexplicable mystery. The instruction about hidden realities is imprinted on the mind, by means of the force of the Spirit; and like writings on a tablet, insight into profound things is engraved on the heart.[25] But if it happens that one be moved to prayer without these <realities>, only the prayer of praise arises in the heart.

23 God's care for him, indeed, shames him every time he wishes to present a different request from that which says: "As You wish and as it pleases You."[26] If he asks for something of his own will, this would declare him to be wiser than God – He who made him worthy of such a gift! – and not as one whom the Spirit knows and guides.

24 When the soul has become limpid,[27] immediately on encountering some subject about God, in that moment the mind is compelled to silence, a spiritual fervor arises in it and a quiet, amazed love. When, indeed, it is amazed in God, the mind is always recollected and easily withdrawn within itself, without compulsion or care about this on his part.

25 Do you desire to obtain these things, my beloved? Attend to the purification of the soul! Do not be moved because of these realities which quickly are destroyed by passion. But honor your neighbor, more than these realities whose lingering or removal from you happen by chance; they are, indeed, earthly realities!

---

[23] Cf. Heb. 2:5; 6:5.
[24] Cf. Acts 2:38; 10:45.
[25] Cf. 2 Cor. 3:3.
[26] Macarius, see note 9.
[27] On limpidity (*šapyûtâ*): see Is.III I.6.

THE THIRD PART

26 Not to love or hate someone on account of his ways, but to love him for himself, beyond searching <his> ways, as God <does>. Indeed, ways may change but you, before someone of your nature remain immutable, in the image of God. Indeed, *in the washing of regeneration*,[28] He has given you His likeness. Made incorruptible in the mystery, take care to have an incorruptible intelligence, according to the model you have received.

27 You desire to receive the gifts which foreshadow the heavenly home, so as to compel nature towards the resemblance which seems glorious. Now then, I will bring you near to what is the mother of labor in the soul. More than any other thing, be concerned about sweetness: it awakens in you all the excellent realities of the spirit and of the body. It makes you remain continually in peace of thoughts.

28 It is, indeed, a sign of the impassibility[29] of the soul: sweetness is the place of condescension which is the fruit of humility. If one does not descend from the height of one's intelligence, he cannot appear sweet to all who meet him. These admonitions make <for> purity in the soul, setting in motion in it the signs of the immortality which you desire and removing irascibility from it, which is the darkness of the soul.

29 The tendency to anger, then, is from pride. Pay attention to this word: every time that you have humble thoughts within you, not even a trace of anger can come near you. Indeed humility knows how to remain without anger in infirmities, in poverty and in the vexations with neighbors. But there is an anger which is from the stirrings of the temperament, which does not show harshness and immediately becomes calm, indeed it is followed by continual compunction. Whoever does not first acquire these things cannot receive *the gifts of the Spirit.*[30]

---

[28] Cf. Titus 3:5.

[29] Impassibility of the soul (*lâ ḥâšôšûtâ d-napšâ*): Is.I 478. Cf. Is.I 513 (*Keph.* I 33), 243, 367, 494, 520; *Keph.* I 41, IV 34, 87; Evag. *Praktikos*, 2 (Bamberger).

[30] Cf.1 Cor.14:1,12 (Peshitta).

THE THIRD PART

30 For Paul, indeed, there is no contradiction at all that we rejoice in the realities of the Spirit, while we journey in what belongs to the flesh.[31]

31 But when not even what is of the intelligence follows the Spirit by eminence of mind or excellent ways worthy of God, then also the soul goes about consenting to what concerns the flesh, even if it is rich in great thoughts from reading and the labor of the body.[32]

32 The grace of the Spirit, then, is not received in the body, but in the heart, and its activity[33] in the interior members of the soul is known by the mind. On that account it is <deep down> within, that we must adorn ourselves,[34] where we who are made poor may receive Christ.

---

[31] Cf. Gal. 5:16–17; Rom. 8:1–12.

[32] Labor of the body (ʿamlâ d-gûšmâ): for the distinction between gûšmâ and pagrâ, see Beulay, Lumière, 30–33. For example, Joseph Hazzaya uses gûšmê when he speaks of the spiritual bodies of the angels. He also uses it to denote the body after the resurrection. Beulay cites Evag. Cent. I.11 as a possible influence on Isaac.

[33] Activity (maʿbdânûtâ) of the Holy Spirit: Is. I.13, 260; Is. II XIV.12, XVI.3, XVIII.3, XXII.9, XXIII.2, XXXII.4. See Keph. I 98, II 14, 51, 54, 90; III 55; IV 85. Brock suggests roots in Macarius 9.

[34] Cf. 1 Peter 3:3–4.

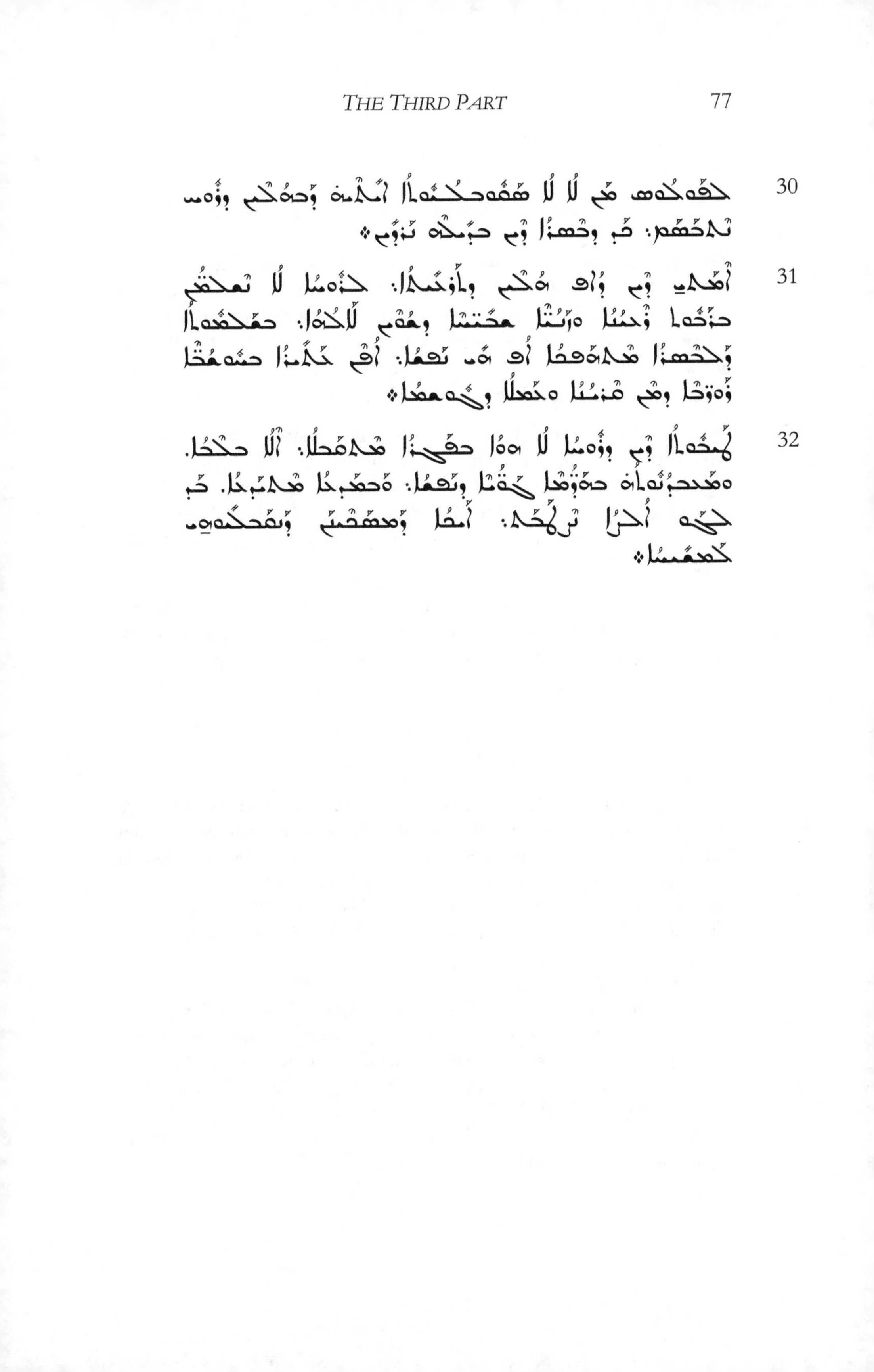

Chapter V

Of the same Mar Isaac. On the creation and on God.

1. Even if there was a time when creation did not exist, yet there was never a time when God did not have love for it[1] because even if it did not yet exist there was never a time when it did not exist in His knowledge.[2] Even if because it was not yet created, <God> was not known to <creation>, yet God knew it always, in all its various parts and its natures. He gave it its existence when it pleased Him.

2. One may know the true love of God for creation from this that after He had finished its structure in all its parts, He brought it altogether into one unity: sensible realities and spiritual ones[3] into one bond and He joined it to His divinity and He raised it above all the heavens and set it on an everlasting throne and made it "God" over all.[4]

3. Yet even according to nature, if creation had received a greater position than this, would this have convinced your nature, O man, as a true sign of the abounding love of God for creation?

---

[1] Cf. Is.III IV.4. On the theme of divine love Brock says that "God's boundless love is a central theme throughout Syriac tradition," from Ephrem to Isaac the Syrian, "Spirituality," 84. Others have commented on the insight of Isaac, that the Incarnation did not occur because of sin but only because God loves the world, see Hausherr, "Précurseur de la Théorie Scotiste," 316–20. See also Louf, "Pourquoi Dieu se manifesta," 37–56.

[2] Cf. Is. II V.11; XXXIX.6.

[3] Spiritual realities (*metyad'ânyâta*): found as early as the Clementine Recognitions; earliest Syriac writer, Narsai; Isaac's usage may reflect Evagrius and Ps.Dionysius. See Brock, "Discerning the Evagrian," 63.

[4] On unity of creation, see Isaac *Keph*. III 81; union of the creation with God, *Keph*. II 19 (Is.II V.18); becoming gods *Keph*.I 62; III 70; throne of the divinity Is. II V.17. See also Evag. *Letter to Melania*, 25–27 (Vitestam); Cent. IV.51 (cited by Isaac in *Keph*. III 57).

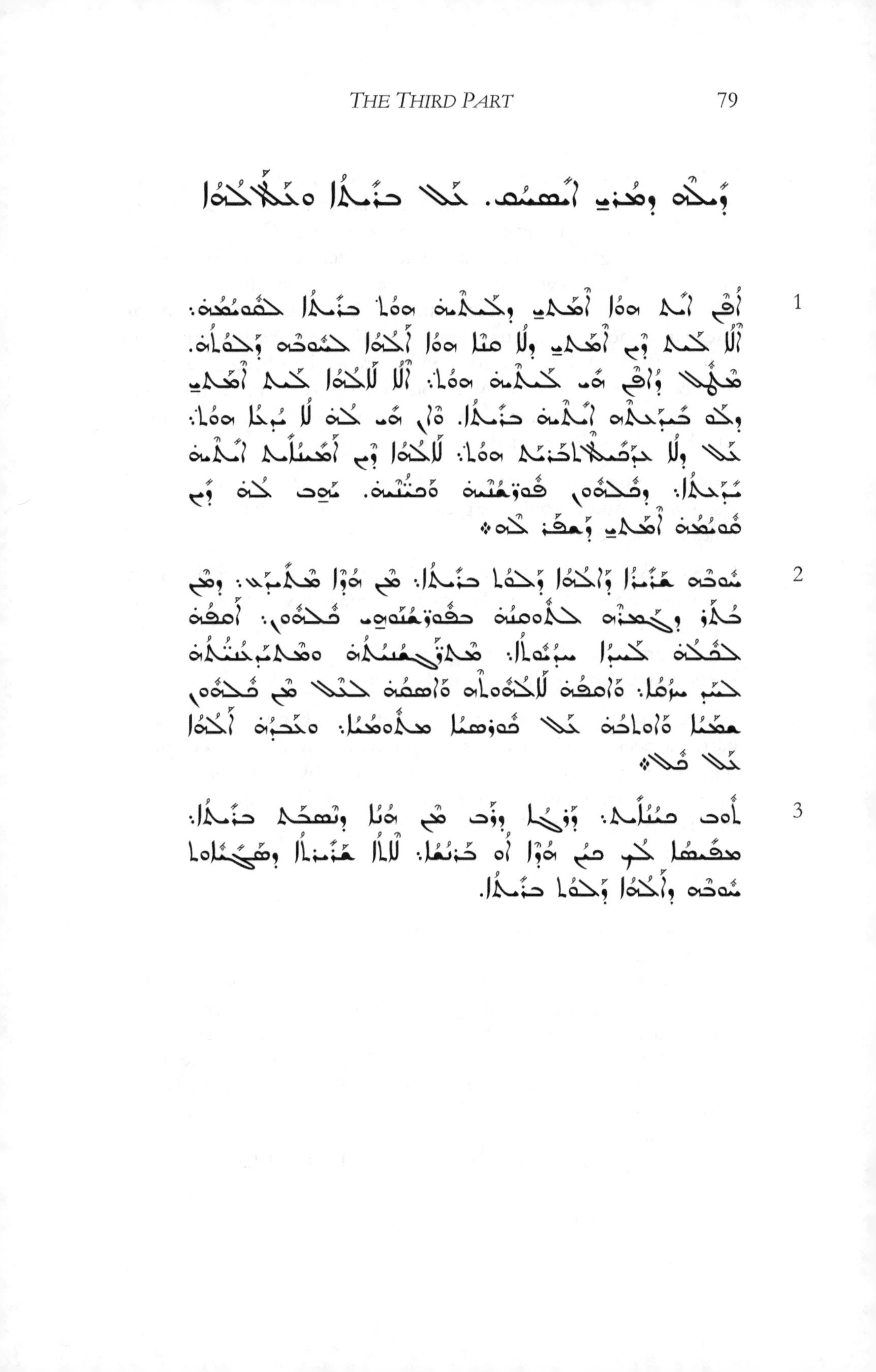

4   With what petition did creation receive this? And what prayer did it present for itself? And when did this arise in its heart?[5] And what way of life did it offer in exchange for becoming "God"?[6] How is it that our thoughts are distracted with aspects of little importance and we do not draw near to the great riches which we have received; we do not even perceive it. That is to say, we do not meditate night and day on our beauty, already we have become gods! Tell me then, O our beloved, if every choice had been given to us to choose for all of nature what pleases us, even what is more noble: who of us would have chosen for oneself or for nature all that which God has determined to do for us.

5   Now is there yet another place above where creation has ascended? But what position could be greater than that of divinity? And behold: creation has become "God."

6   For we do not come to these details with a request, seeking from them testimony of the reality of the mighty love of God for his creation. But we draw near to its extreme riches and to what binds the greatness of the many aspects of His love into one vision, which impels us to consider it collectively.[7]

7   Where our vision is not dispersed by things when we draw near to partial aspects of His love, as the mind stretches out to certain of the various wonders which were done for us by Him, it is possible, indeed, that from any one of these <realities> we approach, a sign of His fervent love for creation may shine forth.

---

[5] 1 Cor.2:9.

[6] On divinization in the Syriac tradition, see Russell, *Doctrine of Deification*, Appendix I. See also the comments indicating the concept of *theosis* already in Ephrem, seemingly independent of Hellenic influence: "He gave us divinity, we gave Him humanity" (*Hymn on Faith* V.15). See Brock, *Paradise Hymns*, 73–74 and *Luminous Eye*, 148–54. See also Vethanath, "Ephrem's Understanding." And see Buchan, "Paradise as the Landscape of Salvation."

[7] For this synthesis of divine love, see Is.II XXXVIII.2.

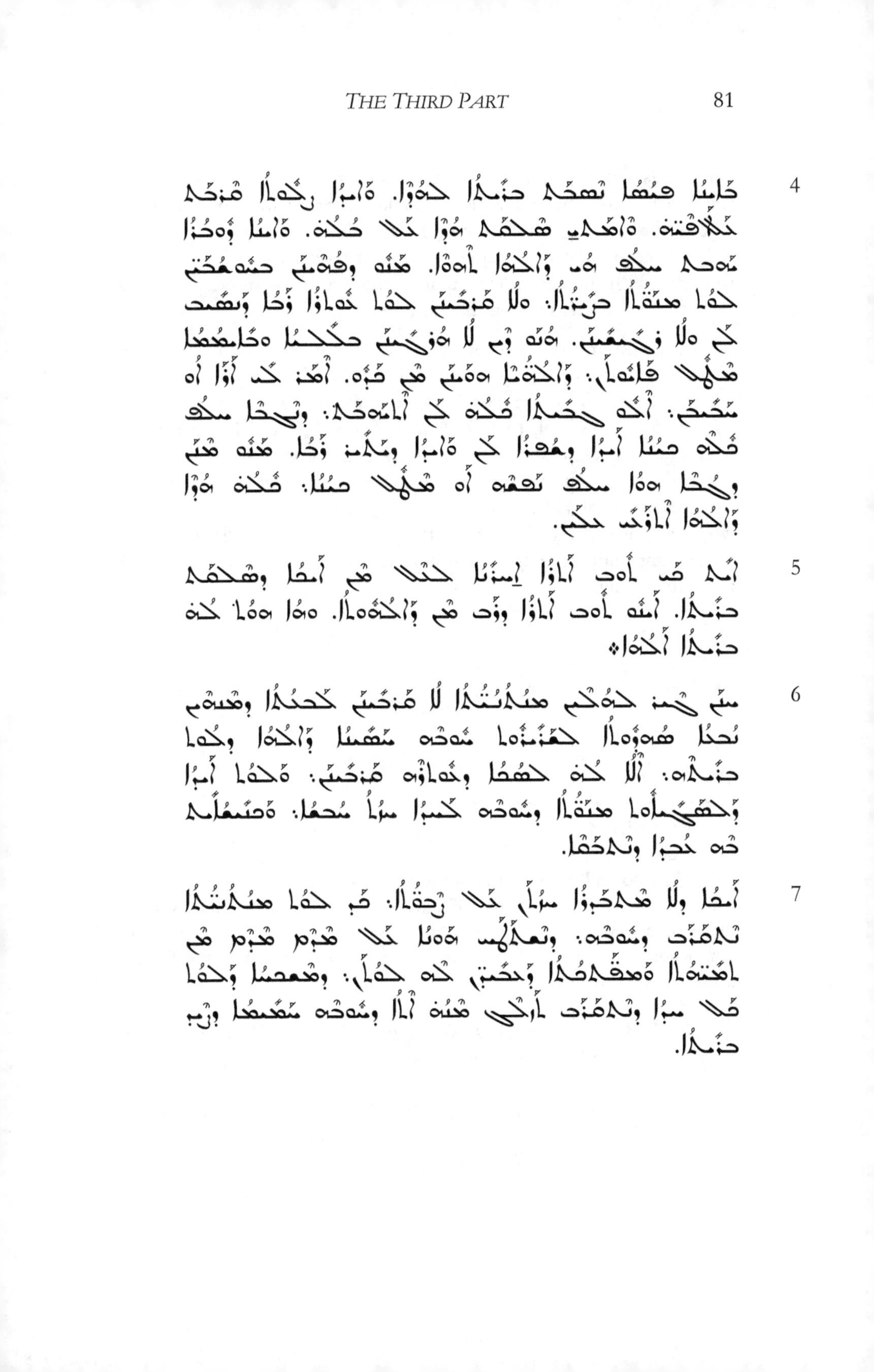

8   But let us draw near to the comprehensive reflection where even the division of other <realities> is taken away from our reflection; where our mind is not distracted by a multitude of things when we seek <a comprehensive reflection>. But wonder,[8] which searches thoughts with the very powerful intercession of the mind, generates collectively a unified vision, not dispersed.

9   At the beginning of creation when God created Adam, although not knowing between right hand and left hand,[9] as soon as he was created he desired the condition of divinity.[10] But what Satan sowed in him as evil, that *you will be like gods*,[11] and he firmly believed it in his childishness[12] – God indeed accomplished it. And at the end of days, he was given the diadem[13] of divinity because of the great love of Him who created him. In the case of the fathers who are moved by the Spirit, the divine power[14] which effects these things and reveals the mystery to them, does well to whisper in them, saying:

---

[8] Wonder (*tehrâ*).

[9] Gen.4:11.

[10] As noted by Brock, this is early evidence of *theosis*, through Adam-Christ typology. For Ephrem: "The Most High knew that Adam wanted to become a god, so He sent His Son who put him on in order to grant him his desire." (*Nisibene Hymns* 69:12). See Brock, "Some Paths to Perfection," 93–4.

[11] Gen.3:5.

[12] Childishness (*šabrûtâ*): *Keph.* II 47; III 71; cf. Is.I 525. See also infantile way of thinking (*šabrût tar'îtâ*): Is. I 529; Is. II XXXIX. 2.

[13] Cf. Wisd.5:16.

[14] Divine power (*haylâ alâhâyâ*): Is.I 489, 553; Is.II IX.11; XI.11,13; XXX. I7; XXXV.13; *Keph.* IV 46. See John Sol.: Rignell, *Traktate*, 22; Macarius 47, 80; Ammonius 571–2, etc.

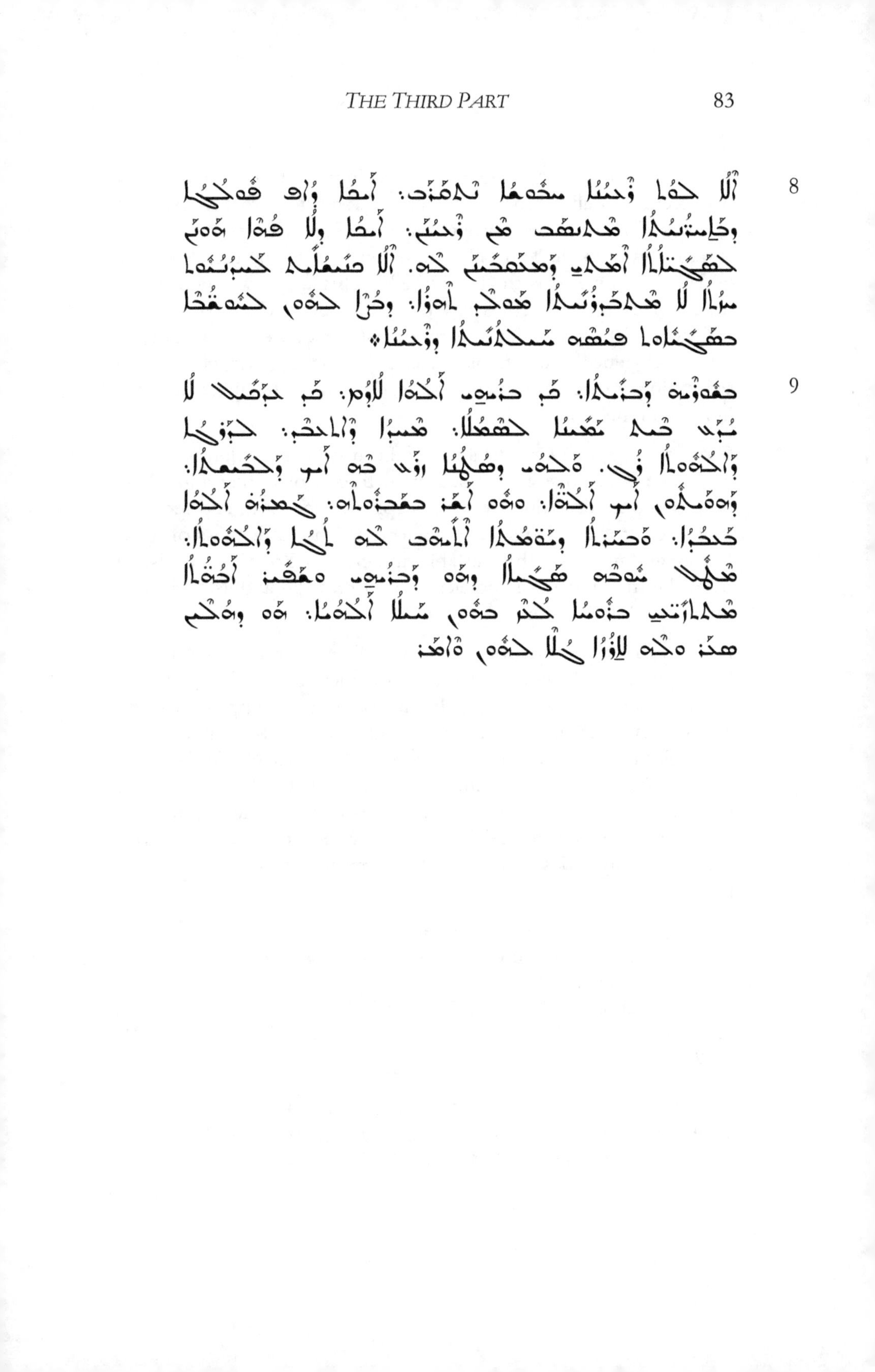

10 "The union of Christ in the divinity has indicated to us the mystery of the unity of all in Christ."[15] This is the mystery: that all creation *by means of one*,[16] has been brought near to God in a mystery. Then it is transmitted to all. Thus all is united in Him as the members in a body;[17] He however is the head of all.[18] This action was performed for all of creation. There will, indeed, be a time when no part will fall short of the whole.[19] For it is not just a matter of this great spiritual intelligence being transmitted only partially, but He will do something greater, once He has made <this> manifest and has indicated it here below.

11 Glory to You, our Creator and our Lord, who by a right contemplation of Your love, have filled me with consolation and joy. You have raised my thinking from the depths of the earth and received it on the throne of Your Essence, to roam in the richness of Your Nature and marvel at the ineffable mysteries of Your love, desisting from the multiplicity of the elements of creation and ascending to the place of its Creator.

12 His invisible aspect inebriates me and His glory makes me marvel. His mysteries stir me and His love stupefies me. He brings me to His mysteries and shows me His riches. When I suppose that my course has concluded, again they pour over me so that they are more glorious than the abodes I have passed through. And when I suppose that I have penetrated within them, I turn back to look at them as they have become a great ocean before me, limitless to cross and pleasant to behold. As I recount this its revelations change, its mysteries increase and its appearances are transformed in the mind.

---

[15] Cf. Evag. Muyldermans, *Admonitio paraenetica*, 7–8.

[16] Cf. Rm.5: 17–19.

[17] Cf. Rm.12:5; 1 Cor.12:12; Eph.5:30. See Evag. *Letter to Melania*, 616 (Frankenberg); see also *Book of Hierotheos* V.2, p.120. And see Is. III X.92.

[18] Cf. Col.1:18; Eph.1:22–23.

[19] Final recapitulation for all creation: Is.I 127; *Keph.* I 10, 19, 62, 68, 91–92; III 77, 81–82. See Is. II XXXIX with quotes from Theodore of Mopsuestia and Diodore; XL. 4–7; XLI 1.

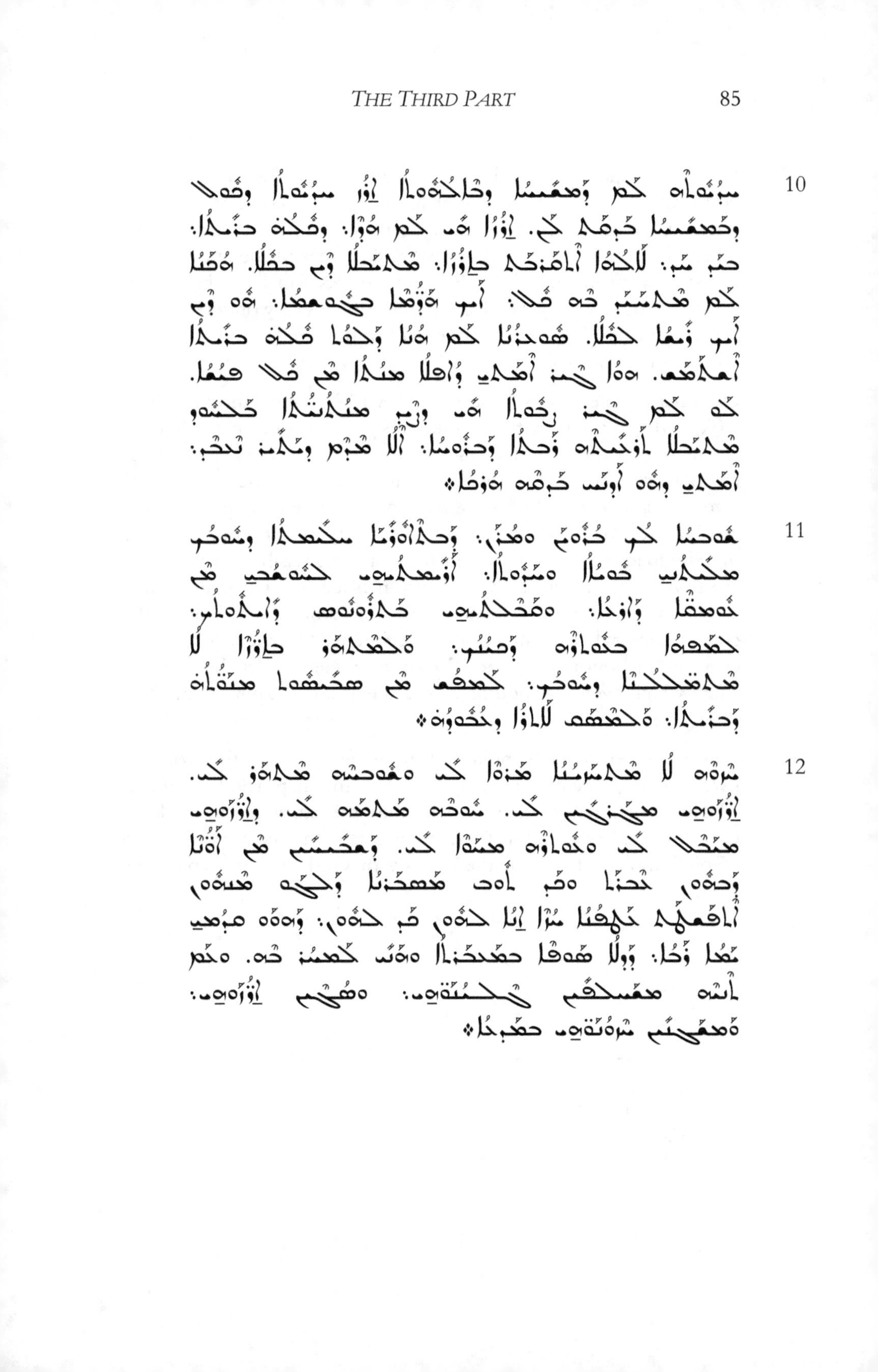

13 If in what concerns us and our nature, His mysteries which He has performed are to such an extent limitless, who would venture towards those of His Nature? And, again, whence could we cite another nature more powerful in insight than that of the angels without straying from their knowledge? If in this which we have seen and felt,[20] the paths of His Economy by means of wonder[21] are cut off from insight before the movement of the intellect, what then of His invisible realities?

14 O immeasurable love of God for His work[22] <of creation>! Let us look at this mystery with wordless insight so as to know that He has united creation to His Essence, not because He needed to but to draw creation to Him that it might share in His riches, so as to give it what is His and to make known to it the eternal goodness of His Nature. He has conferred on it the magnificence and the glory of His divinity in order that instead of the invisible God, visible creation might be called "God" and in place of what is uncreated and above time, God crowned with the name of the Trinity the creature and what is subject to a beginning. On the work of His creation, in honor of its sacred character, He has set the glorious name which even the mouths of the angels are not pure enough to utter.

15 This is the "emptying" spoken of in divine Scripture: the words *he emptied himself*[23] which Paul spoke of with unspeakable wonder, whose interpretation gives insight into the story of divine love. God loved all of creation to such an extent that creation is called "God," and the name of the majesty of God becomes creation's own.

---

[20] Cf.1 Jn.1:1.
[21] Wonder (*tehrâ*).
[22] Work (*ṭuqânê*).
[23] Phil.2:7.

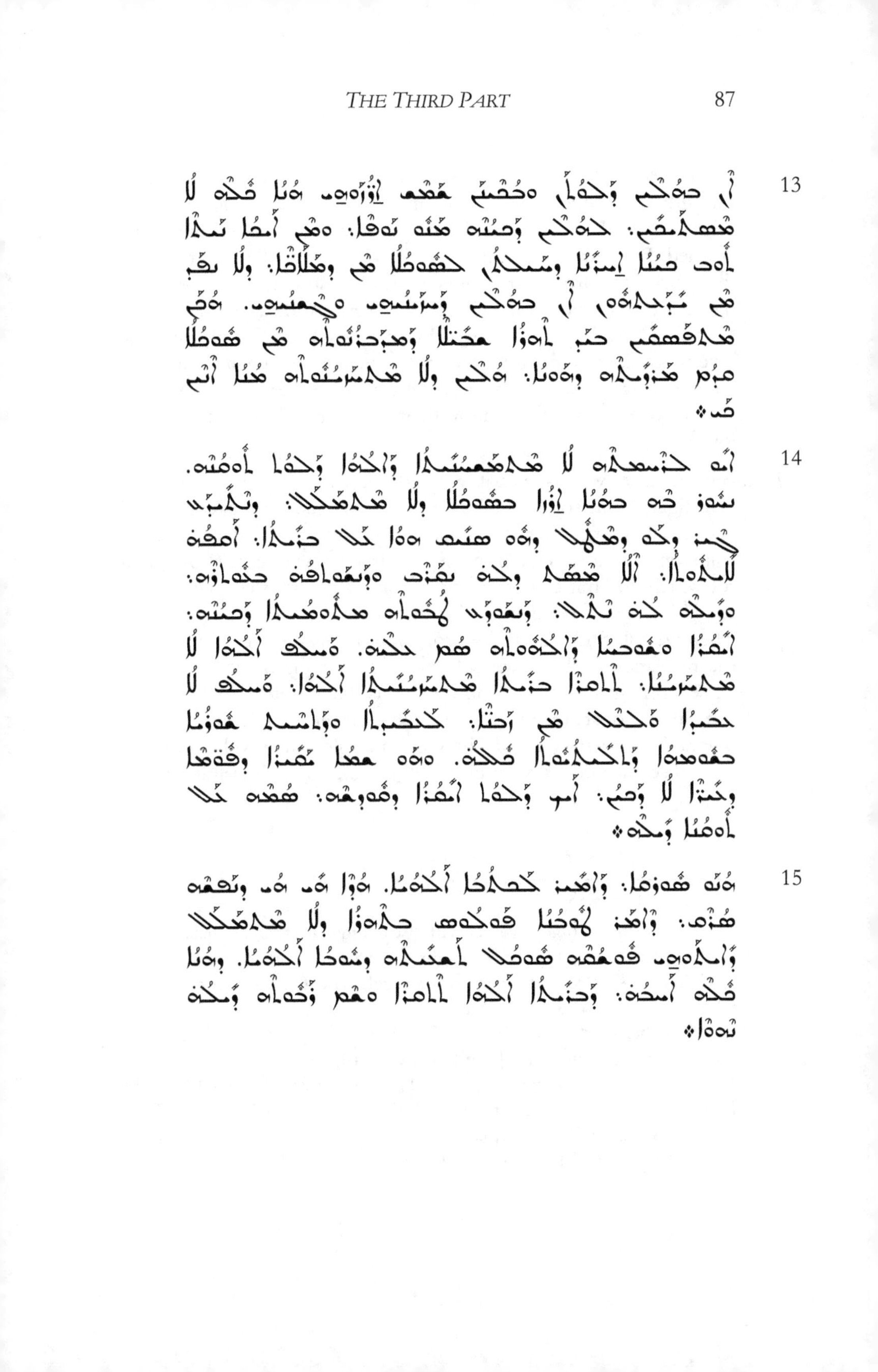

16 *Great is this mystery!*[24] I do not know how I had conceived to swim in this great ocean and who had given me these strong arms for swimming with pleasure in the unfathomable abyss without being wearied. But seeing that the ocean is wide and its limit not visible, the more <the arms> are imbued with pleasure and instead of fatigue, joy leaps up from within the heart. And, again, I am not aware of how I was made worthy of this grace of explaining the love of God, ineffable for a created tongue! Even angelic beings are <too> weak to ascend to the height of its contemplation and are <too> lowly to comprehend in their thoughts, all the riches of His love.

17 But because we have not applied ourselves to this height to investigate[25] but so as to take delight in it, this sweet savor will be given to us swiftly because we have taken account of His aid. So we will stop then and remain in silence after He will have shown that for which no limit can be found, <that is> to say, the love of God for His creation. And until the time comes in the other world,[26] when we will find indeed the prototype of His mystery prepared by the revelation of love, we will conclude our discourse here while persevering in this consolation which is like a mirror <of the other>, in the obscure image of our knowledge concerning love, in our faith, until the day of His great and glorious revelation when we will see our riches, with us and close to us in an invisible way.[27]

---

[24] Cf. Eph.5:32.

[25] Investigate (*bṣa*) together with "searching" (*ʿuqabâ*) are usually seen in a negative sense, that only delight and wonder lead to knowledge of God. This has its roots in Ephrem's struggle with Arianism in matters of faith.

[26] Other world (*ʿâlmâ ʾḥrinâ*): Theodore of Mopsuestia, C.John (Vosté) p.319; Evag. Cent.V.12; John Sol. *Soul* 7, 18, 23, 24, 55, 56, 69 and his *Letter to Hesychius* 57; Babai *C. Evagrius* 126. See Is.I 257; Is.II, X.19, 28, 30; *Keph*. II 65, III 77. It is also found in Ephrem, *Hymns on Nisibis* 46.17 and Jacob of Serug IV 824, 826 (Bedjan).

[27] Cf. 1 Cor.13:12; 2 Cor.5:7; 1 Jn.3:2.

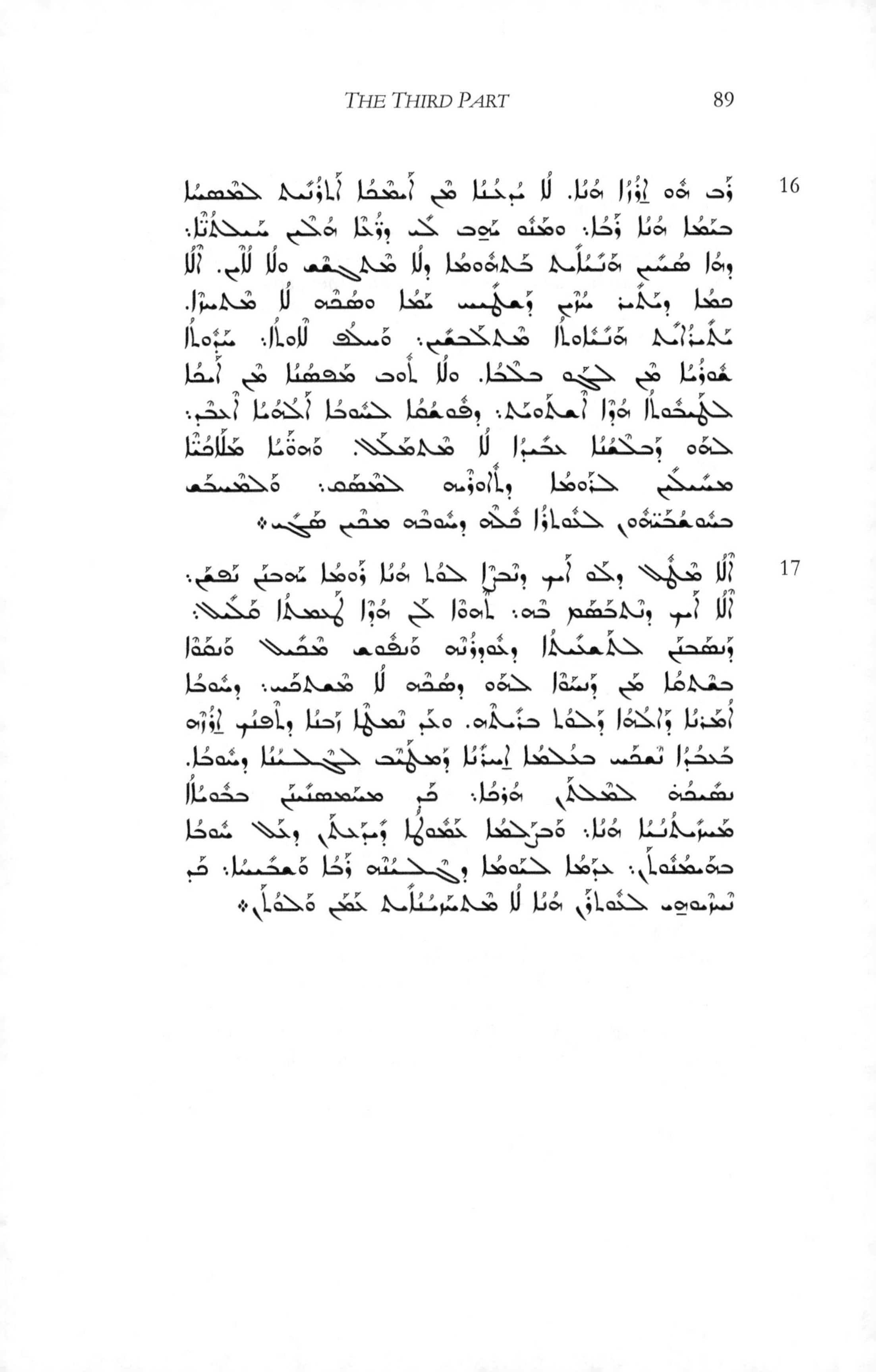

18 Who is capable of the wonder and the joy at these things that <God> has prepared for us without <our> having asked, in His everlasting love and in His immeasurable mercy. As it is said: *God who is rich in mercy on account of His great love with which He has loved us*, etc.[28] To Him be glory forever and ever. Amen, amen.

---

[28] Eph.2:4:
And why was he stretched out on the Cross for the sake of sinners, handing over his sacred body to suffering on behalf of the world? I myself say that God did all this for no other reason, except to make known to the world the love that he has, his aim being that we, as a result of our increased love resulting from an awareness of this, might be captivated by his love when he provided the occasion of this manifestation of the power of the Kingdom of Heaven – which consists in love – by means of the death of his Son.
(Isaac *Keph*. IV 78, trans. S. Brock)

18 ܡܢܗ ܗܩܡ ܟܐܘܙܐ ܡܚܣܪܘܐܐ ܘܚܘܟܝ ܘܗܘ ܘܢܟܘ ܟܡ
ܘܠܐ ܗܢܚܐ: ܚܢܘܚܗ ܡܐܘܗܢܐ ܘܚܬܣܓܘܘܝ ܘܠܐ ܡܚܐܗܡܢܝ.
ܐܟܘܐ ܠܟܡ ܘܟܠܡܢ ܕܬܣܓܘܘܝ: ܡܘܠܐ ܢܘܘܗ ܗܝܟܠܐ
ܘܐܢܬܝ ܘܝܗܢܘܐ. ܘܟܗ ܗܘܗܣܐ ܟܢܘܟܡ ܚܠܩܢܝ: ܐܡܢܝ
ܘܐܡܢܝ ܀

Chapter VI

Of the same Mar Isaac. The purpose of exhortation in agreement with the foregoing <account>: concerning the sweetness of divine judgment and the intention of His providence.

1. Not to cultivate sufficiently what one ought is more tolerable than that one not examine what one has received, so as to know and confess according as one is able. This is often the weakness of nature and the perversion of the will. But the ocean of the grace of God, who confesses it as is due? Even that one who knows then, is not able to confess <it>: the greatness of the realities which the divine Nature prefigures is immense!

2. The grace and the love of this <Nature> with their abundance are poured forth on the intellect in a deluge of marvelous thoughts and the riches of contemplation. They cover the mind at the time of meditation, and it is silenced before the perception of the knowledge of the realities of God; it also desists from the confession <of faith>. Even the power of wonder which occurs in it, ceases.

3. The perception of one's deficiency regarding the <promised> recompense is equal to not understanding the measure of God's love. Perfect recompense is <in fact> the completion of the work which is God's. The fact alone that we perceive that He loves us, is sufficient in place of the work we ought to do if we are not capable of it. And <our> discovery that we are ignorant of the measure of <His Love> is reckoned by Him as the principle of all knowing. When at times we find ourselves in this <situation>, how our soul is enlightened by it! And who is capable of this joy?!

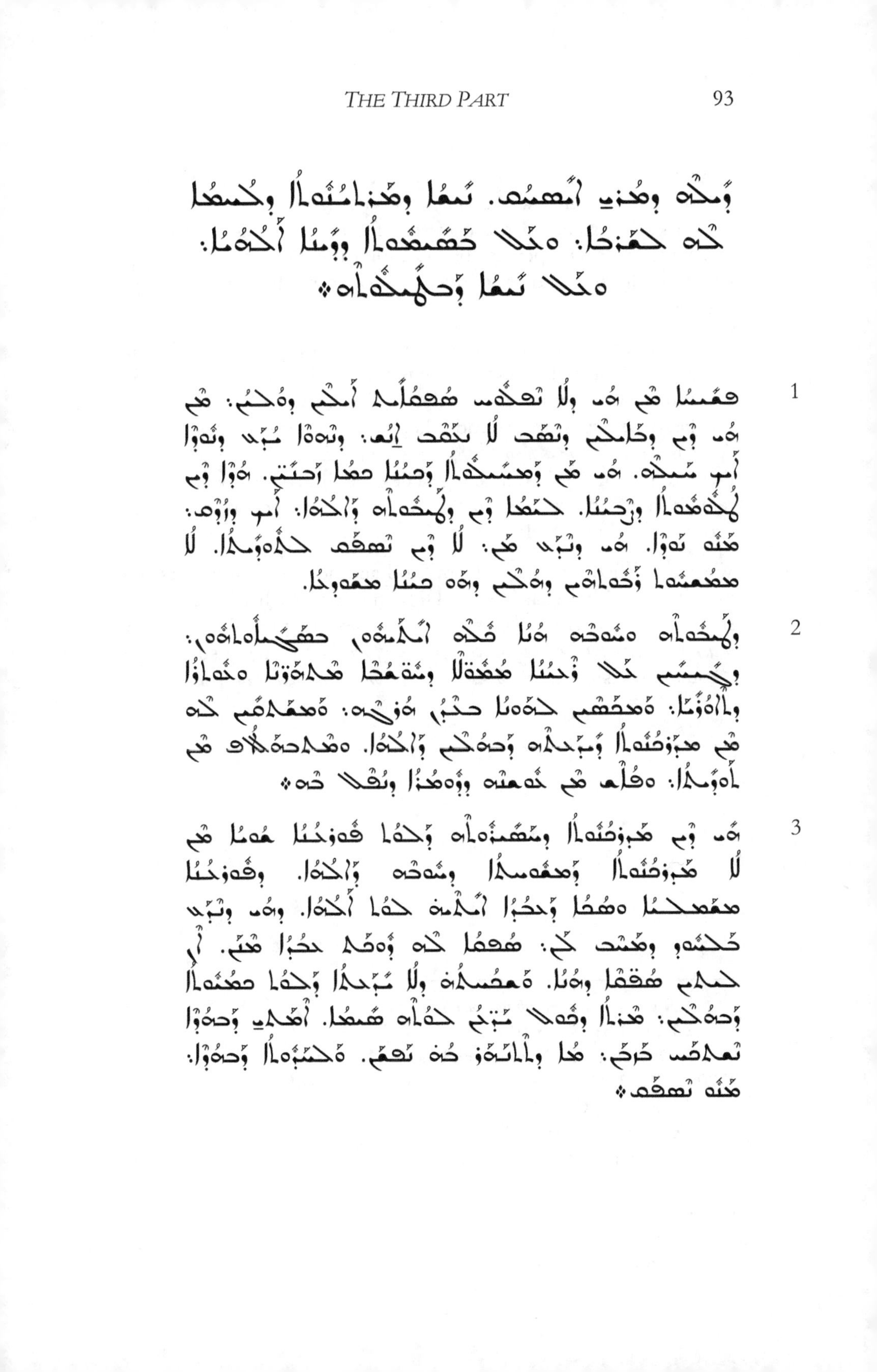

4   About the realities of God, my beloved – as they are, also as their manifold abundance was given – is written down already in this discourse according to the poverty of our knowledge. That brief discourse, by <its> persuasion regarding the truth, is sufficient to lead the diligent mind to wonder and joy in meditating on <those realities>.

5   Let us remain always in the remembrance of these things, and let us delight in them. Let us gather them continually before the eyes of our intelligence[1] and consider them. We are full of joy, and may our heart be lifted up in God when we have known these things. As it is said: *Let him who boasts, boast in the Lord.*[2] This boast <in> these things of God is amazing. They are, indeed, truly worthy of remembrance, more than our life breath. Let us reckon, then, what is ours as nothing at all.

6   We are justified by what is from God and not by what is ours. We inherit heaven by what is from Him and nor by what is ours.[3] It is said: *Man is not justified before God by his works;*[4] and again: *Let no one boast in works but in the justice which is from faith.*[5] This justice, then, <Paul> says is not *from works but only from faith, that is in Jesus Christ!*[6]

---

[1] Nilus, *Discorso di ammonimento* 22, p. 193.

[2] 1 Cor.1:31; 2 Cor.10:17.

[3] On salvation by grace and not by works, see Is.I 315–16; Is.II X.20–21, XI.2. Though works are never excluded, Is.I 302.

[4] Rom.3:20; Gal.2:16.

[5] Cf. Eph.2:9; Rm.4:13.

[6] Cf. Rom.3:22; Gal.2:16.

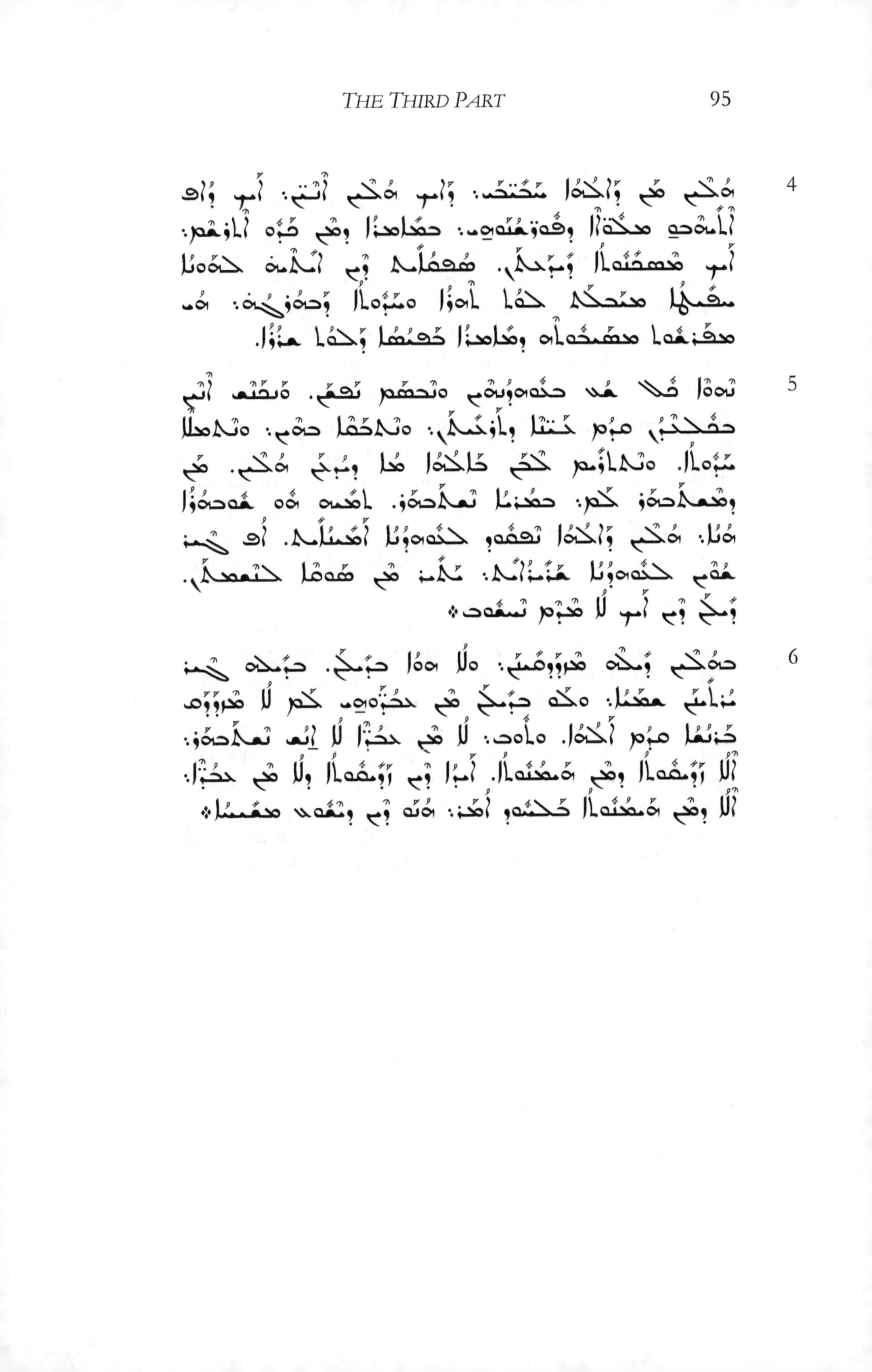

7   This is the interpretation, then, as to how what was said happens, that is, that no one is justified by works.[7] This does not refer only to visible works, that is, the order of the Law. The body, in fact, on its own is not capable of fulfilling all which is commanded <so> as to justify man. By the works of faith one is justified! Listen then to this: if one says he possesses justice according to the Law because of the works of the body, he would be a debtor of all which is commanded by God to be fulfilled. And only then would he be deservedly considered righteous.

8   If then the grace of faith which justifies the conscience does not intervene as mediator, or when works are lacking, or committing a transgression is involved, or one is not able to complete <the works> – the will can take their place. This is not to say that it is impossible to be justified by the Law without need of conversion or pardon; but <the Law> may also declare one deserving of censure.

9   Justice, whether through conversion or conscience, is not given without grace. So that when one is found to be guilty, through conversion suddenly and without works, he stands justified. The Law does not see it this way. In fact, when one has obeyed all <the precepts> but has stumbled in one of them – the one who wished to be justified according to the Law, that is by works and not by grace – not even the precepts which he has done are counted. But for one <precept> he disregarded he will receive punishment, according as the order of the Law has enjoined: "Whoever does not do all which is commanded in this Law will perish, from out of his people."[8]

---

[7] Cf. Rom.3:20; Gal.2:16.
[8] Dt. 27:26; Gal.3:10; James 2:10.

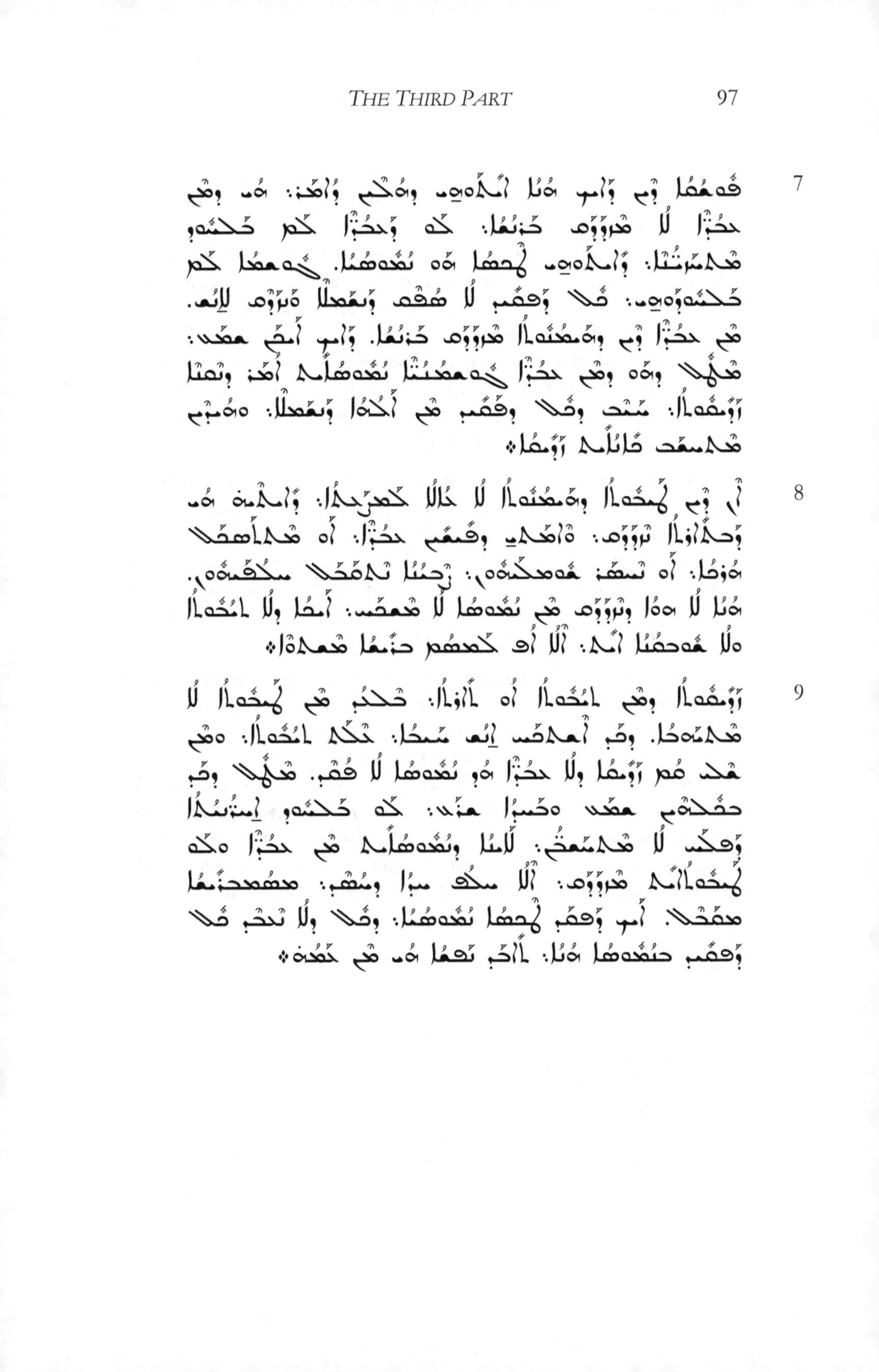

10 Whoever therefore supposes to be justified in accordance with the Law or by bodily works, what righteousness awaits him? For nature is always deficient, and the penalty of its deficiency after being judged according to the Law is determined by divine punishment. Therefore if one would come to expect to be considered righteous before God, this would be a perilous matter, even to the loss of one's salvation. Because human nature is not able to be without sin and to fulfill all righteousness as God desires since *not even one* has been found who has never fallen.[9] Behold, it is written: "Anyone who does not do all which is commanded will perish."[10] This is the righteousness according to the Law!

11 But if you say: "I am justified by conscience and by the will of the soul and I reveal <my> heart to God," behold you have requested grace! While not having accomplished any work, or having stumbled, or having fallen short because of issues, you are convinced that such a conscience is reckoned as a deed. But if you have no work, you who boast about work, why the boast? It is brought to naught. What joy can there be from our way of life?

12 Let every mouth be silenced: the Lord alone has granted victory! One is redeemed by grace and not by works and by faith one is justified, not by one's way of life. In such a way *that one who has not worked, but only believes in the One who justifies sinners, the faith* of his conscience *is reckoned* by God *as righteousness.*[11] This is what the Apostle said: *A man is justified by faith and not by works.*[12] But if righteousness were reckoned <on the basis of> work, it is written: "All who do not do everything which is commanded will perish."[13] Behold the righteousness which is from <one's> way of life!

---

[9] Cf. Ps. 14:3; Rm.3:12.
[10] Dt.27:26; Gal.3:10; James 2:10.
[11] Cf. Rm.4:5.
[12] Gal.2:16.
[13] Dt.27:26; Gal.3:10; James 2:10.

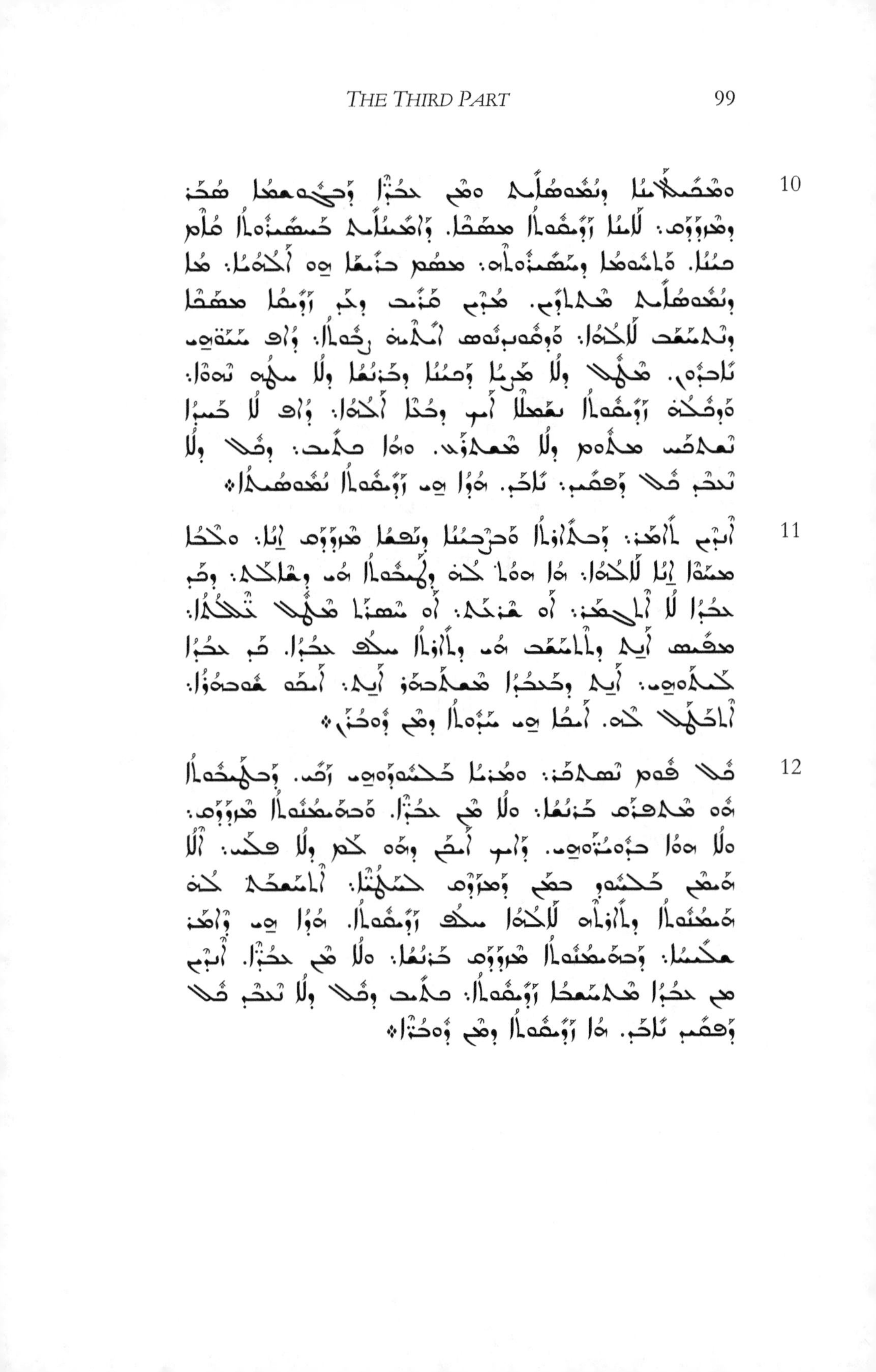

13 This is the righteousness, however, which is from grace when one does a little according to one's strength and fulfills it with one's will, even if the work is not well done. God, on account of His grace, reckons it <as> the fullness of righteousness, ascribing the whole action to him. For myself, even if I am not able to do much, I work according to my strength; certainly I am not able to be without blame or without sin. But O God, for a minimum of work, You give me righteousness!

14 Sometimes I am lacking even this minimum. Not only do I not have a work to give, but many times even that sincere will which I acquired with a good desire, turns aside from You and becomes involved with evil and is separated from You. I am almost emptied of a sincere will towards You. But then when I am empty of works or of will, with only the hint of conversion which You obtained in me, in an instant You give me the fullness of righteousness while the deed is distant – <righteousness> which neither time nor bodily <labor> could yield.

15 But while I remain waiting for all of this, You Yourself receive me, and by means of grace without works, You justify me. You establish me in <my> former high place. And only because of the conversion of <my> will, while I am not capable of anything, You take from me the death of conscience,[14] and You give me righteousness without fault. Who is righteous <so as> to be able to renounce this grace? And by whom have these things not been received along the path of one's way of life?

---

[14] Cf. Heb.9:14.

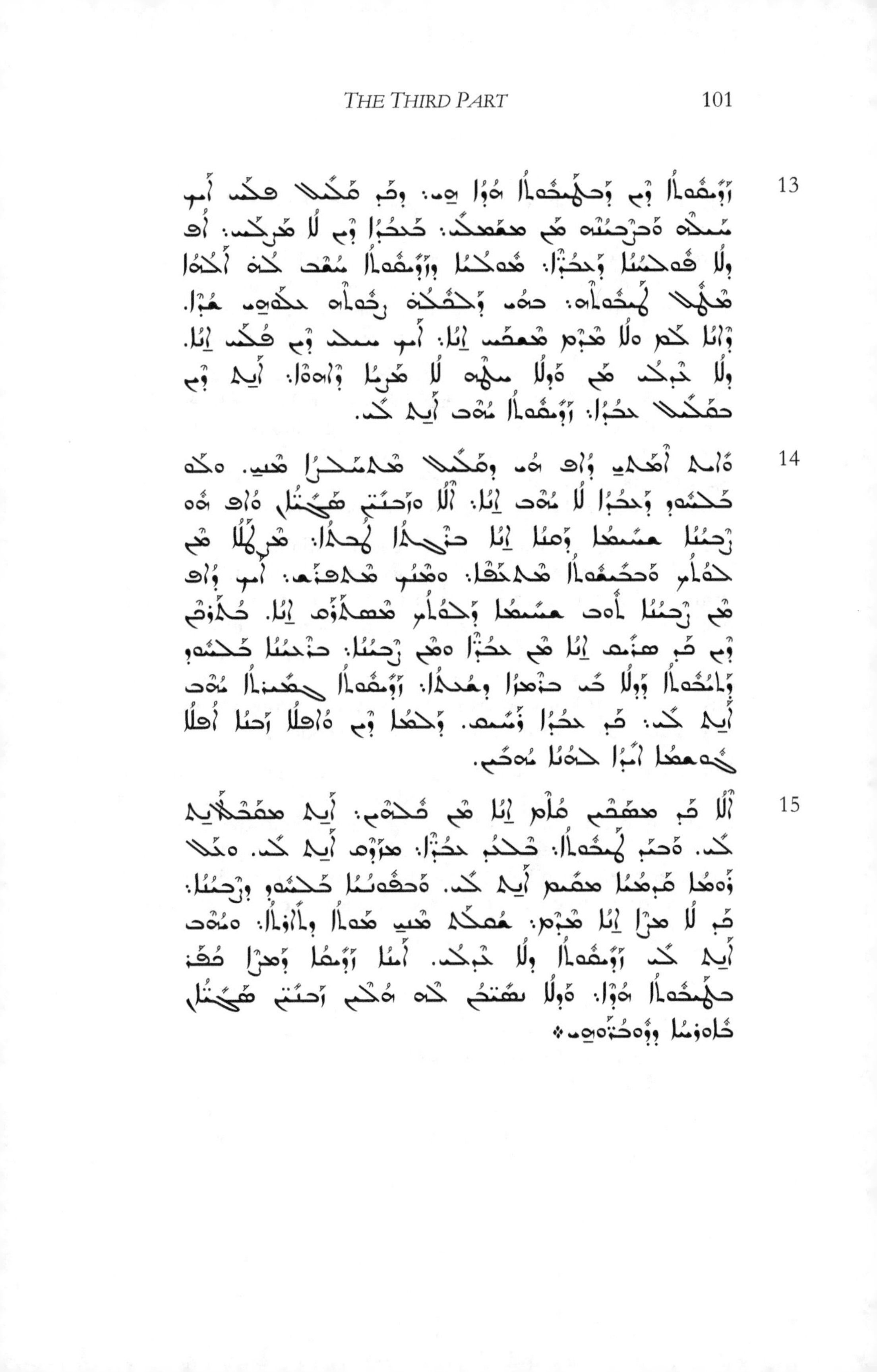

16 Who, then, understands this and faithfully discerns is not able to rejoice in works but only in the goodness of God. And the one who truly recognizes that God's goodness is the cause of his joy, does not hold that his joy be only for himself but rejoices for all creatures. His joy comes to be more abundant than the sea, because it is the goodness of the God of the universe affording such joy, and all creation is a partaker in it, even sinners share in this.

17 So then, he is quick to rejoice even for sinners. He says in fact: "They are <not far> from mercy because of the goodness of the Lord of the universe[15] by which righteousness has been given even to me without works." And again he says: "All like me share in this <great> good because God is good: He only requires a little will <then> He gives His grace abundantly and remits sins."

18 This is the grace which strengthens the righteous, preserving <them> by its being near and removing their faults. It is also near to those who have perished, reducing their torments and in their punishment deals with compassion. In the world to come,[16] indeed grace will be the judge, not justice. <God> reduces the length of time of sufferings, and by means of His grace, makes all worthy of His Kingdom.[17] For there is no one <even> among the righteous who is able to conform his way of life to the Kingdom.

19 But if human realities are to be judged and examined according to justice, yet in listening to the word of Scripture one investigates according to exterior knowledge, not entering into the meaning – where is justice here? As it is said, *He is merciful in all his works.*[18] However, even when He chastises here below or in the life beyond, it is not correct to consider this <as> justice, but <rather> fatherly wisdom.

---

[15] A variant of *Lord of all*, see Is.III 1.3.

[16] Cf. Heb.2:5; 6:5.

[17] On Isaac's eschatology, life after death, etc., see Alfeyev, *Spiritual World*, 269–97. See also Beulay, *L'Enseignement*, 488–510; *Lumière*, 157–58.

[18] Ps.145:17 (Peshitta).

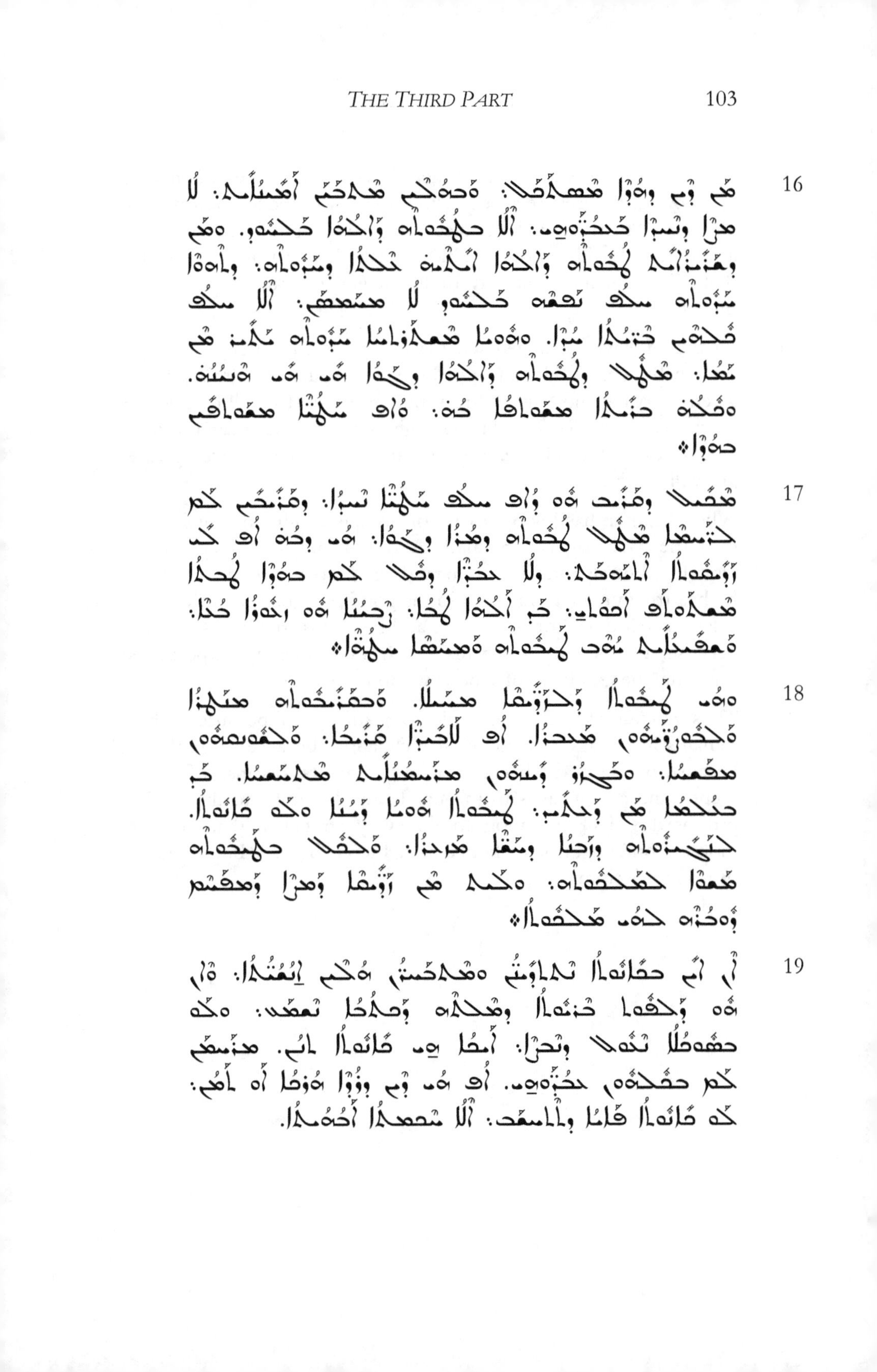

20 Nor do I call "exacting punishment" even those times when God visits one with a severe aspect, either here or in the life beyond, but <rather> "instruction," because they have a good end. On that account, as I said, no one is able to make his way of life resemble that Kingdom and that way of life which is granted <only> by mercy.

21 So then I have explained what was already said, that we inherit heaven by what is His and not by what is ours. And this grace is given every day, not <just> from time to time. If we all receive this grace, let us rejoice in Him who gives it and the greater will be <our> joy! Let us adore and give thanks for it, and an even greater gift will be given.

22 Whoever, then has joy by reason of his way of life, this joy is false, or rather, his joy is wretched. And not only in his joy is he wretched but also in his understanding. Whoever rejoices because he has truly understood that God is good, is consoled with a consolation that does not pass away, and his joy is true joy. <This is> because, as was <just> said his soul has considered and perceived that truly the goodness of God is without measure.

23 Thus human nature is not able to justify itself because daily it remains in need. On account of inclination, because of weakness, because of the body, because of impediments, because of movements, and also what is from outside and is similar to this – God proposed <His> intention to do every stratagem that in every moment one might be reckoned as righteous before Him, as he has heard in <Scripture>.

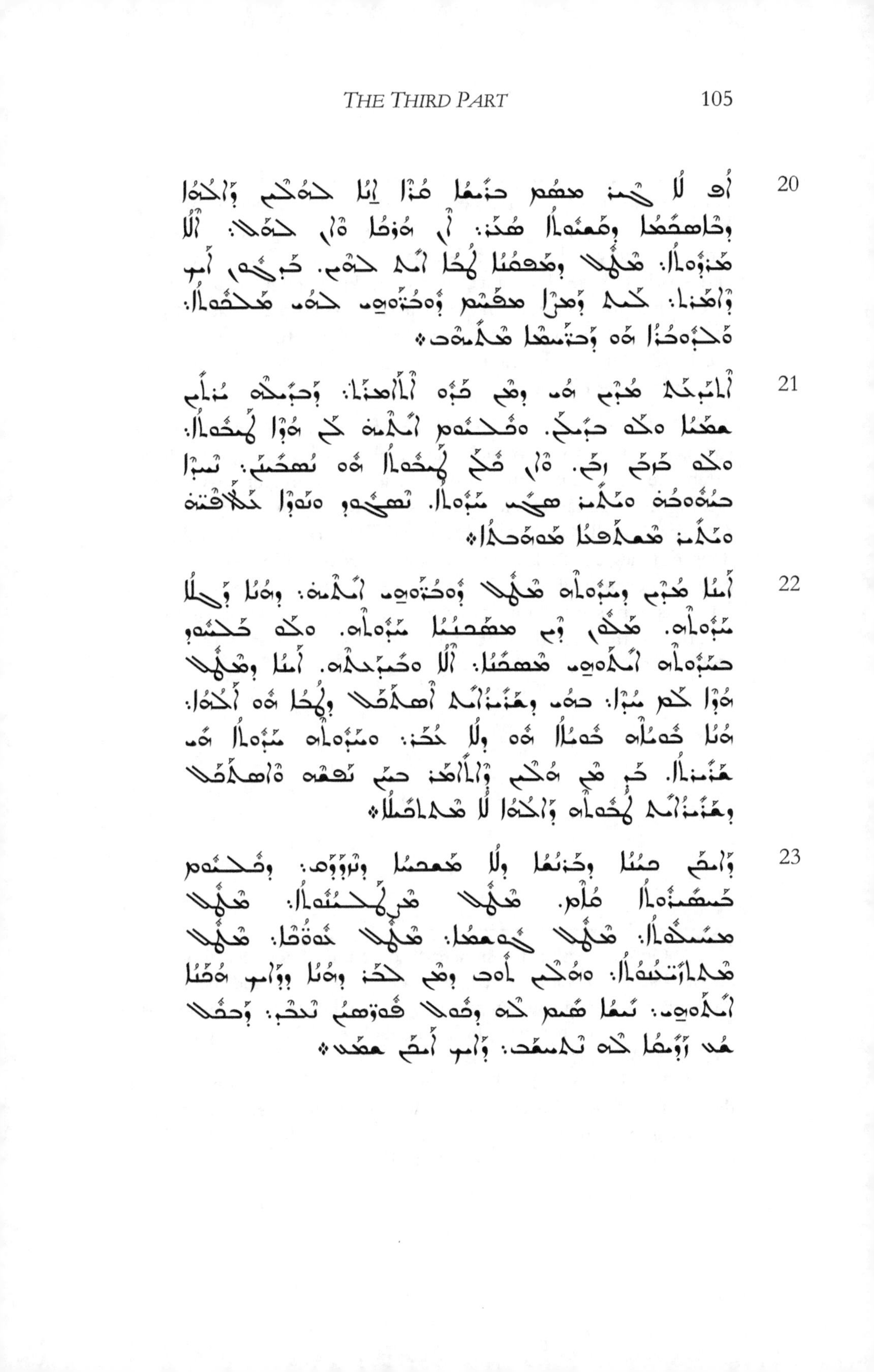

24 For <God>, one sin does not make a sinner.[19] It is pleasing to Him, that as much as possible, one confute the occasions of <sin>. Yet when one goes astray, <God> does not neglect to extend to him His mercy. When one falls into great <sins, God> covers him; and so that these do not come to the knowledge of anyone, He gives a hand to the one who goes astray. As to the greater <sins>, see how God exposes some in order to alarm the dissolute; while the lesser <sins> He leaves exposed, as a rebuke for the greater ones which are hidden.

25 And while one hides hateful and harmful evils, God indicates one's small omissions so as to shake up mankind with them, though how often they are as nothing in proportion <to greater sins>. By attacking his little faults, He indicates the healing of the greater ones. And for a small <act of> righteousness that one is able to do, God does not neglect to honor him and to crown him with a double portion because of it. Indeed, He turns away from <our> sin as much as is possible[20] but looks mercifully on our <lesser> offenses; and for the least diligence which follows, He remits the offense and the continued carelessness.

---

[19] On compassion for sinners: "Cover the sinner even though you are not harmed by him. Indeed, encourage him for life and the mercy of the Lord will sustain you. Support the weak and distressed with a word as far as you are able, that the right hand upholding the universe may sustain you."(Is.I 14). See also Is.I 79, 457.

[20] The discretion shown by God in covering sins is recommended in the *Synodicon Orientale* towards those who have sinned and repented but fear being mocked. The Church must treat them with prudence and mercy, covering their sins. See Canon VI, p. 174–75.

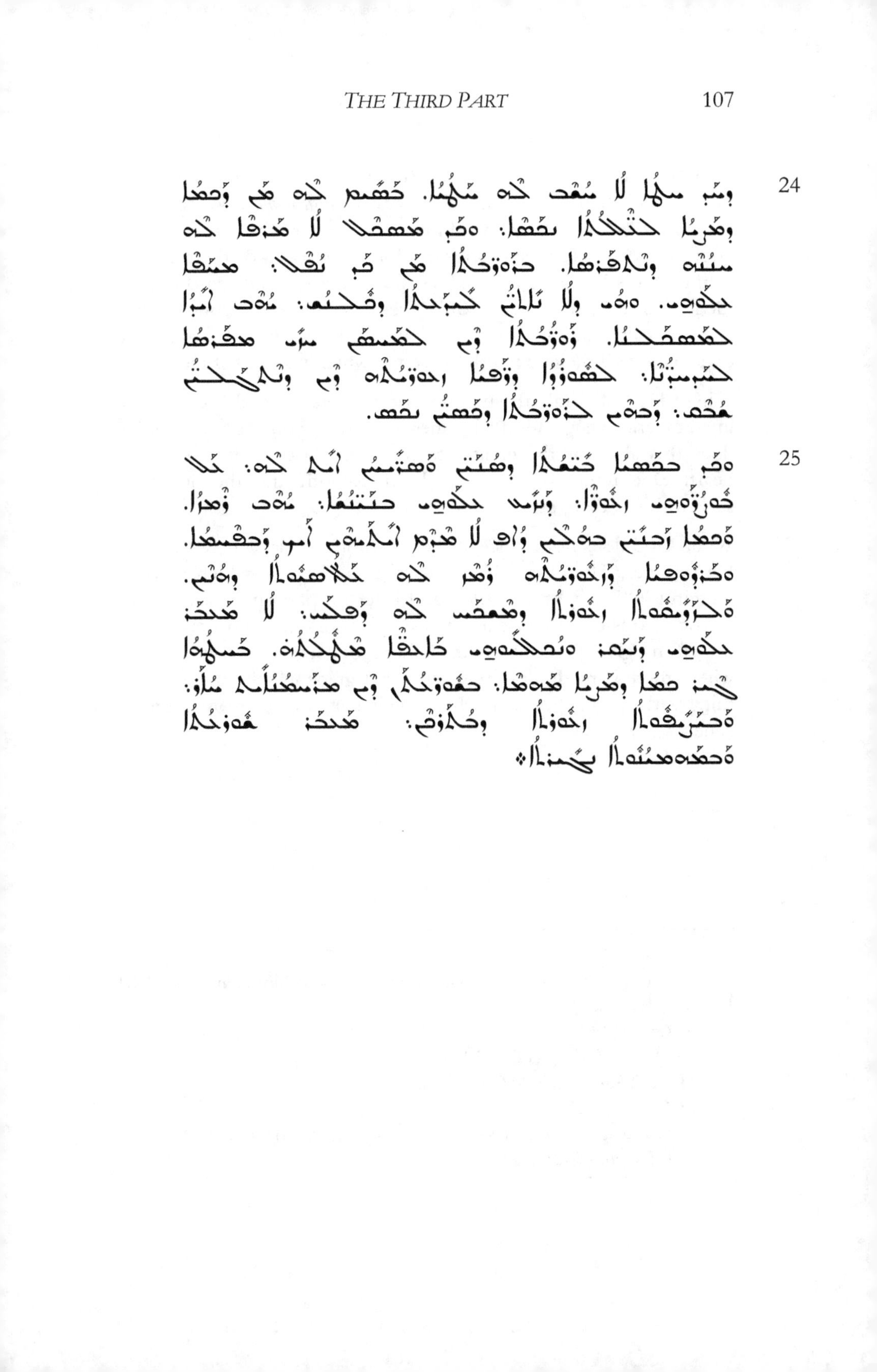

26   And so that no one be considered as a sinner before Him, He prepares a scheme. It is said: *The Lord has also removed your debt: you will not die.*[21] And if there would be an offender who takes no care about remorse, He prepares his pardon on account of the presence of the others,[22] since He loves to offer an occasion for pardon. The mediation and intercession of Moses[23] <intervened concerning> Aaron's calf. And for His own sake and because of David, He overshadows[24] the city <of Jerusalem> which was full of idols.[25]

27   Where He finds only the mention of conversion, and even if it be in an exterior way, <God> inclines joyfully to pour out pardon. He does this also for the greater faults, even though He knows the heart! One remembers the death of Naboth and the deceptive sackcloth of Ahab, etc.[26]

28   While God does not rejoice at the occasions of sin, where they are, He forgives. Therefore He openly shows His will, which is to be merciful:[27] "I delight in pardon and I do not pardon on account of the occasions but because it pleases my goodness – and I take upon myself to give pardon whether there be occasion <of sin> or where there is rectitude – thanks to that grace which covers everything with a veil." So then, when one is naked grace provides what is necessary.[28]

---

[21] 2 Sam. 12:13.

[22] This suggests the power of intercession, also hinted at in Is.III XI 19, 23.

[23] Cf. Ex.32:1–14.

[24] On *overshadow*, see Is.III I. 4.

[25] Cf. 2 Kgs.19:34; 20:6; Is.37:35.

[26] Cf. 1 Kgs.21.

[27] Cf. Evag. *Letter to Melania*, 6 (Casiday; Frankenberg, p. 612).

[28] Cf. Gen.3:7–21.

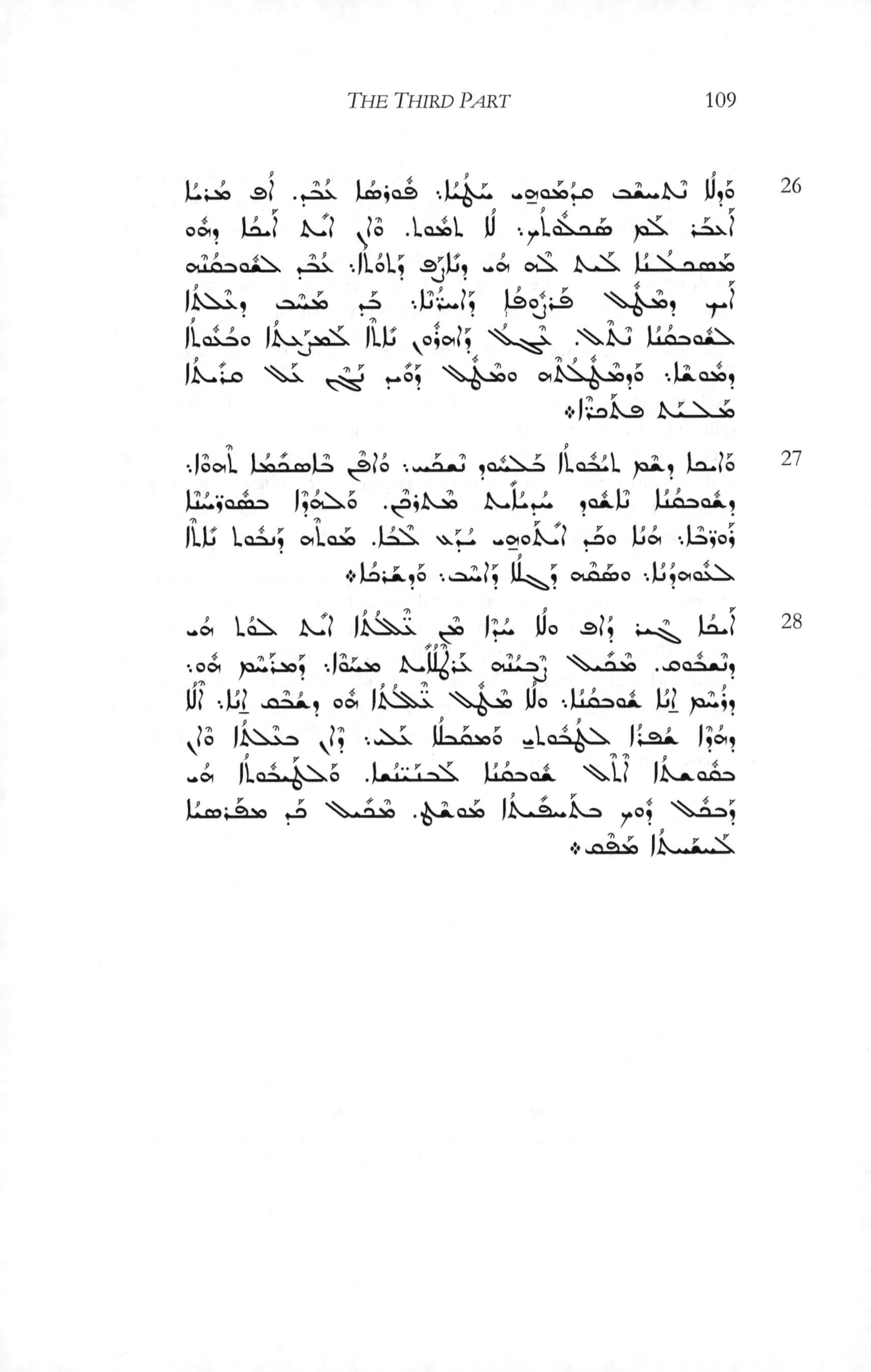

29   There are two debtors of the same creditor who cry out. One owed five hundred dinars and <the other> fifty: this indicates great sins, and partial ones which contain within them also the little ones. Neither of the two debtors had anything to make restitution, so the creditor remitted <the debts>.[29] Here <God> showed clearly that He loves forgiveness and not the occasions <of sin>.

30   His Economy, however, assumes the <burden> of finding pretexts for those who are negligent and do nothing profitably, but only go back to their <sins>. Even if God were to show clearly all His intelligence in this regard, and yet our inclination were not able for this, and on this account the growth of evil increases from this time – this is no obstacle, any where it happens, for His grace to work openly, that is, the grace which He has shown towards the debtors of the five hundred dinars and the fifty.

31   Not because He loved them more did He care for these; because He does not love the others less than them, since it is not the person He loves but <human> nature. And if it is the nature He loves, all persons are included within the boundary of His love, good and bad.[30] And if, without hesitation, while not hiding faults, He granted forgiveness to these whose great number of sins made them unrighteous, all the more reason He will make worthy those whose <sins> are less.

---

[29] Cf. Lk.7:41–42.

[30] Not only the good and the bad, but even demons: quoting Diodore of Tarsus, Isaac says "…of the demons and their great inclination to evil 'not even their immense wickedness can overcome the measure of God's goodness'." See Is.II XXXIX.13–14, XL.2; *Keph*. IV 87.

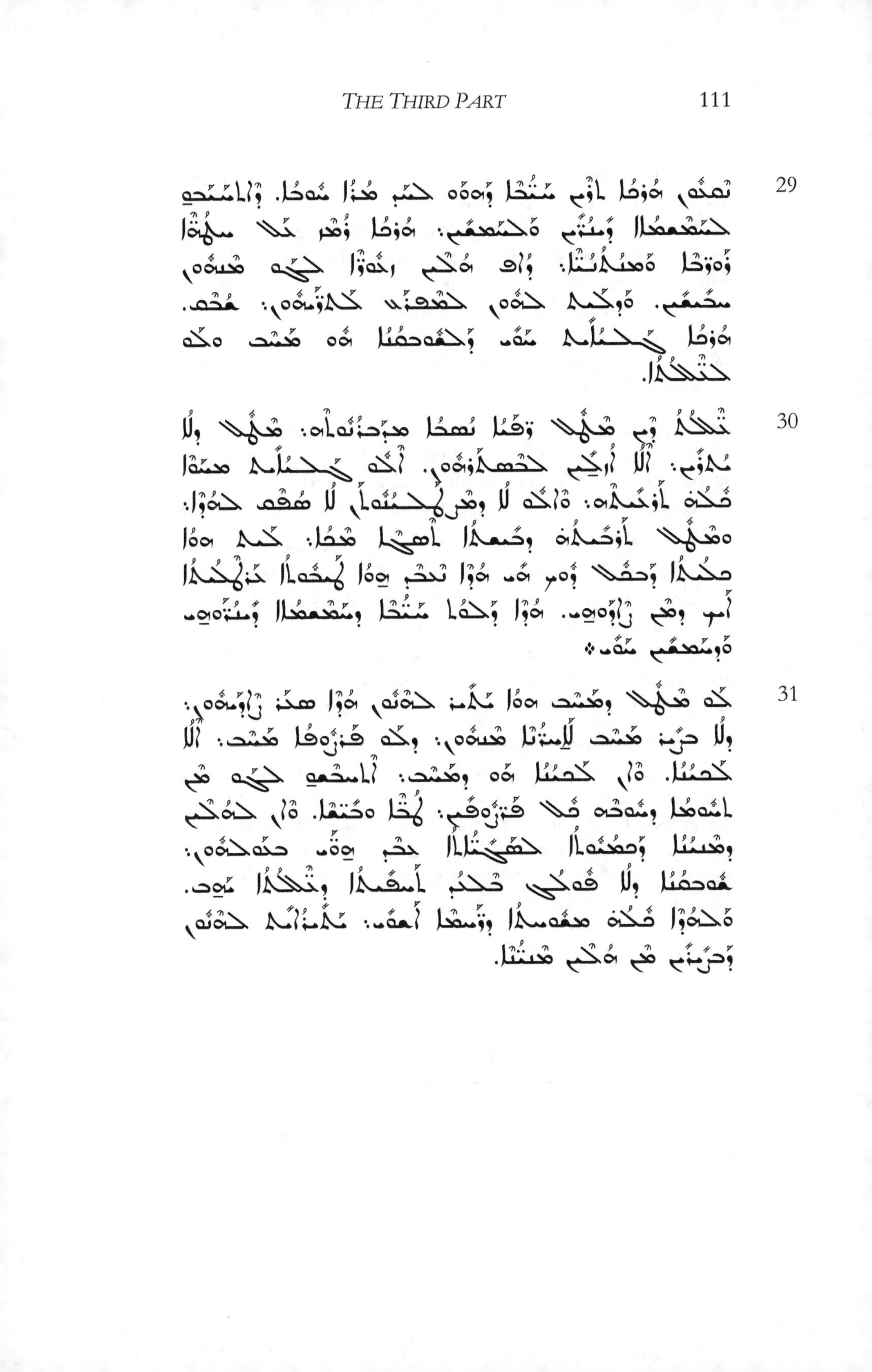

32   He makes worthy of pardon what is extreme and what is insignificant. Such that those who clearly do not <feel> fit to receive it, receive it equally. For <God>, however, both are equal, as he does not bother with calculations. When he pardons the one who has offended more, He is not vexed nor has difficulty more than when He pardons the one who has sinned less. For He loves human beings and does not love justice deprived of mercy. <He says>: *My thoughts are not your thoughts and my ways are not your ways: I am a merciful God.*

33   I considered all these things and I was amazed at the wisdom of the Lord of the universe! I searched His mercy, whose magnificence surpasses the intelligence of all those endowed with reason. This is therefore His will: to pardon everyone in all occasions <of sin>.

34   While being a sinner for a small fault, at once <God> calls him righteous; and because of the good of one day, He pardons all the iniquity of his life. The one who spent all his days in sins, for one good <deed> God decrees him innocent. If only in his conscience he is sorry, God cancels great faults and instead of good deeds, He accepts from him a feeble will. And for the sins of years, weighty and prolonged, sufficient for him is the repentance of one moment.

35   God reckons this as righteousness, even if the body is not able to abstain from previous faults. As if God says: "Do not sin; then for the sins you have committed I will not lay blame. Only recognize the grace I have done for you!" The publican in the temple and the prodigal son testify concerning this: these received a swift pardon though they sinned more than all the others.[31] It is said: *Where sin has increased, there* goodness *has abounded.*[32]

---

[31] Cf. Lk.18:9–14; 15:11–32.

[32] Rm.5:20. In the citation from Romans, instead of grace (*taybûṯâ*) Isaac has used goodness (*ṭâbtâ*), perhaps intentionally.

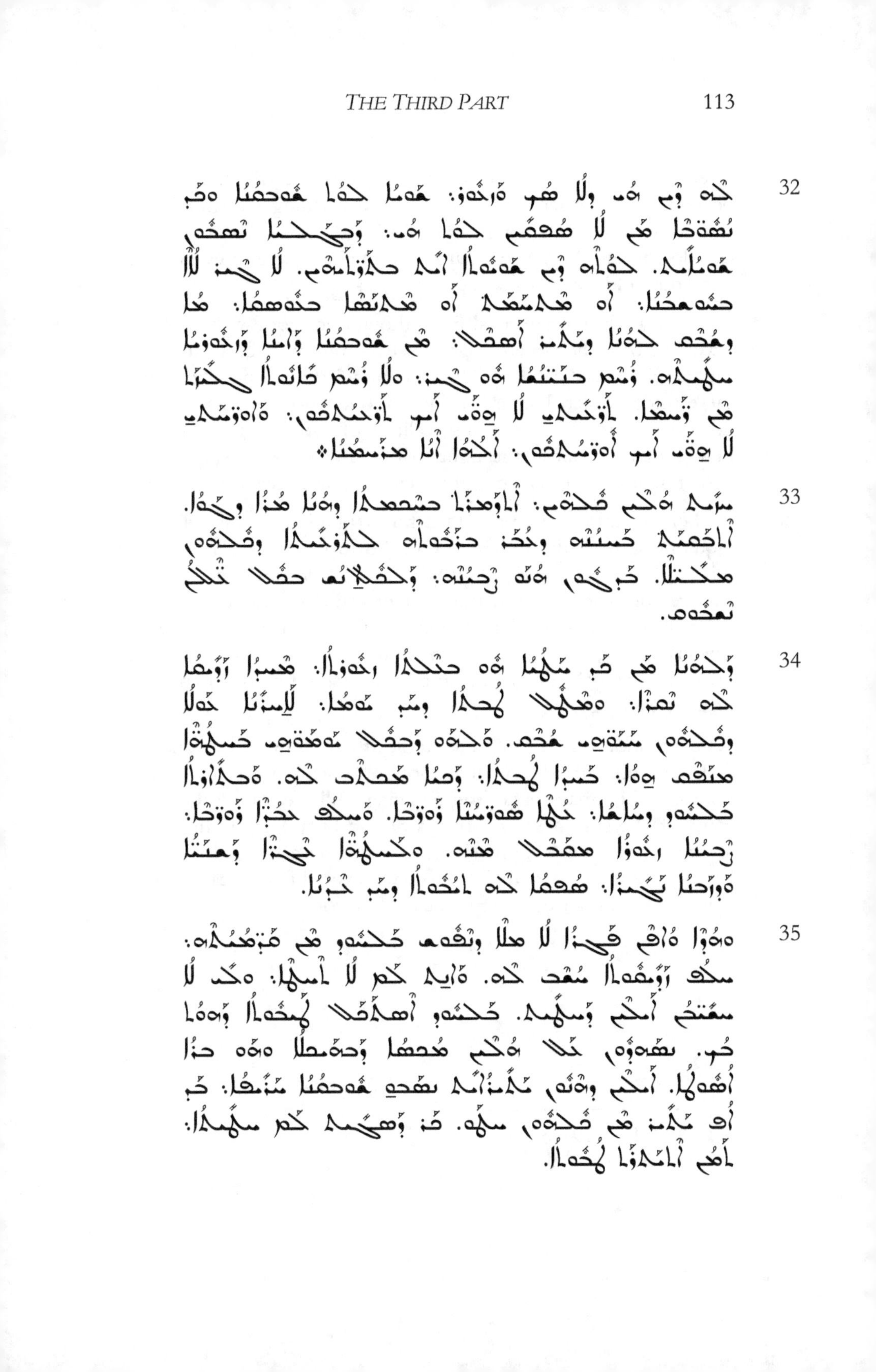

36   Even if it is God who truly gives strength to the will, that it might be able to not consent to sin, and while everything is from Him, yet it pleases Him to call us righteous. As I said, the purpose of this He laid down that by every resource, He might rejoice in everyone as righteous, and <everyone be counted as such>.

37   See how weak our nature is! Even though our good works are few <we take on> the fame of righteousness, but with the least pretext the merciful Lord calls us righteous! Now is there one who doubts these things which I said? Or, indeed, one whose conscience does not witness to these glorious realities of God? Let the remembrance of the thief at the right <of Jesus> be a blessing, as it is known that also he is among the recipients of mercy, freely given.[33]

38   Is there a rational <creature> who is blinded by his will from inquiring into all these things? Or who turns his face from all of this and takes joy in his own way of life? Who is the one endowed with reason who does not search night and day, and does not consider all of these wonders of God and the judgments of His love? That is to say, He does not judge our affairs with justice, but in love subverts right judgment, so that we hateful ones become supposedly well-pleasing.

39   Whoever indeed meditates and studies these things, night and day, and for whom the fount of his joy is to strive to examine these things, and he marvels at God rejoicing while searching the stratagems of His goodness: this one is rich in his poverty! His joy is a joy which <comes> from grace, it is not human. And while not having anything, in faith he possesses everything, because He in whom everything exists, is the cause of his joy.[34]

---

[33] Cf. Lk. 3:39–43.
[34] Cf. 2 Cor. 6:10.

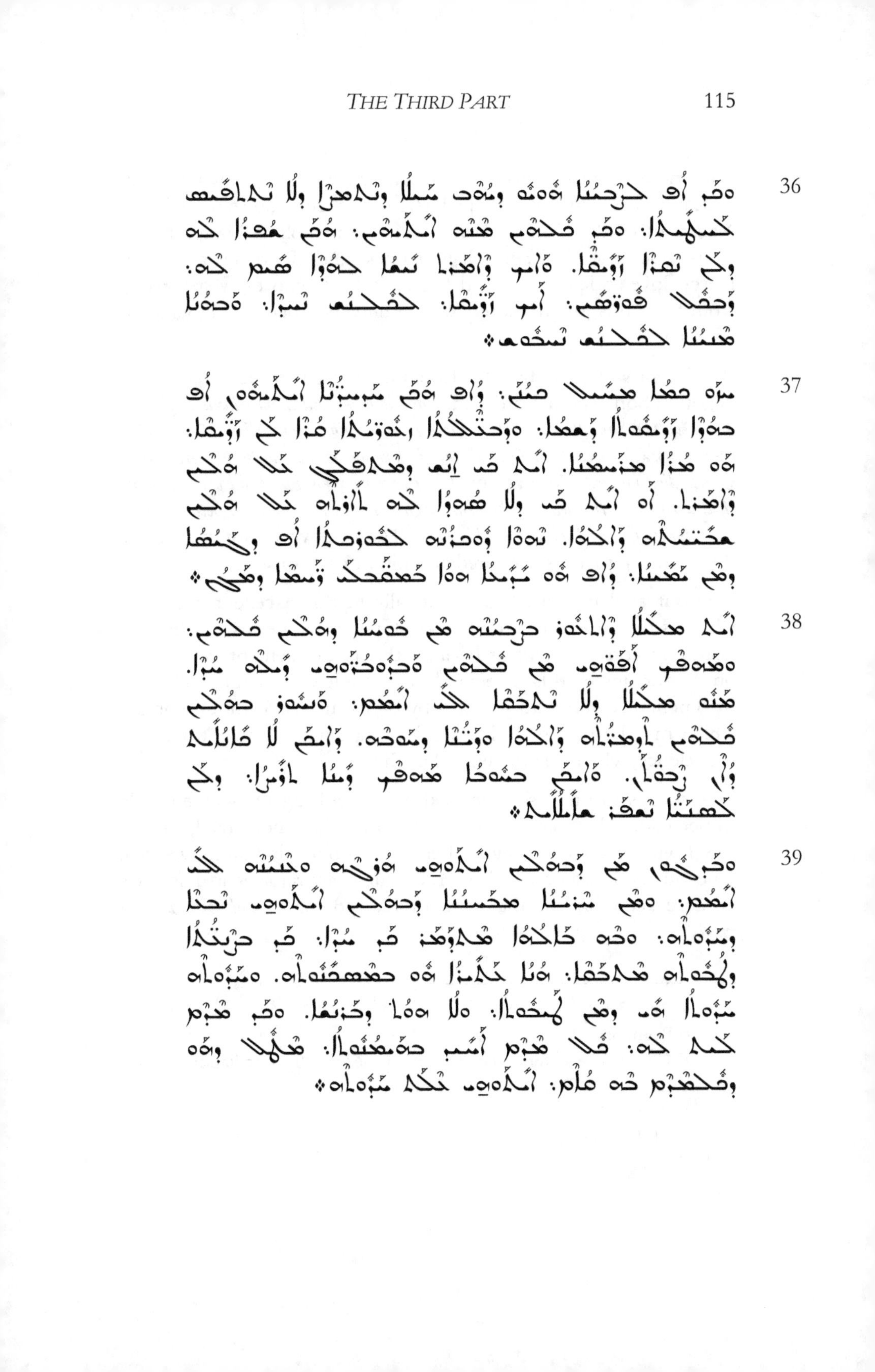

40   For whoever finds all his joy in this, because of this, all which is his is beautiful. This is his only joy! The one, then, who rejoices in the Nature of God and in the riches which that sublime Nature brings to us – because God Himself is richness and His riches are for us mercy, love and goodness – that one, indeed, whose joy springs up from here, this joy of his renews the universe. Because all which is God's is ours.

41   Besides all which is His, He also added the gift to us of His only-begotten Son, as our Lord said: *For God so loved the world as to give his only-begotten Son, that all who believe in him might not perish.*[35] And also blessed Paul said: *Now God shows his love for us that when we were sinners Christ died for us.*[36] And again: *If while we were enemies God became reconciled with us by the death of his Son, then how much more now, because of his reconciliation,*[37] *will we live by his life!*[38] The one whose joy is in these things, this joy of his is the redemption of creation!

42   May our soul be absorbed continually in this excellent reflection which is the remembrance of God's love for us. Let us sanctify our heart[39] in converse with it because this is eloquent prayer. Let us purify our sins by this reflection! Let us renew our soul at all times by repentance and faith – that is by righteousness without works – which may be understood through compunction and the faith of conscience, when we are mindful of this.

43   One speaks to one's soul and exhorts it with encouragement able to persuade: "If today by means of works I was not saved, tomorrow I will be saved by grace." Let us keep our mind attentive at all times in the hope of God's mercy! Our heart rejoices in His love, because according to the word of blessed Paul, *God loves us very much.*[40]

---

[35] John 3:16.

[36] Rom. 5:8.

[37] Chialà here offers a correction to the ms, "reconciliation," based on a reading of the Peshitta text of Romans.

[38] Rom. 5:10.

[39] Cf. James 4:8.

[40] Eph. 2:4.

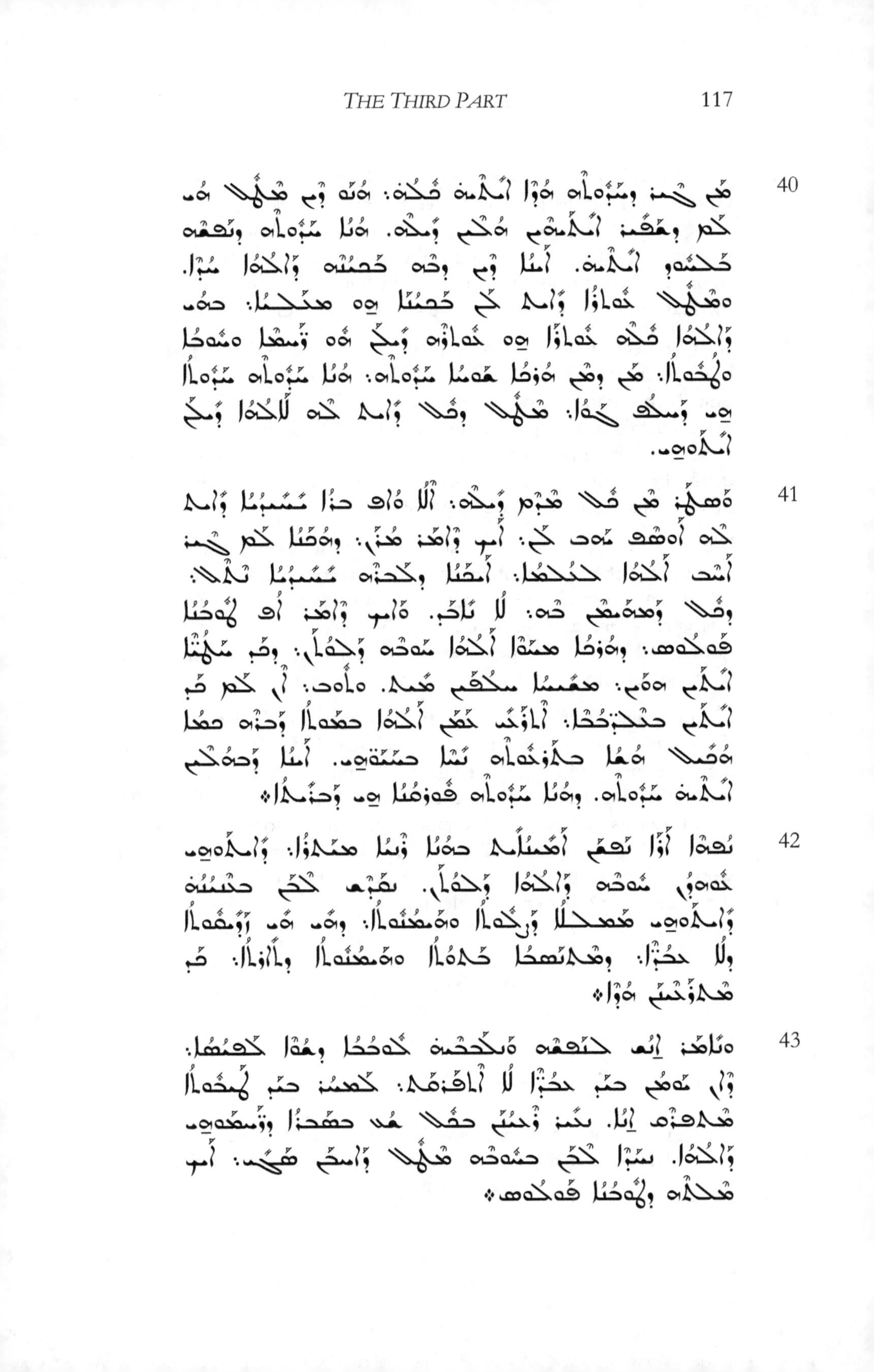

44   May our mind labor continually in reflection on the Economy of God for us. Let us give ourselves to this reflection because of its great insight and its infinite joy. Its labor is the labor of the angels! By this, rational creatures gradually attain *God's manifold wisdom by means of his Church*, as the Apostle said;[41] and also by means of this meditation we grow strong in the knowledge of God's love.

45   If this reflection delights the angels and increases <their> gladness, how much more then for humans. In this, one must remain continually, not haphazardly, with a strong and genuine insight, so that our soul might be a pure temple for God. For on account of our continual remembrance[42] of Him, He dwells in us continually. Indeed, these remembrances greatly help those who <profess> this divine philosophy <in their way> of life.

46   We turn the gaze of our intelligence continually upon all of this, that is, that the divine intelligence[43] was reconciled with us in perpetuity and from before the ages. This was spoken of sufficiently in this very *memra*, and may we always be filled with amazement and hope by it! Those who persevere in converse with these things and in this meditation, emulate the nature of the angels.

47   In our thought, let us also take up the burden of the way of life of the saints of every generation, as a medicinal indication <for healing>. Let us form in our intelligence the purity of their way of life, their excellent life and their constant toil of separation from this world. Let us imitate, by meditation on their reasonings, the glorious reflection of their intelligence, which is continually lifted up in wonder at these things, beyond all of the things of this life and of the remembrance of corruptible things.

---

[41] Eph. 3:10.
[42] Continual remembrance (*ʿuhdânâ ammînâ*): Is.III VIII, *passim*.
[43] Divine intelligence (*tarʿîtâ alâhâytâ*): Is.II XIV.4; XV.2; XXXIX.2.

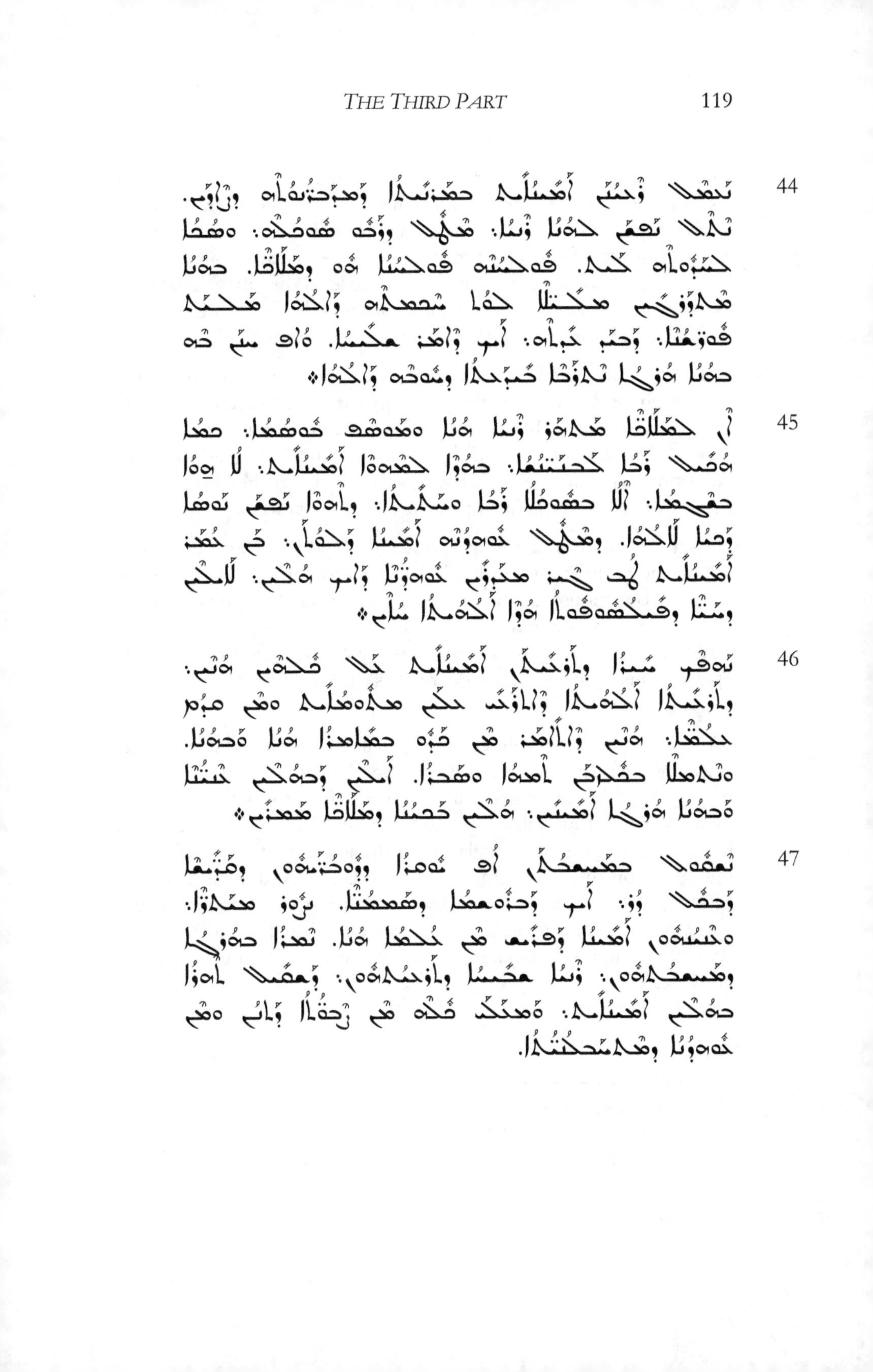

48 They resemble the life of the Spirit, as much as is possible in the way of life here <below>. And while being in the flesh, they are always found above it. Not that they are able to be without food and without what is useful for the necessities of nature – not possible! However when there is also an obstacle to this, they are almost made glad. In their intelligence, they are together with the invisible powers, and in their mind they are found above the world.

49 And with these angelic meditations noted above, they instruct their souls night and day, while the gaze of their mind is always directed towards God. And they await that incorruptible communion with <God>, beyond the world by means of the Spirit, as the holy Ammonas says in one of his letters, when he teaches how one is made worthy of this amazing gift of which the world is not worthy.

50 He says: "Direct your thoughts towards God night and day while asking the Holy Spirit and it will be given to you."[44] Where it says: "Direct your thoughts," he means "mind" instead. Namely: "Weary your mind night and day in meditation on God, because it is necessary that even now you be made worthy of the action of the Holy Spirit." This is the <meaning> of "Ask the Holy Spirit and it will be given to you."

51 While being in these realities, one's intellect is occupied at all times, since by every means it rejects temporal realities; and from here pure ways of life are constantly occurring. From this time, you are made worthy of ineffable communion with God the Father, which happens by means of a revelation in the journey of those who live the migration of the mind,[45] as the fathers say. And in all that concerns you, you show that your way is alien to that of mankind; and while being within a body, in the world, through obedience and <your> manner of thinking, you are <already> lifted up to life, in His Life.[46]

---

[44] Ammonius 586–87.
[45] On *migration*, see Is.III I.8.
[46] Cf. Col. 3:1–3.

THE THIRD PART

52 Not that we have no more need of food, drink and clothes, as I have said <before>; but while it is evident that in all which concerns us we are alien to this world, it is also well-known that all which is ours is opposed to what is <of the world>: in our labor, in our reflection, in our converse, in our word, etc.

53 Some labor to gain possession of this earth but we toil to *inherit the kingdom of heaven*.[47]

54 Some keep vigil and watch at nights to lay up gold and silver, but we watch and weary ourselves by means of our vigil, to taste that way of life after the resurrection.

55 Some adorn themselves for the world and they stumble, but we adorn ourselves for Christ, *the light of the world*.[48]

56 Some become inebriated[49] with wine and so their mind goes astray to their soul's harm. But we become intoxicated with the love of God, and in our intoxication we disregard the corruptible things of this life.

57 Some toil to acquire hurtful knowledge, nothing of which is permitted to go with them in the *future world*.[50] But we weary our soul in the meditation of God.

---

[47] Cf. 1 Cor. 15:50 (Peshitta).

[48] Cf. 1 Peter 3:3–4; Job 33:30.

[49] Inebriated (*rawwîyûtâ*): Is.I 2, 59, 77, 174, 256, 454; Is.II V.21, X.35; *Keph.* I 33, 67, 88; IV 48,82. It occurs in Ephrem, John Sol., Sahdona, Dadisho and Shem'on d-Taybuteh. According to Alfeyev: "*spiritual inebriation* is the single most characteristic mystical theme in the works of Isaac." See Alfeyev, *Spiritual World*, 191, 248–55.

[50] Cf. Heb.2:5; 6:5.

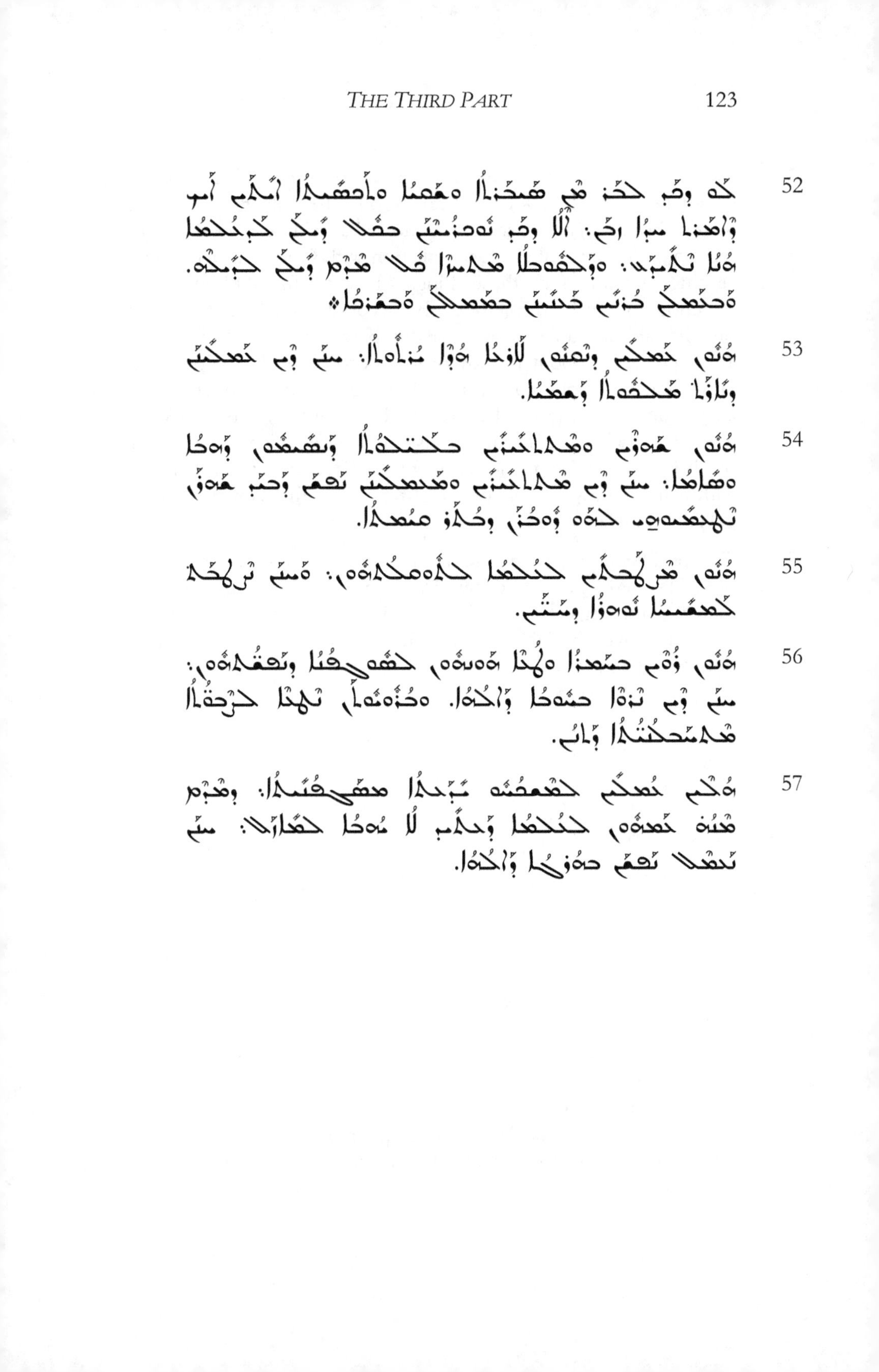

58 Some say absurd and foul things, and words full of ridicule and debauchery. We, however, speak about the salvation of souls: words about judgment; searching into what will be after the resurrection; a discourse about reconciliation with God; instruction concerning salvation – all these things which fill the soul with compunction. We also speak about the accounts which lead to desire sanctity; about studies which make apparent the hope <that lies> after our death; about the joy of our Lord[51] and exultation in the Holy Spirit;[52] about contempt for a corruptible manner of life; about the remembrance that our joy is in Christ; about thanksgiving for our salvation; about the mystery of life which takes place in our body; about the memorial of the sacrifice of our Savior for us, with tears[53] of joy and of suffering together with lips which are impelled in praise of God.

59 We are diligent in all these <matters> because this <concerns> all of God's mercy to be used towards all mankind. Let it not be for us a pretext for neglect, but rather for diligence in righteousness, lest we be reproved by Him because our ways of life are in contradiction <to His mercy>.

---

[51] Cf. Phil.4:10.

[52] Cf. Rom.14:17; 1 Thess. 1:6.

[53] In Isaac, tears (*dem'ê*) accompany purification and rebirth, the eyes are the baptismal font, Is.I 139. See Chialà, *Ascesi eremitica*, 211–13.

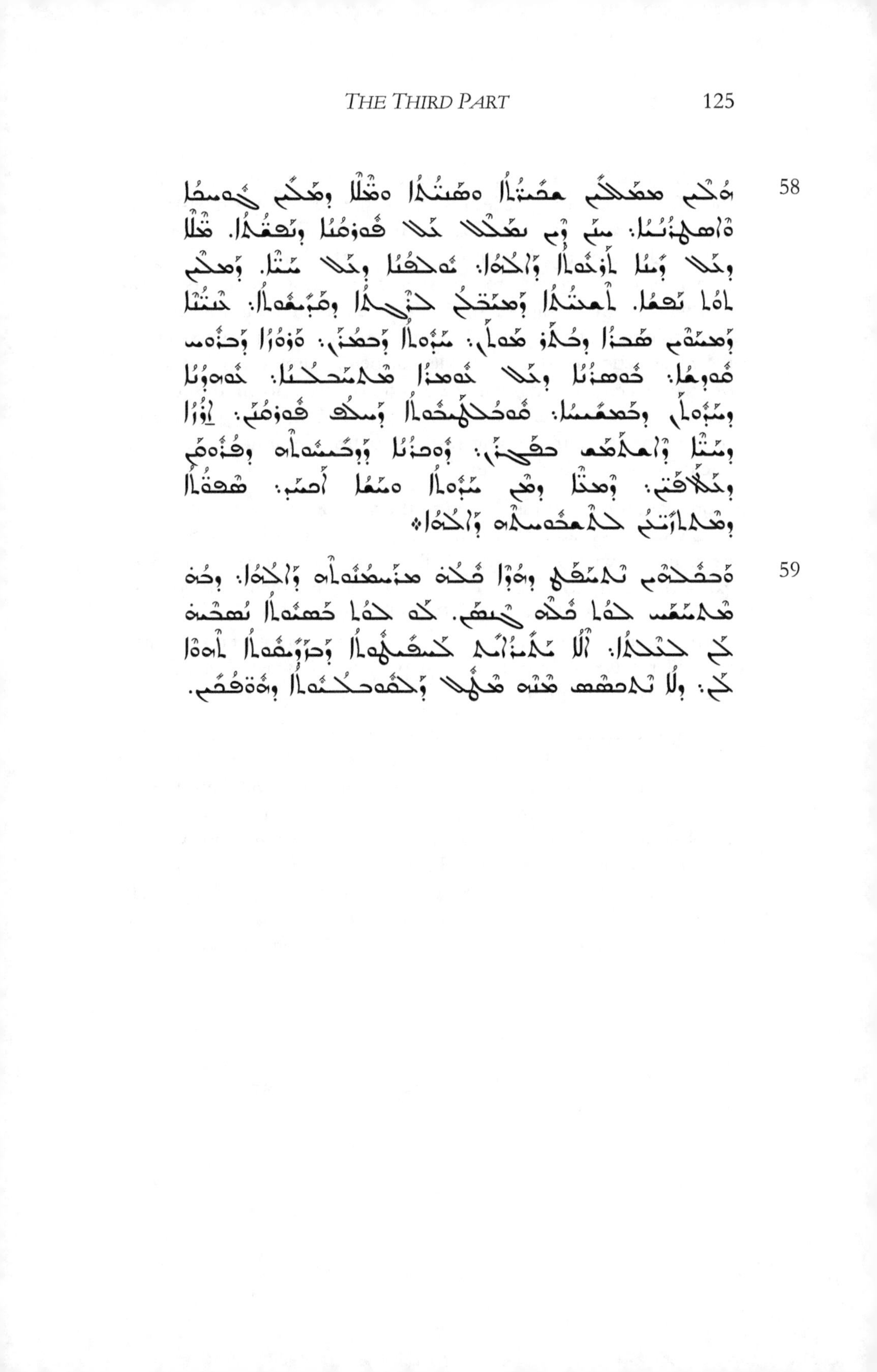

60 As Theodore the Interpreter, marvelous among the saints, said in the <Commentary to the letter> *to the Romans*: "The compassion of God ought not to be an occasion of laxity for those who have received all this mercy, but on the contrary they ought to show great diligence. For we ought to be ashamed to be wrong doers before one who is totally Good. In brief, let us be anxious for all these good things, that our person be adorned so as to arrive properly at the resurrection of the dead, without being summoned to the trial of that decree of judgment reserved for all who in this created world have completely surrendered to evil. But, he says, while the promise of our entrance into rest stands firm, let it not happen that one of us desist from entering."[54]

61 Moreover, not even this is alien to the love of a father: while we act in this world as rational creatures, being diligent about all that concerns us, yet we live this irrationally because we scarcely take cognizance of the life to which we have been led, in which God does not consent to punish for eternity. But when we learn what would have been due in punishment, with what evils we have been complicit, we will receive in ourselves an experience of what <would have been due in punishment>.

62 How great, indeed, is our ignorance! God, then, proceeds with His work according to His eternal intelligence, as becomes His great love. Regarding this, one may consider His entire will from the beginning, by means of insight into what He has indicated in each of His Economies in every generation. So that henceforward we may be roused from <our> sins and after our departure for the life beyond, we will then be chastened especially by the goading of His love. As is said: *The one who has been forgiven much, loves much.*[55] And then will come to pass that word which is written: *God will be all in all.*[56]

---

[54] Cf. Rom.12:1. See Theodore of Mopsuestia, *Commentary on the letter to the Romans*, PG 66 col. 860.

[55] Lk.7:47.

[56] 1 Cor.15:28.

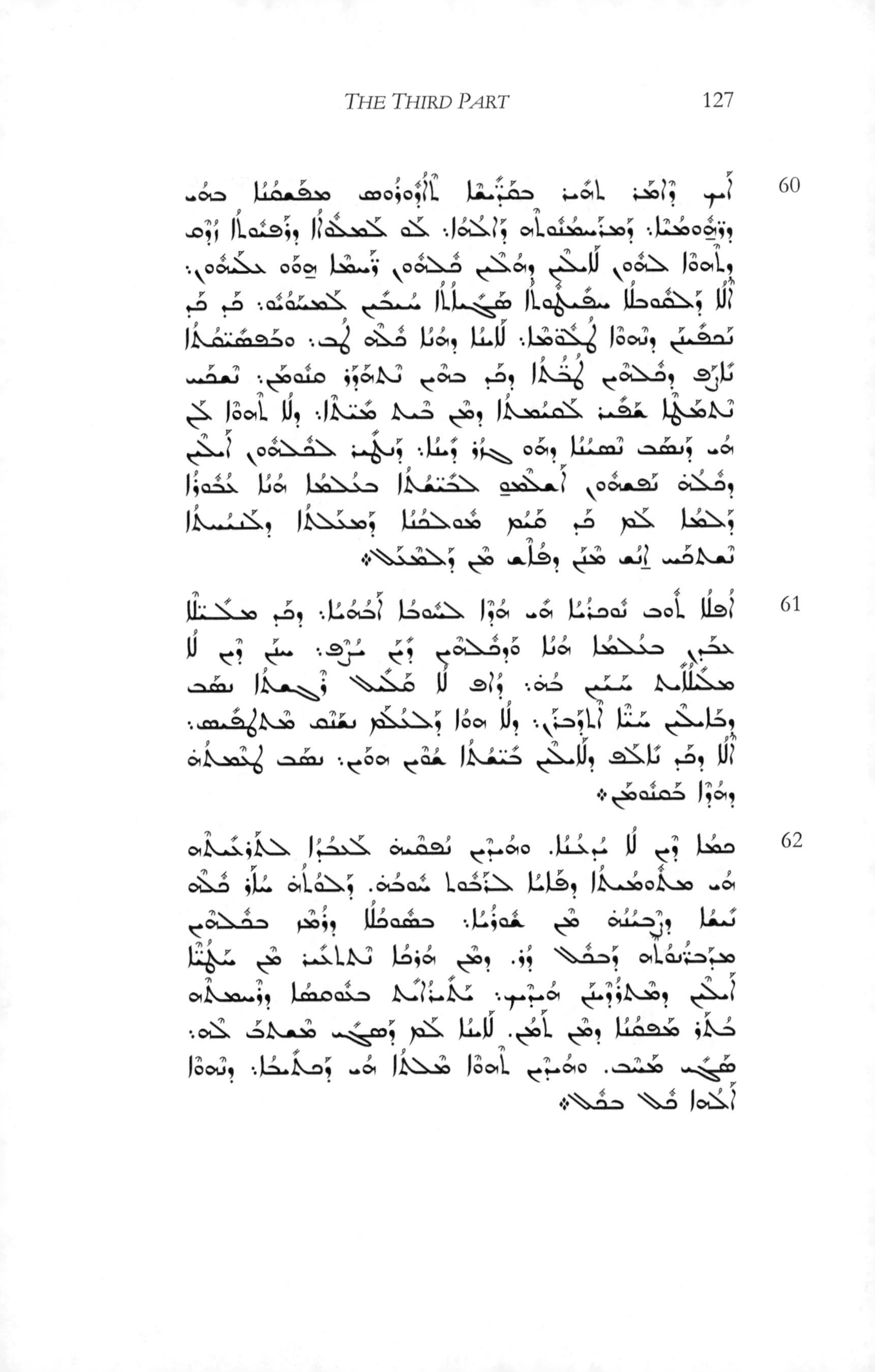

63   To Him be the glory for His wise dispensations which are exalted beyond <all> investigation, forever and ever. Amen.

63 ܘܟܕ ܗܘܝܬܘܢ ܥܒܕܝ̈ܢ ܟܠ ܦܘܩܕܢܘ̈ܗܝ. ܐܡܪܘ ܕܥܒܕܐ ܚܢܢ ܒܛܝ̈ܠܐ ܕܠܐ ܚܫܚܝܢ. ܡܕܡ ܕܚܝܒܝܢ ܗܘܝܢ ܠܡܥܒܕ. ܥܒܕܢ܀

Chapter VII

By the same Mar Isaac. Prayer impelled by the insights of the things which were said. For there is in <prayer> a great signification, from time to time at prayer one turns to contemplate it, then again turns back to prayer. And in the noble passion of the mind, one offers amazing stirrings for the sake of all these great things which are ours.

1   I adore Your majesty, O God, who have created me in Your love and have saved me in Christ from the spiritual darkness which is the ignorance of the soul.[1] You have removed from us the time of error that we may not walk, so to say, in the night in our knowledge of You as in former generations.

2   Glory to You who in <Your> mercy have endured our wickedness; in Your compassion You put right our sinfulness; and in Your kindness You remove our failings. You have given us to believe in You as becomes Your greatness. And You have not paid attention to our faithlessness, which is always before You, because You are a merciful God. And with the dew of Your grace, You always overcome the fire of our sins.

3   What mouth is capable of Your praise? And what tongue is fit to extol You? You have curbed our sins with an increase of Your grace. And instead of the sentence of Your judgment, You have lavished Your treasure also on sinners, because You do not wish *to pronounce judgment on us*[2] but to draw us near to You since we are Your creation. Your grace has surpassed the measure of our understanding: in our stead, the amazing natures of the angels glorify You. <These are> those in whom You have placed a power able to receive the wonderful stirring of Your holiness.[3]

---

[1] Cf. Nilus, *Sulla virtù e sulle passione* 15, p. 285.
[2] Cf. Ps. 143:2.
[3] On angelic mediation, see Is.III VIII.11.

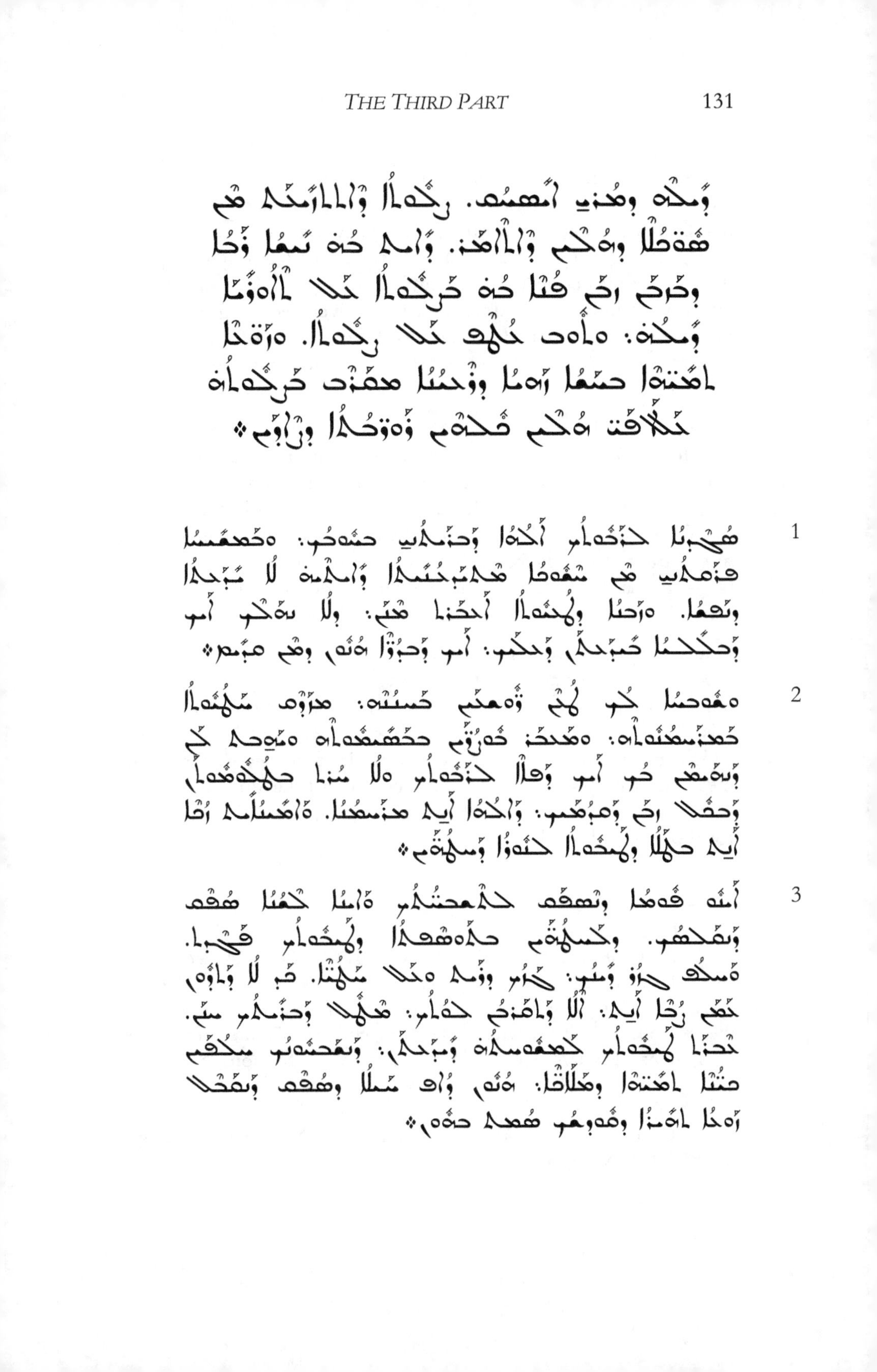

4 Let the angels make You known in our stead, for our nature is too feeble to give you thanks. May the marvelous stirrings of their thanksgiving mingle with our praise. They are truly sorry for our being deprived of You,[4] as You have cut us off from mingling with their assemblies concerning the understanding of Your hidden Being. But without our asking, You have given us the great gift of faith by which we may draw near to the mysteries of knowledge – mysteries by which spiritual beings attain gradually to the Shekinah[5] of Your Essence.

5 By means of the mysteries of faith, indeed, those whom You are near to *in faith and not in vision,*[6] remain upright, my Lord, within the cloud of thick darkness of Your glory.[7] This is received by the illumined mind with great understanding. For it is You who bestow this faith as a gift to those endowed with reason, that their stirrings might attempt to believe in that which is not attainable or knowable – that is the Divine Nature which is hidden from all – by the mysteries that You reveal to them in Your love.

6 I am convinced, therefore, that it is not possible to find You anywhere, O eternal God, neither in spiritual beings nor in weak human company, but only from the fountain of Your love. From this <the fountain>, You pour forth at all times on the assemblies which are above and on those below. In fact, according to the measure of each one of the assemblies, You pour out the treasure of Your mercy <granting> them revelations, as much as possible, for the sake of knowledge.

---

[4] Cf. Lk. 15:10.

[5] Shekinah: Is.I 517; Is.II X.24; XI.5–6, 10, 12, 14, 24. See the Peshitta: 1 Chron. 28:2; 2 Chron. 5:14, 7: 1–2, *passim*; Judges 9:8 (Peshitta 9:11); 2 Macc. 14:35; Sir. 36:15. For its use in rabbinic tradition indicating the presence of God, see Urbach, *The Sages*, ch.3, 37–65. The term appears in Aphrahat, Ephrem, Jacob of Serug, Philoxenus, Sahdona. See Cerbelaud, "Aspects" and Sed, "La Shekhinta."

[6] Cf. 2 Cor. 5:7.

[7] Cf. Ex. 20:21. Cloud of thick darkness of Your glory: (ʿarpellâ d-šubḥâk): Is.II X.17, 24.

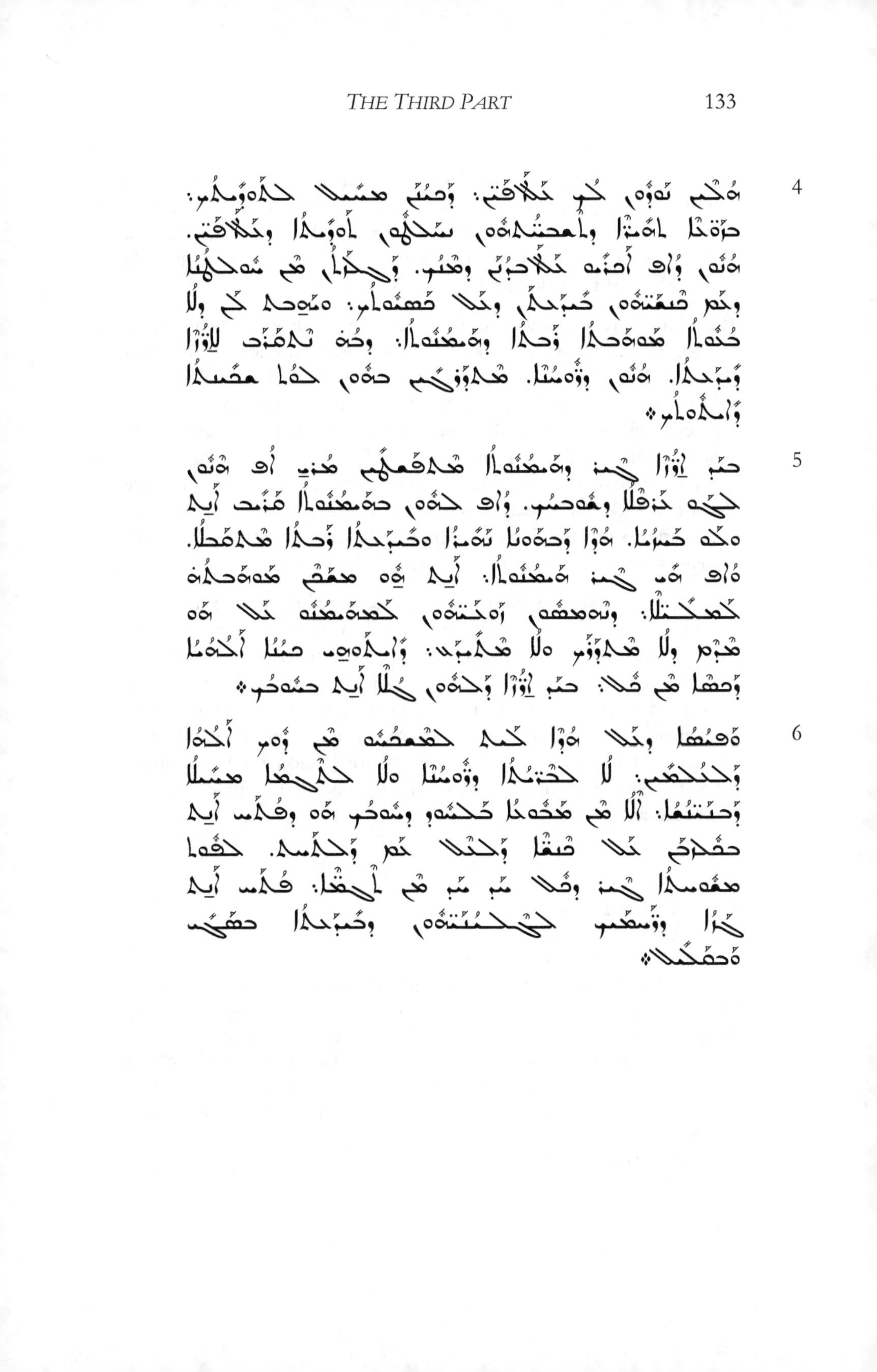

7   The gift of Your grace is a required intermediary, because it lifts our intellect to converse of faith in You. Whereas on account of the great thick darkness which surrounds <Your> holiness, even the eyes of the Cherubim are confused when looking within the secret place of the thick darkness of Your glory.[8]

8   But if they are sustained, more or less, by Your grace to go up to the top of the mountain of faith; this is the knowledge of the Spirit: that is to say, beams of light which shine upon the intellect from that mighty fire which flashes from the interior place of faith, that <place> which is called the inner sanctuary where one adores the magnificence of the glorious nature of the Essence. That is the <place> where no creature has ever entered or will enter there, except that One who was sanctified to enter[9] *by God's foreknowledge*[10] according to His intelligence, which is good concerning all, to continually make atonement for the sins of His people.

9   For it is by faith one enters a place, further within than the Watchers.[11] It is by means of one of them that at one time the mercy of <God> made <Him> enter and dwell there.[12] And from that time forth <God> gives power to those human intellects who are sanctified to enter by faith, I mean near Him. He is indeed incomprehensible and distant, visible not even for a moment, whether for the eyes of the angels or for ours. By revelation then, the angels were first and nearer than us, until You revealed Yourself for our deliverance.

---

[8] Cf. Ex. 20:21.

[9] Cf. Heb. 9:11–12.

[10] Cf. Acts 2:23; 1 Peter 1:2.

[11] The Syriac tradition frequently designates angels as Watchers (Dan. 4:13,17). Watchers figure prominently in pseudepigraphic and later Jewish mystical literature. In Merkabah texts such as 3 Enoch, they are a separate order: "Above all these are four great princes called Watchers…their abode is opposite the throne of Glory…they receive glory from the glory of the Almighty and are praised with the praise." See 3 Enoch 28:1–3.

[12] Cf. Heb. 9:11–12.

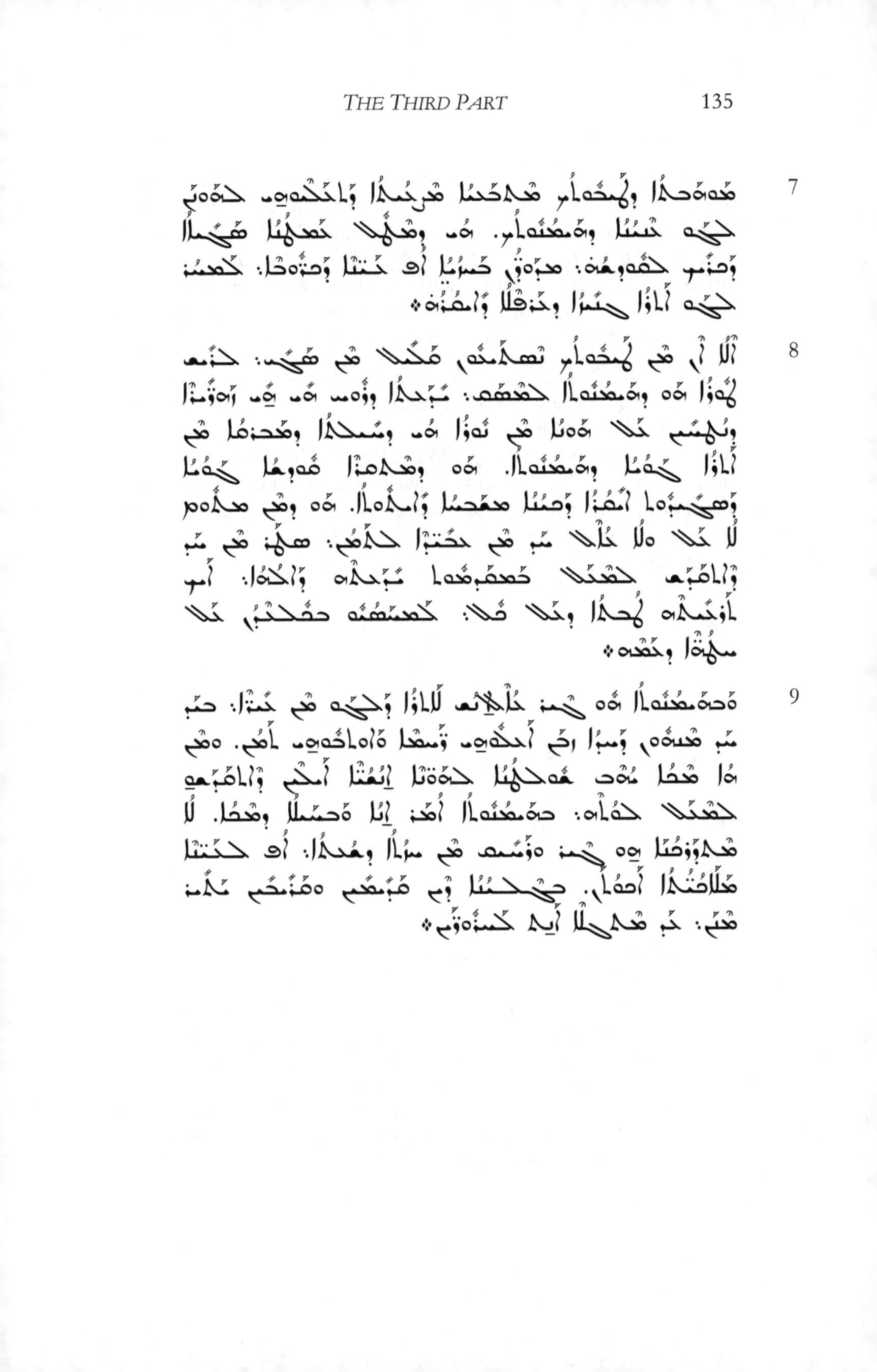

10 Our true hope, the delight of mankind, our nature's boast, steadfast advocate of our weakness who pardons our sins at all times! Your intercession for pardon for us is mightier, my Lord, than the sacrifice of Israel. If the meat of animals and the ashes of their burnt-offerings undeniably purified and sanctified those for whom they were offered in sacrifice, how much more You purify us at all times, You, sacred oblation offered for the world.[13]

11 You offer and You absolve, You are the priest and You are the one consecrated. You are the sacrifice and You are the one who receives it. If that mute metal leaf[14] which manifests the mystery of Your human nature, gave pardon to those who earnestly entreat, how much more You, glorious image of the divinity! And if Your mysteries pour forth all this richness on those in need, how much more will You, true prototype of the mysteries, pour forth on us Your mercy.

---

[13] Cf. Heb. 9,13–14.

[14] Metal leaf (*ṭassâ*): Ex.25:17, 21–2; Lv.16.2, 13–15 (description of the ark). The Peshitta uses *ḥussâyâ* instead of *ṭassâ*. See Is.II XI.14 for Brock's explanation; see also his trans. of Evag. Cent. IV.52: "the spiritual *ṭassâ* is the true knowledge of the Holy Trinity." And see Narsai, *Homily on the Tabernacle*: "With the term *ṭassâ* (Scripture) tells of the humanity of our Lord, and with the *ḥussâyâ* (it tells of) the Being (*îtûtâ*) who has dwelling in him." As referred to in Is.II XI.15, note 15.

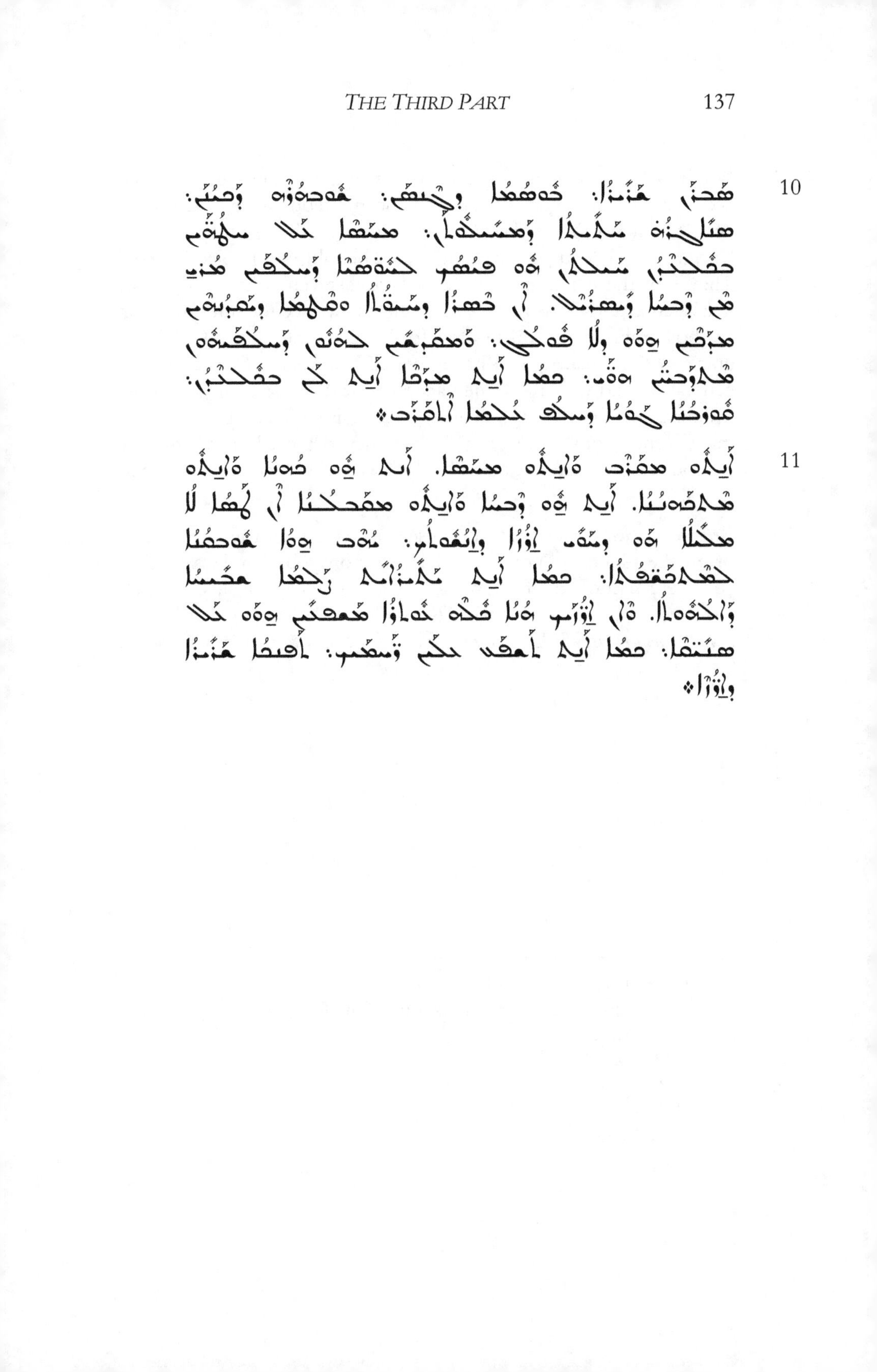

12 For it is You for whom the prophets and the kings have waited according to their generations and the righteous in their descendants.[15] Is it not Your day, O expectation of the Gentiles, for we have received You in our hands and, behold, we rejoice in You! They saw these things in the revelations given them which they marveled at and earnestly desired; whereas we see the interpretation of those mysteries. You poured forth on us the Gihon[16] of Your grace, O our Creator; You have opened Your entire treasury in our generation and we have gained access to it. You have shown us the mysteries of Your Christ. It was by a desire for His Coming that many generations were gripped but they departed from this life without consolation because His days were far removed from their times.

13 *Return, my soul, to your rest*[17] because you have seen the expectation of all the Gentiles. You carried Him upon your hands,[18] in Him you were pardoned of your iniquity and of all your sins. *Bless the Lord, my soul, and all my bones His holy name.*[19] *Praise the Lord, O my soul!*[20] *I will praise the Lord in my life and I will sing to my God as long as I live.*[21] *My heart and my flesh have praised the living God.*[22]

---

[15] Cf. Mt.13:17; Lk.10:24.
[16] Gen. 2:13; 1Kgs 1:33. Gihon, one of the four rivers of Paradise.
[17] Ps. 116:7.
[18] Lk. 2:25–32.
[19] Ps. 103:1.
[20] Ps. 146:1.
[21] Ps. 104:33.
[22] Ps. 84:3.

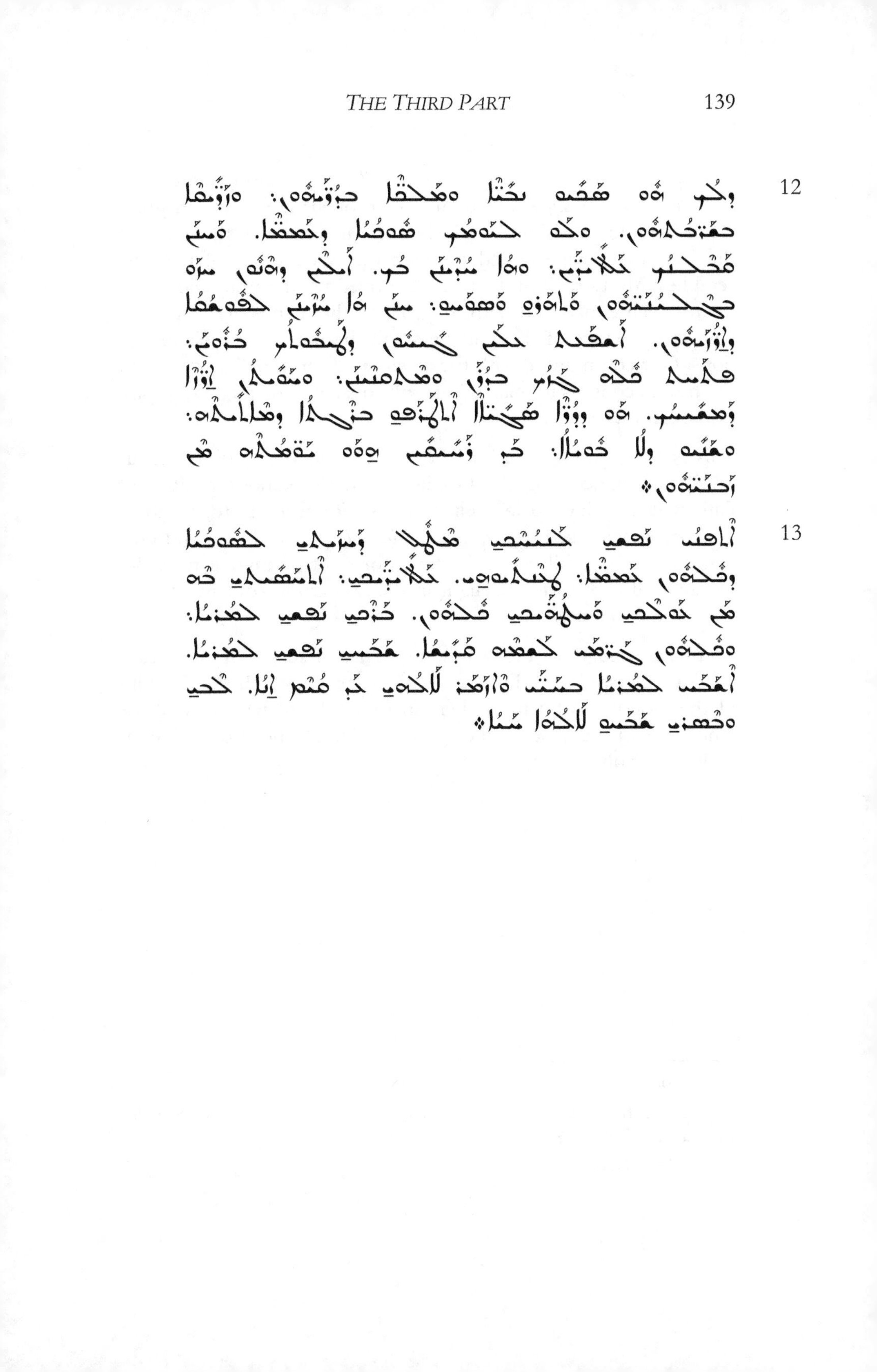

14 I will praise You, Lord, and *my mouth will declare Your righteousness and Your praise all the day*.²³ For You have brought me to the magnificence of Your Lordship. You have associated me with the praise of the angels and have united me with the celebrations of their assemblies. My Lord, You have not deprived us of communion with them which consists in faith, for such is the nature of all spiritual beings: the wings of the Watchers and the mirror of their revelations. Our communion with the angels and our mingling with their assemblies consists in making our will equal with theirs, in the spirit of the faith we have received.

15 This is the praise of spiritual beings, the force of the wondrous revelations concerning the Godhead and the various realities of faith which spring up in their stirrings. For truly, Lord, by them You are experienced *by faith and not by sight*. Your hidden and holy Nature does not fall under the touch or sight of any creature. But by faith, all natures take delight in the rays from Your mercy that flash in their nature.

16 You have brought us near to the mysteries of such glory by means of Your Beloved Son. For You have let us approach the foothills of the mountain of faith – there in the midst of which dwell the nine ranks of the hosts of the spiritual beings,²⁴ and above which is built Your holy city.²⁵

---

²³ Ps. 71:15.

²⁴ On the nine choirs of angels alluded to here, see Is.I 187. See also Ps. Dionysius, *Celestial Hierarchy* VI–X, 200c–273c.

²⁵ Heb.12:22.

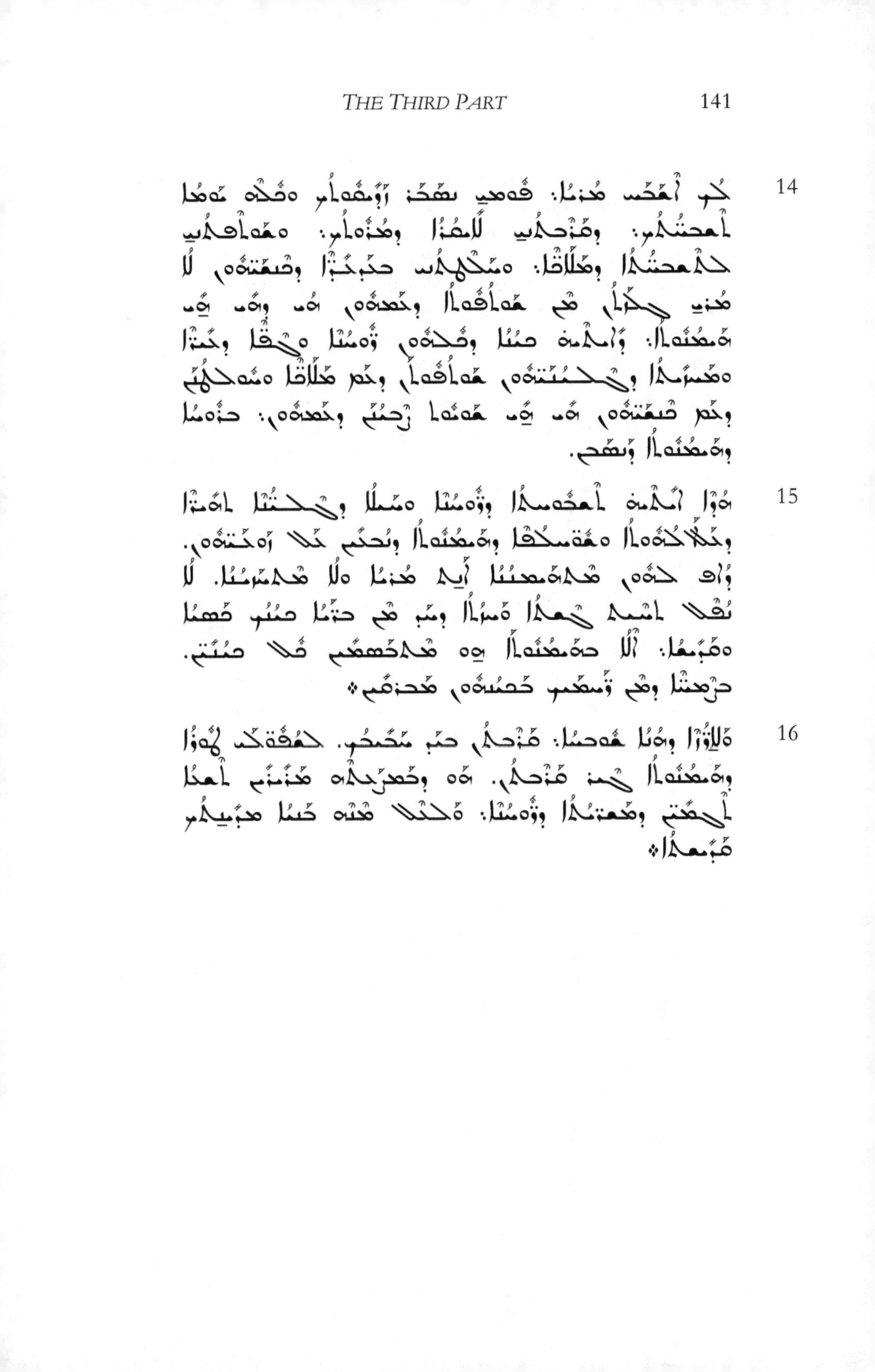

17 Our God, Living and Lifegiving, this is the mountain Your apostle and servant Paul announced to us when he said: *You have come near.* For You have come near to the mountain of Sion[26] – which is faith and knowledge of the Lord – *to the city of the living God, to the heavenly Jerusalem.* This consists in participation in the divine contemplation[27] *with the assemblies of the archangels.*[28] For the mind which shares in the revelation with them is in ascent on the ladder of faith to Sion, the mountain of God.

18 <To bring> an end to our evils, You have brought us to this, O God Just Judge,[29] who is not always angry but turns and refrains from looking at our sins.[30] You did not spare Your Beloved Son, but You gave Him up for us all[31] that His death might justify us. You have made known to us in Christ hidden aspects of Your eternal wisdom and You have brought us to the knowledge of faith in You.[32]

19 Do not abandon me, my Lord, depriving me of this mercy which is upon me! For You have called me without my asking, and brought me in Your eternal love to Your glorious kingdom.[33] Let me not be deprived of meditation on this love. Send Your power, my Lord, to assist me and rescue me from the sea of temporal life. O Sea of help, continue to help me and do not abandon me to the abyss of evils.

---

[26] Ascent to Sion: Evag. Cent.V.6; VI. 49.

[27] Divine contemplation (*te'ôryâ alâhâytâ*): Is.I 23, 31, 161, 198, 571; Is.II XIX.5; *Keph.* IV 48. Brock lists occurrences in Ps.Dionysius, Sergius, Babai, Gregory of Cyprus – and notes its absence in Evagrius.

[28] Heb. 12:22.

[29] Ps. 9:5.

[30] Ps. 85: 3–7.

[31] Rom. 8:32.

[32] Rom. 16: 25–26.

[33] 1 Titus 2:12.

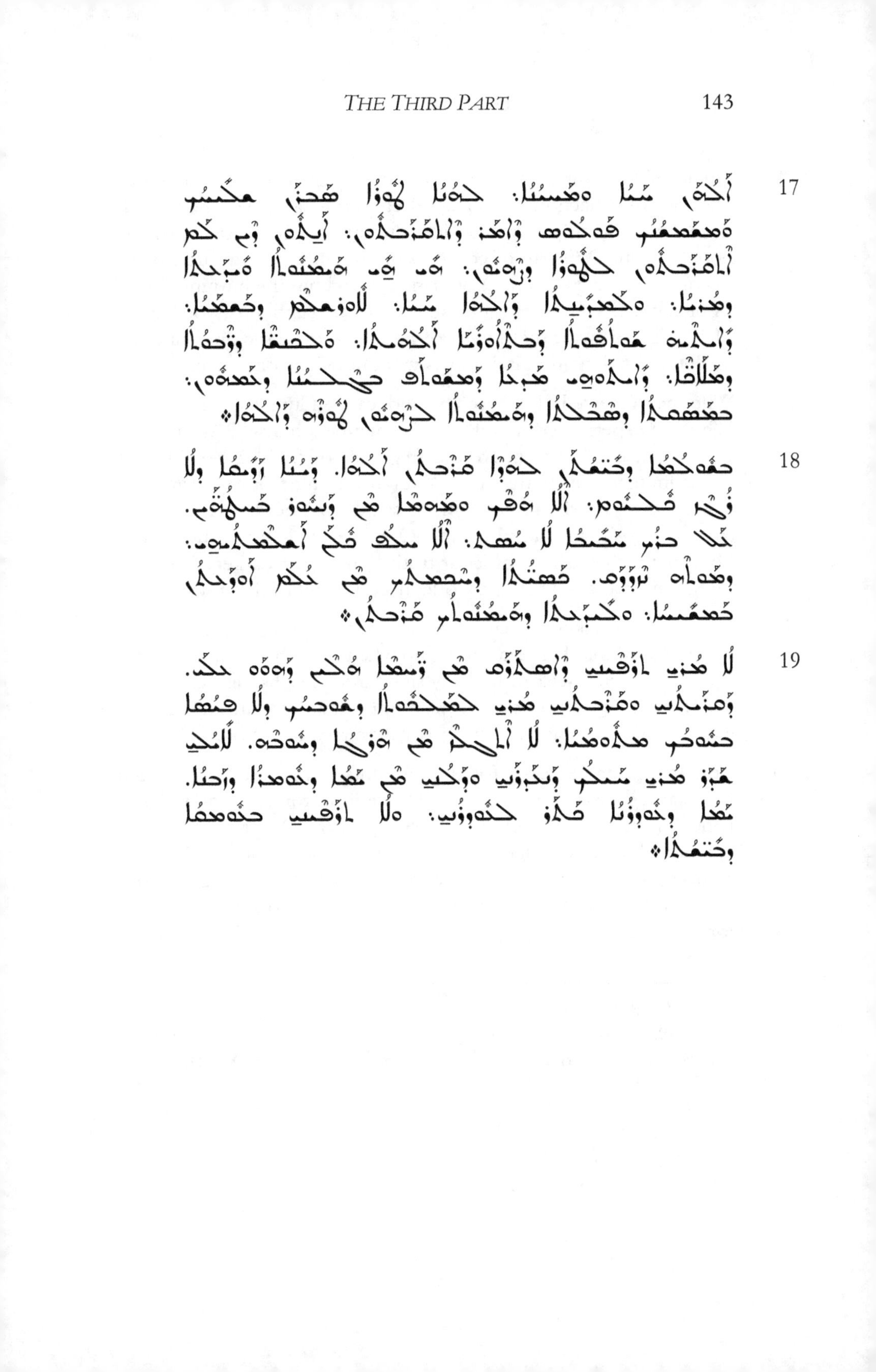

20   Guide of Life, direct my mind to You: open before my thoughts the door of reflection on You. O Renewer of all,[34] You have gladdened me with Your knowledge. Stir up in my heart a genuine hope in You. O Ocean of compassion, rescue me from the anxiety of wandering away from[35] You. Bring me within the burning fire of Your faith. Give me to drink the wine of perception of your hope. Make me worthy of that fervor of heart that once the drop of hope in You has fallen upon it, it burns without being consumed.[36]

21   Who has received this thought and can endure its vehemence? Who has experienced it and again remembers himself? What body or thought can even endure the fragrance of faith in You? Christ the culminator of truth, make Your truth shine *in our hearts*.[37] O Power who have shown forth in the saints, by Your love I have *overcome the world*[38] and its pleasures. O Power who have put on our body, make the insights of Your truth shine in my darkened soul. O Ocean that has sustained the world, draw me out of the stormy sea.

22   My Lord, You know that I am sad because my sins are always before You:[39] hidden tears spring up when I see the weakness of my soul. But when I seek to heal my sins through sighs, desires rush in with them to change in ruin my pain of heart and to turn my thought away from intercession and my meditation regarding You.

23   You are a capable healer for the torments of my heart. Strengthen my heart against the passions which are in it, for You know that it is not in me to overcome in this struggle. It is Your might which conquers but which ascribes the victory to me. Conquer in me, as You know how, and reckon the victory to me according to Your wisdom! For those who have conquered in this goal, it is their victory.

---

[34] Cf. Rev. 21:5.

[35] Wandering away from (*pehyâ*): here seen in a negative sense but may also be understood positively as "pondering," see Is.II XVIII.3.

[36] Cf. Ex. 3:2.

[37] Cf. 2 Peter 1:19; 2 Cor.4:6.

[38] Cf. 1 Jn. 5:4.

[39] Cf. Ps. 51:5.

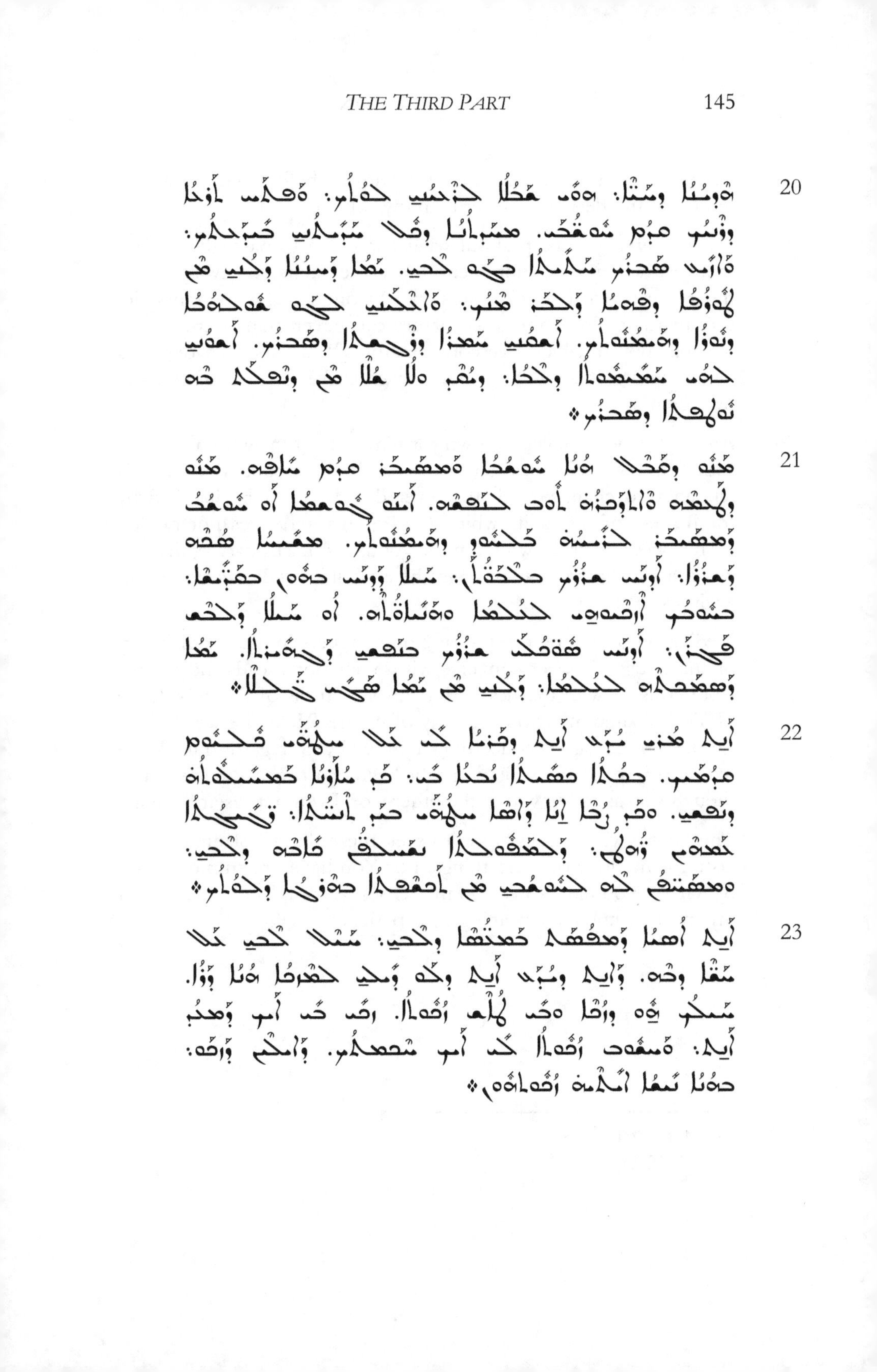

24 Let my heart's compunction be a witness before You, that the tumult of the flesh is stronger than my will.

25 While everyday I weep about what has come to pass, there is no moment when I do not incur the same faults, renewing those things for which I seek conversion. O Conqueror, who grants victory to the guilty whose own nature can never grant victory, give me that power which overcomes nature. While its own defeat is within nature, it is said to conquer by grace, yet it knows no victory by it own nature

26 Another power weaves a crown for him:[40] that One who has wisely formed his wretchedness so as to reveal His goodness, knows his tendency to change. Such that everyday, he must be justified by forgiveness of his faults which God grants and does not hinder. <This occurs> to show in him the goodness of His nature, that the weakness of human nature might be a herald of His sweetness and a witness of His mercy.[41]

27 Meditation on the perception of You conquers in me the difficulty of the struggle. Sweet converse with Your hope leads me captive from consent with the flesh. May this sweetness of the knowledge of You separate me from the way of nature. Make me worthy, my Lord, of true insights concerning Your will with regard to us. Make me worthy of that meditation which, in the process, transfigures thoughts so as to see within the other world without resembling it.

28 The power which teaches me to seek these things, plants in me a taste for the love of these things. For You have drawn me to You by what <You have sown> in my senses: accomplish in me, within my spirit, to know its meaning by experience.

---

[40] Cf. 2 Tm. 4:8.
[41] Cf. 2 Cor. 12:9.

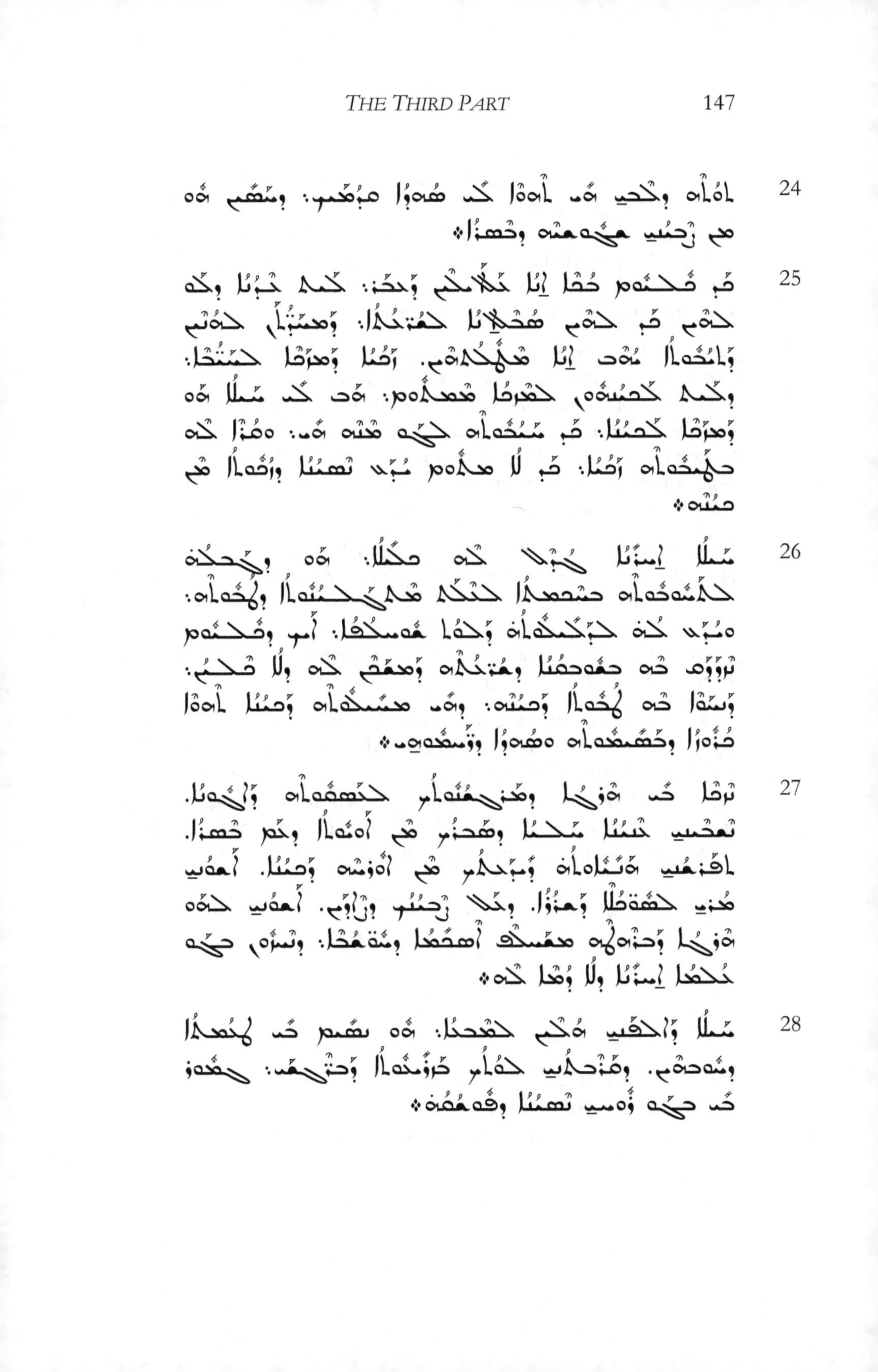

29 Since You have associated me in the mystery of Your glorious divinity, strengthen me in this hope by the assurance of faith. Because, my Lord, by means of Your Beloved Son You have drawn me to this understanding, instruct me in a hidden way that I might think about Your majesty. Give me a sound mind that it may flourish continually by means of a clear reflection regarding You.

30 Remove from me an ignorant mind which thinks silliness; stir up in me how to think rightly about Your splendor, so that I do not begin to give praise concerning Your divine judgments in a human manner subject to passions about the ways of Your intelligence, Savior of our souls! Prepare in me the paths of Your wisdom and open to me the door to meditation on Your glorious will, for I do not know, my Lord, how to enter there.

31 O Christ, door of the mysteries,[42] make me a sharer in the apperception of Your mysteries. By You, my Lord, I enter to the Father and I receive insights of the grace of Your Holy Spirit. O Christ, key of the mysteries and end of the mysteries: by You, my Lord, the door is opened for us to the mysteries which from of old were hidden in Your Father.

32 Make me worthy to receive You within me, that by You I may open the mysteries past and future and enter there. O Lord, You make me worthy of the sweetness of hope in You. Whoever tastes this cup will persevere in controlling himself and return again to his true self. This cup, indeed, becomes sweet in the heart of those who receive it, like the juice of the grape.

---

[42] See Is.I 544: "The cross is the gate of the mysteries; here takes place the entrance of the mind unto the knowledge of the heavenly mysteries."

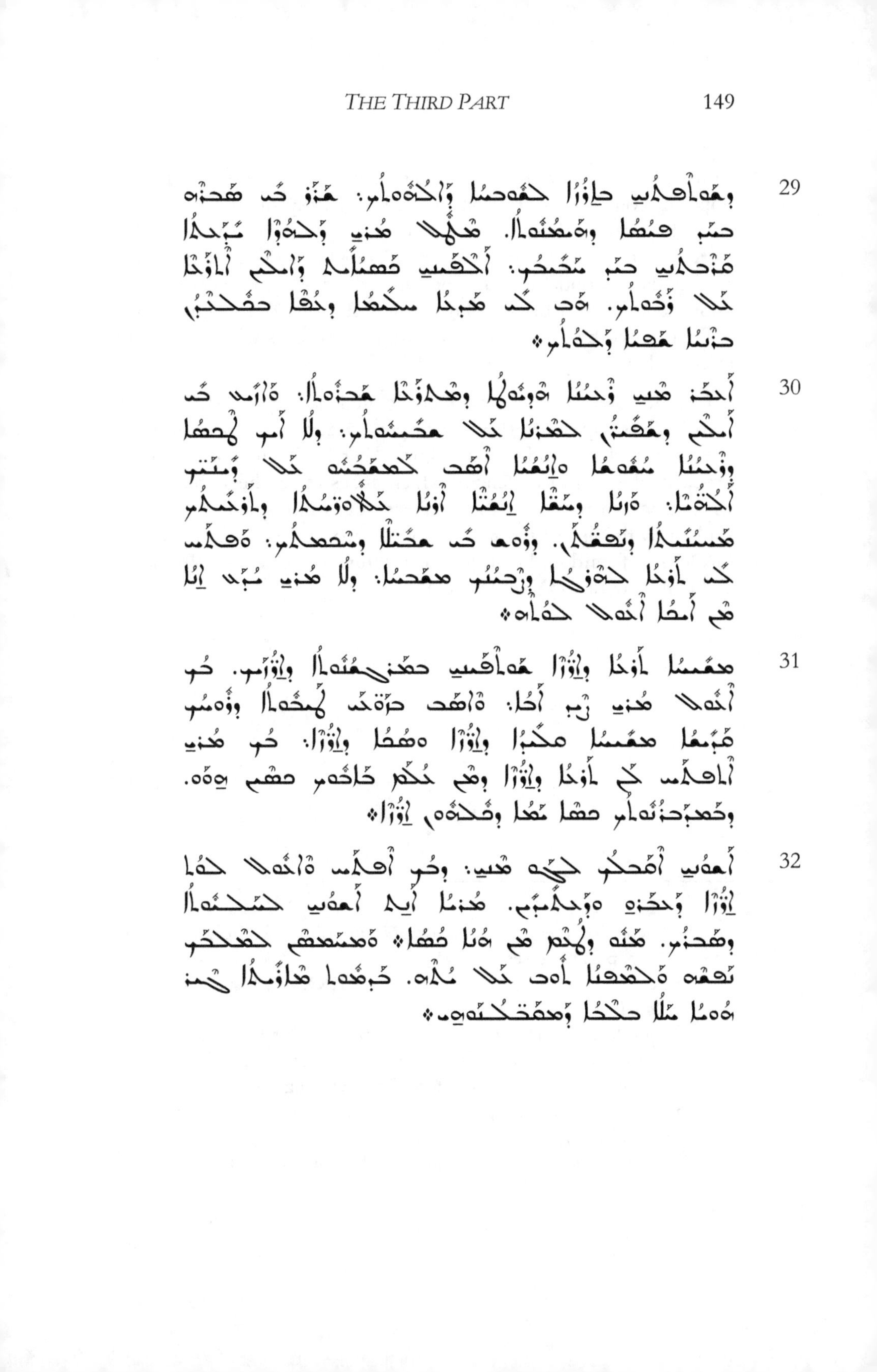

33   You who make all things new,⁴³ renew me by the apperception of hope in You. Joy of creation, make me worthy of that joy which arises beyond the flesh and is received in the silence of the soul.⁴⁴ Bury within my members the fire of Your love. Place on my heart the bonds of wonder at You. Bind my stirrings in the silence of the knowledge of You because knowledge of You consists in silence. Make me worthy to behold You with opened eyes which are more interior than the eyes of the body.⁴⁵

34   Create new eyes in me, You who created new eyes for the blind man.⁴⁶ Close my exterior ears and open hidden ears, which hear the silence and the sounds of the Spirit, that by Your Spirit I might proclaim the word of silence⁴⁷ which arises in the heart but is not written, which moves in the intellect but is not spoken – though spoken by the lips of the Spirit and is heard by incorporeal hearing. O Ocean of pardon, begin to wash nature's uncleanness from me and make me fit for Your sanctuary.

---

⁴³ Cf. Rev.21:5.

⁴⁴ Silence of the soul (*šetqâ d-napšâ*): in John Sol., Bettiolo, "Sulla preghiera," 5, p.81. And see Is.III IV.7.

⁴⁵ See interior eye (*'aynâ gawwâytâ*) Is.II XXXV.4; Keph. IV 67, cf. And see Is.III I.11.

⁴⁶ John 9. See Christ as Creator in Ephrem. For Ephrem, "God is the source of healing and he sent His Son into the world to heal humanity and fulfill what was lacking in nature. The fulfilling and healing of the world is considered by Ephrem as a second creation." See Shemunkasho, *Healing in the Theology*, 381–387; 407–21.

⁴⁷ Word of silence (*melta d- šetqâ*): cf. John Sol. *Letter to Hesychius* 1.

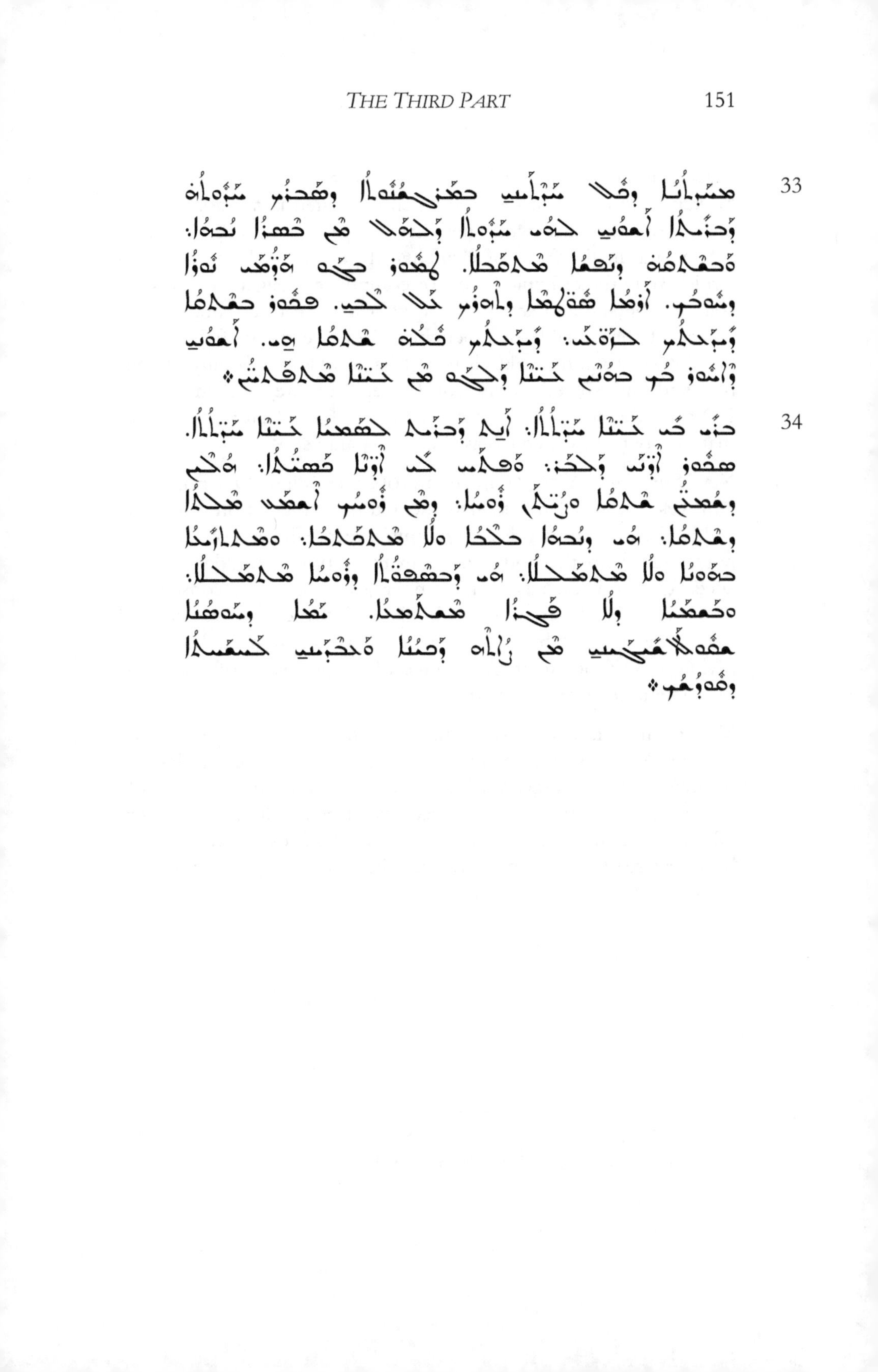

35 My Lord, You have not formed me like a clay vessel that when broken cannot be restored and when encrusted is not able to take on its former polish when new. But in Your wisdom, You have created me in the form of elements of gold and silver that when tarnished, in the refining sorrow of compunction, again imitates the color of the sun and shining is brought to its former condition by means of the crucible of repentance. You are the craftsman who polishing our nature makes it new. I have soiled the beauty of baptism and I am sullied, but in You I receive a more excellent beauty. In You is the beauty of creation: You have brought it back again to that beauty from which it was altered in paradise.[48]

36 New Sun, light Your lamp in my obscure mind! O Christ who removes nature's lament, give me hidden lamentation and tears within the eyes from a discerning mind: tears whose moisture does not exude from the body but from the fervor of hidden repentance. This fervor leads to true inner joy and to the consolation which silences the mouth and holds out to the heart an unusual nourishment. It establishes it as a true witness within the body, testifying at all times to the guarantee of forgiveness[49] of one's sins that one has received by mercy.

37 My sins are many, my Lord, but Your compassion is greater than my sins. My wicked deeds increase in number but they are incomparable to Your mercy. Your love is greater than my sins. I look, my Lord, at my sins and I am speechless at how willful I have been. Observing Your deeds towards me, wonder seizes me, how I have been rewarded by You in a way opposite to what I have merited.

---

[48] Cf. Gen. 3.
[49] Cf. 2 Cor. 1:21–22; 5:5; Eph. 1:13–14.

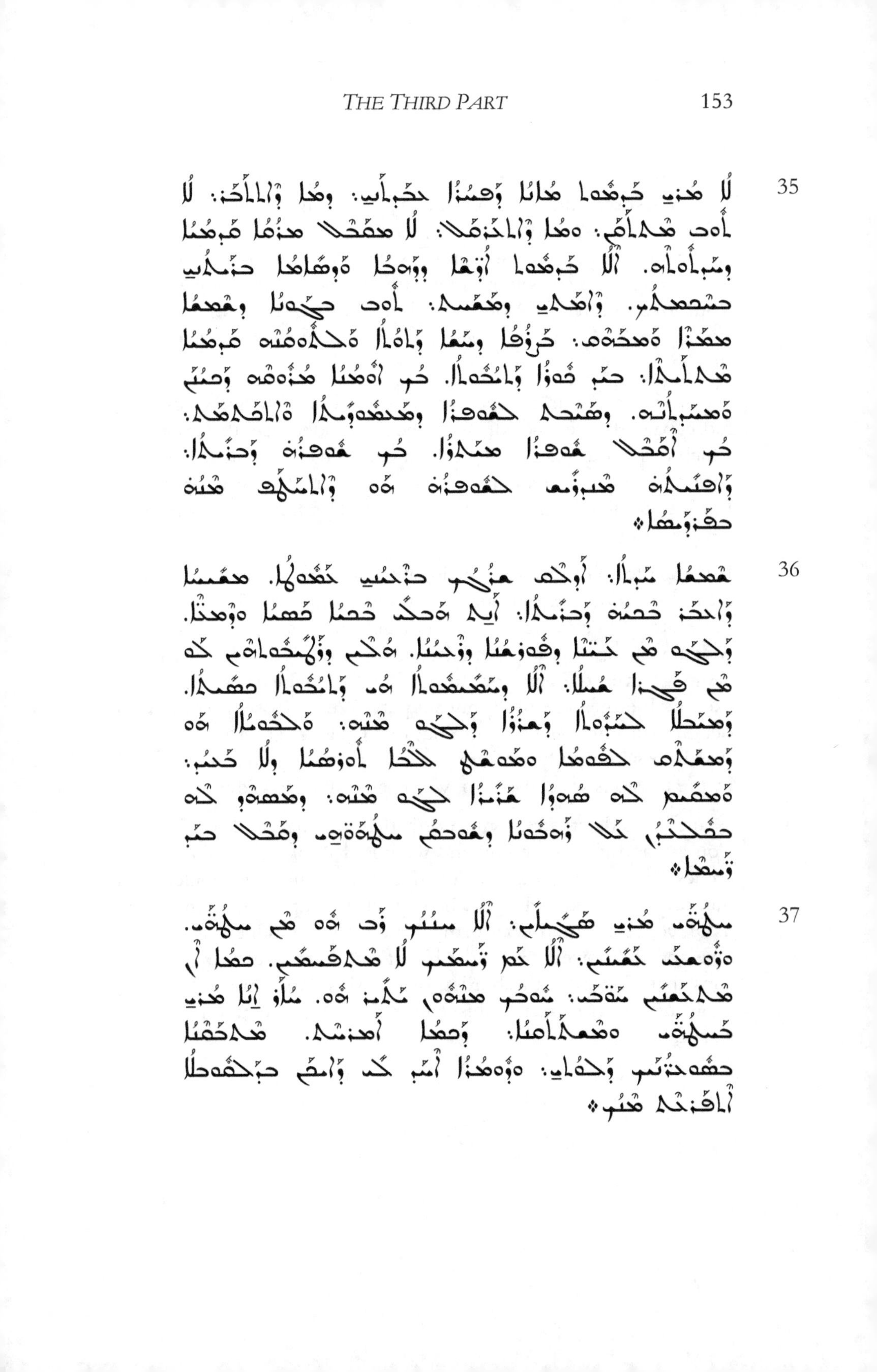

38   Your gift has brought me to the knowledge of You and not to Your chastisement. In Your mercy, You have watered me with Your sweetness, without the help of ascetic labor. You have clothed me with a fragile nature which each day is a witness to Your grace. Your wisdom shows us, by means of our weakness, Your love towards us. You have placed in us an inclination to be a witness of Your Nature which is more patient than our faults and sins.

39   My Lord, has Your patience no other way than to inflict us with more pain than expected? We never consider that the goodness which is in Your Nature might be a bad thing. If a stirring like this dare enter in us, it would be by ignorance that it springs up. My Lord, untroubled You put up with us and without constraint You bear our sins.

40   It is easy for You to bear our iniquity as it was simple for You to bring forth our creation out of nothing. For us, my Lord, both of these are difficult since we are not able to bear even a small sin which we happen to see. And according to our judgment, my Lord, we judge even the great ocean of Your love which with its waves exceeds the measure of all our iniquity. We suppose, according to our human intelligence, that You, our Creator, are afflicted when You bear with us. Our suffering is a mirror to see what is in us, and by the passions we consent to, we weigh, my Lord, Your richness.

41   Grant us understanding, my Lord, that we may look on You as You are and not as we are, and we might think about You as becomes You, Giver of all our gifts! This is Your great opulence in our favor: true knowledge which is stirred up in us concerning Your concealment. Because my Lord, Your goodness and Your love and the power for good which is in Your nature, are the reasons that You carry the burden of our sins. And on this account, while not even expecting his conversion, You grant time to the sinner.

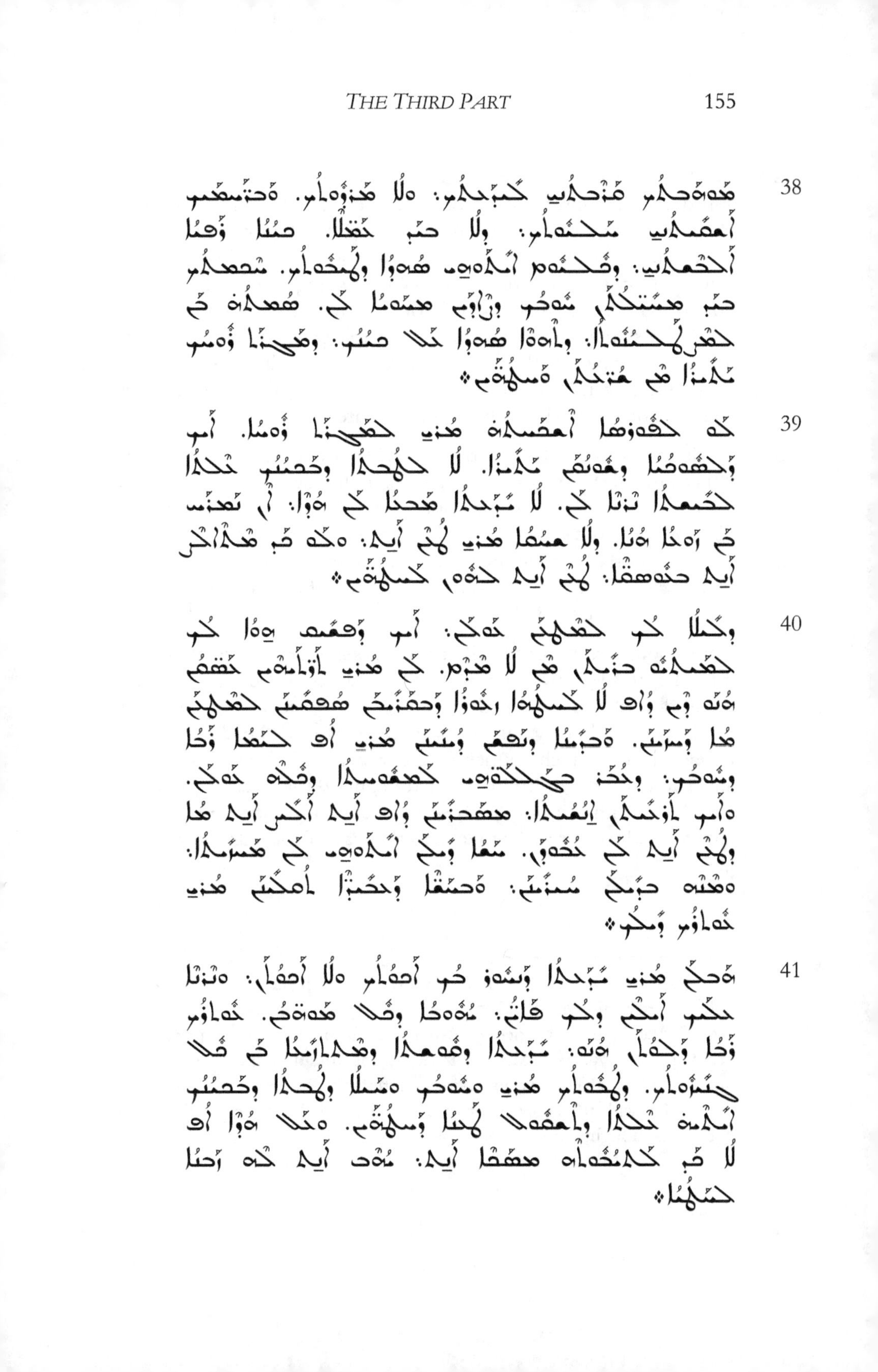

42   My Lord, may we not proceed with our insights in an exterior approach to Scripture which only denounces occasions of sin. But make us worthy of Your truth which is within Scripture. Grant us to search unceasingly in wonder, the reason for which You endure sinners. Not when wanting to know something You do not know, do You give time while waiting for it to happen, or not. For this would be shameful, my Lord, to think this about Your prevenient intelligence which with its knowledge precedes all the stirrings of our nature, even before our formation.[50] This only befits servants who do not know what will be in the future.

43   While this is true, it is right that we reflect on Your holy Nature. It is because of Your goodness and Your limitless mercy that You tolerate the sinner, even that one whom You know will not convert. You endure this not like one who does not know, awaiting possible good deeds, but because of Your compassion; as One who knows all, everything is manifest to You. Infinite, our Creator, is Your love for humanity!

44   Your goodness, my Lord, which You pour out on everything, may it not be for me a pretext for evil, that because of Your sweetness I might do evil. Hold me with the reins of Your mercy, that I might be able to stand up against the stirrings which assail me and against the accidents[51] which happen to me. Send me Your holy guardian angel and heal the infirmity of my thoughts,[52] for <being> mortal I am filled <with infirmity>. Keep my steps from the snares the enemy has hidden for me,[53] to lead to the way of wickedness of a sinner.

---

[50] Nature (*ṭuqânân*): cf. Is.II XXXIX.6. God foreknew our structure before our creation, cf. Ps.138.

[51] Accidents (*gdêšê*): occur to spur one on, or to test, train or reward. See Is.I 175, 496, 503. More commonly the tradition speaks of "variations" (*šuḥlâpê*): afflictions, adversities, sufferings.

[52] Cf. with the angel of providence in Is.I 433 who in times of trial "provides thoughts of righteousness."

[53] Cf.Ps.142:4.

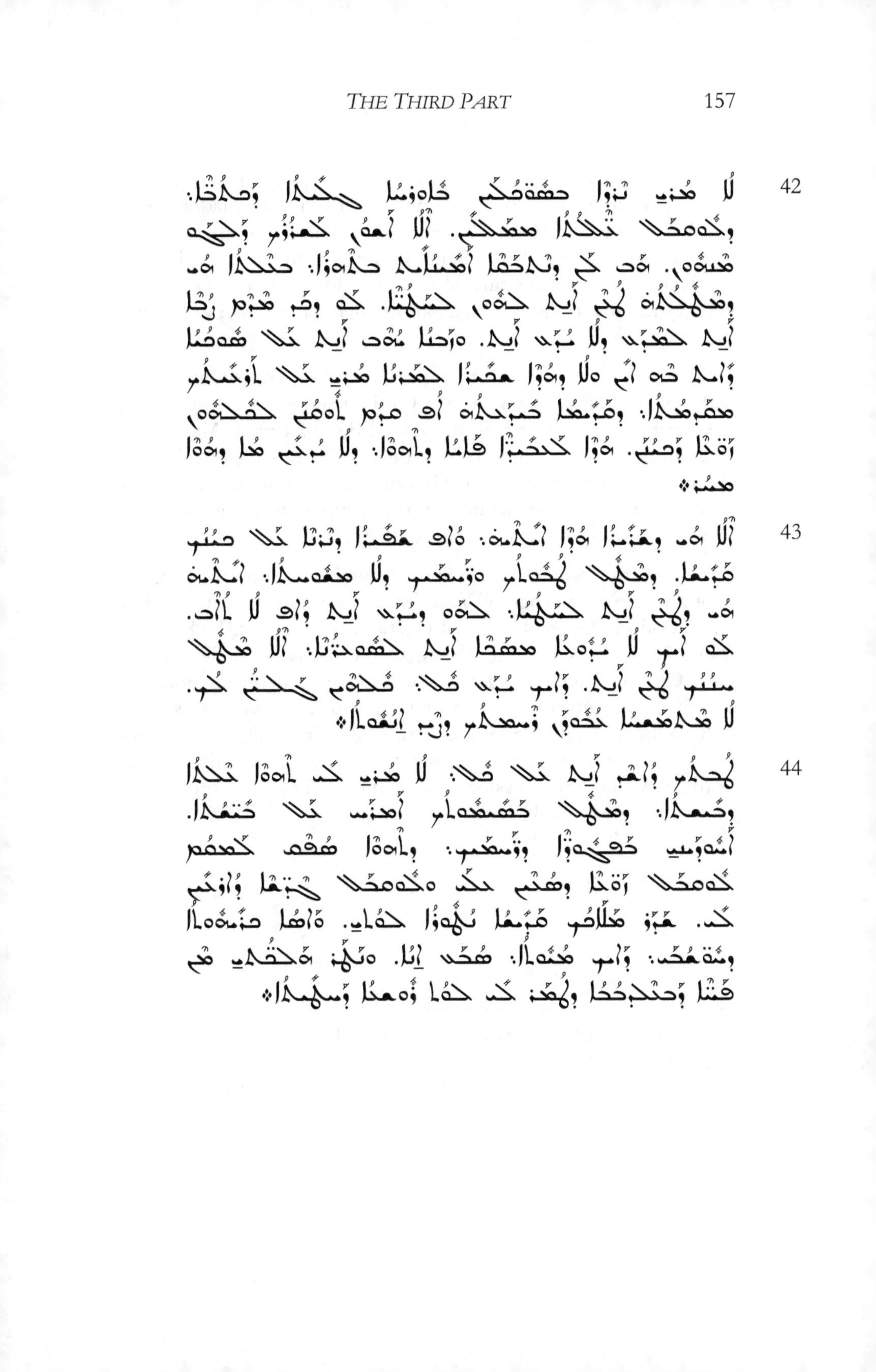

45   Most of all, my God, keep me from all stupidity of the intellect which reasons with erroneous opinions, filled with madness and worthy of weeping. Before Your majesty it thinks about Your Essence with an abominable opinion. Grant me, my Lord, the humility which knows the measure of nature and the misery of its weakness. Grant me a mind of right knowledge, proper to rational beings.

46   Guide of the living, reveal to me my thoughts and show me the paths of converse with You. My Lord, create for me, within me, the spiritual light[54] which is the knowledge of Christ. May I find Your truth in it, and think right thoughts about Your divinity and about the matters of my soul. My Lord, let me not be tried by my adversary and become derided by the demons, for those who are tempted by pride are delivered up to them.

47   But under the protection of humility which created me, I grow strong in the knowledge of You, by the help which is from Your grace. I adore the great Light of creation, Jesus Christ,[55] which has shone forth in its time according to the ineffable intelligence of God, Creator of all. Intelligence which thought, before all moments and times to send forth the magnificence of creation and its joy – only-begotten Light[56] from the nature of that intelligence – completing His work *in the consummation of this world*[57] and it rises in our hearts.[58] At the time pleasing to His will, the Light has brought us near to His great intelligence.

---

[54] Spiritual light (*nuhrâ d-ruḥânâ*), see *Keph.* I 13.

[55] Cf. Gen. 1:16; Jn. 8:12.

[56] Only-begotten Light: occurs in Ephrem, *Hymns on the Crucifixion* VIII.12.

[57] Cf. Gal. 4:4.

[58] Cf. 2 Pt. 1:19; 2 Cor. 4:6.

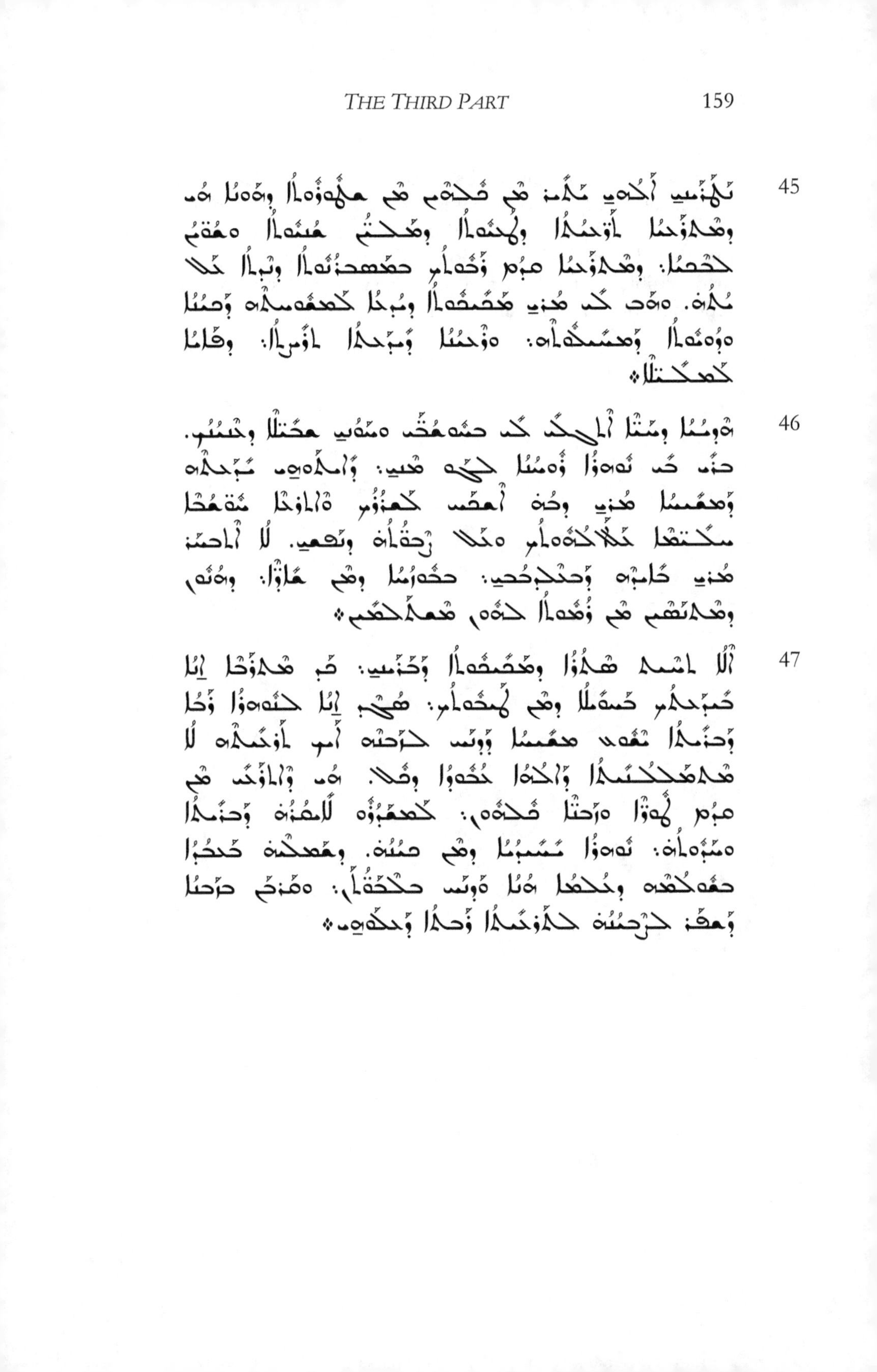

48   This Light has brought me back to the *house of my Father*[59] and has shown me that He also prepares for me an inheritance of glory beyond the confines of the worlds. Because of this He has created me, that the principle of Good and His creative action might be made visible, which brings all into existence. Blessed be this magnificence forever and ever. Amen

---

[59] Cf. Lk. 15:17.

48 ܘܐܦܢܝ ܠܚܡܐ ܐܟܠ܂ ܘܡܝܡܝ ܘܐܢ ܡܙܐܘܐܠ ܘܦܘܕܚܢܐ ܠܗܘܠܐ ܗܘ ܗܦܘܟܢ ܢܠܚܩܐ ܟܕ ܢܟܘ. ܘܡܢܗܠܐ ܗܘܐ ܐܢܫܝܢ ܟܚܙܢܟܐ ܘܢܐܠܣܪܐ ܗܘܡܐ ܐܚܙܢܟܐ ܘܐܟܐ ܘܣܝ ܠܦܠܐ. ܚܢܝ ܦܗ ܐܢܦܗ ܠܢܟܡ ܢܠܦܝ ܐܡܝ܂

Chapter VIII

Again of the same Mar Isaac. On how the saints are set apart and sanctified by the inhabiting of the Holy Spirit.

1 The temple of God is a *house of prayer*.[1] The soul, then, is a house of prayer in which the memory[2] of God is celebrated continually. If all the saints are sanctified by the Spirit to be temples of the adorable Trinity:[3] the Holy Spirit sanctifies them by means of the constant remembrance[4] of His divinity. Constant prayer,[5] then, is the continual remembrance of God. Therefore, by means of continual prayer, the saints are sanctified, becoming a dwelling for the action of the Holy Spirit.[6] As one of the saints said: "Be mindful of God always and your intelligence will be a heaven." [7]

---

[1] Cf. Is. 56:7; Mt. 21:13.

[2] Memory (*dukrânâ*).

[3] Cf. 1 Cor. 3:16.

[4] Constant remembrance (*'udhânâ ammînâ*): Is.I 35, 253, 258, 321, 508; Is.II VIII.15; XXIX.7; XXX.4,13.

[5] Constant prayer (*ṣlôtâ ammîntâ*): Is. I 304, 441– 42, 544; *Keph*.II 97. Cf. *ammînûtâ da-ṣlôtâ*): Is.I 15, 107, 259, 557; Is.II XIV.41–42 (including references to Evagrius, Theodore of Mopsuestia, Macarius, Babai, Sahdona, Dadisho, Shem'on d-Taybuteh); *Keph*.IV 34.

[6] Activity of the Holy Spirit (*ma'bdânûtâ d-ruḥâ d-qudšâ*): here Isaac specifically links the action of the Holy Spirit to prayer and remembrance of God. When the Spirit takes its dwelling place in a person, one does not cease to pray because the Spirit will constantly pray in him. See esp. Is.I 259. And see Is.I 70, 353; Is.II V.33; Is.III VI.45. Cf. Is.III IV.32.

[7] Also cited anonymously by Sahdona II, 8,59. Cf. Nilus, *Perle* 2, p. 10 and see Joseph Hazzaya, *Lettres*, 138, "firmament of the heart."

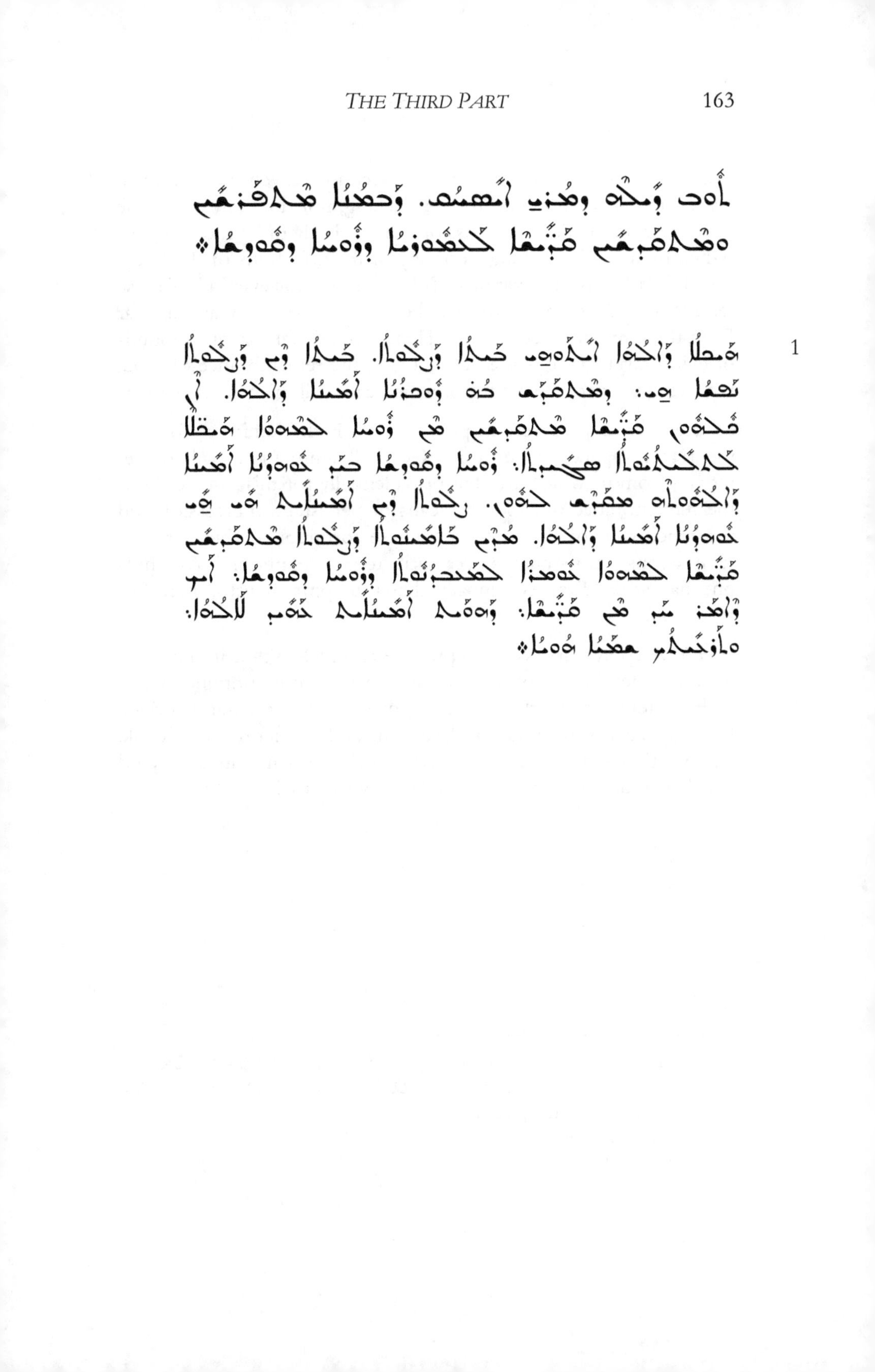

2 Therefore, if our soul becomes a second heaven by continual prayer, in heaven no good thing is lacking, nor does any evil come there, nor temptation, nor passions of the body or of the soul, nor remembrance of evil things, nor any of the afflictions of the body, nor the darkness or vexations of the soul. If, however, all of these temptations do come to us, it is because we go astray and are far from the remembrance of God. Hence we err, falling into all kinds of evil. Prayer, then, is the definition of the remembrance of God, removing the occasions of error which cause all the evils we suffer.

3 So then, let us persevere in prayer which is the luminous form of the remembrance of our Lord God: all temptations will be removed from us which are sent providentially for this – to set in us the remembrance of God by means of persistent intercession and the crucifixion of the intellect.[8] These torturers – which are the temptations – constrain us necessarily to make <prayer>. As a holy one has said: "Pray continually that the spirit of error may flee from you."[9]

4 When we apply ourselves to <prayer> and make space in ourselves for the remembrance of the Lord by means of our continual prayer to Him, temptations flee and passions cease. Even Satan is driven far away; adversities find no place in us and afflictions grow weak. All evil things give way, somehow, to the remembrance of God which is in us; shouting, they flee from before their Lord.[10]

---

[8] Crucifixion of the intellect (*zqîfûtâ d-hawnâ*): Is.I, 15–16, 223, 232; Is.II XXX.6. See Abba Isaiah *Ascetical Discourses* XXVI.4. See also de Andia, "Hèsychia et contemplation," 28–34.

[9] Budge, *Paradise* II, 439.

[10] Cf. Mk.9:26.

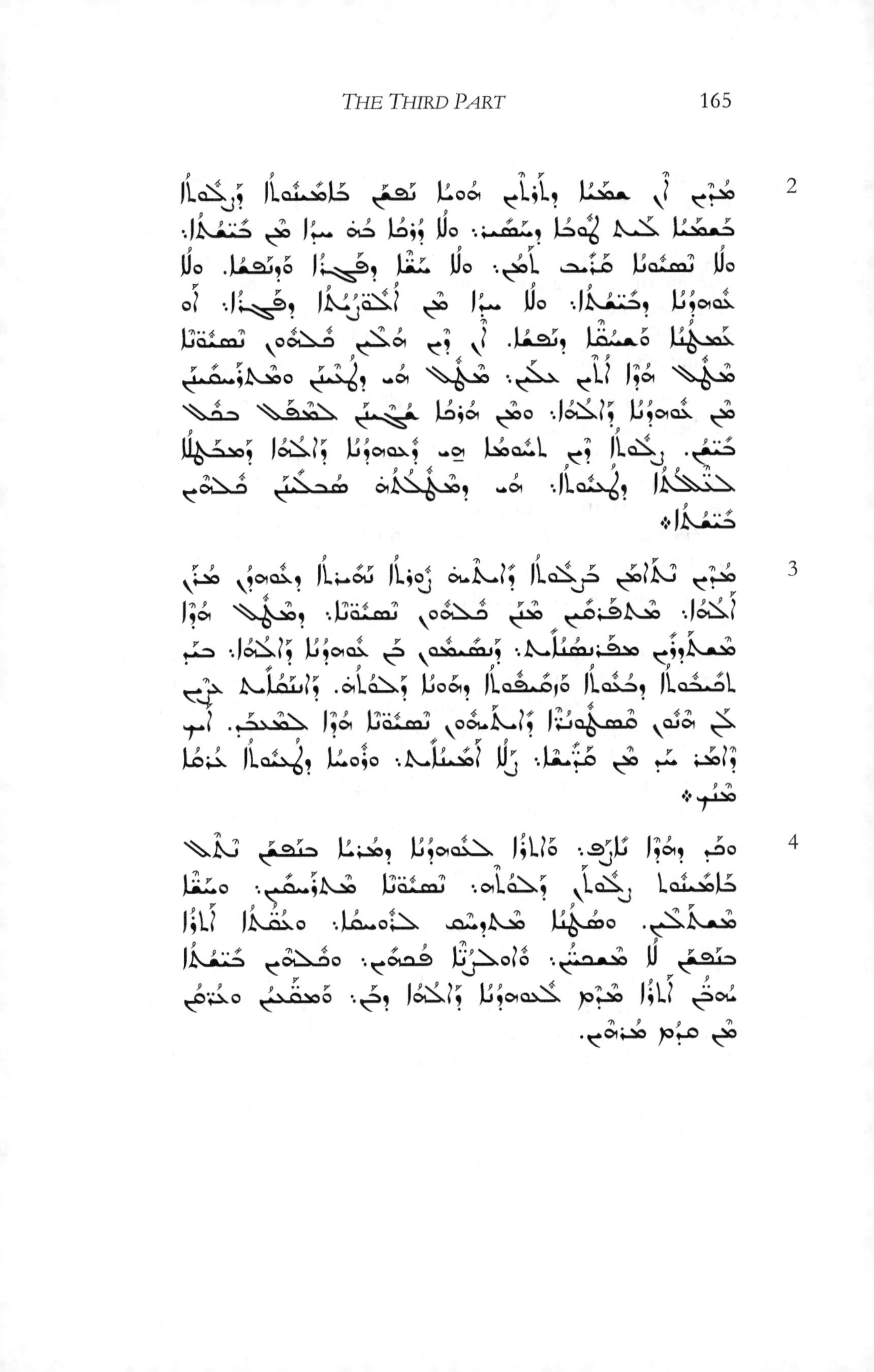

5 The angels celebrate in that house where the holy altar is set for the continual mystery of their Lord. The continual remembrance of God is in fact an altar which is established in the heart,[11] from it all the mysteries ascend to the sanctuary of the Lord;[12] one finds there not one of the contrary events we have set forth. They are, indeed, fearful before the splendor of the divine light which burns in the midst of the mysteries. And as it were, naturally, all adversities are conquered where God is named.

6 But sometimes, even when we are diligent about <prayer>, some of these realities are allowed to remain and show their impudence to vex us, because we have not begun in a right way this continual remembrance of the Lord. And so because of our failure, they even have the opportunity to assail us. <Whereas> the annoyance of the adversaries is not able to approach the house of the king when he is there.[13]

7 The divinity, however, dwells in human beings not with its Nature. For its Nature is infinite, and not limited or contained in a place. Heaven and earth, indeed, are full of it yet there is no place sufficient for it.[14] It is in every place yet remote from every place, because of the immensity and sublimity of its Nature. It is said that God dwells in a place by the will and by the action of His power, as it is written: *I will dwell in them and I will walk among them*;[15] that is: "I will manifest in them the power of my action." As it is also written that <God> overshadows[16] the temple in Jerusalem or the tent which was erected by Moses.

---

[11] Cf. Heb.8:2.

[12] On the heart as altar see Is.I 167; on the altar of prayer and prayer being sacrificed, Is.II XIV.20, XXI.4. See *Book of Steps* XII.1–4 and John Sol. *Soul* 88. See also Evag. Muyldermans, *Parénèse*, 27; Macarius 344 and Sahdona III 24. See Brock, "Spirituality of the Heart."

[13] Cf. Mt.12:29.

[14] 1Kgs. 8:27. Cf. Theodore of Mopsuestia, *Homélies* V 4.

[15] Lv. 26:11–12.

[16] Overshadows (*aggen*), see Is.III I.4.

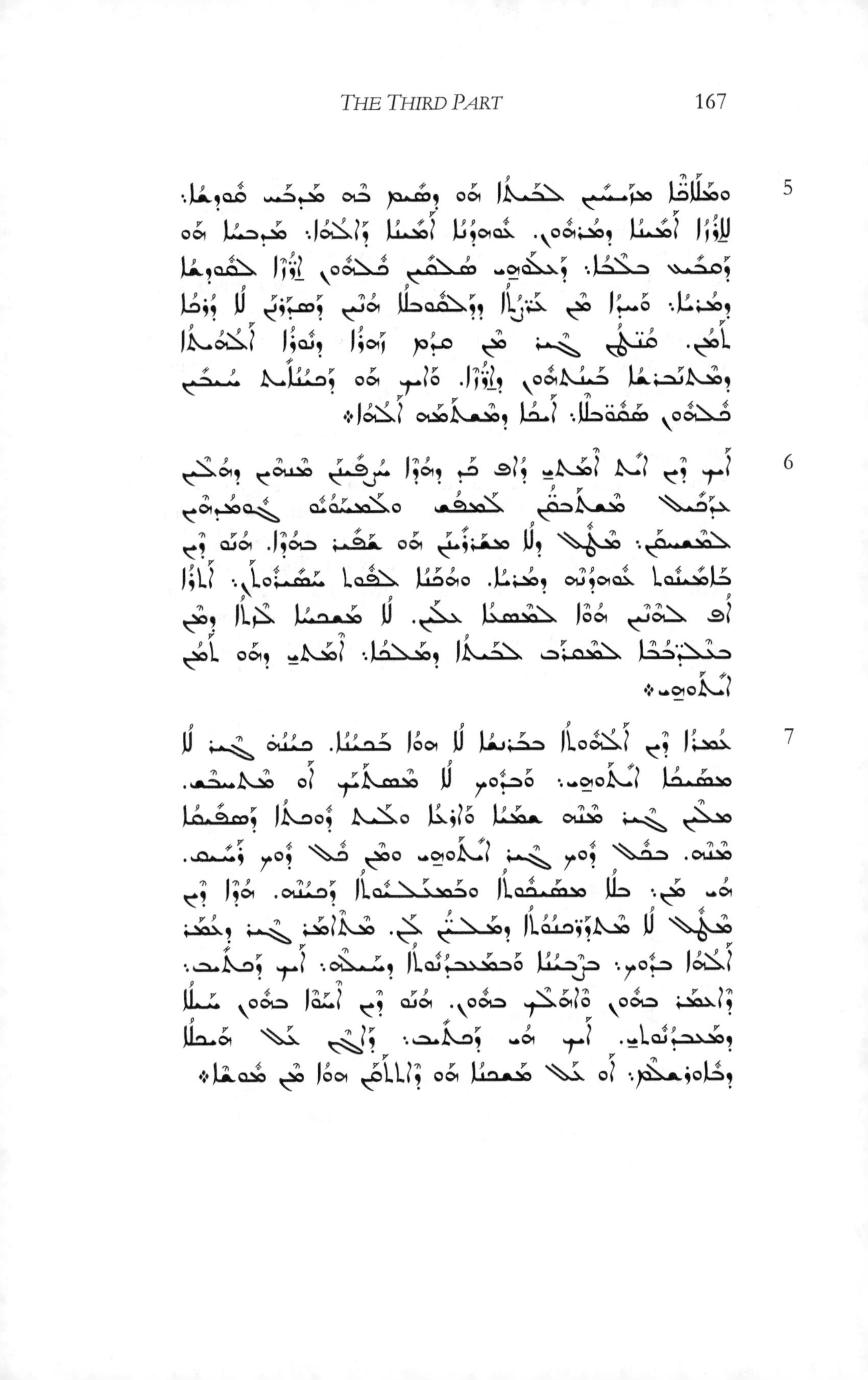

8 When the house of <God> was built and completed by Solomon, it is said that his Shekinah[17] overshadowed it and the house was filled with his glory;[18] it is also said that the priests went out from the holy place, from before the Shekinah of the Lord, because they were not able to serve in that the whole house was filled with the cloud of the glory of the Lord.[19] This was the sign that God was well pleased by it and dwelt in it. It is like this for the soul which has been built upon virtue, when at the time of prayer it perceives this cloud which overshadows the intellect at prayer.

9 This happens in a concealed way, and the one who prays is not able to complete the recitation of his prayer. Therefore, one becomes tranquil and is speechless in stupor before the glory of the Lord, which is revealed by an intuition of the intellect. This is a sign that the Lord is well pleased in him and has overshadowed him! This is like what Ezekiel saw when it was shown to him in a vision concerning the building of the temple. After the house was finished, which had been constructed in his presence – it was shown to him as in a divine revelation[20] – then also he saw the divine *Shekinah* which overshadowed the temple, and it was filled by it.[21]

---

[17] Shekinah, see Is.III VII.4.
[18] Cf. 2 Chron. 7:1–2 (Peshitta).
[19] 2 Chron. 5:13–14.
[20] Divine revelation (*gelyânâ alâhâyâ*): Is.I 161, 371, 391, 545, 549; Is.II XVI.5; Theodore of Mopsuestia *WS* VI 239; John Sol. *Soul* 61. It also occurs in Narsai, Dadisho and Sahdona.
[21] Cf. Ez. 43:5.

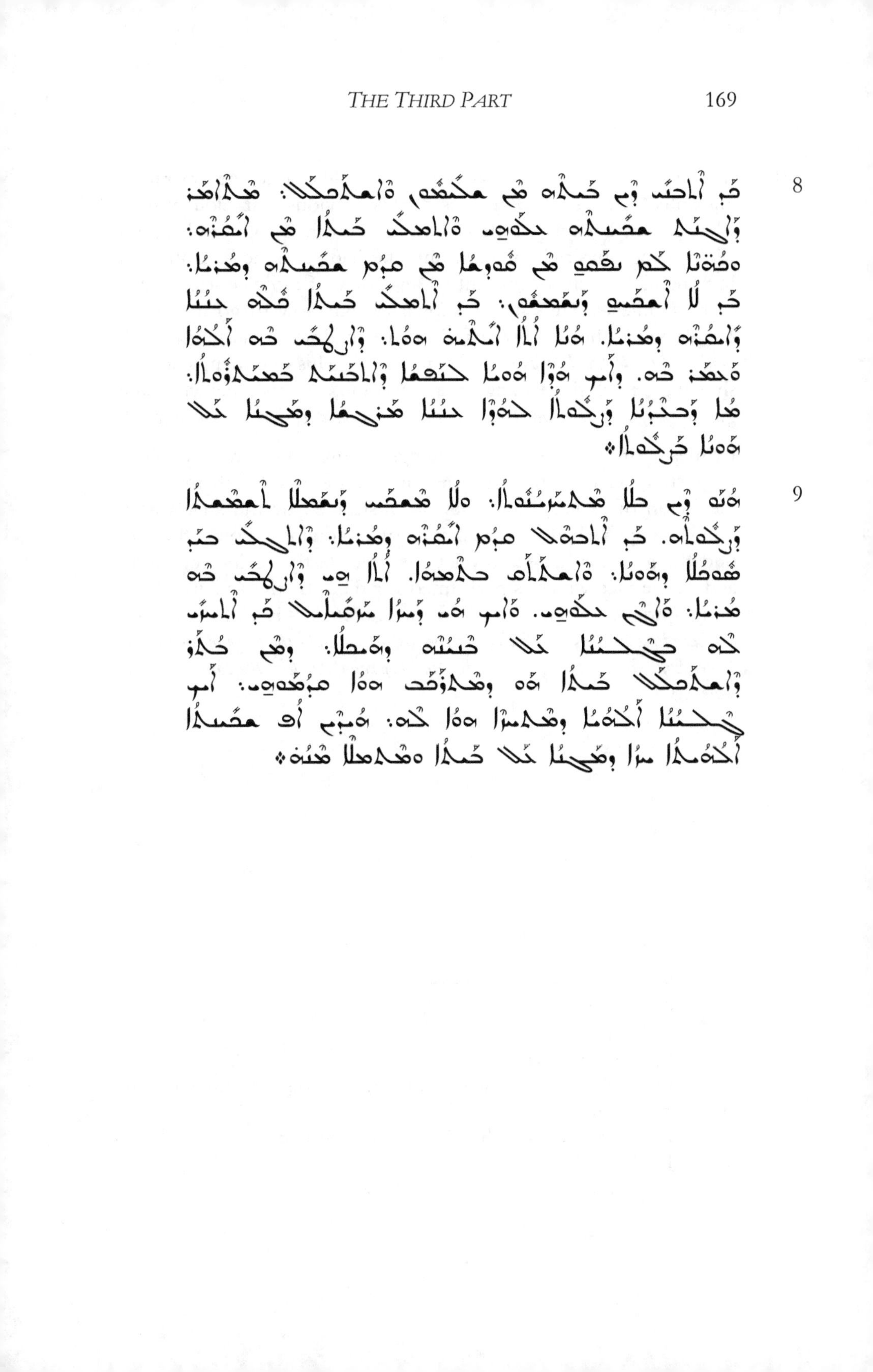

10   In the vision which he saw, there was like a divine operation imprinted in his soul. By means of this previous marvelous vision, what he saw became visible to him before it had come to be. And while being physically in Babylonia, he had seen the revelation in Jerusalem,[22] which was distant by a journey of more or less <three to four miles>. Thus it was shown to him how to go up to the temple while the *Shekinah* of God overshadows it, as he says: *He conducted me to the door which looks to the east.*[23] This one then, who was showing him all these things in a revelation, was an angel who said: *Put in your heart all which I show you because I have come as a proof to you.*[24]

11   By means of these visions, two things are made known to us: all of the visions which happen to the saints were done for them by the mediation of angels,[25] and they are instructed by the angels until one has approached the revelations of the divine vision;[26] the second thing is that angelic revelations precede the divine revelation and the service which is performed for them by the activity of the Holy Spirit, as is here made known. Therefore <Ezekiel> says: *He conducted me to the gate which faces the east and behold the glory of the God of Israel came from the way of the east, and his voice was like the sound of many waters.*[27]

---

[22] Cf. Ez. 40:1–2.

[23] Ez. 43:1.

[24] Ez. 40:4 (Peshitta).

[25] On mediation of the angels in Isaac, see Hansbury, "Insight without Sight," 68–70.

[26] Divine vision (ḥzâṯâ alâhâyâ): Is.I 161; *Keph.* I 72.

[27] Ez. 43:1–2.

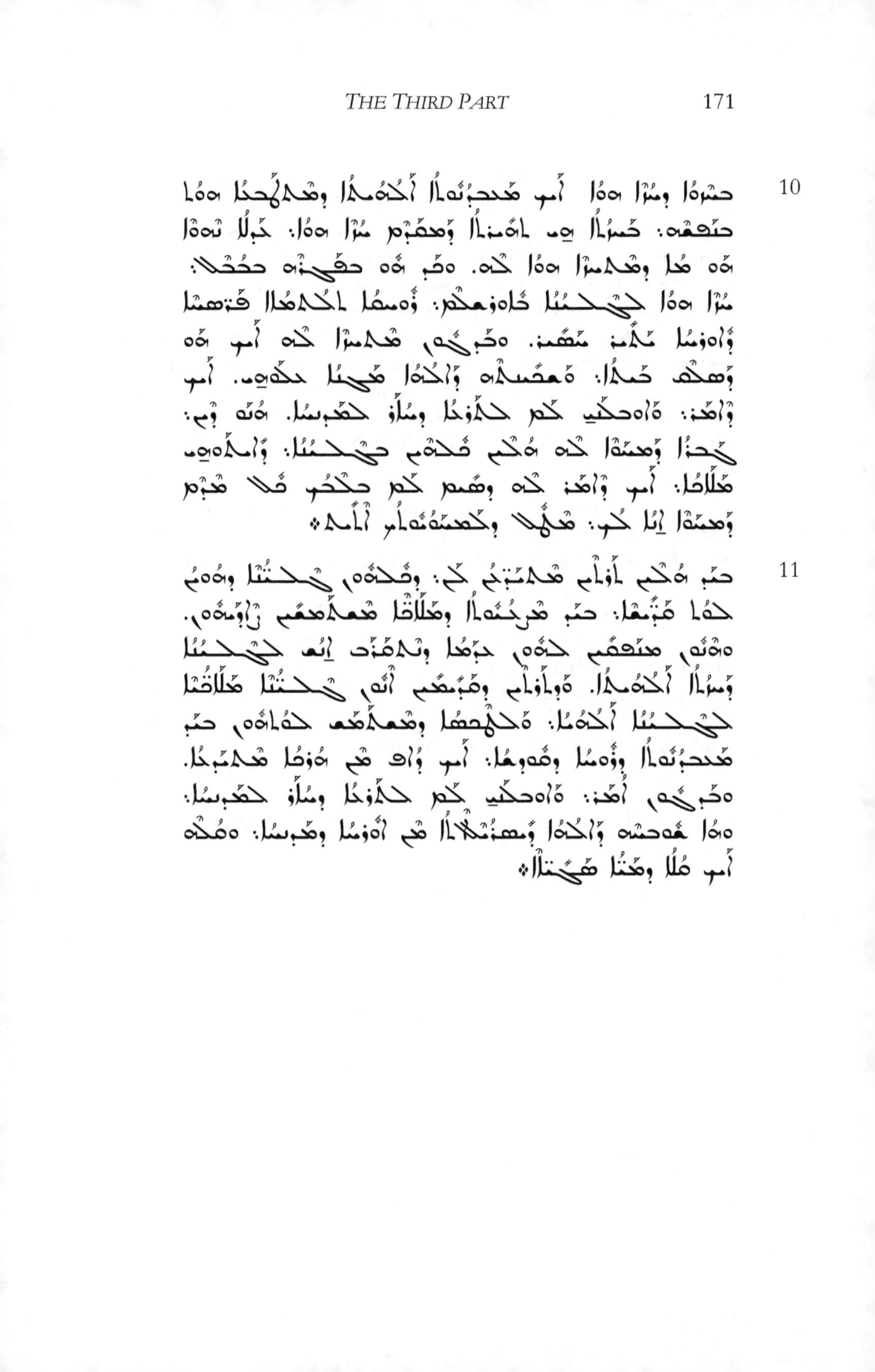

12 Also that revelation which <God> shows him is according to the order of the life beyond. It says in fact: *The earth has shone with his glory*; and, *I fell on my face and the glory of the Lord entered the temple.*[28] Again in another place it says: *The inner court was filled with the cloud and the glory of the Lord went up above the cherubim and the house was filled with the cloud.*[29] Also: *The inner court was filled with the splendor of the glory of the Lord*;[30] and other similar things which the Scriptures make known concerning the working order of the *Shekinah*, whose power overshadows the place set apart for the Name of His holiness, and in which His memory is sanctified at all times. Thus the <Scriptures> manifest the action of His glory by means of a clear vision, so as to instruct.

13 As to how it is said that <God> abides or dwells, it is not in His Nature but in His glory and in His energy that He abides, in the place set apart for His holiness – whether this be in a building made by hand and in things not endowed with reason called vessels of His sanctuary, or in the rational temples which are the souls. It is the power and energy <of God> that sanctifies and sets apart from the other souls that soul in which the Lord is sanctified, by means of the remembrance of Him: by the manifestation of a revelation and the knowledge of the mysteries revealed in it, and not by an inhabiting of the divine Nature <in us>.

---

[28] Ez. 43: 2–4.
[29] Ez. 10: 3–4.
[30] Ez. 10:4.

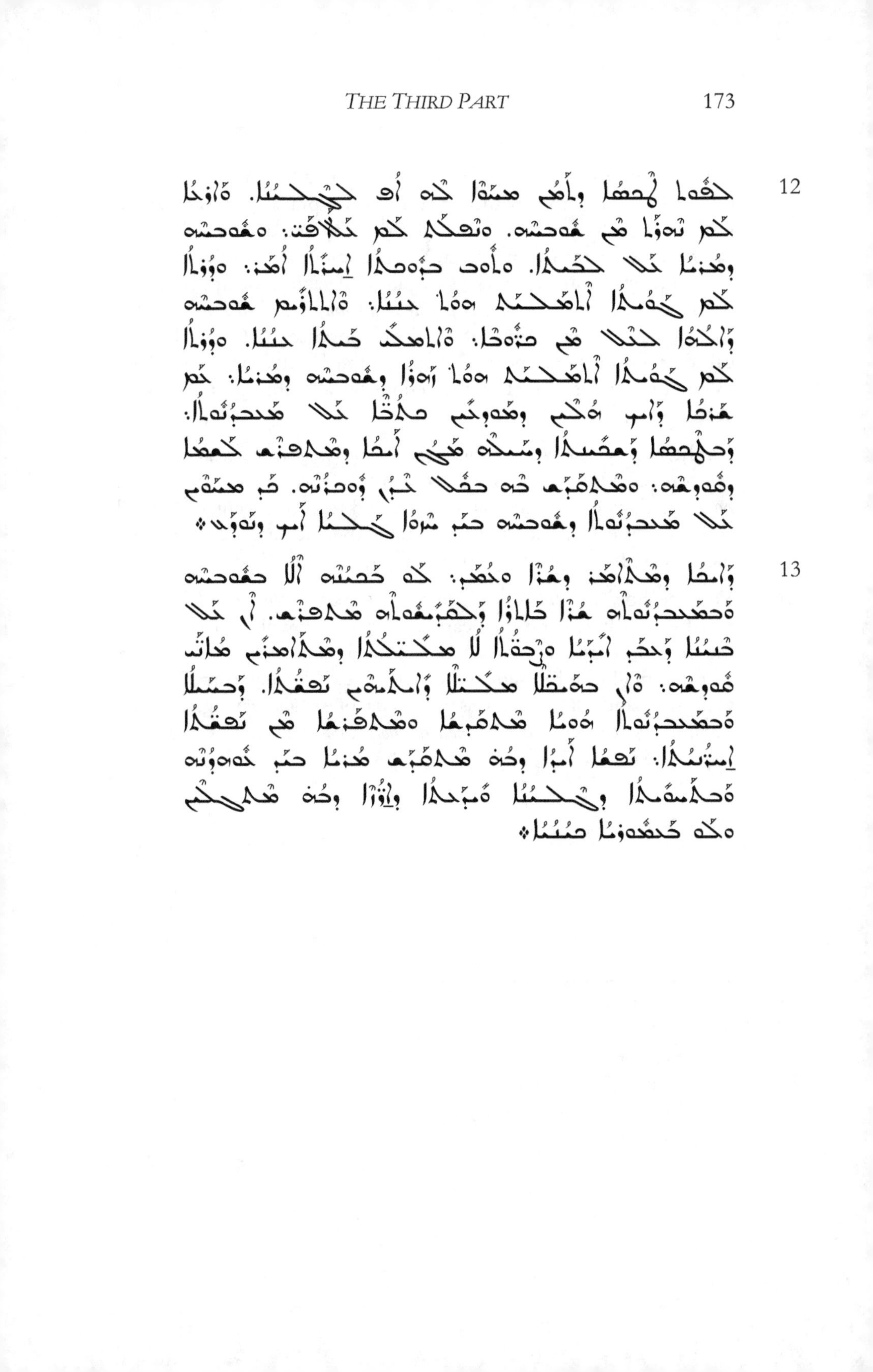

14   Let us earnestly desire this good and continually sanctify the parts of our body, together with our soul, in the praise of God. Let us sanctify ourselves by the continual remembrance of Him which we call to mind by means of prayer. We become holy temples by prayer,[31] to receive within ourselves the adorable action of the Spirit. As the Apostle says: *Everything is purified and sanctified by the word of God and by prayer!*[32] By means of the remembrance of God which is called to mind there and the Name of the Lord which is invoked over him,[33] one is sanctified and renounces all defilement and every alien power.

15   Surely, *In every place where you remember my name, I will come to you and I will bless you.*[34] Let us continually remember God and our mouth will be blessed, as one of the saints once said to some seculars: "Stand and greet the solitaries that you might be blessed! Because their mouths are holy since they continually speak with God."[35]

16   You see how the mouth which always speaks with God is made worthy of holiness and the heart is sanctified in which the Name of the Lord is blessed continually! Bless God continually in your heart that you might be blessed, and do not cease blessing Him. Sanctify your soul and all your limbs with His blessings, saying: *Bless the Lord, O my soul; and all my bones, his holy name*;[36] also: *I exalt you, my Lord and King*, etc.[37]

---

[31] Cf. 1 Cor. 3:16–17.
[32] 1 Tim. 4:4–5.
[33] Cf. James 2:7.
[34] Ex. 20:24 (Peshitta).
[35] Budge, *Paradise* II, 634, p.148.
[36] Ps. 103:1.
[37] Ps. 145:1.

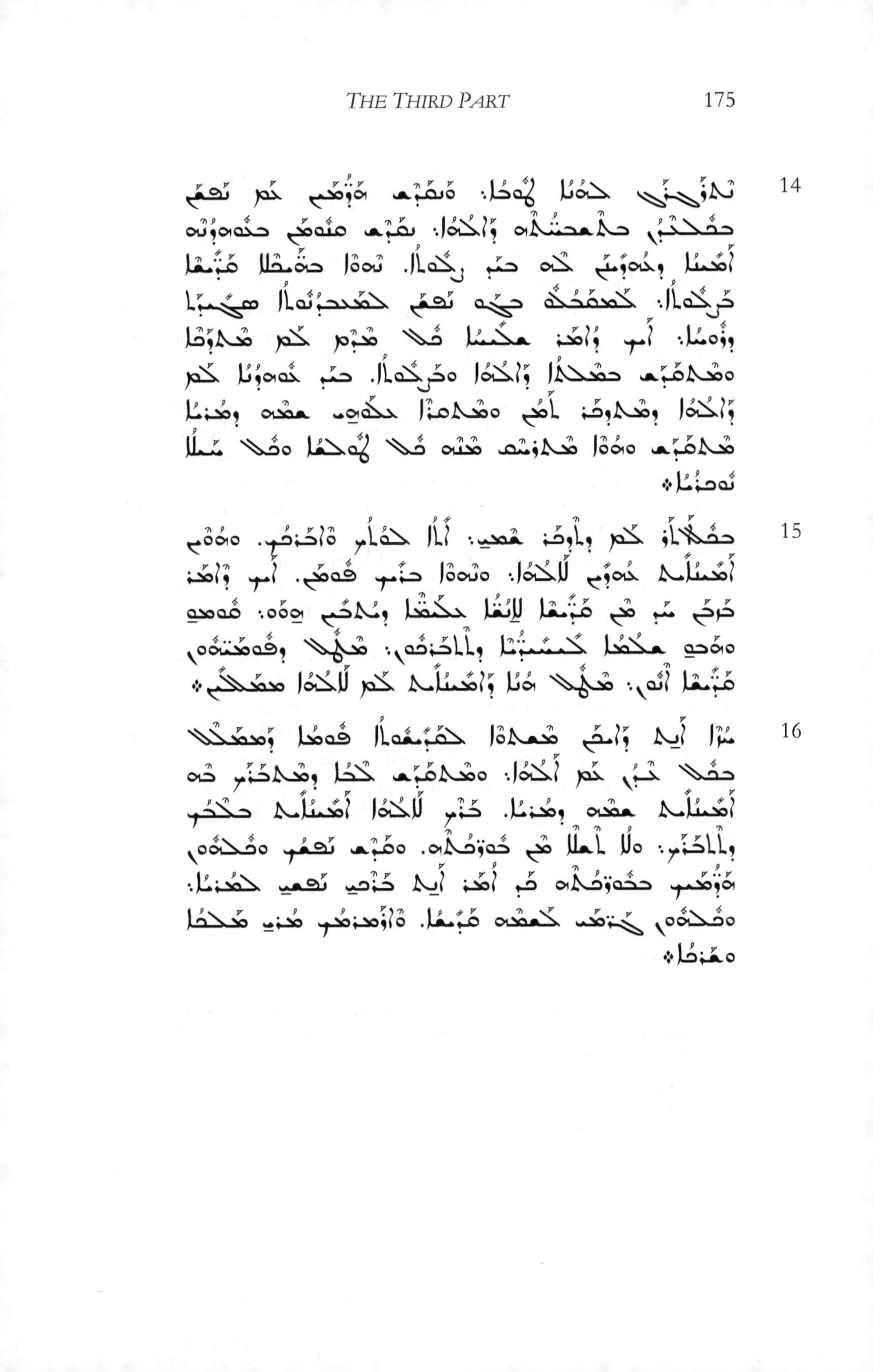

17　Speak His praise with your mouth and never be sated of His glory, in order that His magnificence and His excellency might fill your soul. May God always be exalted in your heart, and may you never be sated of His magnificence and His blessings, not even of that splendor which the prophet saw dwelling over Jerusalem – so also your soul will be filled with it. He said in fact: *The earth has shone with his glory*. It also has been said: "Always remember God and your intelligence will be a heaven."[38]

18　Let us ardently desire this magnificence, to be temples of God[39] by means of continual remembrance of Him in prayers and praises. As the holy bishop Basil said: "Pure prayer is what causes the continual remembrance of God in the soul. Thus we will be temples for God in that He dwells in us by the continual remembrance with which we call Him to mind."[40] Those who are a *house of prayer*[41] are made worthy of this heavenly glory. And the temple in which the continual memory of the Lord thus dwells, gives light such that the rays from it shine forth and show clearly even from a far.

19　The continual remembrance of God is the mystery of the *future world*:[42] there we receive fully all the grace of the Spirit.[43] And there the remembrance of God will no more depart from us because we will be wholly His temple. The saints on earth ardently desire that mystery of the future joy, by means of constant absorption in prayer. Of these realities we are made worthy, by the grace and the mercy of *Christ our hope*,[44] *together with all of His saints*,[45] forever and ever! Amen.

---

[38] Nilus, *Perle* 2, p.10.

[39] Cf. 1 Cor. 3:16–17.

[40] Basil of Cesarea, *Lettere* II, 4. See Is.I 353 where Isaac cites the same passage of Basil. See also Brock, "Traduzioni siriache," 175–76.

[41] Cf. Is. 56:1; Mt. 21:13.

[42] Cf. Heb. 2:5; 6:5.

[43] Cf. Mt. 13:17.

[44] Cf. 1 Tim. 1:1.

[45] Cf. 1 Titus 3:13.

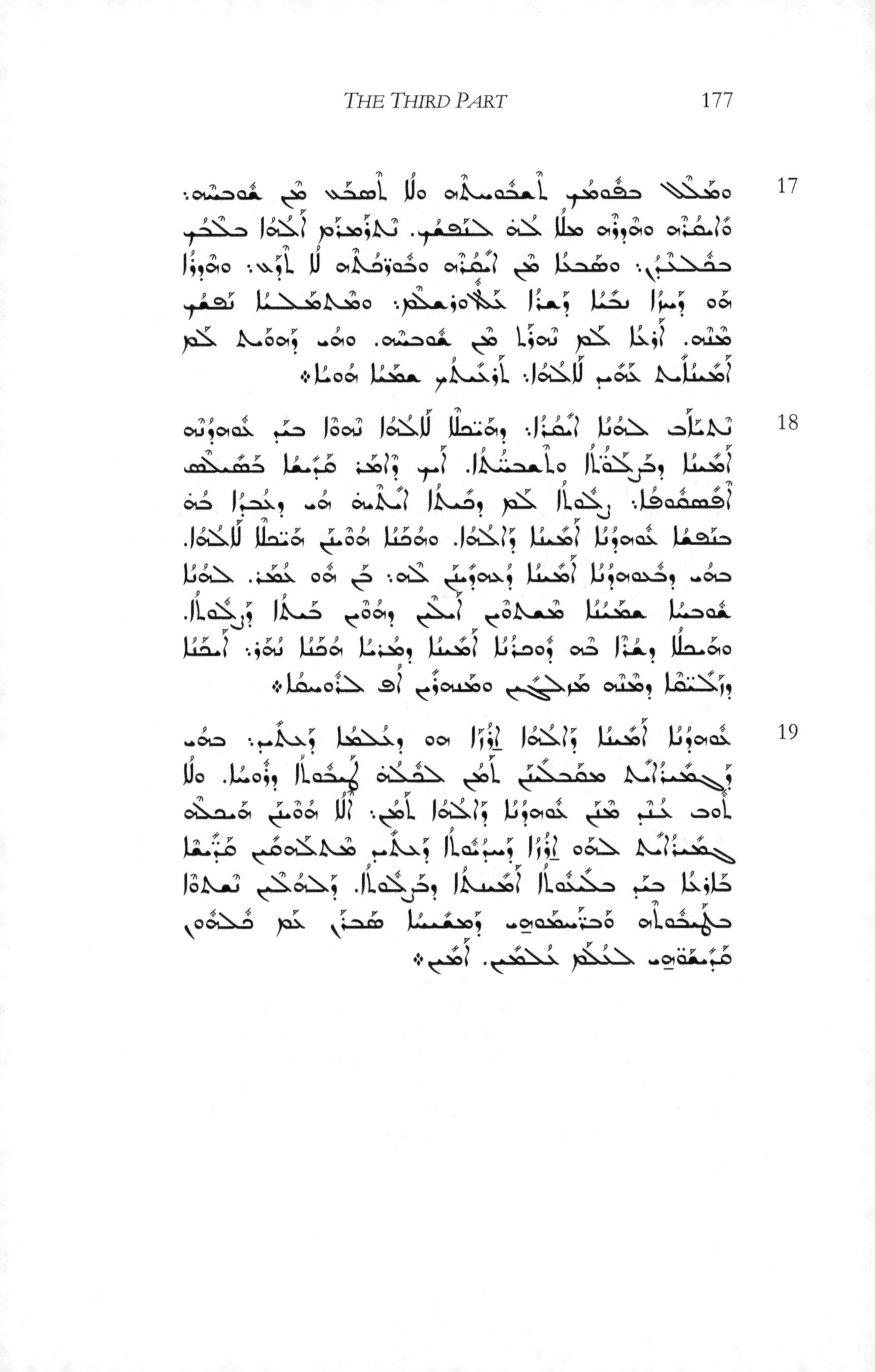

Chapter IX

Of the same Mar Isaac. A synthesis of all kinds of labor concerning the part of the mind: what power and action belong to each one of them.

1. Prayer is the place of the soul where the fulfillment of the bodily way of life occurs. The way of life is from the working of the body: fasting, the office, alms, labors, chastity, service to the sick, silence, weeping, obedience, renunciation, mercy, with the rest of what is similar; and there are yet many other realities such as these.

2. These ways are the limit for <bodily> activity. Prayer, however, is the contemplation of the soul,[1] which is above the body and visible things and the understanding of what is in them, which are more profound than what can be examined but are intelligible, though not being of the earth. When solicitude for prayer is not joined to these ways <of life>, they remain in the order of bodily labor. And even if they are beautiful things, found in the parts of the soul, this labor is only for visible things.

3. That which the power of prayer is to the way of life, reading is for prayer. Every prayer, then, which is not sustained by the light of the Scriptures is offered with bodily understanding.[2] And even if one makes supplication for good things and noble stirrings arise from it, so as to lean towards the hidden realities that by means of the mind one cannot know, and what one asks for <with> desire be acceptable to God – this is of a lower degree than the knowledge <from Scripture>.

---

[1] Contemplation of the soul (*te'ôryâ d-napšâ*): Evag. Cent. II.15; V.41.

[2] On the importance of Scripture in the life of prayer: Is.I 52–53, 124–5, 135. Is. II XXI.13; XXIX.5–11. *Keph.* I 66–67; IV 63. See John Sol. *Letter to Hesychius* 24: "Pay attention to the reading of the words of Scripture, in order to learn from them how to be with God…In this way you will be illumined in prayer as a result of your reading." And see Sahdona II 8, 51.

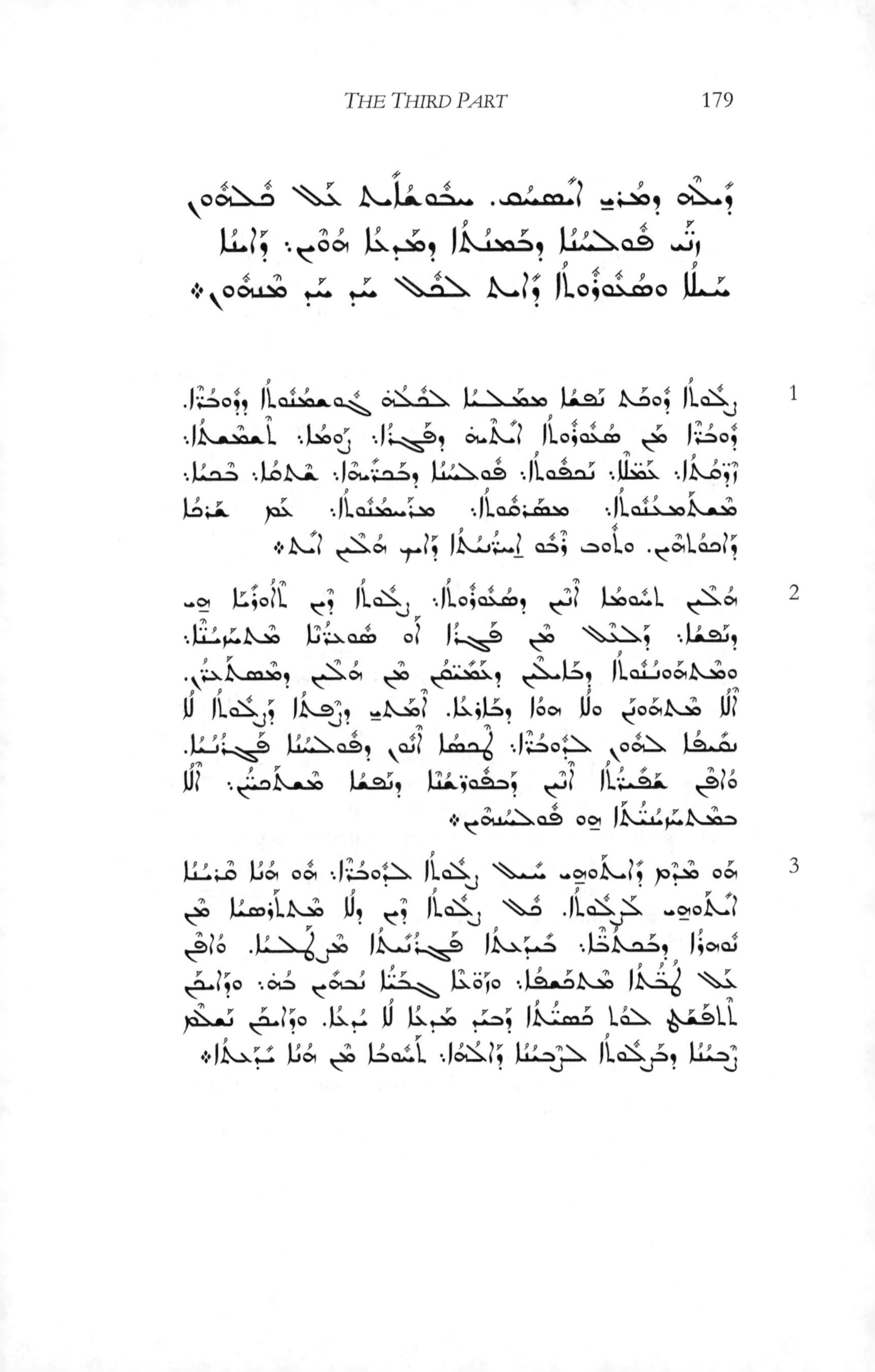

4   Indeed, this is because while meditating on glorious things and seeming to be occupied with amazing realities, <such a one> is <really> far from God. And so he is not able to attain to the beautiful things for which he hopes, but walks keeping his own counsel and reflects on his own will: the admonition, then, which is from the true knowledge of the light of the Scriptures does not <affect> him.

5   The way of life is the body, prayer is the soul but the vision of the mind is of the spiritual order.[3] Vision of the mind,[4] I call revelation of hidden things, and the understanding of incorporeal things, and that certain understanding which is <given> by the Spirit. These realities receive power from reading regarding knowledge – its deepening and progression from insight to what follows which is more amazing and more luminous. As to prayer, which is excellent intercession of the soul and salutary petitions offered up, it is said: "It is good that these things (intercession and petitions) be provided by the soul and remain with it."

6   Meditation, then, consists only in the reflection on what is in God, while marveling only at what is of <God>, seeking out only Him and His majesty, and that the mind be occupied only with Him without a reflection on what is beyond, nor a remembrance of beautiful and excellent things concerning the body or corporeal things. The <mind ought> only be occupied with meditation on the Essence while not associating this with a reflection on <other> realities, or the thought that something might happen to me from you or from another place. This meditation has indeed scorned all which is of <human> nature – whether excellent realities or what might be alarming – by means of the memory[5] of God alone, which is sanctified in the mind.

---

[3] On the stages of the life of the soul – corporeal, psychical, spiritual – in John Sol., see Hansbury, *On the Soul*, Introd. xi–xiii.

[4] Vision of the mind (*ḥzâtâ d-ʿreyânâ*): Is.I 49; Is.II XIV.2.

[5] Memory (*dukrânâ*).

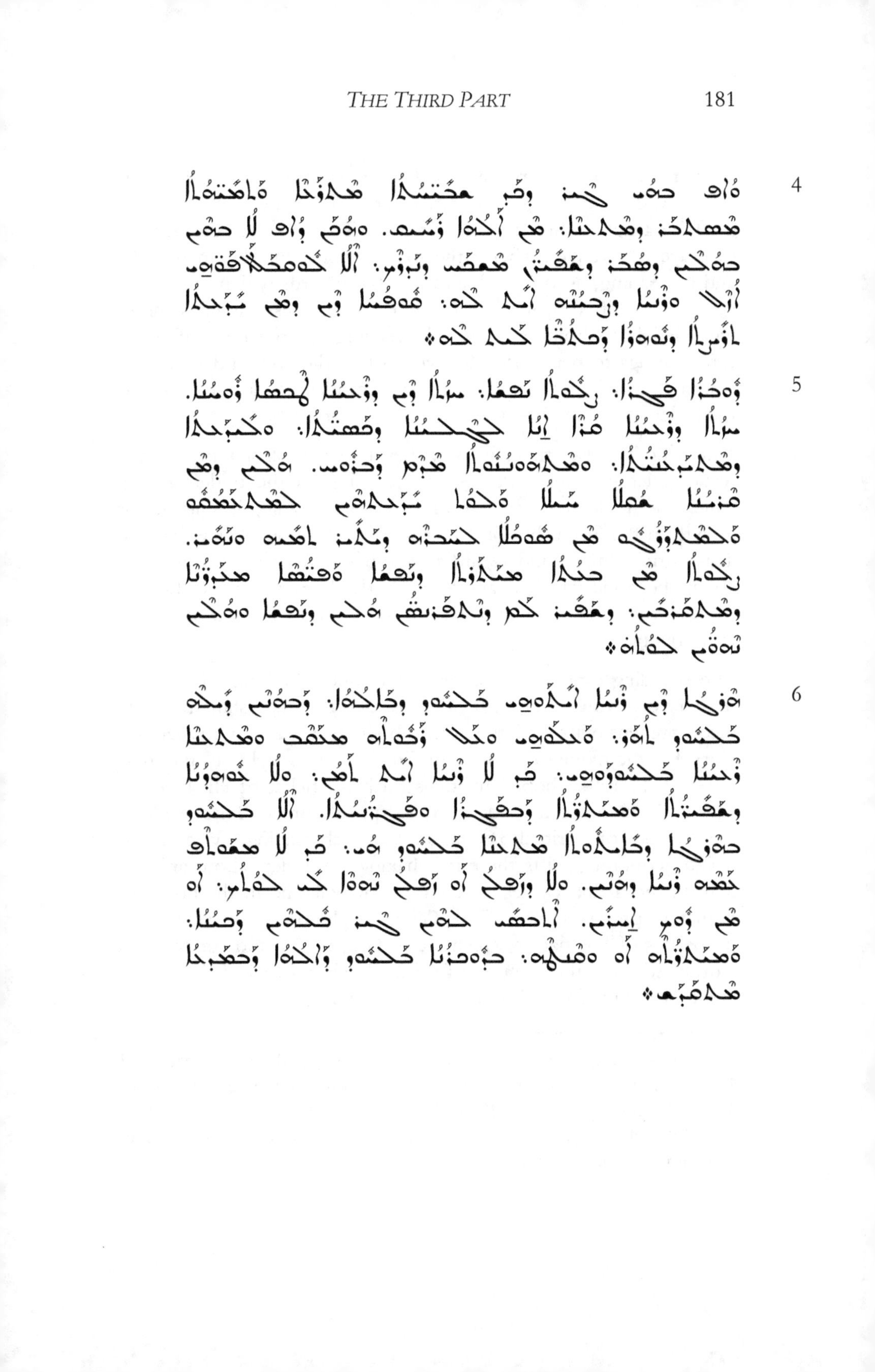

7 How many times in prayer, meditation such as this is brought forth. And from here, there is the entrance of the mind near the ineffable height, while the spirit by grace is sustained in the realities of prayer. Moreover, when <the spirit> is sustained by meditation and by reading, no one is able to discuss towards which marvelous stirrings it is lifted by intercession, and to what desire it leans and in what delight the mind remains. The reading of a portion <of Scripture> brings to perfection this work of meditation, and it is <the reading> which assists with marvelous realities, so as to last. See to the order of reading because it is useful for this labor.

8 One who is wise, then, who wishes to grow strong in spiritual realities, let him read the lesson according to the understanding which the meditation generates. Not just any reading is suitable for growth in the Spirit, but only that which tells about divine realities. This enriches the mind regarding spiritual mysteries, and instructs about the hope which is above the body. It transfers the thought from earth to the world above, so as to raise it to that way of life of immortality.

9 The <reading> moves the senses of the soul to look into the hidden mystery of divine wisdom. It brings one to the understanding of its incomprehensibility and the truth about its nature. It makes one marvel at the hidden Essence and direct one's thoughts to the mysteries of the future hope.[6] It brings forth the riches of His love, revealed to all and ready, indeed, to be spread abroad. These realities are the root of spiritual meditation, to which reading, by means of insight, continually lifts the mind making it wander[7] about and delight in the divine virtues which are above all, and in the hope for humanity preserved near God. Giving a glimpse, God shows the properties of His nature which are in Him for us and for the two worlds, whether the creation of spiritual beings or all of those who are in need in the world of mortal humanity.

---

[6] Future hope (*sabrâ da-ʿtîd*): Is.I 418, 430, 438, 508; *Keph.* I 38, 84; II 17. Cf. Is. II XXIX.11. John Sol. returns often to the theme of hope, see *Soul* 71,73; Rignell, *Briefe* 21, 29, 35, 51, 101.

[7] Wander (*pehyâ*): here wander is intended in a positive sense, may also be understood negatively.

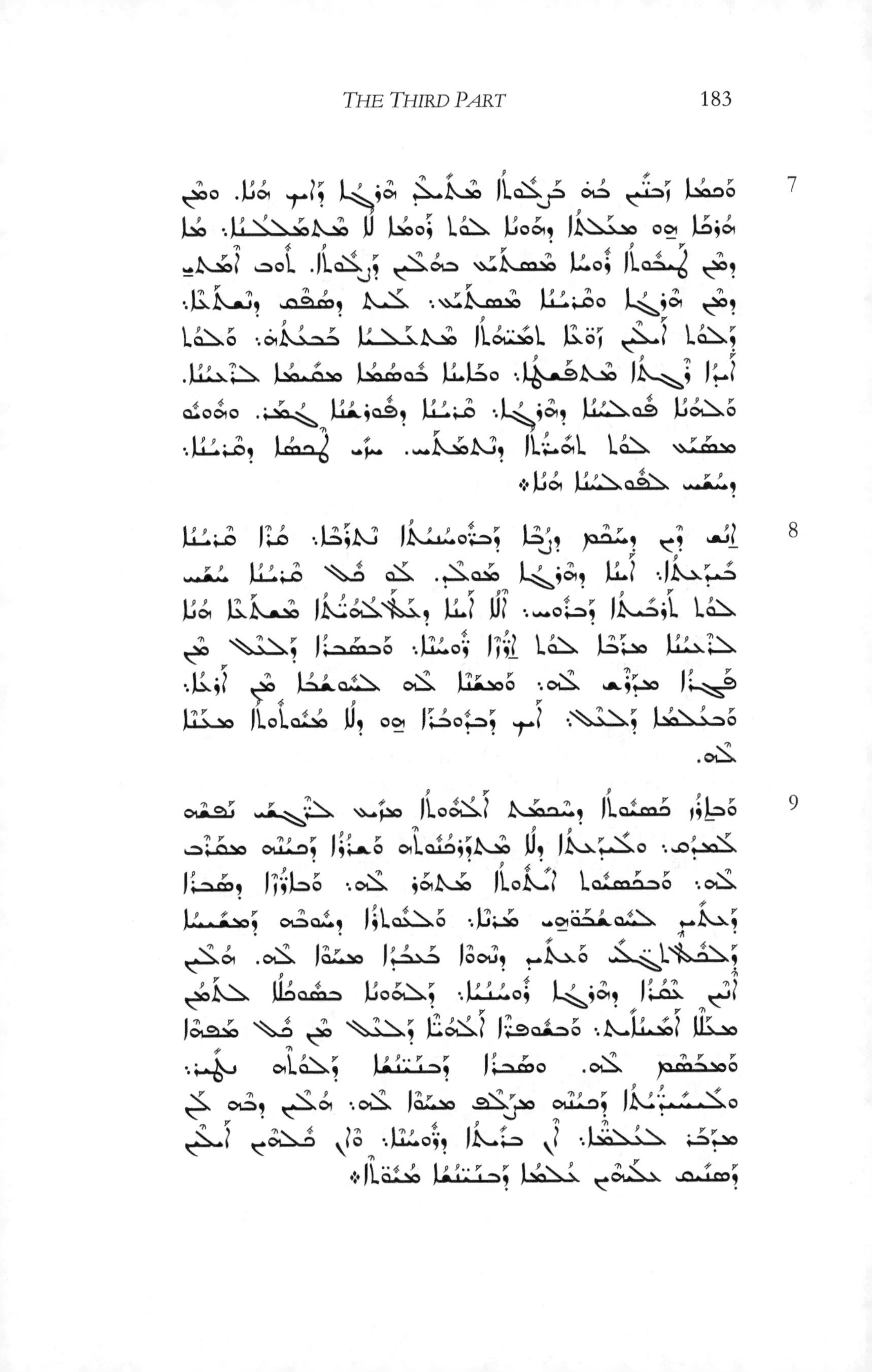

10 When, then, this labor <of meditation> grows strong and is consolidated in the soul, at that time there is not much need for reading. Not that one may be entirely without it but there is not much need for extensive reading. Which is to say that a continual meditation on the Scriptures is not necessary, although Scripture ought not to leave one's hands. In that, even when one is occupied with a small matter in these things, by means of the power that one draws out of a few verses, one is captivated with the Lord in contemplation.

11 Even if the reading is such as this, it is meditation and it is prayer. It is meditation in that it is not just part of the tongue, but its only intention is to bring the mind to discernment. And it is prayer in that by the memory[8] of God, it always captivates and fills within and without, with the desire and the meditation of heavenly realities. Then the <reading> moves completely with prayer which concurs with these impulses because an effortless exaltation stirs through the mind in the hidden part of the intellect. This is the prayer which occurs without the body, which we call incorporeal, in that it is not moved by sensible realities and is not visible by the body.

12 From this reading, limitless prayer is generated, whose meditation arises secretly in the mind and continually fills the intellect with God,[9] and as I said, it always captivates and attracts the mind with the realities of the Lord. This order of prayer is sublime, more than all ways of life, in that it is <prayer> which gives life to them with the life which is in God. <Prayer> is <the means of ascent> which lifts up to heaven as far as the order of revelation, in the place of a ladder.[10] This is its work, lifting up to whatever high place requested.

---

[8] Memory (*dukrânâ*).

[9] The intellect as a dwelling of the Trinity, see Evag. Cent. III.71.

[10] Cf. Gen. 28:12, ladder of Jacob. On prayer as a ladder (*sebeltâ*), see Evag. Cent. IV.43.

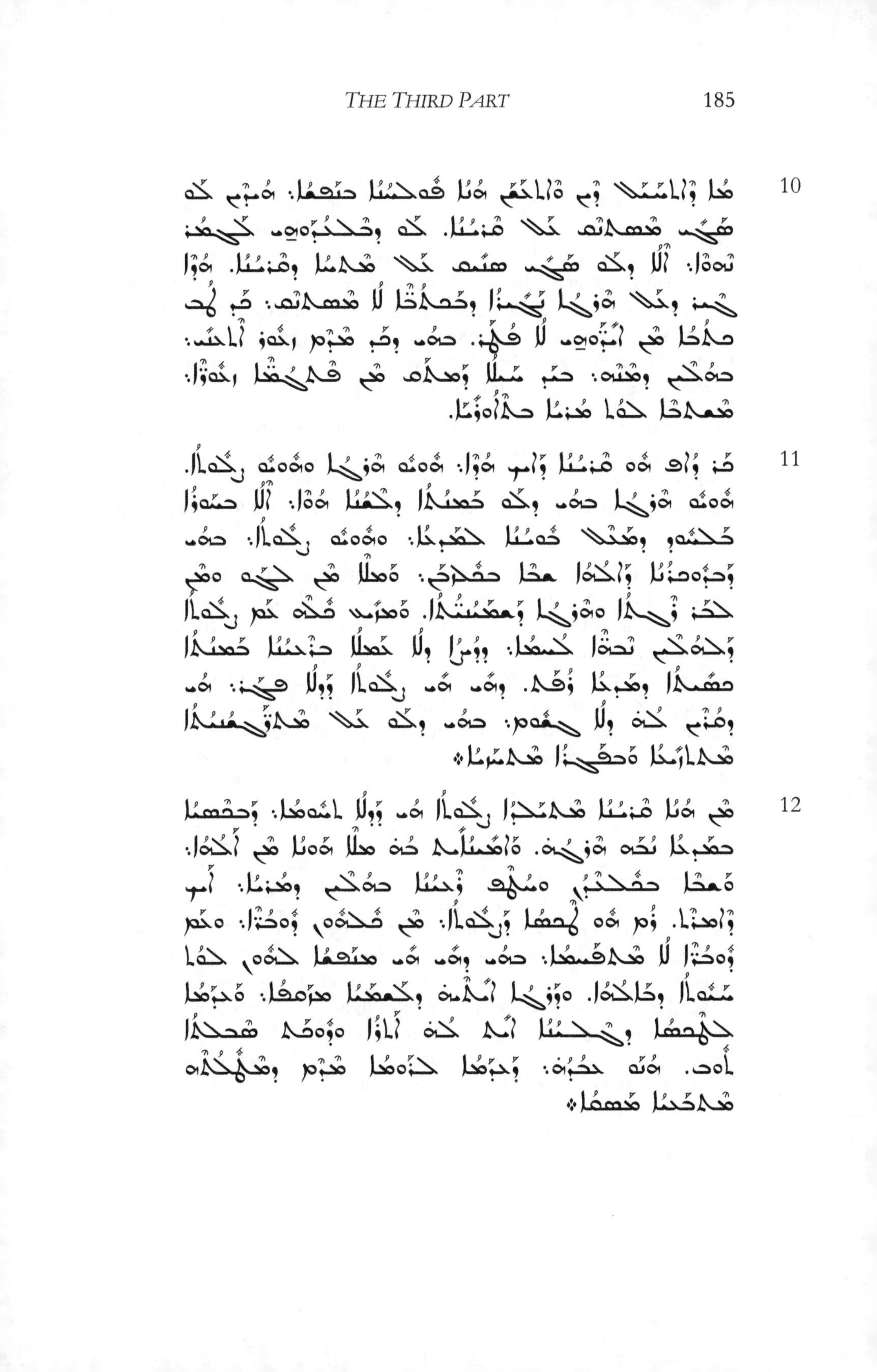

13   When, however, one has ascended to that place, then prayer will have another use there: at once the use for which it *went up on the roof*[11] has arisen for it, and until it descends again to earth, its function of ladder is no longer needed. But if prayer is a figure of a raised ladder which lifts up to heaven, by which the intellect ascends continually – prayer satisfies the purpose of a ladder for the intellect – therefore as long as we are on earth, we always need this ladder which is prayer, by which we ascend at all times to God, so as to be made worthy by it of the heavenly light.

14   Meditation also strengthens, refines and grants victory to the prayer of the heart. It shows the intellect the way of heavenly and mysterious realities, for it is moved towards them at the time of prayer. Then this prayer rises up like a ladder and makes the intellect ascend.

15   Prayer, however, of itself, without meditation and reading is <too> weak and obscure to make the intellect ascend and come together with the heavenly realities. But because in place of the offering and the sacrifice which those of former times were offering, an excellent grace was given to us by God: we sacrifice the stirrings of our intelligence instead of dumb objects[12] – that is, thanksgiving and praise – by means of prayer which is the *acceptable sacrifice*![13] That is what we offer to Him as Lord, cause of our salvation[14] and guardian.

---

[11] Cf. Acts 10:9: Isaac on Peter's ascent in the context of revelation, see Is.I 154–61; cf. 172–73. On Acts 10:11, see Evag. Cent. IV, 46. Theodore of Mopsuestia comments on the ascent of Peter and its relation to revelation, see Nahum 1.1 in his *Commentary on the Twelve Prophets*, 249–50. Isaac, like Theodore, uses Peter's ascent to show how a life of prayer leads the soul to revelations of hidden mysteries, as the prophets were led to the knowledge of things beyond description, see Is.I 156 where he quotes Theodore. See Hansbury, "Insight without Sight," 63–67.

[12] Cf. Heb. 10:1–18.
[13] Cf. Phil. 4:18; Ps. 50:23; Heb. 13:15.
[14] Cf. Heb. 5:9.

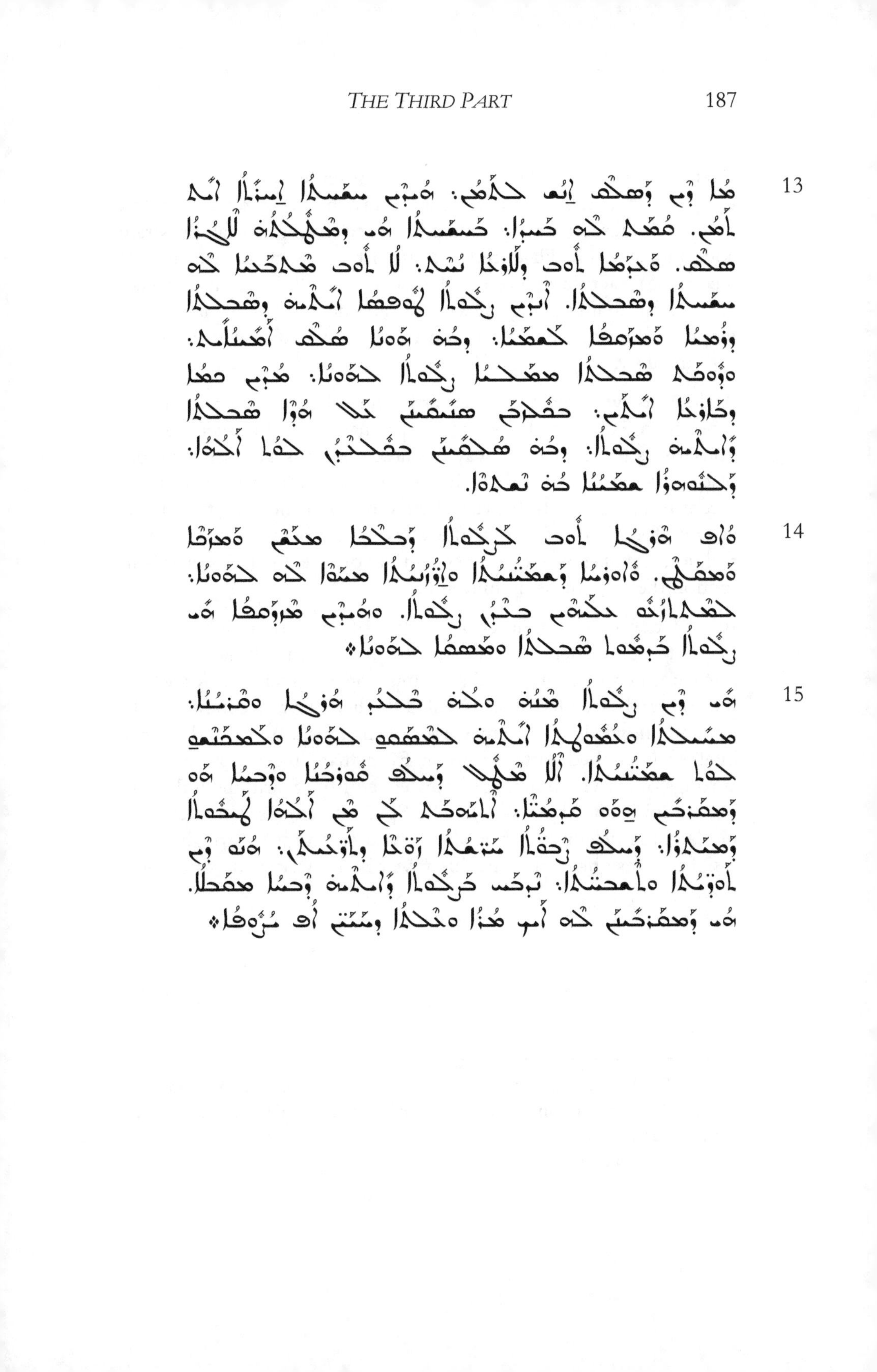

16   Even if <such a sacrifice> is dark and obscure, we do not neglect to offer <it>. And even if we are not ravished by a revelation, but by one of these causes considered as excellent, let us fall prostrate continuously with diligence.[15] Let us offer in sacrifice stirrings of incorporeal sacrifices, owed to the Creator of all. Let us not neglect to pour out thanksgiving for what we are indebted, while laying our faces on the ground. This is the function which prayer performs for humanity.

17   As long as we remain on the earth, the function of prayer is for those who exist here below and continually seek to ascend to the house-tops.[16] Prayer is the way of nature and it is the ascent to that place which is above nature, that is heaven. Without it, there is no ascent to that place. In heaven, then, it has no other function. Prayer, therefore, is the queen of the ways of life: because from earthly realities, it makes heavenly ones and in corporeal realities, it sets in motion the state of being fully alive.

18   Its order, however, is inferior to that of revelation. When, then, prayer has come near to this place <of revelation>, it has no space, nor care, nor memory, so that it must again ascend above where the soul had ascended. This is called the height of incorporeal realities and knowledge of the mysteries of the Spirit. When, indeed, the intellect is clothed with the Spirit, from that time it possesses the stirrings of the cherubim, the knowledge of the Spirit, the reflection of the Spirit and the vision of the Spirit; it remains completely in God, in the delight which is above nature. And it is brought from insight to insight; and from this towards the vision of contemplation.

---

[15] On kneeling and prostration during prayer, see Is.I 341–43. And see Chialà, "L'importance du corps dans la prière," also Hunt, "Praying with the Body."

[16] Cf. Acts 10:9.

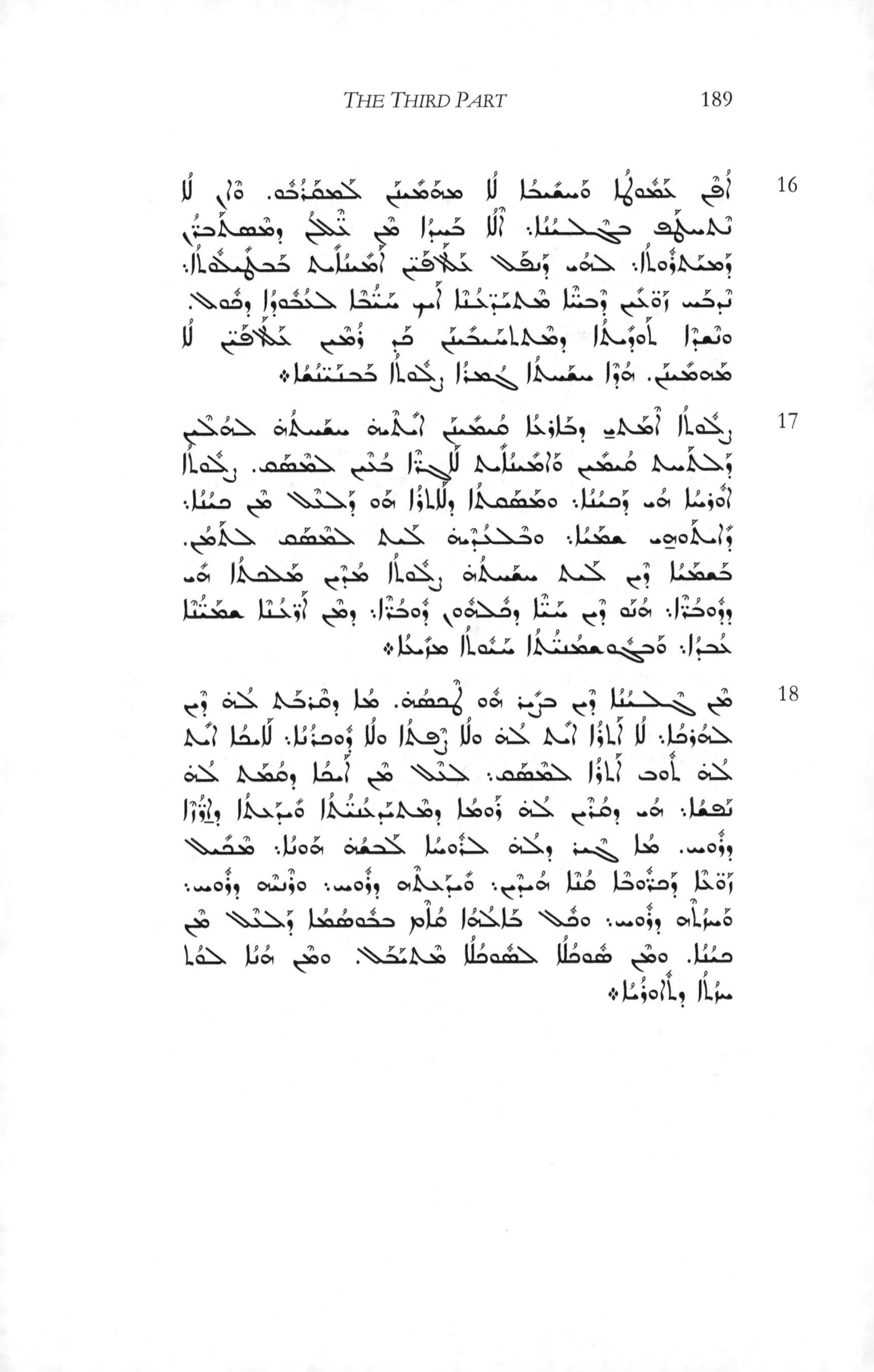

19 Contemplation is said to be sublime or imperfect by what leads it from insight to insight, according to the sense of the things which are moved in them. These realities are of the order of the revelation of the mysteries. Of all which is accomplished in the soul, this is the most sublime. It is the way of the Spirit[17] and not a stirring of the soul. Yet without prayer, <such realities> do not come to pass; and <prayer> without these does not shine and is not strengthened, since to pray is of the soul.

20 The one, however, who is directed towards hidden realities, remains in the Spirit and in the revelation of the intellect[18] which <is from> God. By revelation, then, I do not intend realities visible to the eyes or audible to the ears, and not even something which can be perceived on earth while among others. What place is there for sensible realities in a spiritual revelation and in the stirrings of the intellect which are enlightened by the Spirit, as the fathers say who were lifted up from earth and from the flesh?[19]

21 These realities which are conceived through vision, or hearing or in the presence of the senses, by angelic action, are useful for this world and for the way of life beyond because they increase the growth of the fear of God in souls. They are similar to those <realities> realized by means of the visible revelation entrusted to the Economy through Moses, by means of that angel to whom the Economy of that people was entrusted and the glorious things shown in their midst.

---

[17] Way of the Spirit (*dubbârâ d-ruḥ*): best understood here in the context of John the Solitary's tripartite division; see *Soul* 12, 17, 24, 60, 64, 66–67. See Is.I 303, 368, 376. Is.II VII.2; X.2; XX.2,5,6,10. *Keph.* I 28, 36, 37; III 14, 46; IV 12,13, 15–16, 47, 92. Chialà notes an Evagrian influence.

[18] Revelation of the intellect (*gelyânâ d-hawnâ*): Is.I 161; Is.II XV.7; *Keph.* I 80.

[19] Cf. 2 Cor. 12:2–3.

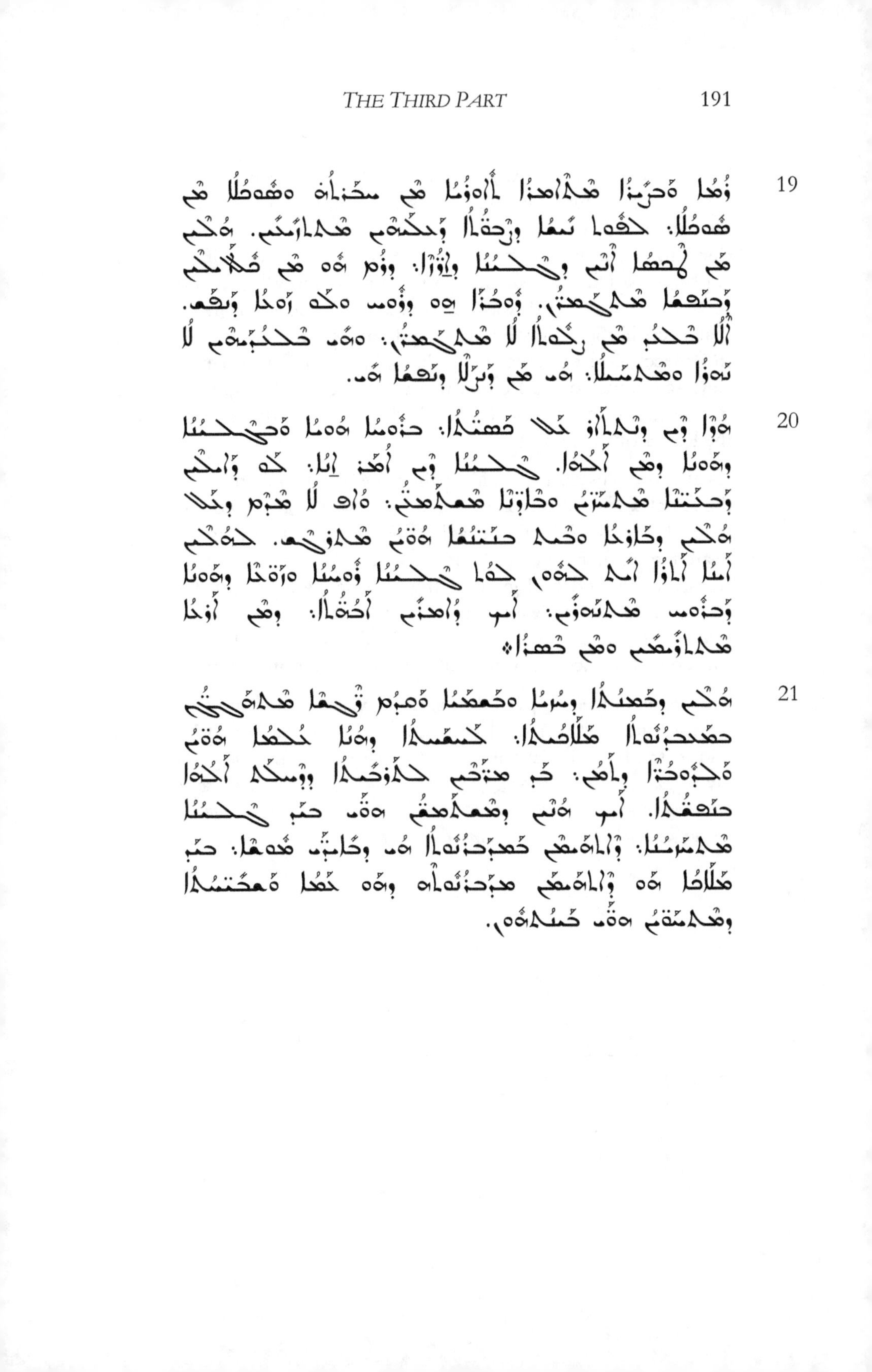

22 These are similar to what had already been realized regarding Moses, as Scripture has said: *Moses was tending the flock of Jethro, his father-in-law, and conducted the flock to the desert, and he came to the mountain of God, to Horeb. The angel of the Lord appeared to Him in a flame of fire from within a bush; and <Moses> saw that the bush was not consumed.*[20] Clearly it may be seen, that even if the vision be attributed to the presence of God, and the speech and the amazing realities be realized in a supernatural way, according to the Economy, nevertheless the action happened by means of an angel who was showing to <Moses> that he was the leader of the people.

23 As also the blessed Paul said: *If then the word spoken by means of the angel was confirmed, etc.*[21] And as also Stephen said: *God sent them this Moses, chief and savior, by means of that angel who appeared to him in the bush. It is he who led them out, working signs, in the land of Egypt, at the Red Sea, and in the desert for forty years,*[22] thus clearly indicating that it was an angel who revealed himself to Moses in the bush, that one to whom was entrusted all this Economy and all these dreadful things done there.

24 The angel, indeed, appeared in various ways, with mighty and great visions, and performed all these things in the name of God, as is said in the book of Exodus: *Behold, I send my angel before you to guard you in your way and to bring you into the land which I have prepared. Pay attention to him and listen to his voice. Do not strive against him lest he not forgive your debts, because my name is in him.*[23]

---

[20] Ex. 3:1–2.
[21] Heb. 2:2.
[22] Acts 7:35–36.
[23] Ex. 23:20–21.

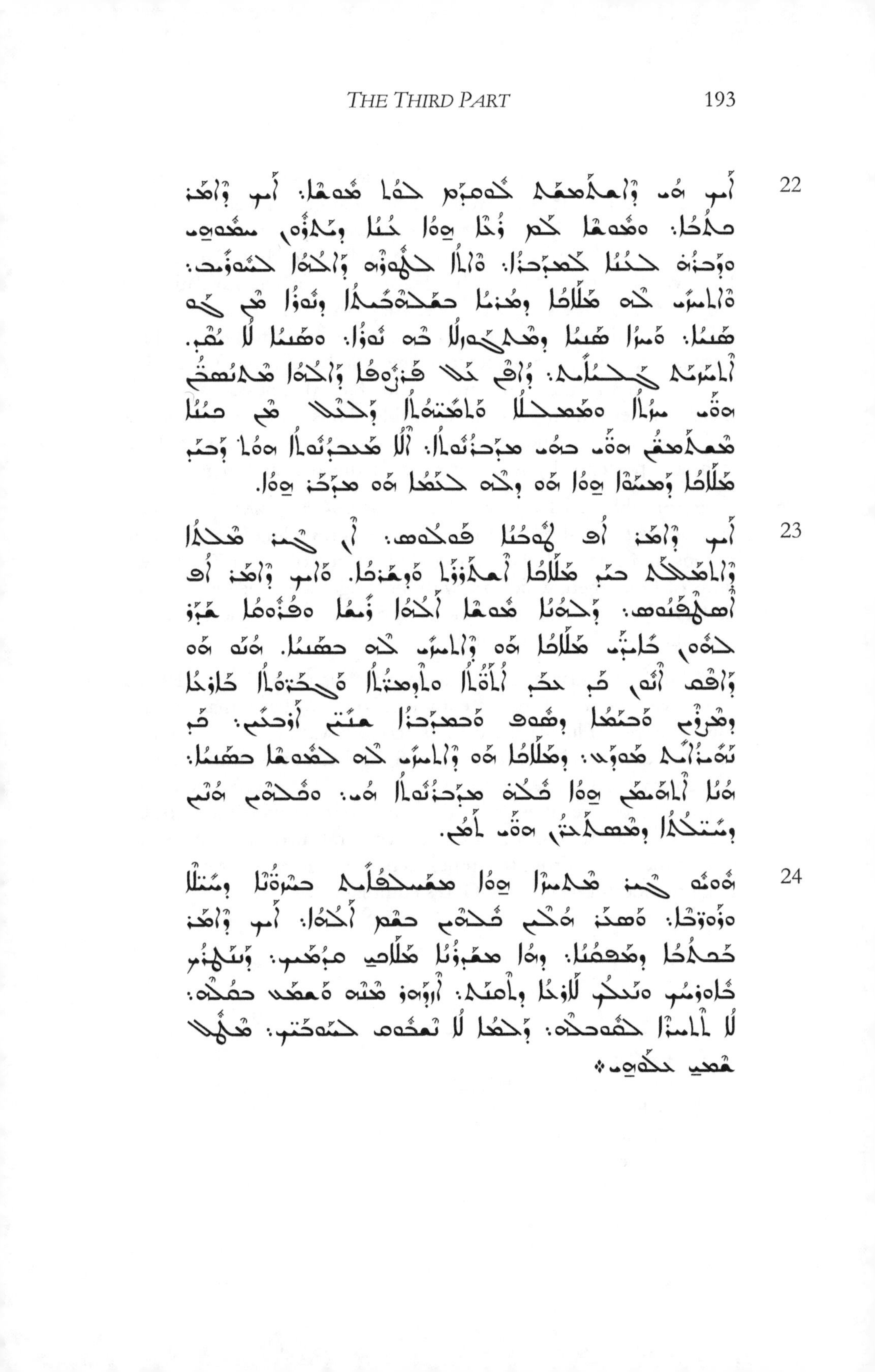

25 Clearly Scripture has shown that all these things were spoken there by the command of God. And whether that great revelation on the top of Mount Sinai, or all those which were spoken of in the Law to Moses, they are as from God Himself. And the words of the Law which were celebrated by them are an angelic revelation, as God said: *My name is in him.*[24] Because in the name of God the angel was visible, spoke, visited, admonished and affirmed the Law, leading <the people> whether in the cloud or in the fire, in dark night, or in the vision of smoke and thick darkness,[25] and in all these realities which were made visible. Thus <the angel> guided the divine flock by means of visions and revelations of every kind, signs and portents, by voices and words, dreadful and mighty.

26 Therefore, blessed Paul says: *If the word spoken by means of the angel was confirmed,*[26] to show that it was not God revealing Himself in the visions and images but an angel. This is not of God! The revelations of God, then, which are without images are invisible and ineffable; and the revelations of the Holy Spirit are in silence. They are delights <in> the stillness of nature, and not visions.

27 As <God> is elusive and invisible, thus also are His revelations. There were none before the coming of our Lord as a man; as also, then, the way of life of the world to come[27] was not known, nor yet had the fullness of the grace of the Spirit been given until after the descent of the Paraclete on the Apostles.[28] At that time the revelations of hidden realities and the future mysteries which are not like what is of this world, began to be given and made known to each one of the saints. From this time, then, the angel was showing all of these wonderful realities by God's command.

---

[24] Ex. 23:21
[25] Cf. Ex. 13:21–22; 19:18; 20:21.
[26] Heb. 2:2.
[27] Cf. Heb. 2:5; 6:5.
[28] Cf. Acts 2.

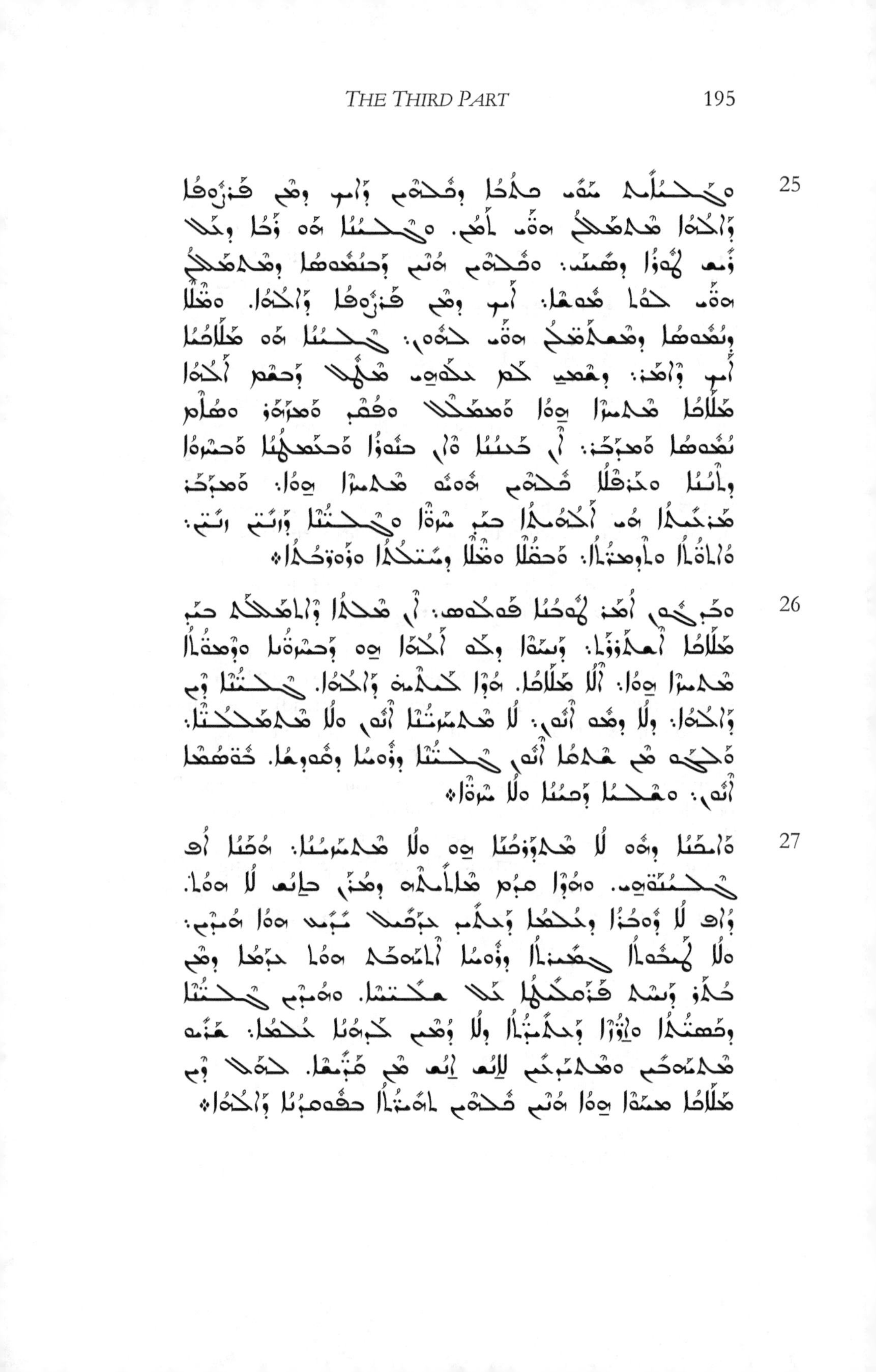

28   God was not transformed into images. God forbid! As our Lord said to the Jews: *You have never heard his voice, nor have you seen his form.*[29] And because this is from an angel, the word spoken through him was confirmed by means of the tablets with the writing, and with the voice on the mountain, lest the sons of Israel transgress <the word>.[30] The Apostle said: *Anyone who has heard it and transgressed it, has received a just retribution; how can we escape if we neglect these realities <of> salvation which have begun to be spoken by our Lord.*[31]

29   Thus <the Apostle> showed that these present revelations are not similar to those previous ones; there, indeed, an angel was showing them but here it is God Himself, Word by human means.[32] It is said: *The distributions of the Holy Spirit are conceded according to His will,*[33] that is to say, that the revelations now are by means of the action of the Holy Spirit, while the previous ones were an angelic action. Those previous ones were useful for the way of life of this world because they led <only> to the knowledge of the fear of God and not to the knowledge of revealed realities.

30   The revelations, however, which are made known by the Holy Spirit, lead to the knowledge of the future world.[34] This is as Moses said to the people. When that great and dreadful revelation appeared on the top of the mountain, it was before the eyes of all the people, with flashes of thunder, fire, hurricane, clamor of horns sounding and proclaiming an amazing sound full of terror. But the people greatly feared those dreadful realities, and could not endure the awful vision and the intensity of the sounds of the angelic horns which became terrible. Moses was encouraging them and made known the reason for the revelation and its terrible might, saying to them: *Take heart because God has come close to you, so that the fear of Him be in you and you do not sin.*[35]

---

[29] John 5:37.
[30] Cf. Dt. 5:22.
[31] Cf. Heb. 2:2–3 (Peshitta).
[32] Cf. Jn. 1:14.
[33] Heb. 2:4.
[34] Cf. Heb. 2:5; 6:5.
[35] Ex. 20:20–21; cf. 19:16.

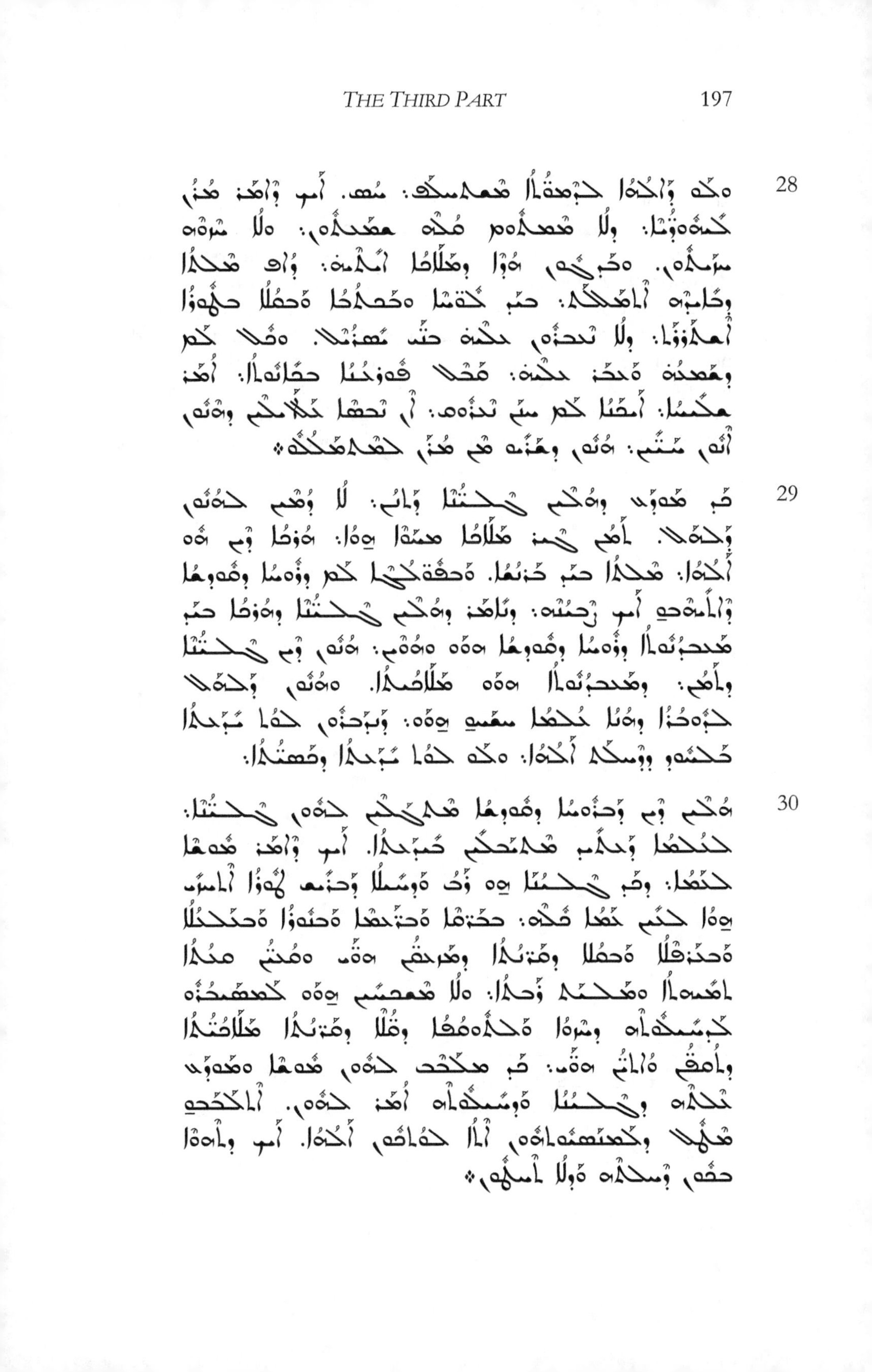

31 With all of this <Moses> made known that the visible and perceptible revelations are of use in the way of life here below, for the growth of faith and the fear of God. As for what is of the mystical part and which is in the mind – that is, the understanding of incorporeal realities and the delight of silence – it is for the of use for the perfect.[36] In this, we speak of the highest place of prayer, to which one is raised up by means of prayer. In this a mirror[37] of the new world[38] is received, making us taste by means of the Spirit that life beyond, which we shall receive.[39] Only the Spirit is able to make known this His mystery; He who by His power is prepared to give that greatest way of life which is beyond words. To Him be glory forever and ever. Amen.

---

[36] Cf. 1 Cor. 2:6; Phil. 3:15.
[37] Cf. 1 Cor. 13:12.
[38] Cf. Mt. 19:28 (Peshitta).
[39] Cf. 1 Cor. 2:10–11.

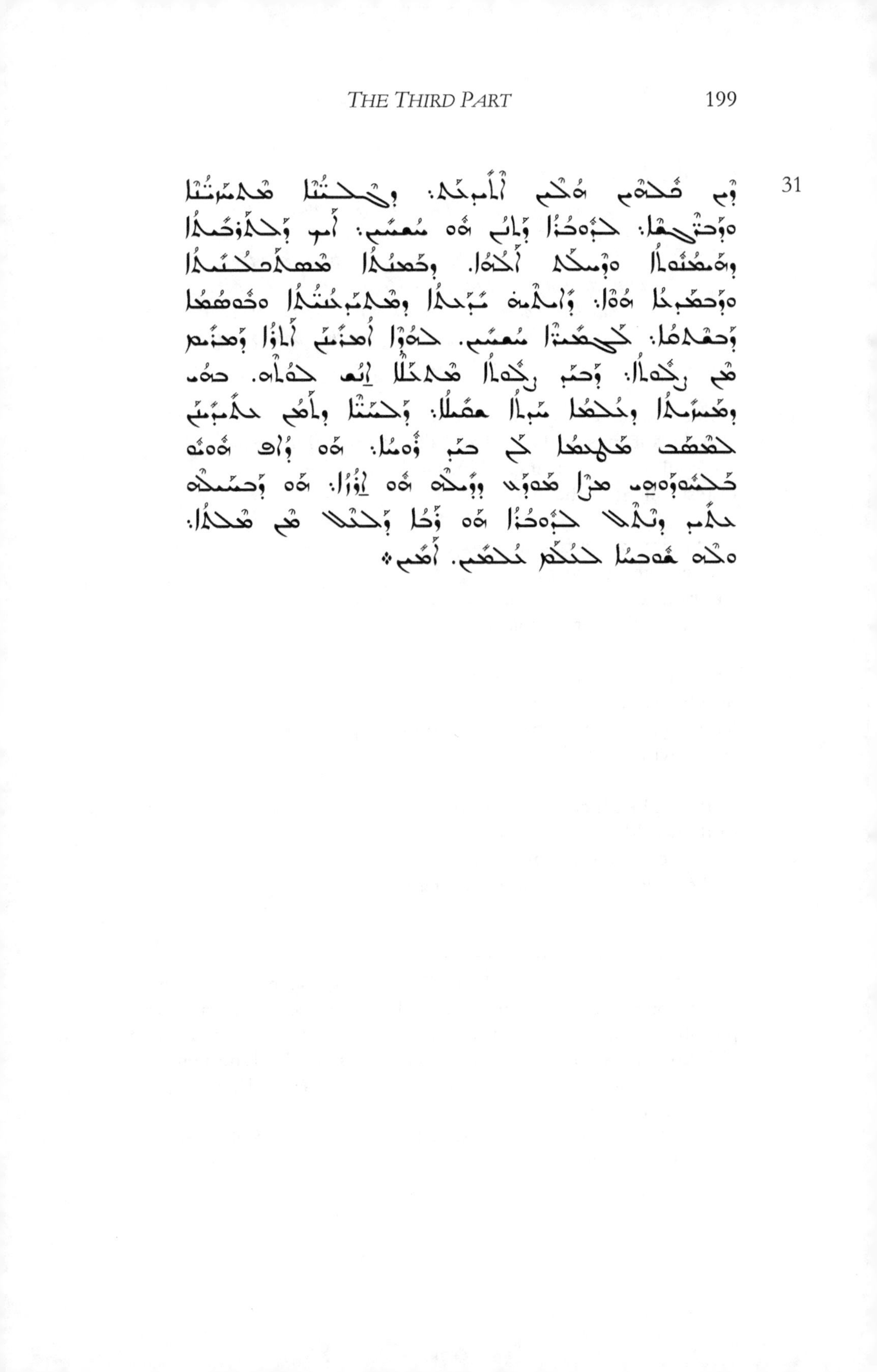

Chapter X

Converse of prayer[1] of the solitaries, composed with metrical speech and according to the limits of insight. Words which seize the heart and restrain from the distraction of earthly things. <Words> composed for the consolation of solitaries with which they converse at night, after the time of the office, that their body might be relieved of sleep.[2]

1. At night when all sounds are still,
also the stirrings of the soul and all sorts <of things>,
our soul, with its stirrings, shines in You,
O Jesus, light of the just.[3]

2. At the time when darkness abounds
over all like a garment,
Your grace, my Lord, shines for us
Instead of the perceptible light.

3. The light of the material[4] sun
delights the eyes of our body:
Your light, which surpasses the sun in its greatness,
shines within our darkness.

4. In the night which calms all the efforts
of the world wearied by affairs,
receive our soul, astonished by You,
in that stillness which is greater than silence.

---

[1] See Chialà's Introd. to Is.III (CSCO) for questions of authorship of this chapter, Isaac or Ephrem, etc. Chialà concludes that the chapter probably is not by Isaac, but perhaps was intentionally included here by him. Concerning authorship, see also Bou Mansour, "La distinction," 7.

[2] Compare with Preface to the chapter of prayers: Is.II, V.

[3] Cf. Ps. 112:4.

[4] Material (from the gr. στοιχεῖον): Is.I 50, 304–05, 460, 471, 478; *Keph.* I 9,13; II 59; IV 89.

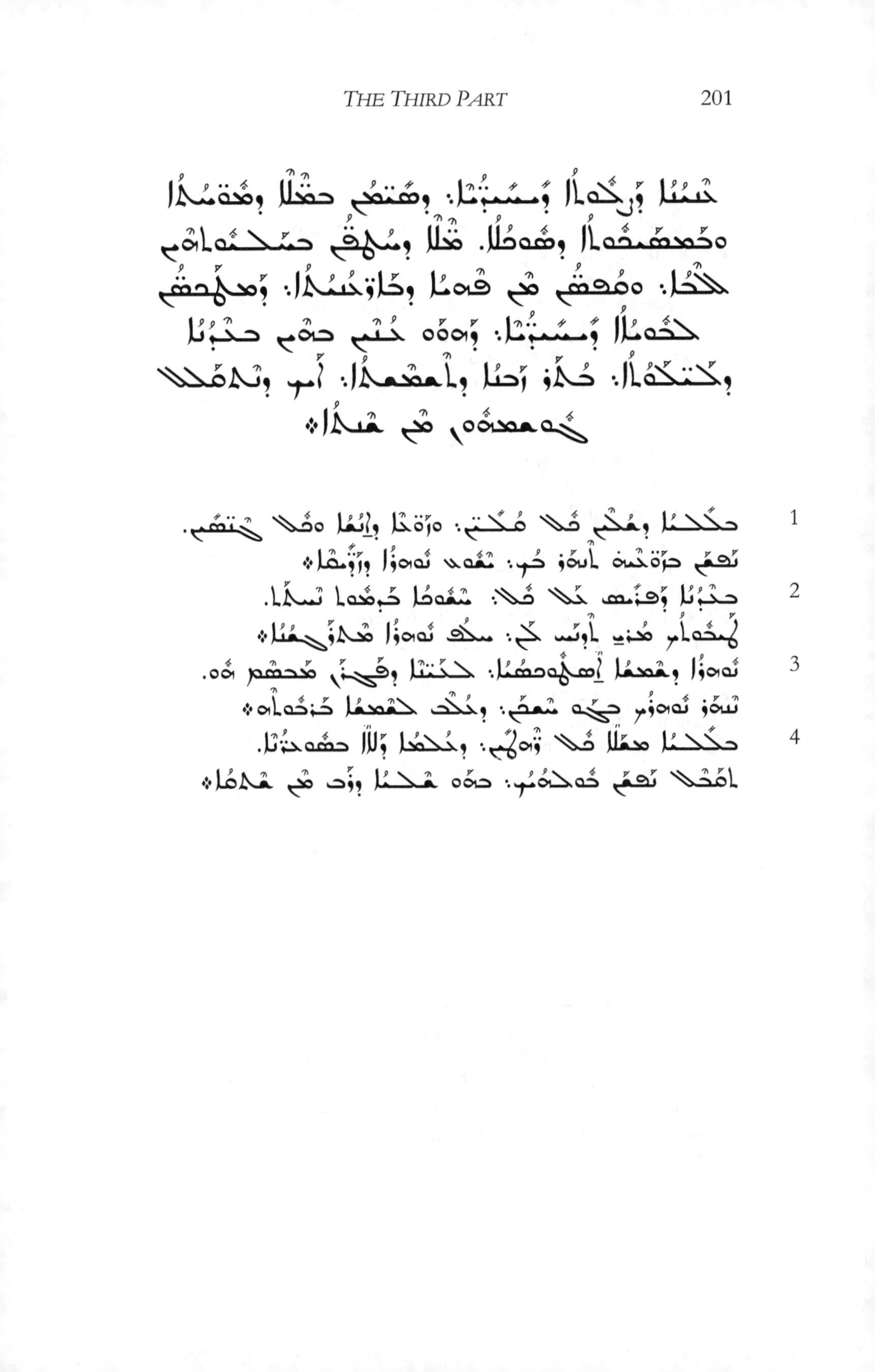

5   At the time which gives rest to the weary,
    by means of sleep which makes everything sweet,
    in You, my Lord, our thoughts become drunken,
    in You, delight of the saints!

6   In the hour when all sleepers break forth
    for corruptible deceptions,
    awaken, our Lord, in our souls
    that knowledge which does not go astray.

7   At the moment when each one
    puts clothing on his limbs,
    clothe with joy, our Lord,
    our inner person.[5]

8   By day, when all are called
    to earthly work,
    make us worthy, our Lord, to take delight
    in our way of life which is in heaven.

9   When each one removes
    his night garment,
    remove, our Lord, from our heart
    the remembrance of the passing world.

---

[5] Cf. Rom. 7:22 (Peshitta); 2 Cor. 4:16; Eph. 1:13–14. Inner person (*barnâšâ gawwâyâ*): Is.I 125, 244, 483, 562, 575–76; Is.II V.31, VIII.I, 2,16, XIII title, XXXI.1; *Keph*. IV 60. It occurs occasionally in Evag. Cent. VI.39 and frequently in Macarius, e.g. 9, 12, 66. See John Sol. *Soul* 7, 8, 23, 39, 41, 91; *Letter to Hesychius* 28. See Ammonius 637. Cf. Aphrahat *Dem.* 6:1 and Ephrem, *Hymns against Heresies* 32:12.

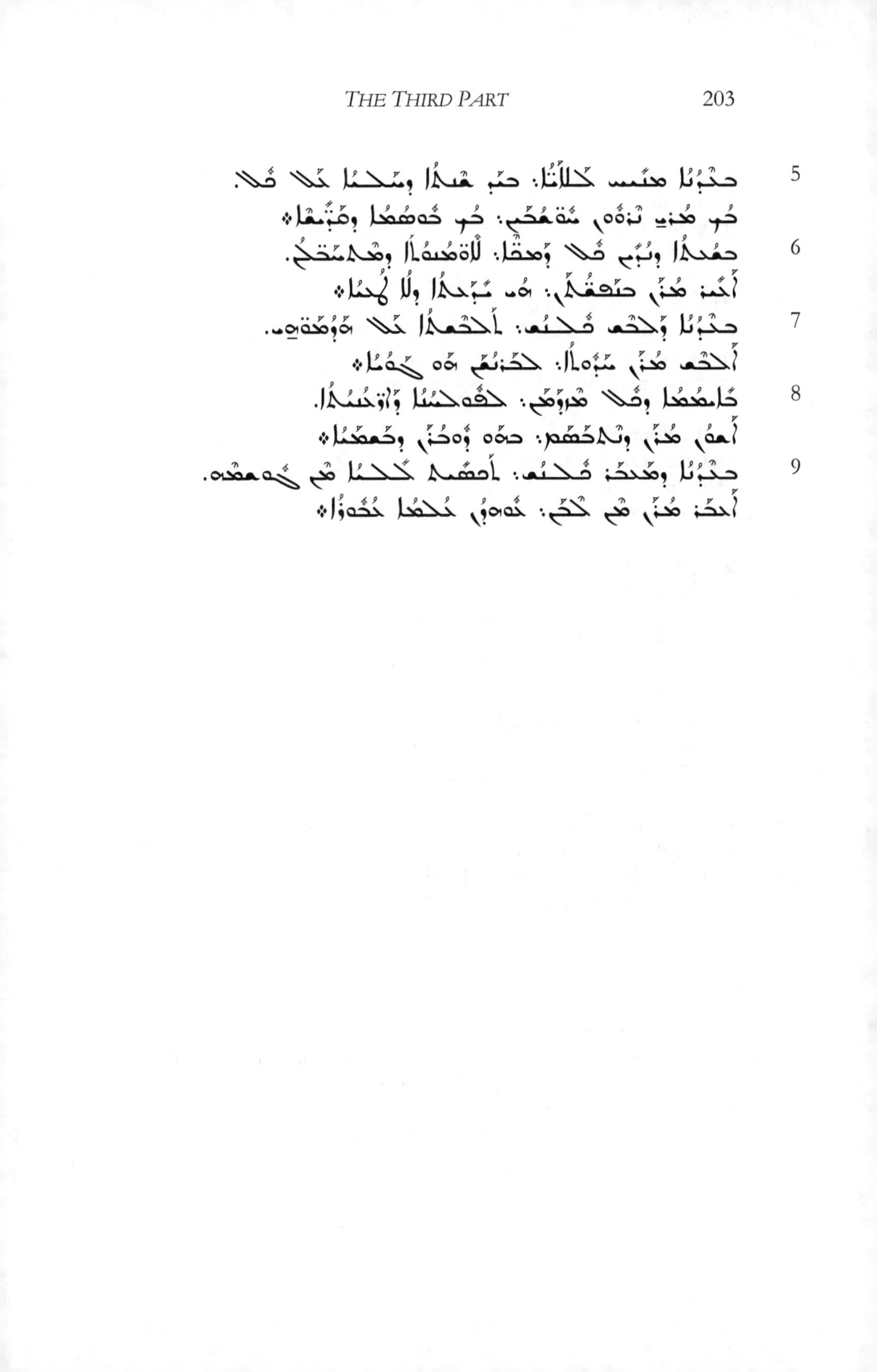

10 In early morning, when sailors
    begin <to work> in the world,
    in Your harbor,⁶ my Lord, our souls
    are at rest from all stirrings.

11 At the hour when all begin
    distressful worldly work,
    make us worthy, our Lord, to be enfolded
    in that consolation which does not pass away.

12 In the hour when darkness comes to an end
    and each one begins work,
    grant us, our Lord, to delight
    in the stirrings of that future world.⁷

13 Origin of the luminary course,
    head of mortal labor,
    place, my Lord, the foundations in our mind
    of that day that does not end.

14 A new sun shines for us
    in the hour of darkest night,
    in which is prefigured that understanding
    kept for us <until> the resurrection.

15 Grant us, our Lord, to imitate
    that vigilance of the resurrection,
    that by night and by day, my Lord,
    our mind may be attentive to You.

---

⁶ Your harbor (*lmênâk*): Is.I 105, 217, 317, 325–26, 346. 408. Is.II V.14, VII. 2–3, XVII.12, XVIII.19. *Keph*. I 80; II 12, 79, 96; IV 31,93. Cf. Macarius 49; Shubhalmaran 45v, 1 XII,7

⁷ Cf. Heb. 2:5; 6:5. Future world (*ʿâlmâ da-ʿtîd*): see "world to come," Is.III I.1.

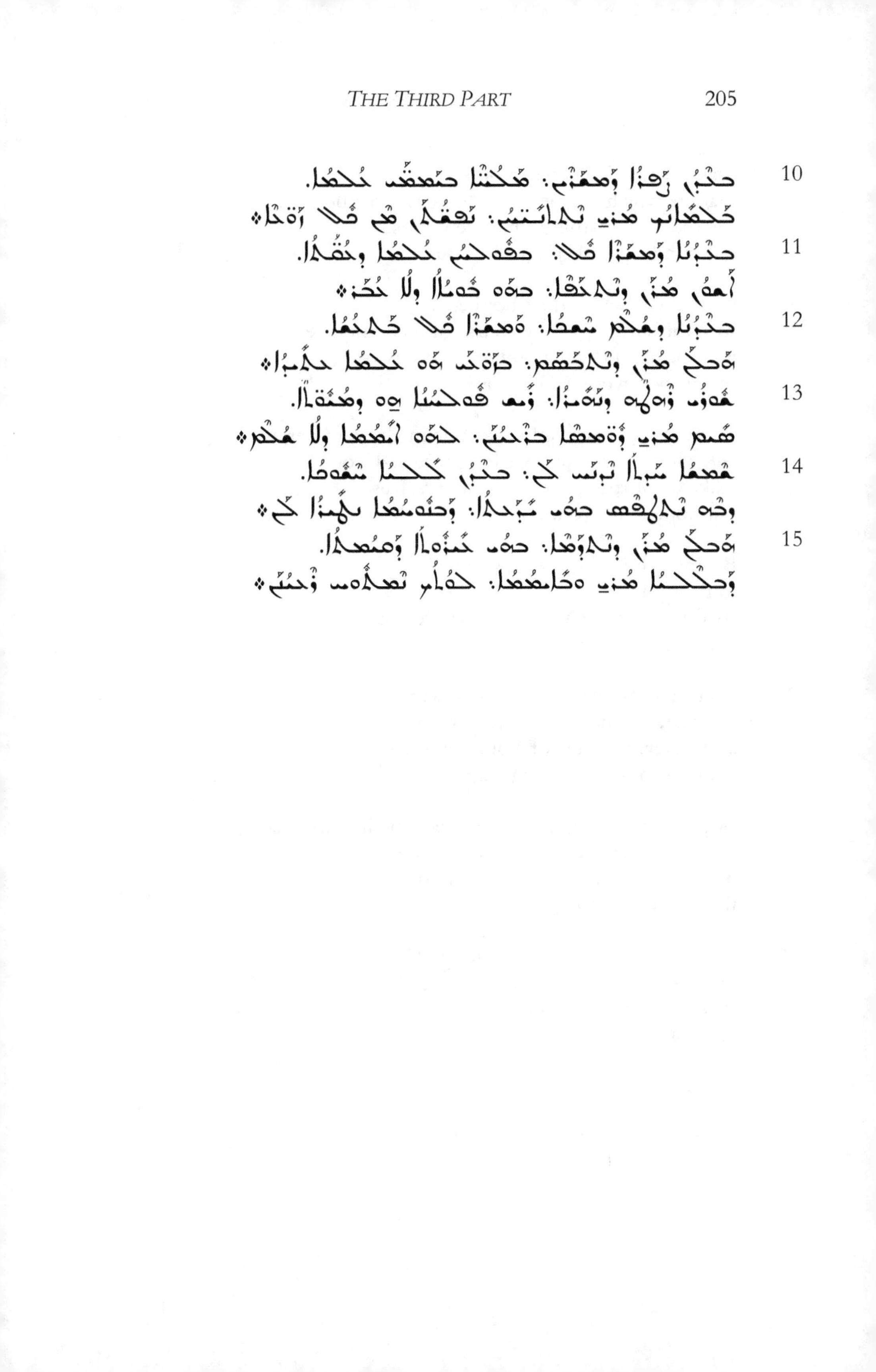

16 Make us worthy to see in ourselves
    that life which will be <after> the resurrection,
    lest there be anything which separates
    our mind from delighting in You.

17 Of that day which does not begin
    with the stirrings of the course of the luminaries,
    inscribe, my Lord, its mystery in our person
    by our persevering with You.

18 Everyday we have embraced You in Your mysteries,
    and within our bodies we have received You;
    make us worthy to perceive in ourselves
    our hope in the resurrection.

19 Be, my Lord, wings for my thought
    to fly in the air,
    so as with <these> wings to be present
    at our true abode.

20 You have hidden Your treasure within our body,[8]
    by means of the grace which dwells
    at the elevated table of Your mysteries:
    grant us to see our being made new.

21 Because, my Lord, we have buried You in ourselves,
    <having eaten> at Your spiritual table,
    may we feel, our Lord, in that deed,
    the future renewal!

22 May we see the beauty of ourselves
    by means of Your spiritual beauty,
    that which within mortal nature
    stirs immortal signs.

---

[8] Cf. Mt. 13:44.

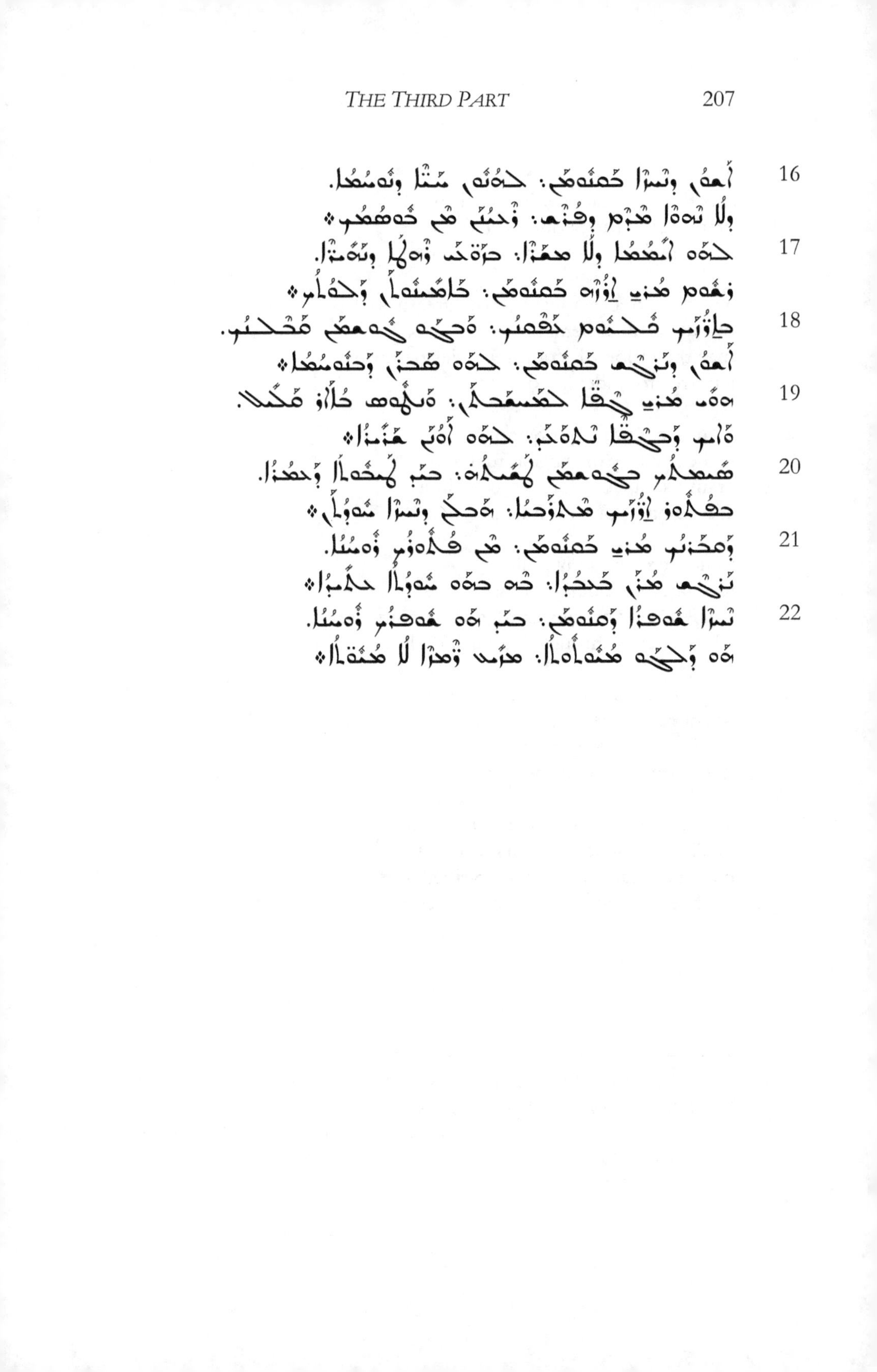

23 Your crucifixion, our Savior,
    was the boundary of the bodily world:
    grant us to crucify our mind
    in the mystery of Your spiritual world.

24 Your resurrection Jesus, is the greatness
    of our spiritual person:[9]
    may the vision of Your mysteries be for us
    a mirror to understand it.

25 Your Economy, our Savior,
    is the mystery of the spiritual world:[10]
    grant us, our Lord, to proceed in it
    according to our spiritual person.

26 Our wretched body pulls us
    to swim in the dark world:
    make us worthy, our Lord, of that converse <with You>
    which breaks through the thick darkness.

27 May our mind, my Lord, not be void
    of spiritual reflection on You,
    nor in our limbs grow cool
    the warmth of Your delight.

28 The mortality which is in our body,
    behold, it belches forth its foulness:
    may the great joy of Your spiritual love
    cleanse the trace of it from our hearts.

---

[9] Cf. 1 Cor. 2:15. Spiritual person (*barnâšâ ruḥânâ*): Is.I 245, 332. Cf. Is.II XXI.14; *Keph*. III 92; John Sol. *Soul* 12, 14, 16.

[10] Spiritual world (*'âlmâ ruḥânâ*): Is.I 454; *Keph*. I 13. See John Sol. *Dialogues* II, p.19.

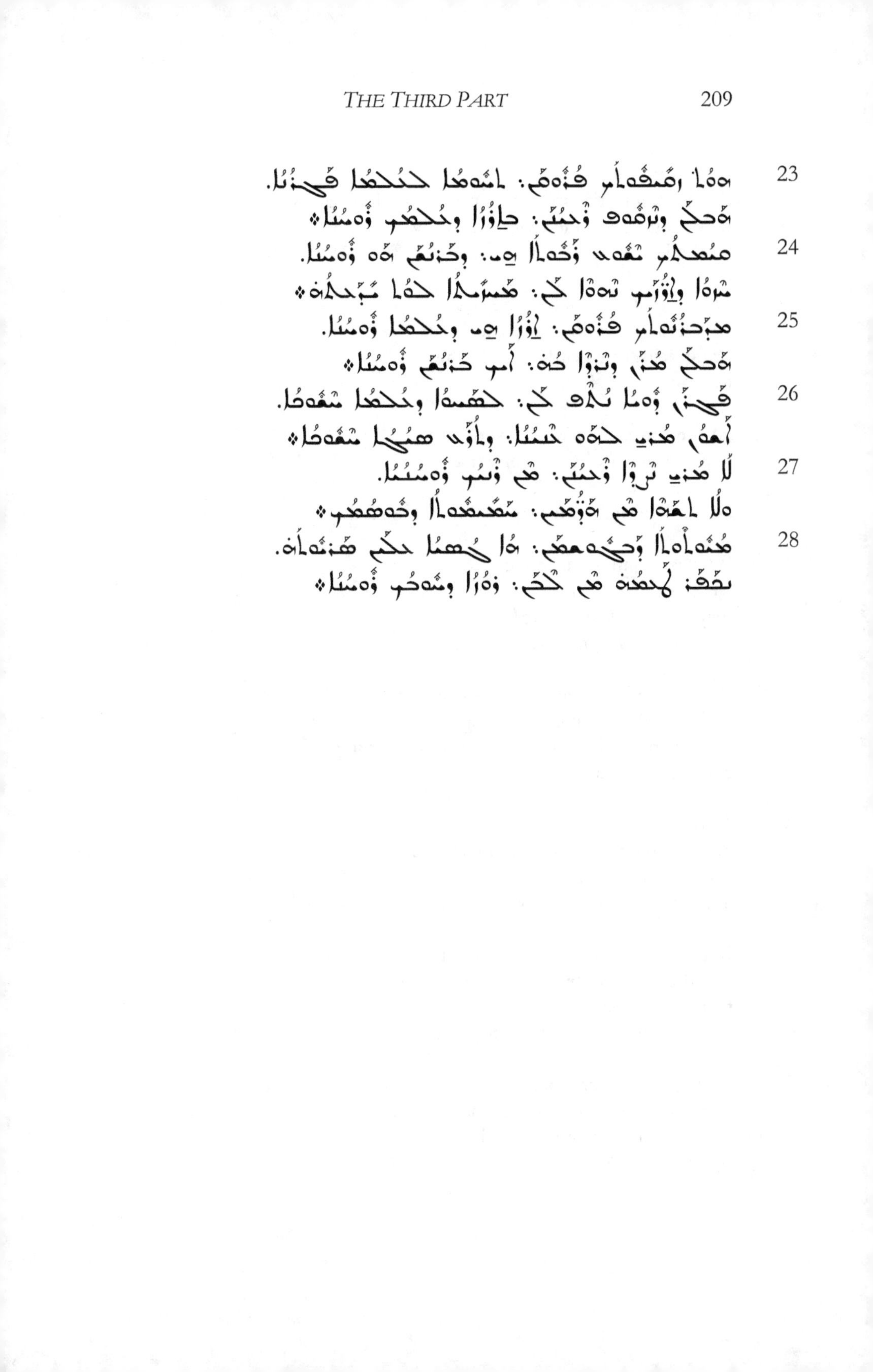

29 As in a prison,
    the hateful things in our members hold us captive:
    may their odor fade from our body,
    by the intoxication which <comes> from Your gift.

30 Our body is for us like the sea
    which always submerges our boat:
    bring near, our Lord, <our> ship
    to Your divine harbor.

31 At the time when we are separate
    from others and their converse,
    be our gain, our Lord,
    and in You may our sadness be made glad.

32 By trusting in Your grace
    we go out to be alone:
    may we see clearly, our Lord,
    the power of Your aid at work.

33 Pour forth Your peace on our hearts
    and Your calm on our stirrings,
    so that the night which is beyond all darkness
    may be for us as the day.

34 At that time in which we are left destitute,
    because night has hemmed us within its darkness
    and we are separate from everyone,
    in You, my Lord may our consolation grow.

35 In that place which is void of all
    and there is no voice in it which encourages,
    fortify our mind, our Lord,
    within the bulwark of Your grace.

36 Rouse us up, our Lord, from our sloth
    with that knowledge which does not go astray,
    lest our mind be submerged
    by the deep sleep of desires.

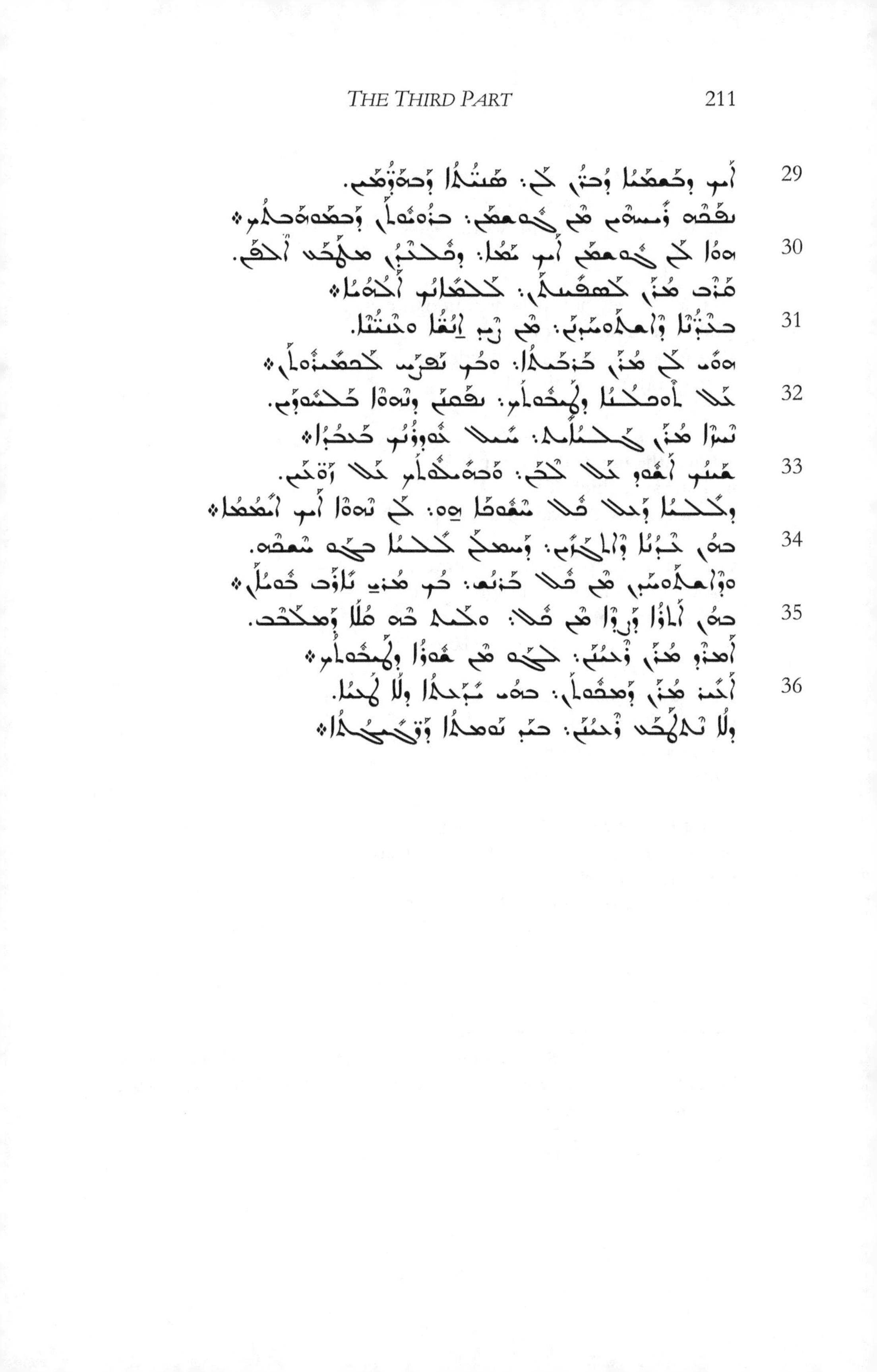

37 Our Lord, make us worthy by Your grace,
together with the wise virgins,
that being prepared with works <like> theirs,[11]
our way of life be vigilant.

38 So that we may not dwell within darkness,
while our minds are obscure,
<rather> may we see a reflection of Your grace,
in our prayer, at all times!

39 The day of Your knowledge, my Lord,
follows the night of our mind:
in Your sun, chief of lights,[12]
may we renew the way of life of our chastity.

40 Grant us to keep vigil in our prayer,
together with the just at night,
so that our lamps be lit
towards the sun of Your revelation.[13]

41 At night the just are inebriated
with the love of God;
at night-time, provide
consolation to our weakness.

42 Grant that our mind might labor
in the memory of Your holy manifestation,
while our souls shine
in the fervor of Your love.

---

[11] Mt. 25:1–13. See Jacob of Serug, "A Homily on the Ten Virgins Described in our Saviour's Gospel," Bedjan, *Homiliae Selectae* II, 375–401; trans. in *The True Vine*.

[12] Cf. James 1:17.

[13] Cf. Mt. 25:1–13.

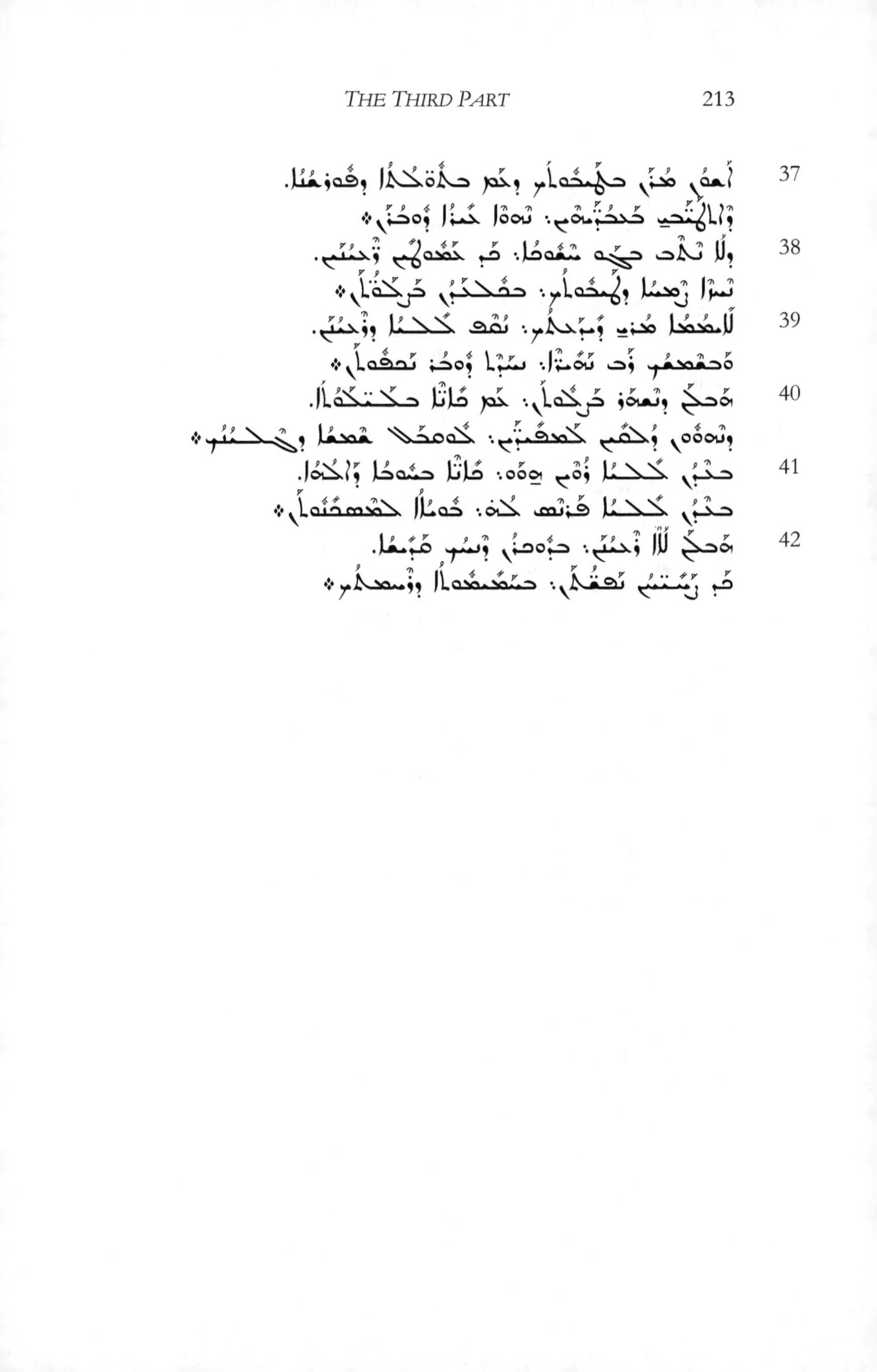

43 In this hour, the saints
    labored at prayers;
    make us worthy, our Lord, to share
    in that consolation of their vigils.

44 Grant us to feel in our self
    and to receive in our way of life, the fragrance
    of that consolation which they shared in,
    during the journey of their minds.

45 O Christ, who watch for us
    in prayer with <Your> Father,[14]
    grant us to feel a pledge
    of pardon[15] for our iniquity, during our prayer.

46 O Christ, who sweat at prayer
    for us, during the night,[16]
    make us worthy that our mind may perceive
    Your suffering for our salvation.

47 O Christ, who have poured out <Your> gift
    on the saints at prayer[17]
    gladden, our Lord, our intelligence
    by means of the perceptions of Your grace.

48 O God, to whom are
    the days and the nights,[18]
    make us glad, our Lord, by means of hope in You,
    when the night is dark.

---

[14] Cf. Mt. 26:39.
[15] Cf. 2 Cor. 1:21–22; 5:5; Eph. 1:13–14.
[16] Cf. Lk. 22:41–44.
[17] Cf. Acts 2:1–2.
[18] Cf. Ps. 74:16

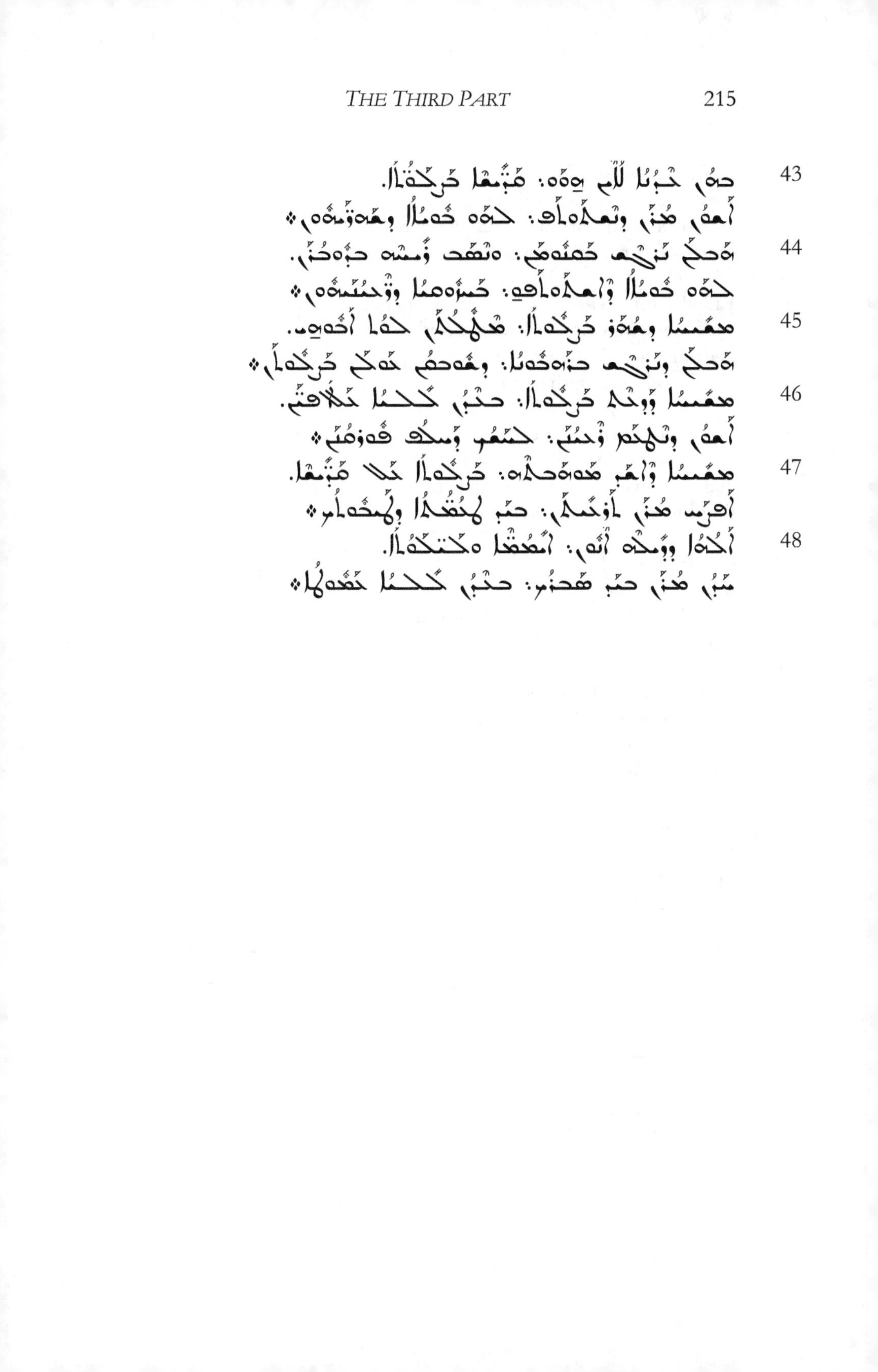

49 In the converse of prayer with You,
    we draw near while bowing down:
    <breathe> on our mind and gladden it
    that by our prayer, it may communicate with You.

50 Enlighten the stirrings of our intelligence
    so that we may observe with wonder,
    and our thought be enfolded in You
    for the whole length of our prayer.

51 At the dawn of Your coming
    our mind receives Your manifestation,
    and its power of reason anticipates
    that incorporeal way of life.

52 Grant us, our Lord,
    to hasten to our holy city,
    and like Moses from the top of the mountain,
    may we <foresee> it by means of Your revelation.[19]

53 Even if the body afflicts
    and by means of its miseries brings us low,
    may Your grace my Lord,
    overcome in us the law within our flesh.[20]

54 Our Lord, with my mind
    I love Your spiritual law,[21]
    but *a law* which is placed *in my members*[22]
    leads me captive from being occupied with it.

---

[19] Cf. Dt. 34:1–4.
[20] Cf. Rom. 7:23.
[21] Cf. Rom. 7:14.
[22] Cf. Rom. 7:23.

THE THIRD PART

55 <it is> as if the soul were led captive
    by hateful works,
    or as if it were pulled away
    by compulsion from spiritual converse.

56 But <the soul> does not wish
    to be enslaved in the tent of the body's passions,
    and it calls for help while groaning,
    and its misery is indescribable.

57 Like the widow who, wronged,
    passionately cries for help to God;
    she, whom in that Gospel is promised
    satisfaction, <according as she desires>.

58 *Avenge me* – she says in prayer –
    from my body which is *my adversary*.[23]
    And that sweet judge
    gives a reward for her compunction.

59 As we are swimming in the ocean
    of our bodily stirrings at all times,
    wash, our Lord, our mind
    from the stains of hateful things.

60 To You we call from out of the waves,
    O our wise Mariner:
    cause to blow on us a serene breeze,
    but if we sink, draw us out.[24]

---

[23] Lk. 18:3. Cf. Is.I, 107. See also Nilus, *Sulla virtù e sulle passioni* 17, p. 286.

[24] Cf. Mt. 14:24–31.

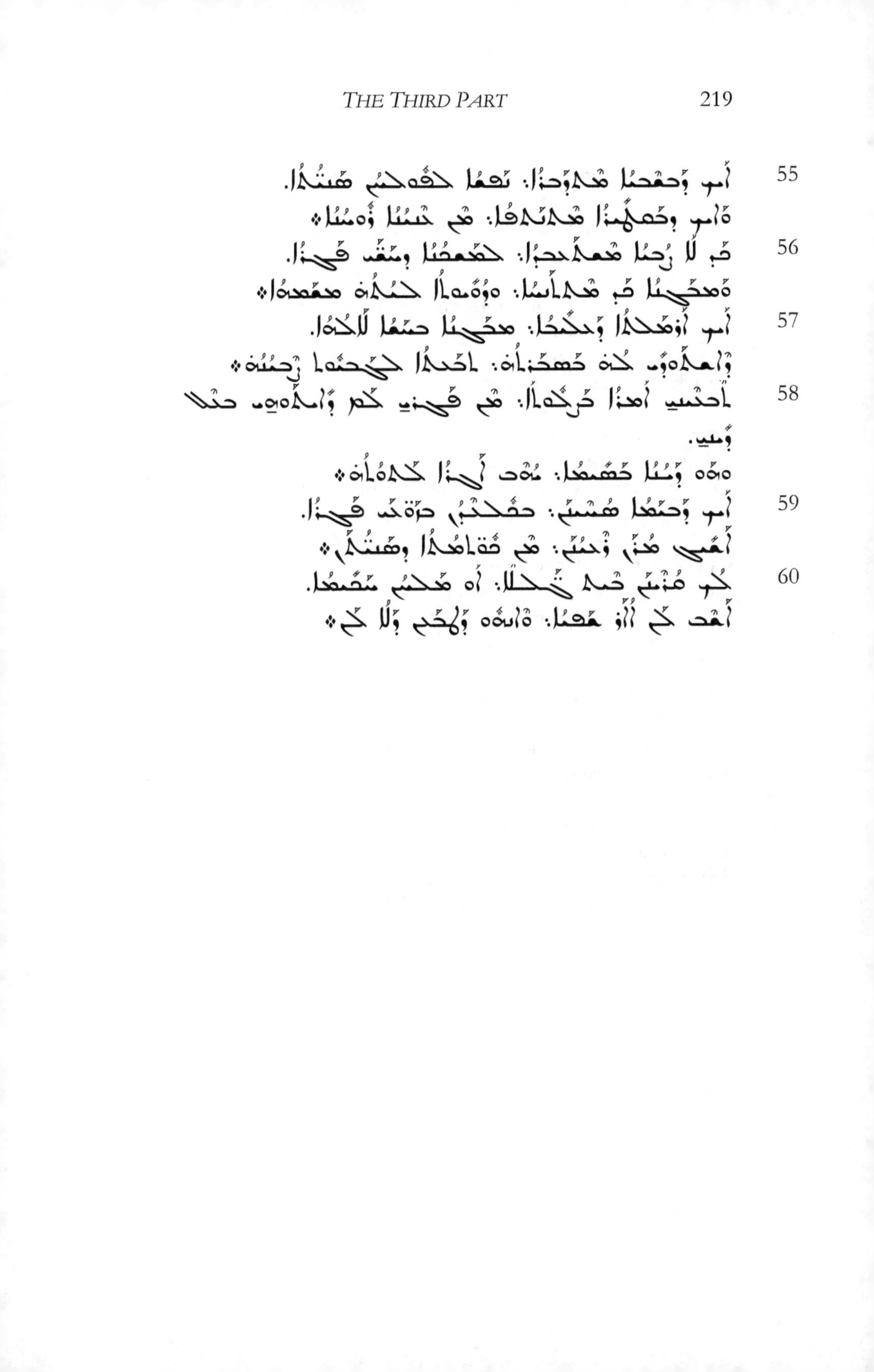

61 In the middle of the night I rose up, my Lord,
to announce You with great passion
and to offer You a sacrifice of praise,[25]
to You, *just judge*.[26]

62 Because You have not forgotten our dereliction
and our humiliation at all times,
<just> how eager our mind is
for what is excellent, is manifest to You.

63 Even if our weaknesses prevail
a thousand, thousand <times> all day <long>
and we immerse ourselves in their hateful things,
we do not desist from converse with You.

64 Our Savior, who have come to wash
the impurity of the sinful world,
grant us compunction at all times
that we might cleanse the impurity of our thoughts.

65 Sanctify our hearts, my Lord,
and fill <them> with the Spirit of Your glory,
and by means of the holy remembrance of You
may they receive the Spirit of joy.

66 Create in us, my Lord, *a new heart*,
infuse in us *a new spirit*,[27]
that by the renewal of our mind
we may put on the garment of the Kingdom.[28]

---

[25] Cf. Heb. 13:15.
[26] Cf. Ps. 9:5.
[27] Ez. 11:19.
[28] Cf. Mt. 22:1–14.

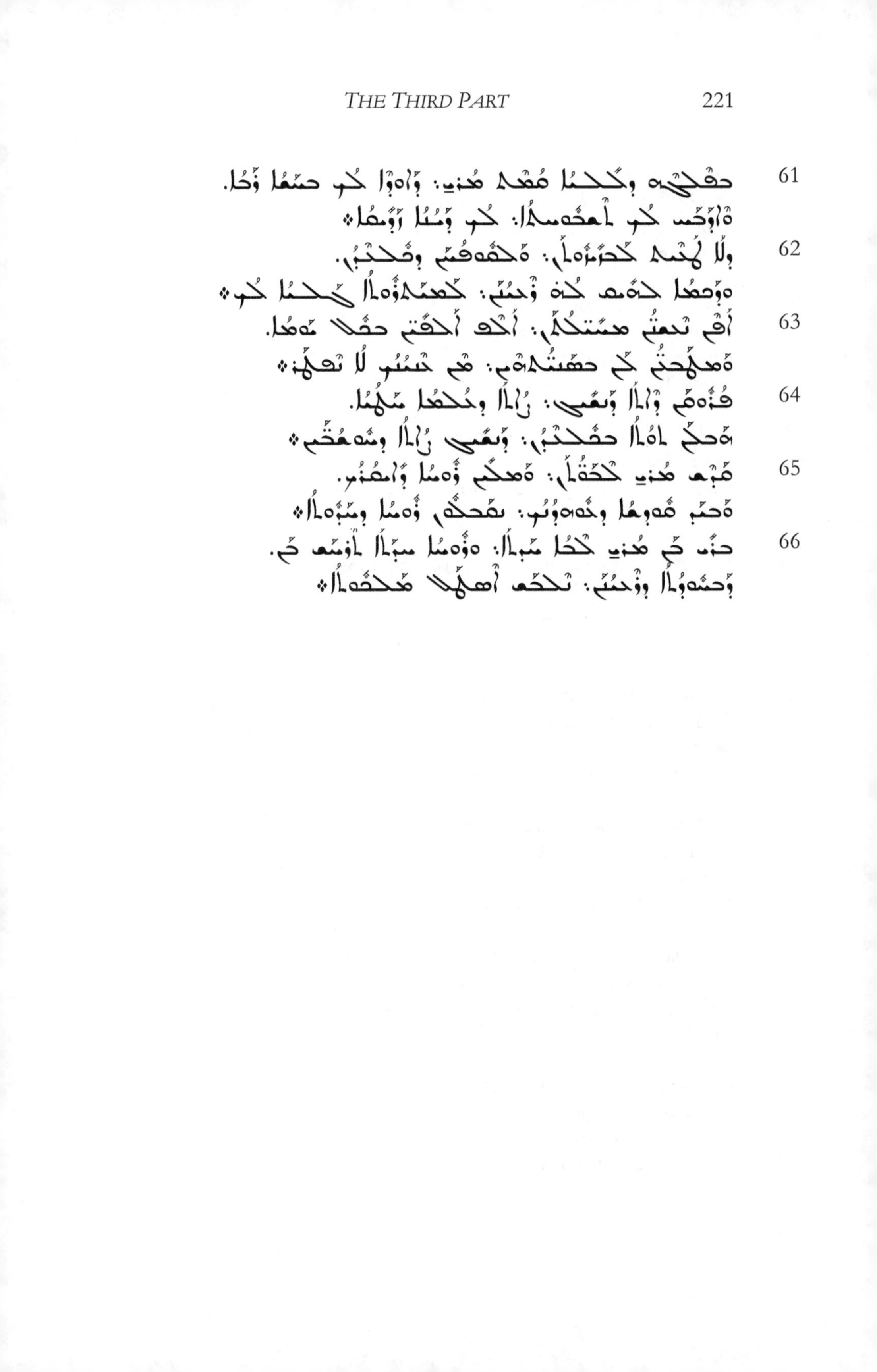

67   By the mysteries of Your Spirit, we are renewed,
and by Your grace, we are sanctified,
while we continually forget everything,
by means of the converse with You.

68   And that holy hope of ours
we always feel in our prayer,
when we are led by it continually
<far> from the corporeal world.

69   The mortal world is <too> weak
to receive all of Your gift:
from Your abundance overflows
fullness on its weakness.

70   My Lord, our souls are thirsty for this hope,
as we are afflicted:
gladden our souls, our Lord,
that we may see Your favor in our substance.

71   In this world we are separate
from humanity and its converse,
be for us a guide, our Savior,
and a companion at all times.

72   In this time that we are deprived
from <being> with the world and its business,
be consolation for us, our Lord,
and may we not be deprived of Your love.

73   Because our heart is full of adversities
and we are always sad
make us worthy, our Lord, of Your consolation
which is beyond all adversities.

74   Our souls are full of weeping
and it is always bitter for us:
gladden, my Lord, our sadness
and refresh our burning heart.

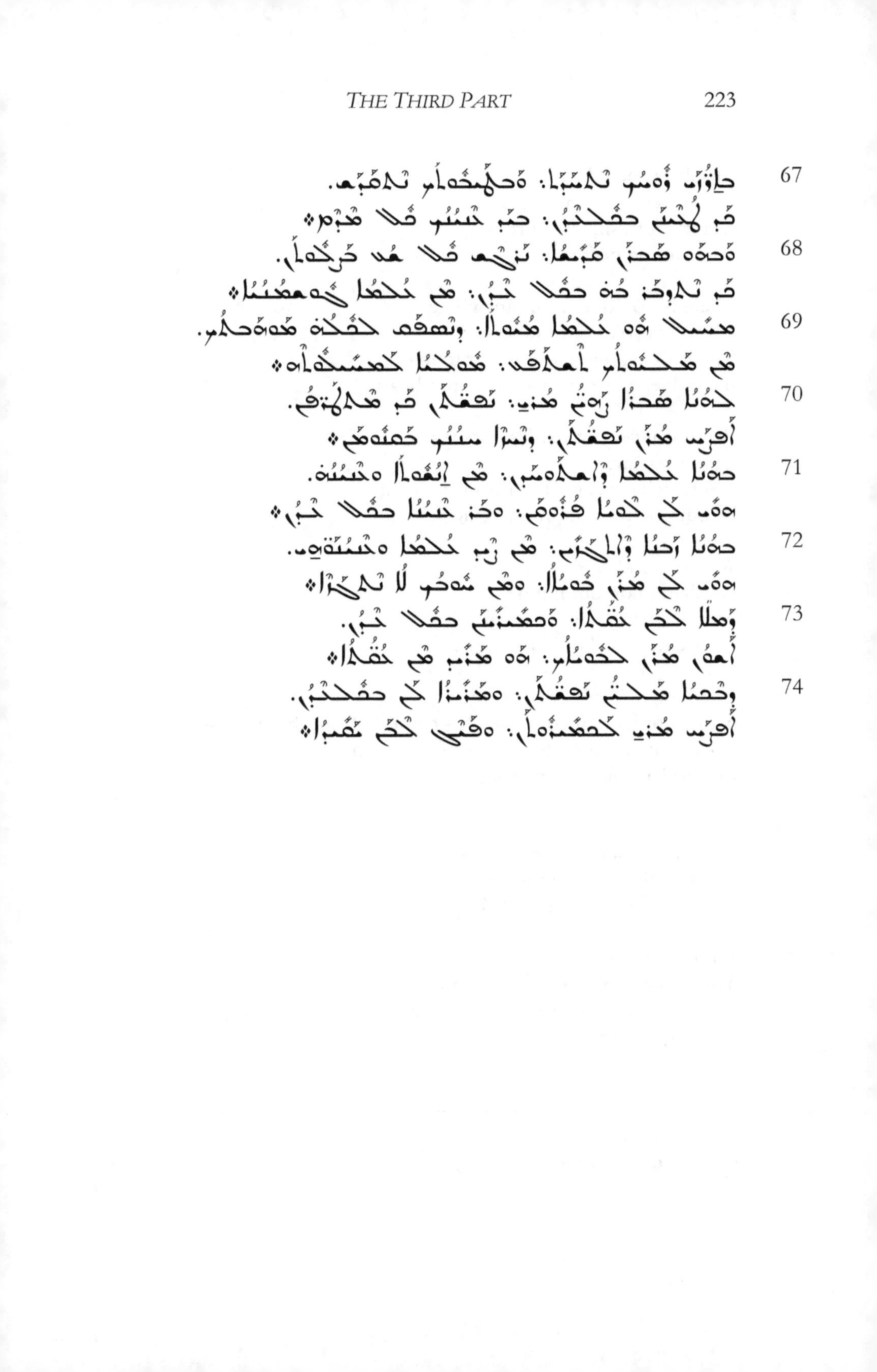

75   Troubles encircle us
and suffering, night and day:
secretly refresh, our Lord,
our burning hearts.

76   There is no hope for us anywhere
which consoles our sadness:
Savior of all, may Your finger touch
the hidden sorrow which is in our heart.[29]

77   Because incessant battles pursue us
night and day,
and they have cut off our hope in You:
be our commander in the struggle!

78   Weeping and tears in secret
are shed upon our mind,
because we are always fearful
lest we deprived of Your hope.

79   Encourage, our Lord, our souls
with Your hidden voice which <comes> from the stillness,[30]
when You teach us, by means of the Spirit,
the hidden aim of our struggle.

80   May our mind not be lacking
in Your encouragement, our Savior,
lest it be drowned in the sea
by the waves which cut off hope.

81   For that true hope
You show us, our Lord, from afar,
so that by seeing it we might be strengthened
and defy all miseries.

---

[29] Cf. Lk. 16:24.
[30] Stillness (*šelyā*).

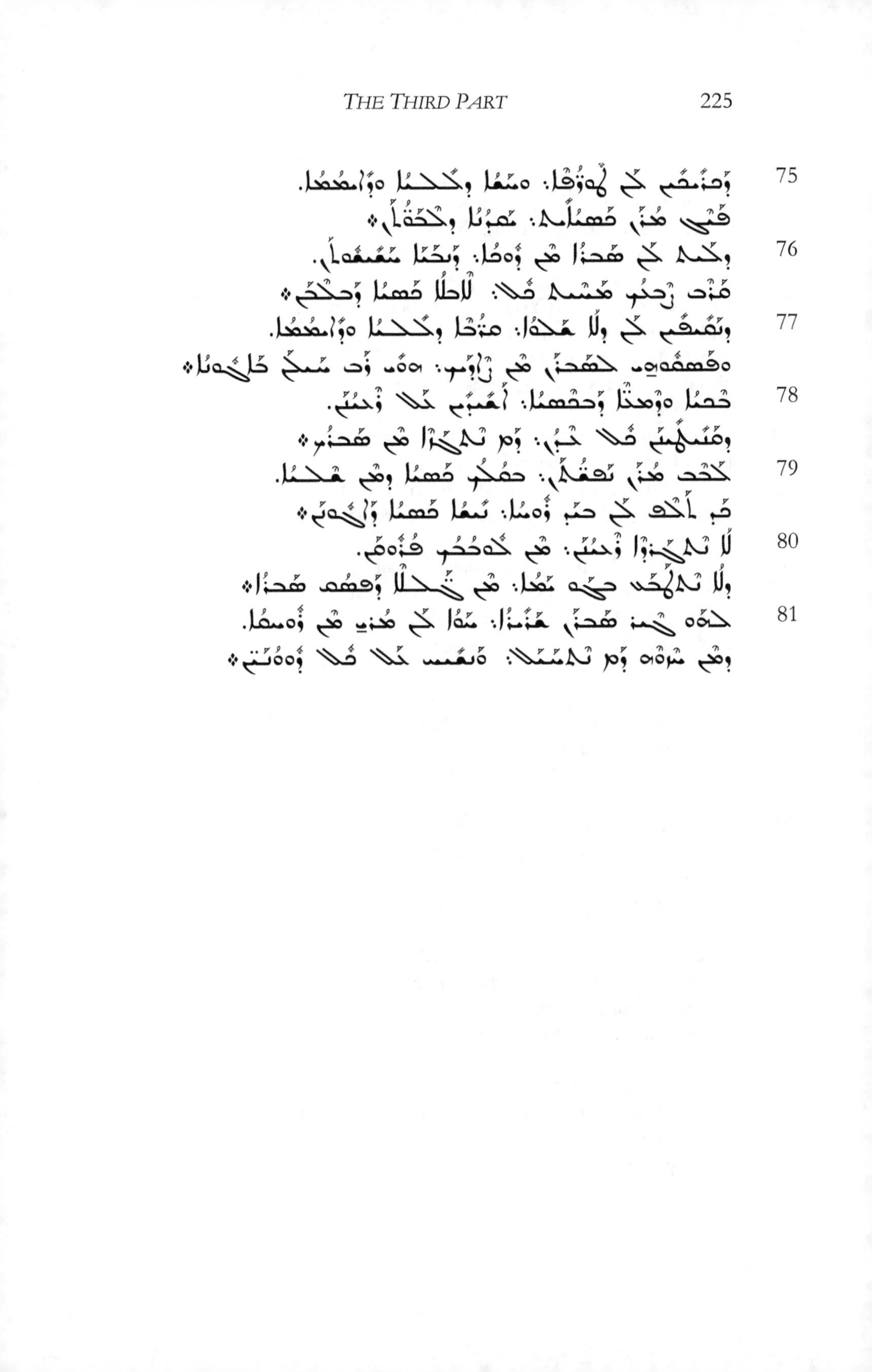

82 We are inexperienced in the struggle
    to resist at the times of battles:
    make wise in You our childishness,
    <even> in this <our> spiritual maturity.

83 From converse with You we have become wise,
    and we receive help from Your Spirit
    which always instructs us
    about the path which ascends to heaven.

84 Anoint, my Lord, our heart with Your Spirit,
    that we might be priests in secret,
    and fulfill the priestly ministry for You with our stirrings,
    in the Holy of Holies of the knowledge of You.

85 May the coercion of Your grace prevail
    upon our intellect, through the stirrings of our meditation,
    and may we be led, by means of Your gift,
    to the dwelling of the incorporeal beings.

86 In that house of rest of the saints,
    and the elevated place of the pilgrims,
    let us come together in the faith,
    assisted by the power of Your grace.

87 By means of Your revelation may we become wise
    about the way which leads to our city;
    sustain our journey to it,
    <far> from the world of struggles.

88 O Jesus, whose majesty descended
    to raise up the lowly that they might be exalted,
    increase Your gift with us
    that we may attain to Your love.

89 Grant us a holy mind
    that we might receive Your likeness in our deeds,
    and depict the true model
    of Your humility in our person.

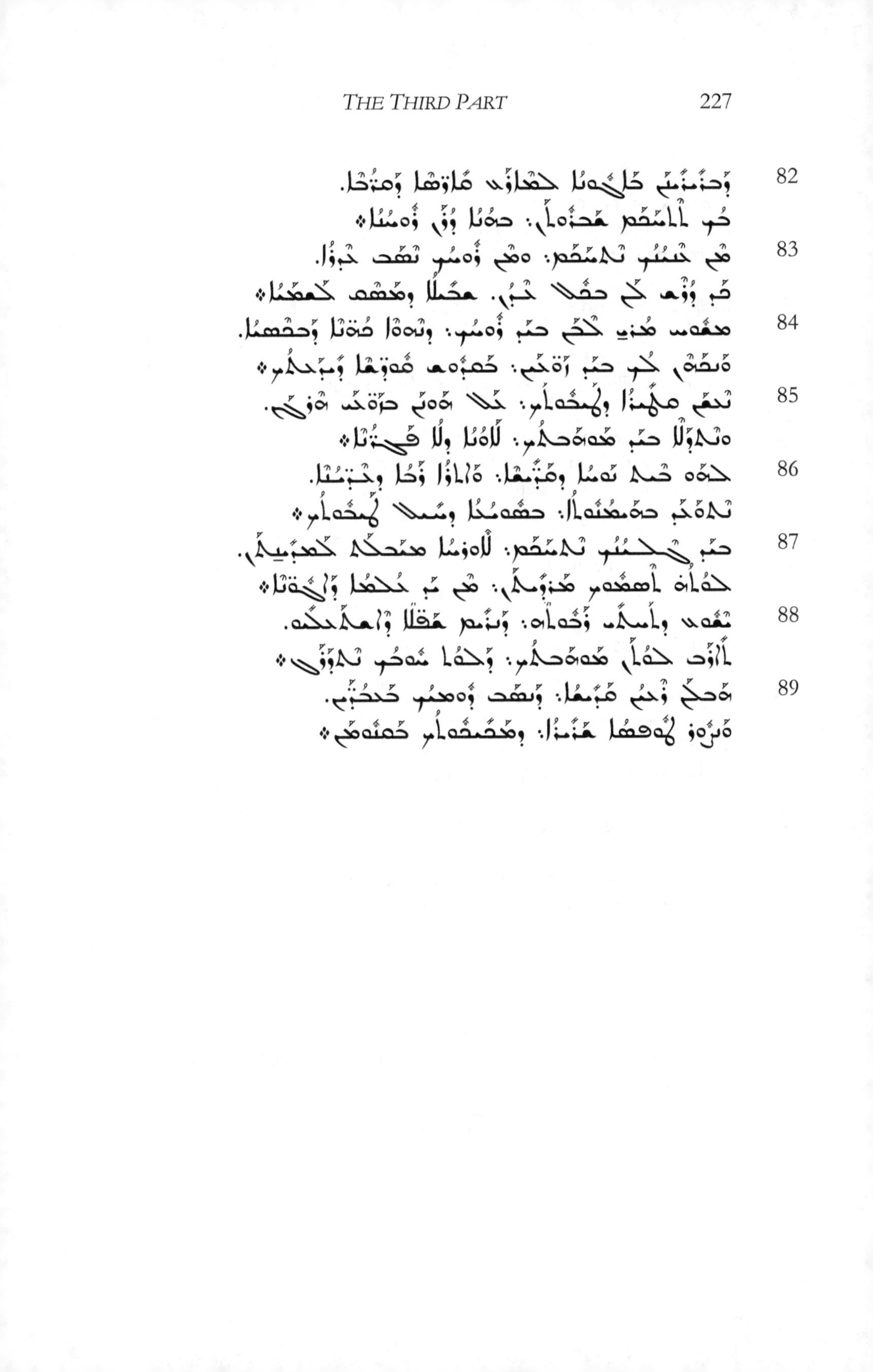

90   Grant us to perceive mystically
the taste of Your sweet love,
and may our mind fly to You,
by means of its savor at all times.

91   Moisten our arid soul
that it may bear fruits of praise,
and may it be a holy temple
for the dwelling-place of Your glorious realities.

92   Make our members, our Lord,
partners with You, head of the whole body,[31]
lest one of us be alienated
from communion with Your gladness.

93   O true Son of our race,
who goes to receive the Kingdom,[32]
do not renounce Your kindred
when You rise upon the clouds.[33]

94   Our souls are thirsty for Your manifestation
and the revelation of Your great dignity:
grant us confidence, from this time,
in the *pledge*[34] of our communion <with You>.

95   Even if we are wretched
and our race is dust,
raise up our soul according to our greatness,
because we have become God's kin.[35]

---

[31] Cf. Rom. 12:5; 1 Cor. 12:12; Eph. 1:22–23; 5:30; Col. 1:18.
[32] Cf. Lk. 19:12–15.
[33] Cf. Mt. 24:30; Mk. 13:26.
[34] Cf. 2 Cor. 1:21–22; 5:5; Eph. 1:13–14.
[35] Cf. Acts 17:29.

90 ܠܗܿܘ ܕܥܐ ܕܣܘܥܪ̈ܢܐ ܕܫܡܝܐ܆ ܘܚܟ݁ܡ ܘܢܓ̈ܝܗܐ ܕܥܠܡܐ܂
ܘܢܦܢܶܐ ܠܗܘܢܿܗ ܘܢܬܠ܆ ܕܢܣܰܒ ܠܗܢܿܦܗ ܚܕܐ ܬܡܪ܀

91 ܘܐܶܝܟ ܚܢܦܐ ܘܚܟܝܡܐ܂ ܘܐܠܬܐ ܩܐܪܐ ܘܐܗܕܘܣܪܐ܂
ܘܐܘܕܐ ܠܕܗܐ ܛܒ̈ܥܐ܆ ܟܣܢܕܘܙܢܐ ܘܡܚܬܢܫܡܪ܀

92 ܥܕܐܕ ܗܕܝ܂ ܘܘܒܘܚܪܝ܆ ܟܪ ܢܦܫܐ ܘܦܟܕܗ ܟܘܗܥܪܐ܂
ܘܠܐ ܠܐܢܐܕܐ ܠܒ ܗܒܝ܆ ܚܥܕܐܘܟܘܐܠ ܘܕܘܘܩܥܪ܀

93 ܐܘ ܟܕ ܠܝܘܗܝ ܗܢܪܐܠ܂ ܘܐܪܙܠ ܥܝܢܕ ܥܕܝܗܐܠ܂
ܠܐ ܐܗܦܘܕ ܕܚܬܫ ܚܝܢܨܝܕ܆ ܗܕܐ ܘܪܐܣ ܐܒܝܗ ܕܚܢܫܢܐ܀

94 ܠܒܝܢܝܕ ܪܗܡ ܢܗܦܟܪ܆ ܘܚܝܚܡܢܐ ܘܘܘܡܖܕܗܝ܂
ܘܚܟ ܗܨܐ ܐܘܡܟܢܐ܆ ܚܙܘܚܕܢܐ ܘܥܕܐܘܟܐܠ܀

95 ܐܥܝ ܐܢܠܝ ܗܗܨܬܢܐ܂ ܘܝܗܘܗܝ ܐܢܠܕܘܗܝ ܘܢܣܫܢܐ܂
ܠܐܐܘܕ ܢܗܥܝ ܟܙܘܘܕܗܝ܆ ܘܐܠܠܘܗܘܗܝ ܟܠܟܕܗܐ܀

96 What mercy not able to be measured!
    What sea of total compassion!
    What grace without limit!
    What love, greater than the world!

97 Our vision of Your love is imperfect
    because we encompass its riches with our understanding!
    O the depth of Your grace, our Creator,
    for creatures!

98 It is not for the good of a few:
    the Son of our human race was the Son of the King,
    but He went to prepare
    a Kingdom for all our nature.

99 Even if I be despised or mocked
    ten thousand times for this,
    never, my Lord, will I deny
    the greatness of our hope in You.

100 My folly is greater than the word,
    and the sea is not able to wash it away!
    I said this and I say it <again>
    Your love is greater than my debts!

101 The waves of the sea are less
    than the number of my sins,
    but if we weigh <them> against Your love,
    they vanish as nothing.

102 I am a dwelling-place for all evils
    and the mountains are slighter than my iniquity,
    yet with Your love,
    I do not fear to call myself just.

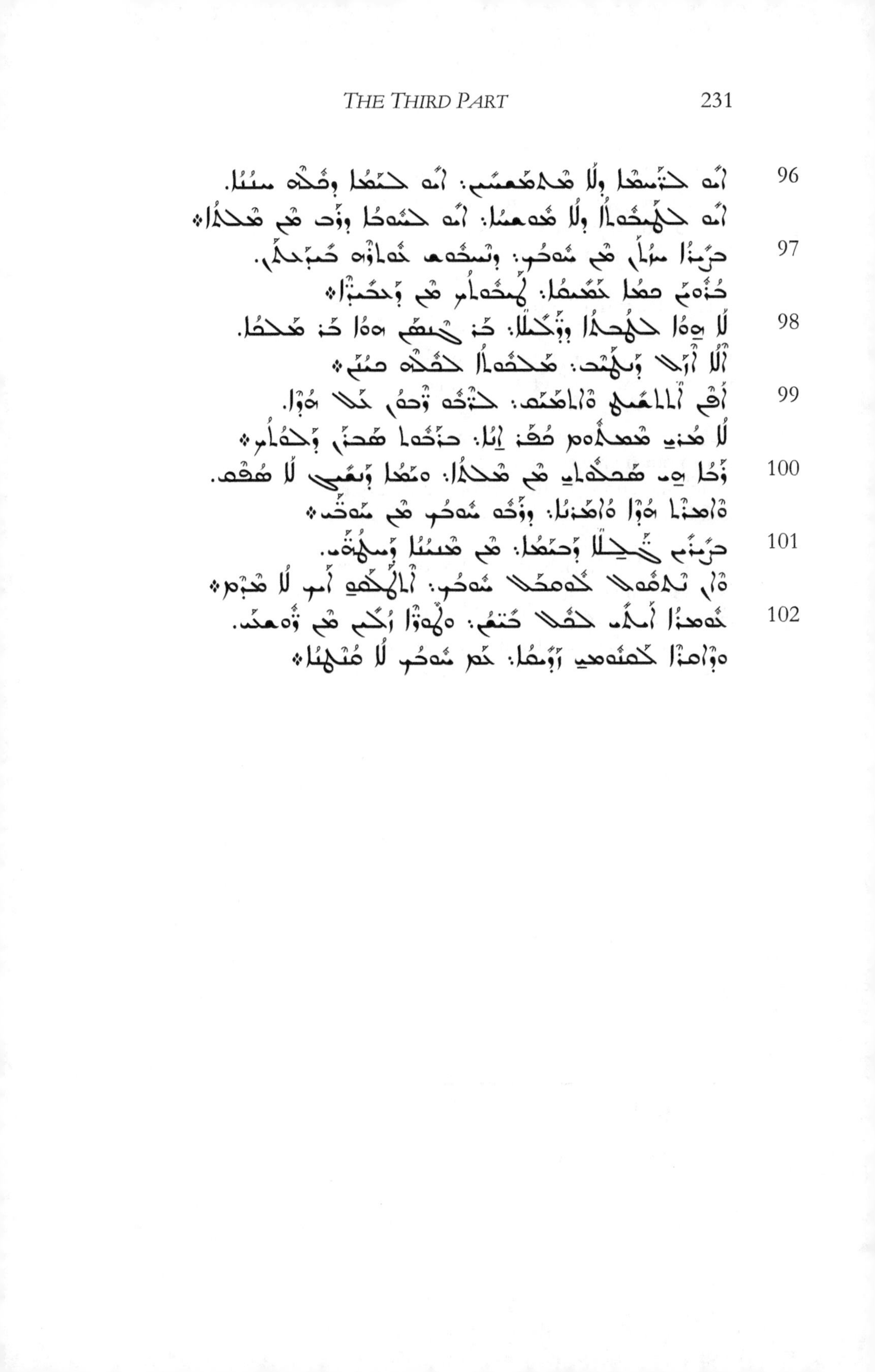

103 To You thanksgiving from all of us,
    the *remnant*[36] of our wretched human race;
    and to You from our race is due
    loving adoration at all times.

104 The benefits transmitted
    to us by Your hands are ineffable:
    we adore the foot stool of Your feet,[37]
    with weeping and joyful suffering.

105 Because our mouth is <too> weak to praise You,
    may Your mercy recompense us
    which has shone forth over our mortality,
    and has taken up and embraced our foulness.

106 For Your love which is joined to our nature,
    is not ashamed that we call ourselves <Your> members,[38]
    and has attached our filth to <Your> body,
    glory <to this love> from all creatures!

---

[36] Cf. Rom. 9:27–29.
[37] Cf. Ps. 110:1.
[38] Cf. Heb. 5:30.

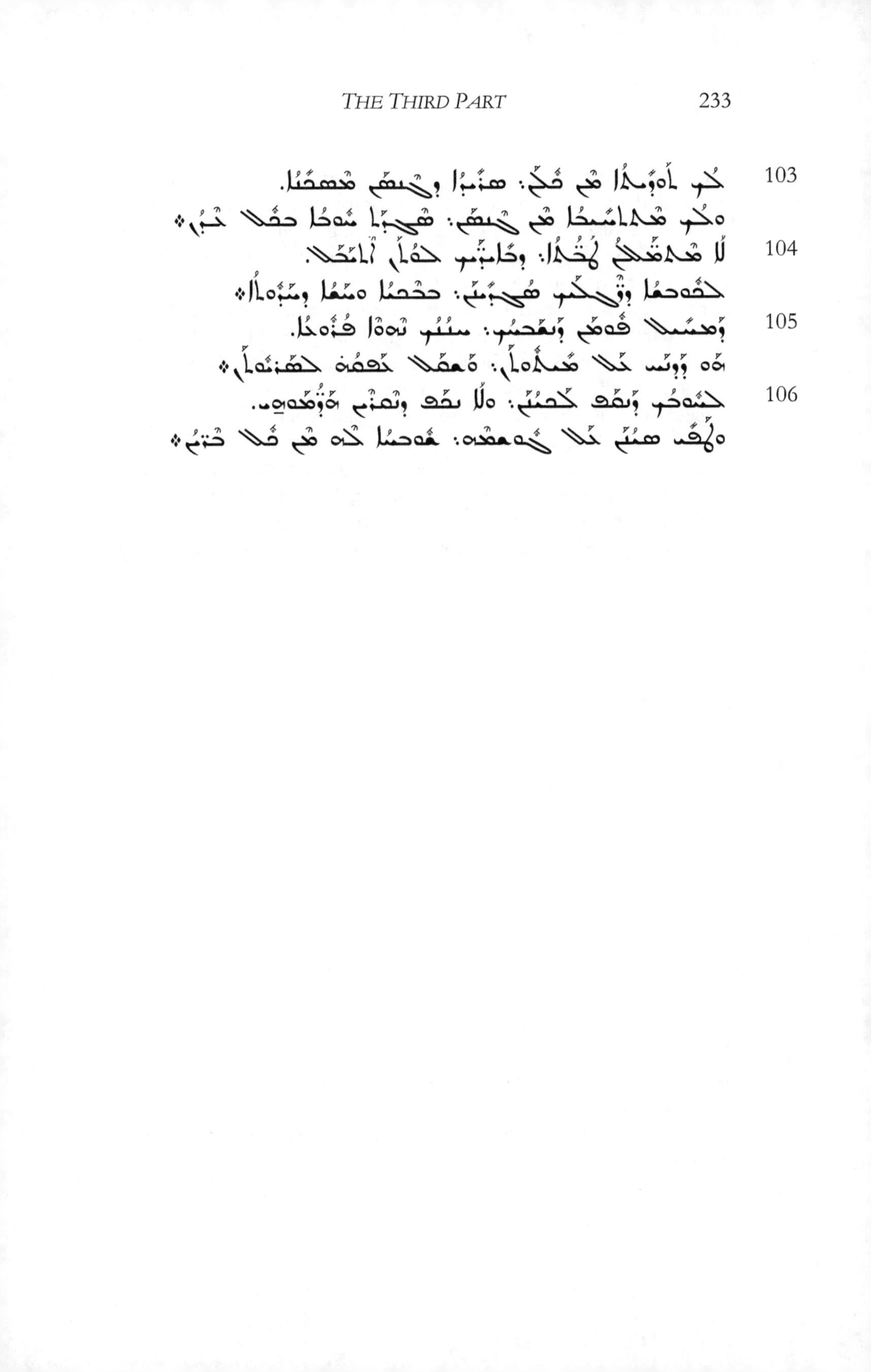

107   These <words> my beloved are full of spiritual meditation for the mind, and they are converse in the Spirit with our Lord! Let us make some place in our soul for these things that, by means of our quiet rest, the mind might discern and enter into converse with our Lord. For all of you, it is clear that converse with the world is contrary to converse with God. Therefore your wisdom must make this separation and honor the part which is good.[39] Indeed, if there are one or two persons who seek this mystery of spiritual converse, and they meet together with one another once a week, while quietly engaged in this divine converse – the gain, when they are enlightened, is even greater than the advantage which they receive from their solitude. This is because they help one another by means of the light they receive from one another, but without a mediator. This becomes perfect stillness, if accidental things <do not occur> which might dislodge them from their goal, and <that they> keep themselves also from worldly words.[40]

---

[39] Cf. Lk. 10:42.

[40] According to Chialà, this paragraph is probably an addition made by Isaac, cf. Is.II V.31–33.

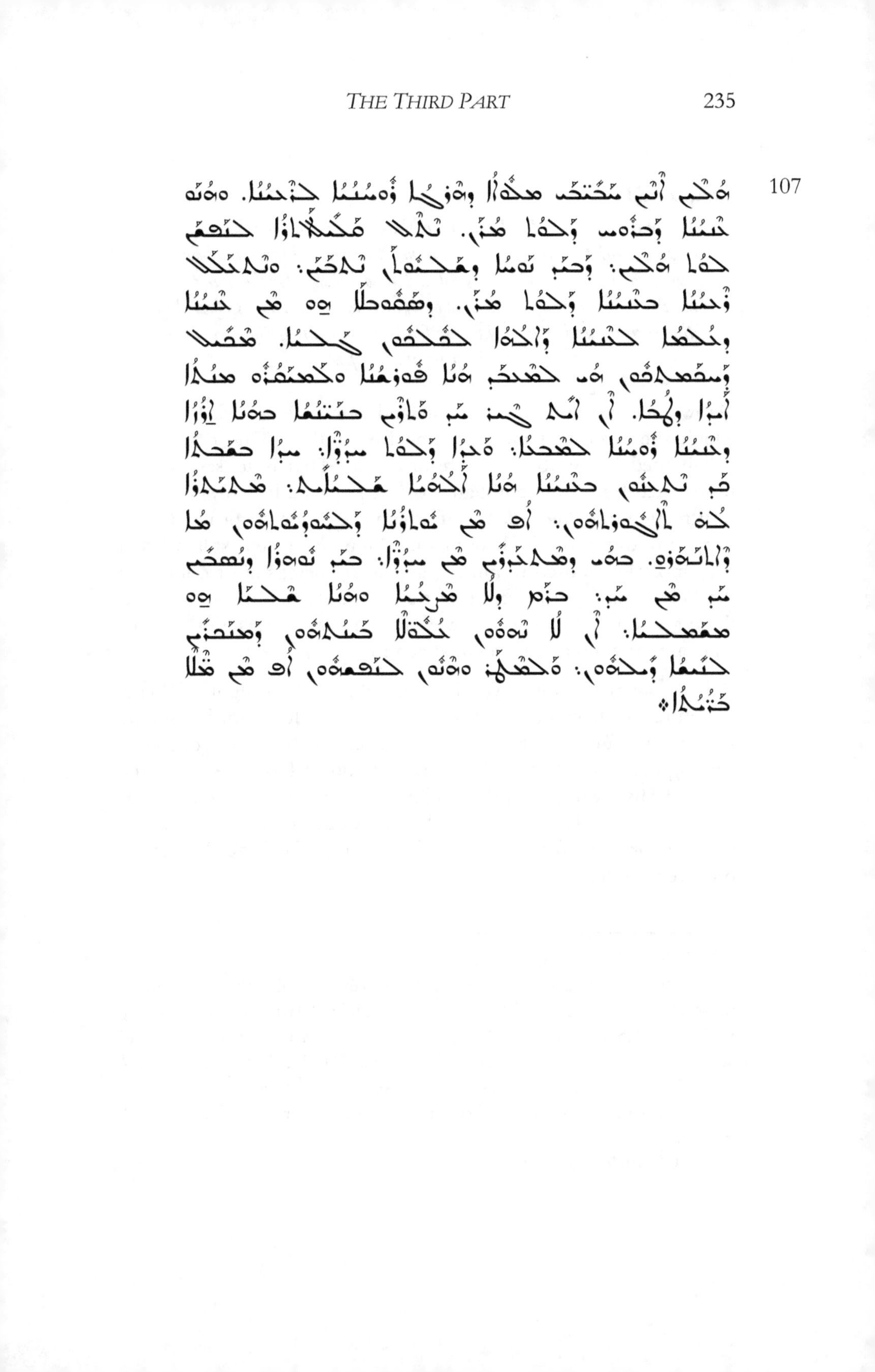

Chapter XI

Again of the same Mar Isaac. Concerning that: "you have been raised with Christ,"[1] as said by the divine Apostle; and concerning this divine sacrifice which the holy Church accomplishes for the living and the dead for the sake of the hope of what is to come: what is effected by this sacrifice and in a special way for a believing lay person because of the firmness of his hope.

1 "How indeed is our resurrection and our renewal[2] visible in us which the Apostle Paul proclaims frequently?"[3] Those who are enlightened know about our resurrection. That is to say, we are resurrected but in the faith; and we are renewed in a mystery. The resurrection and the renewal of which the Apostle speaks do not happen to our body, for behold, our <human> race is still afflicted with mortality and corruptibility, and living beings are troubled by the flesh capable of suffering in this world. How can one say that these are resurrected and renewed, for behold the miseries of mortality are lifted up against them at all times?

2 But we ought to look beyond the flesh with the insight of divine Scripture. We have risen by a virtuous way of life; we have risen by faith in the future realities; we have risen in the knowledge concerning the divine Nature, in the perception of His Essence, in the glory of His greatness, in the height of His Nature, in the hope for the good things kept for us, in the knowledge of the mysteries of the *new world*,[4] in faith in the marvelous transformation[5] which is prepared for creation.

---

[1] Col. 3:1; cf. Eph. 2:6; Col. 2:12.

[2] Renewal (*ḥuddâtâ*): renewal of the universe, of all (*kul*), of the inner person. See Is.I 127, 256, 374, 471; Is.II V.1, 6,7; VIII.16; X.19; *Keph.* I 90; II 19; III 21,82; IV 46, 59, 61,78. John Sol. *Dialogues* X, pp.122, 125 and *passim; Letters*, p.3 (Rignell, *Briefe*); Evag. Cent. III. 48,51; Nilus, *Discorso di ammonimento* 41, p. 202; Theodore of Mopsuestia, *Homélies* VI 12.

[3] Cf. Col. 3:1; Eph. 2:6; Col. 2:12; and on "renewal," cf. Rom. 12:2; Eph. 4:23; Tt. 3:5.

[4] Cf. Mt. 19:28 (Peshitta).

---

⁵ Transformation (*šuḥlāpā*): found frequently in Isaac, Is.I 4, 12, 25, 127. Is. II VIII.7, 15; XXII.7–8; XXXVIII.2. *Keph.* IV 57.

3   Rightly then does the Apostle proclaim to us a true resurrection in Christ, as a reality in which we already exist. That is to say, we have risen by the renewal of the mind.[6] In the former generations, there was no remembrance of God; indeed remembrance of Him was completely dead. As to the intermediate generations, even while knowing Him, they knew Him in a limited way.

4   We, indeed, have been renewed in our mind[7] by a new knowledge that was not revealed to them. For we have known this Being who has neither beginning nor end. And again, they had a childish way of thinking about God: that He is hard, vindictive; that He requites and is just when He requites, irascible, wrathful; that He remembers *the debts of the fathers in the children of the children.*[8]

5   But we possess a greater sense of God and we have an elevated knowledge of Him. Indeed, we know Him as one who pardons, who is good, who is humble. Even for one good thing <done>, if only in thought or compunction, He pardons the sins of many years. And the sins of others He does not remember, lest they be associated <with ours>. But even those who have died in their sins and passed over already, He rends asunder the greater part of their sins[9] by means of His mercy.

---

[6] Renewal of the mind (*ḥuddâtâ d-madʿâ*): see Is.I 469; *Keph.*IV 54. On resurrection as a progression in knowledge, see Evag. Cent.V. 22, 25.

[7] Cf. Eph. 4:23.

[8] Cf. Ex. 34:7. Elsewhere Isaac criticizes this infantile way of thinking (*šabrût tarʿîtâ*) as not recognizing "His kindness, goodness and compassion." And that one "should not understand everything (literally) as it is written, but rather that we should see, (concealed) inside the bodily exterior of the narratives, the hidden providence and external knowledge which guides all…" – an aspect of Isaac's exegesis. See Is.II XXXIX.2, 19.

[9] Cf. 1 Peter 4:8.

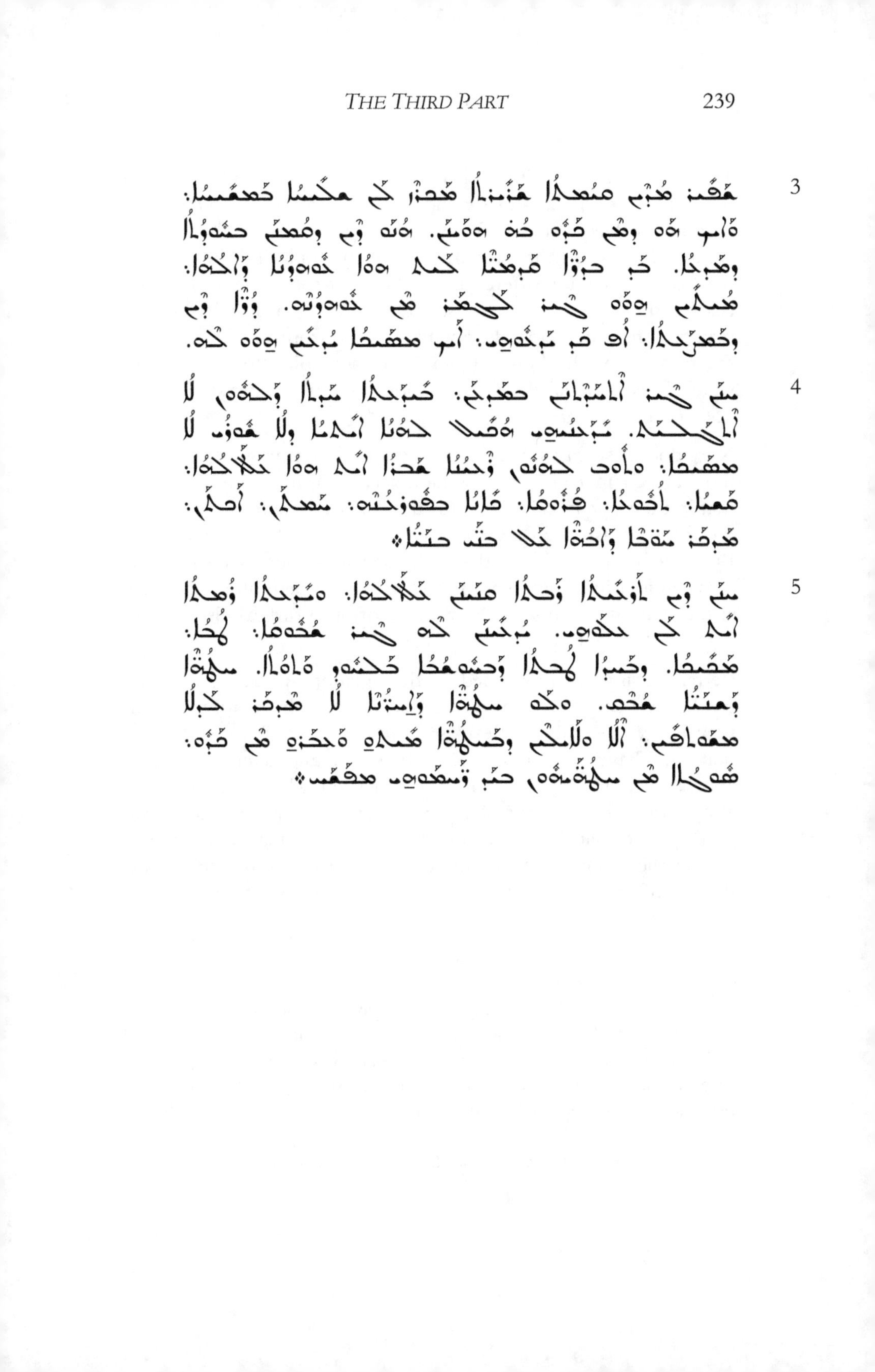

6   There is also the offering which is the best of all for our atonement – swift for the living and for those in the afterlife – which in His wisdom he has prepared for all. The oblation offered up in the Church witnesses to it – the mystery of the body and the blood of the Lord – which is offered in the hope of forgiveness of the deceased, the sinful race of those already departed. But if the dead may no longer be helped by anything, what profit to offer for them the mystery of the body of our Lord, according to the tradition which is held by all the Church: oblation for the departed in the hope of atonement?[10]

7   Now does it seem to you that this tradition is empty or an ignoble thought? Or indeed is it a tradition according to an interpretation: that in the mystery celebrated for the departed, there is the hope of the forgiveness of sins? Or is it profitable only for the righteous? But then what would be the advantage to sinners for whom the oblation is offered, and with it the prayer and petition of the priest at the altar, in which with the sacrifice of our Lord, he also remembers the dead one concerning this hope?

8   Certainly, sinners are assisted by the oblation and it reduces their burden. Whenever it is offered on account of the quantity of sins, they are greatly assisted. Besides, there are those whose fault is not that they have sinned but have shared in ungodliness and have apostatized; or they have blasphemed even while sharing in the <mysteries> of salvation. I think that it is to separate these from participation that the expression is heard, according to church custom at the moment of the mysteries: "And for all the children of the Church who are worthy to receive this oblation before you."[11]

---

[10] Cf. 2 Macc. 12:43–45. See the homily of Jacob of Serug, "On the Memory of the Dead and on the Eucharist," Bedjan, *Homiliae selectae* VI, 535–550. For trans. see Connolly, *Downside Review*. Full title: "On the commemoration of the departed and on the loaf brought for the Eucharist, and that the departed profit from the offerings and the alms that are done in their behalf."

[11] See Vadakkel, *Anaphora of Mar Theodore, Qanona* p.79.

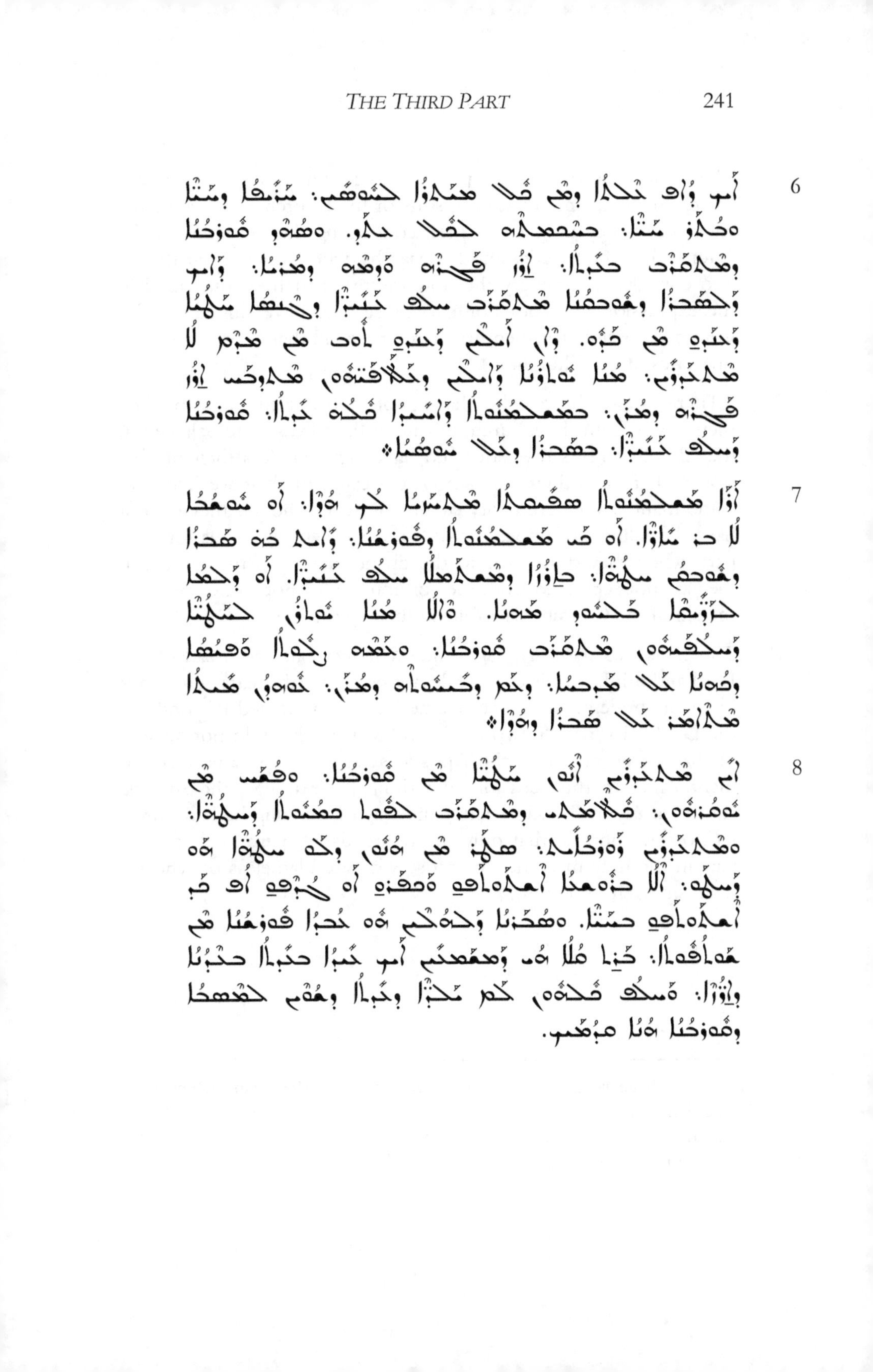

9   This expression does not separate sinners, but those who are not worthy to be counted with the sons of the Church, because of the wickedness they have committed concerning the mysteries of the Church; like the heretics and heresiarchs, who among other things, also consider as ordinary the holy mysteries of the Church.[12] But the expression does not point to those who have sinned, as if it were not possible for them to share in the aid that comes from the mysteries of the Church.

10 <There are> those who have not apostatized or separated themselves from the Church, but in all their lives have believed in the Church and its mysteries and have kept stainless their profession of faith and their baptism. Yet because of their weakness, in some manner they are guilty of sin. But even though they do not have the fullness of hope, as <do> the excellent righteous for their part, when they draw near to the divine Nature in their intellect, they are not separated from the communion of hope in Christ, and the aid of the Church <is> fully in their spirits.

11 This is like what the Apostle said: Whoever eats the bread of the Lord and drinks of his cup, while not being worthy, eats and drinks his own condemnation, because he has not discerned the body of the Lord.[13] In fact, "unworthy" and "worthy" here do not depend on bad or good deeds, the Apostle says, but on mental discernment. And on the occasion of writing these things, the Apostle shows clearly in the same letter the way of thinking he laid down: let no one suppose that only the righteous are permitted to have part in the holy mysteries, or those who are blameless or who remain sincerely repentant.

---

[12] Chialà suggests that Isaac refers here to Messalians which elsewhere he names: Is.I 171, 495; Is.II XIV. 22, 47; *Keph.* IV 31,34. See Hagman, "Isaac of Nineveh and the Messalians."

[13] 1 Cor. 11:27–29.

9 ܀ ܀ ܀ [Syriac text]

10 ܀ ܀ ܀ [Syriac text]

11 ܀ ܀ ܀ [Syriac text]

12 But if it were not so, one must completely cease partaking of the mysteries in the city, since in these places it is difficult to find one occupied about conversion or <even> concerned about things such as these. Those who understand the words of Scripture <implied here> wrongly, relying on their own opinion, do harm not only to themselves but many <others> are led astray by them, since there are many who follow because of the ignorance concerning this apostolic word. But we learn his doctrine from the order of the text.

13 Blessed Paul wrote this discourse to the Corinthians on the holy day of Sunday, when they were gathered in church; that the rich who were among them shared equally with the poor, in the holy mysteries according to the order held to by the Church. But after this, each was sitting down and eating and taking delight in what each had prepared at home. The poor, then, would sit while hungry and looking at the rich who were drinking and enjoying themselves.

14 Blessed Paul heard about this and he wrote to them that while they shared in the nourishment of the mysteries together, as to bodily nourishment, however on their own they judged that the poor are not worthy to share with them. This shows that the ordinary table for them was more important than the table of the mysteries. Paul made known to them that: "If the mystery is considered by you as an ordinary reality such that it does not even seem to be like the ordinary table, well then it is to your condemnation that you eat the bread and drink the chalice of the table of the Lord."[14]

---

[14] Cf. 1 Cor. 11:17–34.

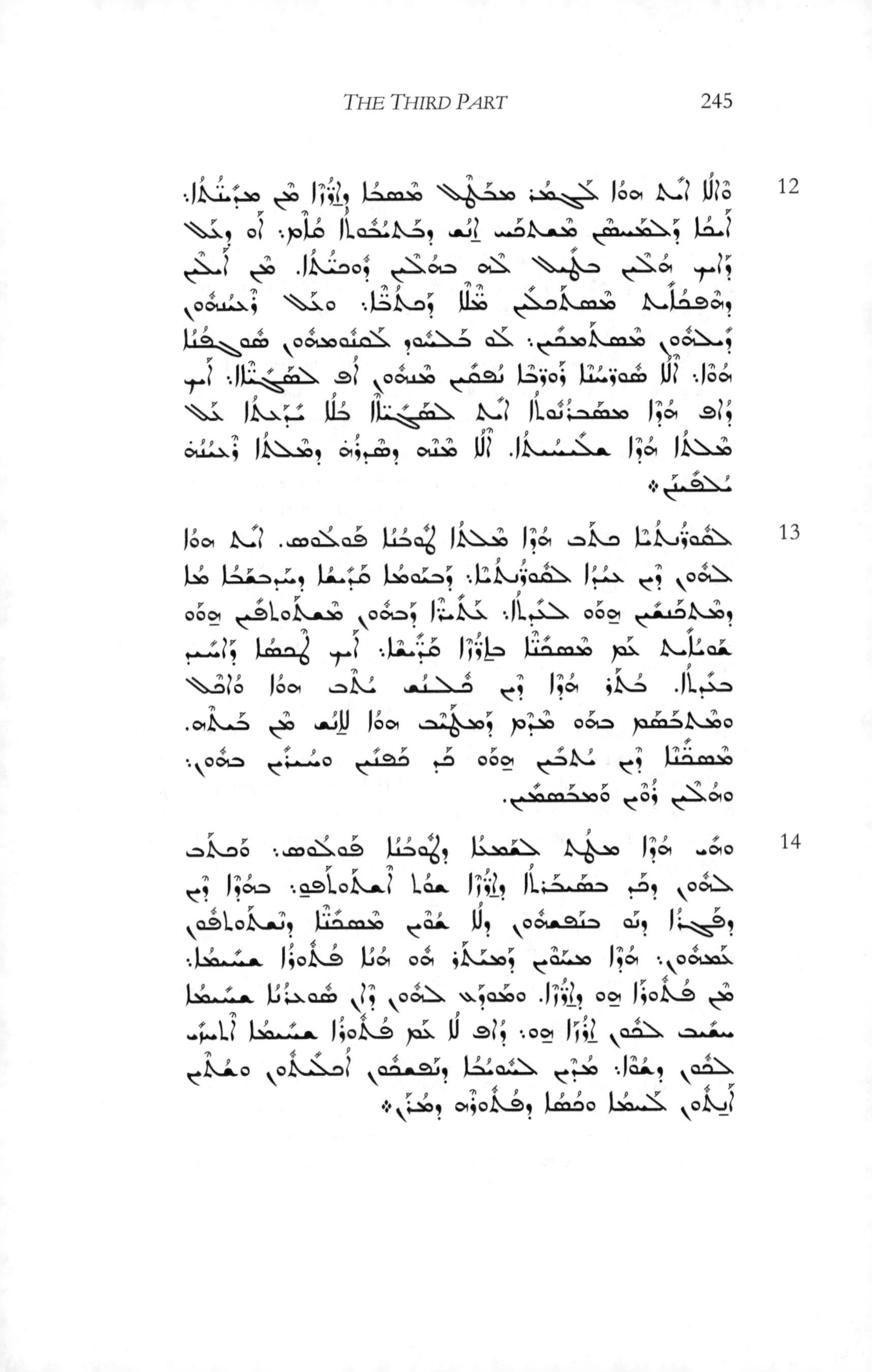

15   Also the blessed Interpreter, in his commentary where he explains the thinking of the Apostle, brings forward and also affirms the things which we have said above. And after having shown its cause, he explains the meaning of Paul's discourse saying: "This is clearly what the Apostle wishes to make known: it is right that the mysteries be offered with a perfect mind and not slackly as if it were ordinary bread;"[15] and at the very end of his discourse, the blessed Interpreter says: "Whoever has perfect faith regarding the mysteries of Christ – for which the Apostle lays out his discourse – I think he is never deprived of the expected good things."[16]

16   You see, O mankind, that the Apostle does not condemn nor declare alien to the blessing expected from the mysteries, those who by their way of life are not worthy, but rather those who are not worthy of the mysteries because of the corruption of their mind. There is great harm for an unprepared mind to rely on its own insight into the word of holy Scripture. Therefore we do not give heed to an imperfect human way of thinking, but I said and I say again and I don't deny: there is help for deceased sinners from the sacrifice of our Lord on their behalf!

17   And if only for the righteous is remembrance to be made, why does the priest also bring to God, in prayer before the altar, the memory of all sinners of Adam's race? I, indeed, do not deny these holy and acceptable sayings, full of redemption, which the priest repeats with great passion near the offerings while inclined before the altar.[17] I am not in error on account of them, nor am I a transgressor.

---

[15] Theodore of Mopsuestia on I Cor. 11: 27–29 not found but see Isho'dad of Merv: Vol. IV, Bk. XVII. p.36.

[16] Cf. Theodore of Mopsuestia 1 Cor. 11:33–34 in PG (Migne) 66, col. 889.

[17] Inclined (*ghîn*) before the altar: in the *Anaphora of Mar Theodore* there are four *gehanta* cycles each including a specific *gehanta* or prayer recited while inclined. The third *gehanta* concentrates on the Economy of Christ and concludes: "…we are gathered together, even we, your humble, weak and miserable servants, that by the permission of your grace we may celebrate this great, respectful, holy and divine mystery wherein is

---

realized the great salvation for the whole race of mankind." See Vadakkel, *Anaphora*, text 56, p. 87.

18 Nor do I regard it burdensome to put the *sedra* in this place, that everyone might know the power which is in the mysteries of the body of Christ; so as to send the help of grace even to the dead, that the bright lights of its strength might descend even to Sheol. Let it be known to those who are ignorant, that not one of the mysteries set by the holy Church, was set and confirmed unadvisedly or by chance.

19 But all of these <mysteries> are full of hope, and great discernment is hidden in them for those who fulfill them. How great is the power of faith and how exalted the knowledge of Christians and what intelligence they have of God! We believe in fact that the power of the mysteries of the Economy of the Only-Begotten is able to give absolution even to the dead, and even in Sheol to help those who believed in it during their lives. From this, those who concerning the resurrection hold that such hope is also for their deceased, have received instruction and with great faith make petition for this and ask absolution also for the dead.

20 And as if it were already indeed a reality placed in his hands, the priest with undivided faith presents the offering, and makes petition to God in the remembrance of the sacrifice of Christ for the pardon of sinners, living and deceased, so that they might be purified: the living by receiving <the sacrifice> and the dead by the remembrance on their account. For the priest says without hesitation: "Thus, our Lord and our God, accept from us according to your grace, this sacrifice of praise which is the reasonable fruit of our lips."

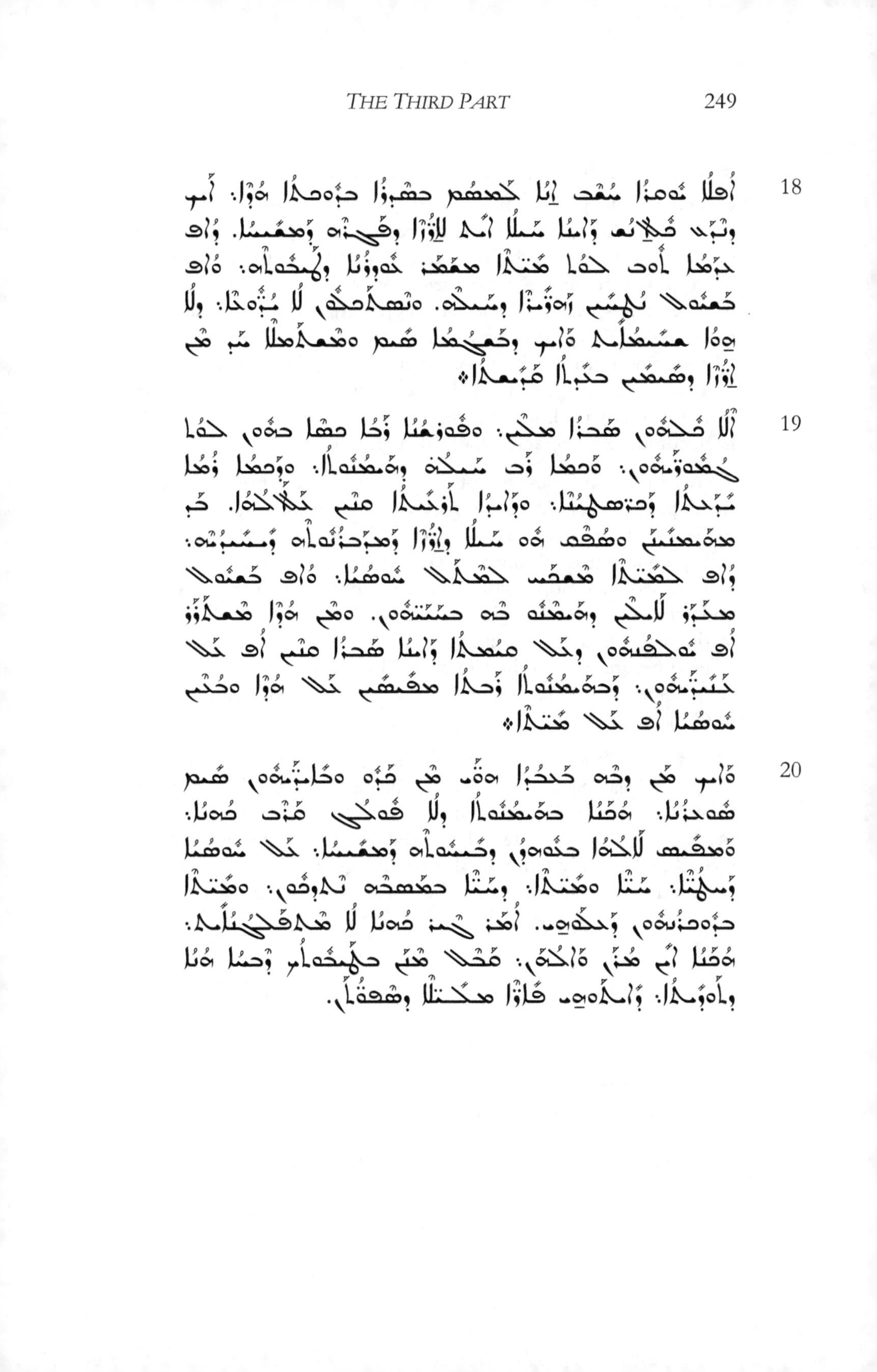

21   Why? He says: "That before you there might be a memorial of the righteous of former <times>, of the holy prophets, of the blessed apostles, of the martyrs, of the confessors, etc."; furthermore: "and of all the sons of the holy Church who have departed from this world in the true faith."[18] You see how he describes the word faith: he does not speak of those who departed without sins and who have passed from this world in righteousness. Rather he says: "Those who in their faith have departed from this world and cleave to your grace, my Lord, pardon all their sins and transgressions which in this world, in a mortal body and in a mutable soul, they have committed and acted foolishly before you."[19]

22   You see that the priest is not ashamed to speak about the sins of the departed and ask pardon of God. You heard how he presents to God this powerful request, without hesitation at a forceful moment, while not doubting that God holds this in reverence. Have you learned what hope is placed in the Church of Christ? Have you understood the way God has taught mankind, and how He has put in them the faith concerning His will, which is set in prayer and offered before Him in the Church? Why do you consider this prayer as bold? Are you lacking in faith? Or are you indeed an adversary of God's will?

23   That there is some means which God offers, the Holy Spirit has taught by placing in the Church, through intercession, the great power of Christianity and God's gladness for our earthly nature. All the will of God is externally revealed, in a symbolic way,[20] by means of His holy Church. But the haughty and the ignorant do not want to believe in the mystery of His good will for our race.

---

[18] Fourth *gehanta*, Vadakkel, *Anaphora*, text 70–71, p. 90.
[19] Fourth *gehanta*, Vadakkel, *Anaphora*, text 77, p. 91.
[20] In a symbolic way: from *remzâ*; cf. Is.II IX.6, XXXIII.2.

21 ܠܥܘܢܐ: ܘܡܢ ܟܠ ܡܕܡ ܕܐܕܢܐ ܚܪܘܦܐ ܡܒܚܢܐ. ܘܡܢ ܟܠ ܡܕܡ ܘܡܢ ܟܠ ܡܕܡ ܘܡܢ ܟܠ ܡܕܡ ܘܡܢ ܟܠ ܡܕܡ.

22 ܡܐ ܐܝܟ ܘܠܐ ܐܝܟ ܘܠܐ ܐܝܟ ܘܠܐ ܐܝܟ ܘܠܐ ܐܝܟ ܘܠܐ ܐܝܟ ܘܠܐ ܐܝܟ.

23 ܘܗܕܐ ܘܐܝܟ ܘܐܝܟ ܘܐܝܟ ܘܐܝܟ ܘܐܝܟ ܘܐܝܟ ܘܐܝܟ ܘܐܝܟ.

24   Let it not be that we doubt, my beloved, concerning these verses full of holy things about God. Being in accord with the will of God, they are placed with the thanksgiving for the mysteries set by the Church, and with the holy divine things. As such, God the Lord of all is especially pleased, and because of this, <the verses> are placed with the mystical words of the sacrifices of revelation. Let it not be that we deny the word or the meaning concerning the power of this perfect and divine prayer, which is full of hope for all mankind.

25   I have not written these things so that relying <on them> you become remiss but in order for you to grow strong in your hope. Thus may your mind grow <continuously> in God and the future ways increase in your soul, while earthly things be despised in your eyes. May your mind be filled with wonder at God,[21] and the fire of His love shine in your soul while it proceeds in meditation on the insights of His mysteries, towards the place which is above the world.

26   However it is not right because of fear of being slack to hide or to diminish understanding of the mysteries of our worship, or to deny the power of the confession of the marvelous Economy on our account. Nor should fear make us cease from marveling at God, nor from giving glory with incomparable joy. If someone believes that being without faith and knowledge is able to be more helpful, let him earnestly take pains with this for his <own> soul.

---

[21] Wonder at God (*tehrâ db-alâhâ*): Is.I 304–05, 376, 492; Is.II XX.10–11, XXI.7; *Keph*. I 36, II 55, 89, IV 47.

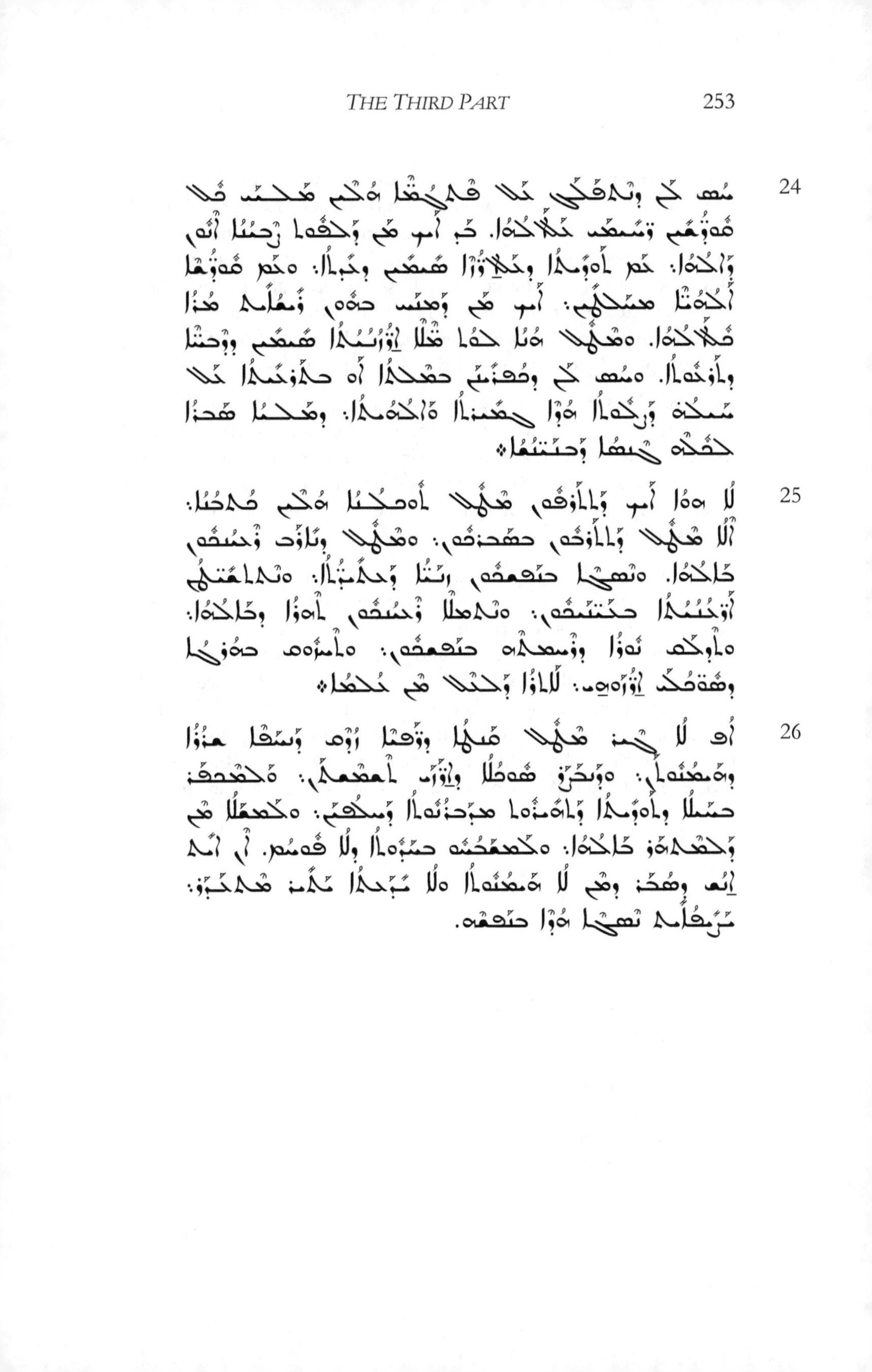

27 But we are saved by faith! And by it we are moved and regenerated to immortal and *true life*,[22] while we marvel at God's mercy, how He has arranged everything for our benefit, by that salutary wisdom towards our sinful race. He it is who has openly revealed the accomplishment of all the good of His will, eternal and mysterious, by means of the Economy of Christ, our Lord. He appointed for us an incorruptible advocate: the body and blood of our Savior; He who is not guilty of any one of the sins of creatures.

28 Let it not be <thought> that I am defending sin! However, I lift up the power of the advocate of sinners who is in heaven![23] And I make manifest the great hope within the liturgy for Him which the Church fulfills, more excellent than the word or the power of creatures. The knowledge of our <human> race is not able now to possess or draw near to the whole truth about its hope.

29 And not without inquiry, I endeavor to show the effect of sin while I myself marvel at God's wisdom. I am amazed at this Economy of Christ and at the power of His mysteries, while with this insight, I approach <in> amazement[24] and I turn to silence. How <the Economy> is full of salvation for mankind![25] Because of this Economy, a *multitude of sins* is pardoned[26] by means of the sacrifice of the body of Jesus[27] offered for them. And not only, but because of the sacrifice, the judgment concerning them will be merciful. Not even one ten-thousand of what <punishment> they are worthy of will be required.

---

[22] Cf. 1 Tim. 6:19.
[23] 1 Jn 2:1.
[24] Amazement (*temhâ*).
[25] Cf. 1 Tm. 2:4.
[26] Cf. 1 Pt. 4:8.
[27] Cf. Heb. 10:10.

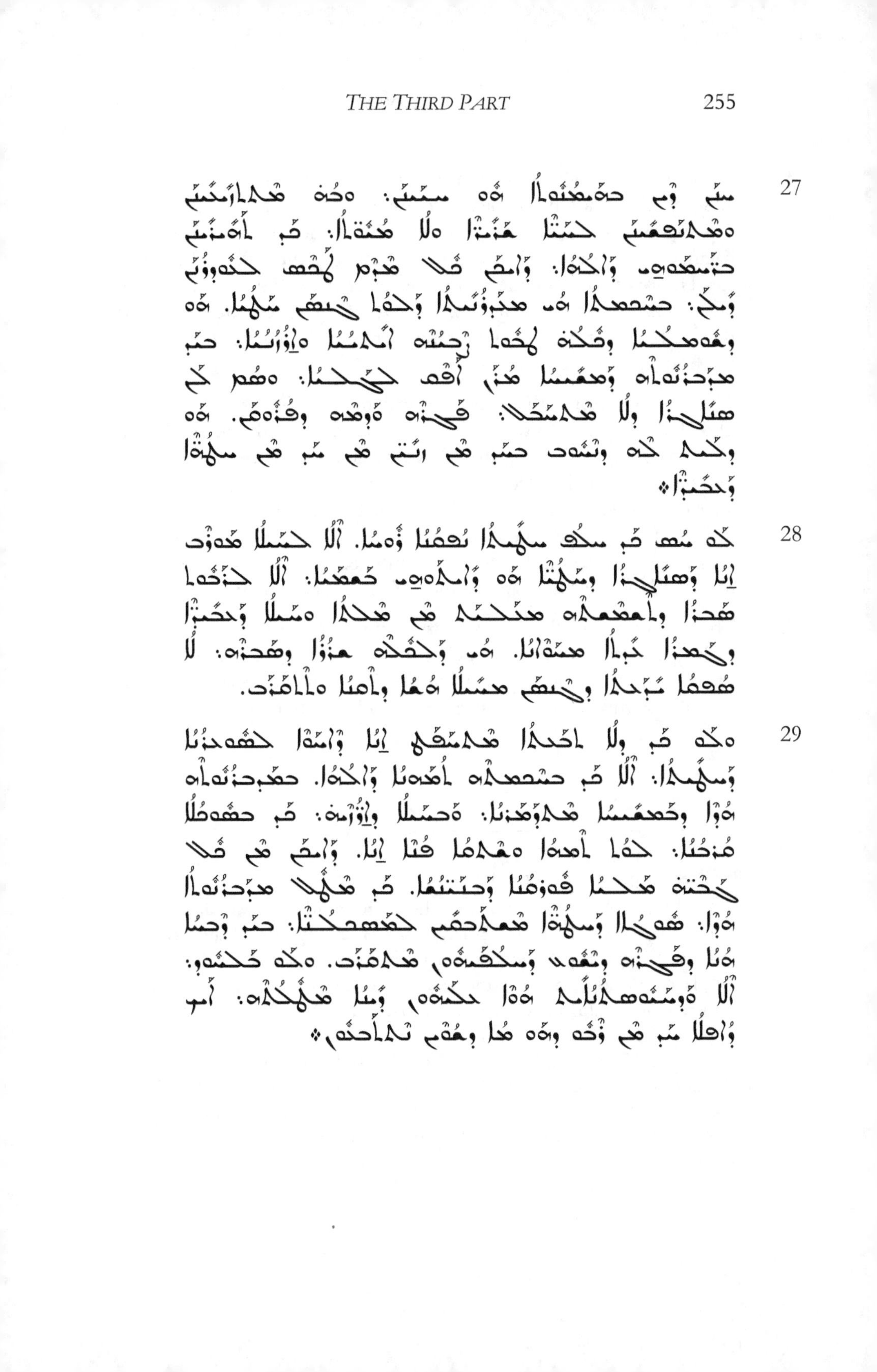

30 Perhaps those whose sins are very few and of slight quality, <God> does not hold them accountable. Even for those whose sins are of a great number, He diminishes the torments from the balance sheet for a reason centrally placed by the will of the Creator. He loves to show mercy by means of that One whom *God has predetermined for atonement by faith in his blood*.[28] But few are worthy of this faith and of the understanding of the mysteries, in the hope of the body and blood of Jesus.

31 This is therefore the true resurrection which <occurs> by knowledge, by an assured faith and the renewal of the mind. Those who were baptized in Christ[29] have received it in the hope of the *future world*.[30] The blessed Paul says: *<Christ> raised us up and made us ascend and sit with him in heaven*. Whoever has entered the thick darkness[31] of the knowledge of faith and has known the power of its mysteries, is always in heaven in his intellect, and sits with Christ by means of the continual appearance of His marvelous Economy.

32 This Economy in all its parts is often in the mysteries which are full of hope, to signify that our belief in the *knowledge of truth*[32] is a gift of God. Those who are pleasing to God believe because of Him and not by the power of nature or the will and human discipline.

---

[28] Cf. Rom. 3:25.

[29] Cf. Rom. 6:3; Gal. 3:27.

[30] Cf. Heb. 2:5; 6:5; hope of the future world (*sabrâ d-ʿâlmâ da-tîd*): Is.I 41, *Keph.* IV 78. In John Sol. *Soul* see *sabrâ da-ʿtîdâtâ*, 21 and *sabrâ da-ʿtîd*, 73. All who have written about John Sol. have noted the importance he places on hope; hope in the world to come for him is based on the resurrection of Christ and the grace of baptism.

[31] Cf. Ex.20:21.

[32] Cf. 1Tim. 2:4; 2 Tim. 3:7; Heb. 10:26. Knowledge of truth (*îdaʿtâ da-šrârâ*): Is.I 430, 494. Is.II VIII.1; IX title, 2, 4; X.15,16; XIII.1; XIV.33, 34; XXV title; XXXV.5; XXXVII.3, 4. It is common in Evag., see Cent. I.14, 52, 89; II.10, 19. See also Theodore of Mopsuestia, Vadakkel, *Anaphora*, text 70, p. 89.

THE THIRD PART

33   Who is able to receive the fountain of His mysteries? That one before whom is opened an entrance to its intuitions, which like a fountain springs up and flows for the delight of his soul, and which always finds new things in the treasure of his mind![33] This is what was said by our Savior: *The one who believes in me, as the Scriptures said, streams of living waters will flow from within him.*[34] To Him be glory for ever and ever. Amen.

34   The end of the *memra* on the holy mysteries of our Savior, composed by blessed Mar Isaac, solitary and orthodox,[35] who was bishop of the city of Nineveh.

---

[33] Cf. Mt. 13:52.

[34] John 7:38.

[35] According to Chialà it may have been a copyist who mentions Isaac's orthodoxy, or one of his disciples, given the insistence in this chapter on prayer for the dead and how God pardons the sins of the deceased in His mercy and the possible polemical interpretation of this. But elsewhere Isaac gives a similar assurance of his own orthodoxy, see Is.I 127; Is.II XXXIX.7.

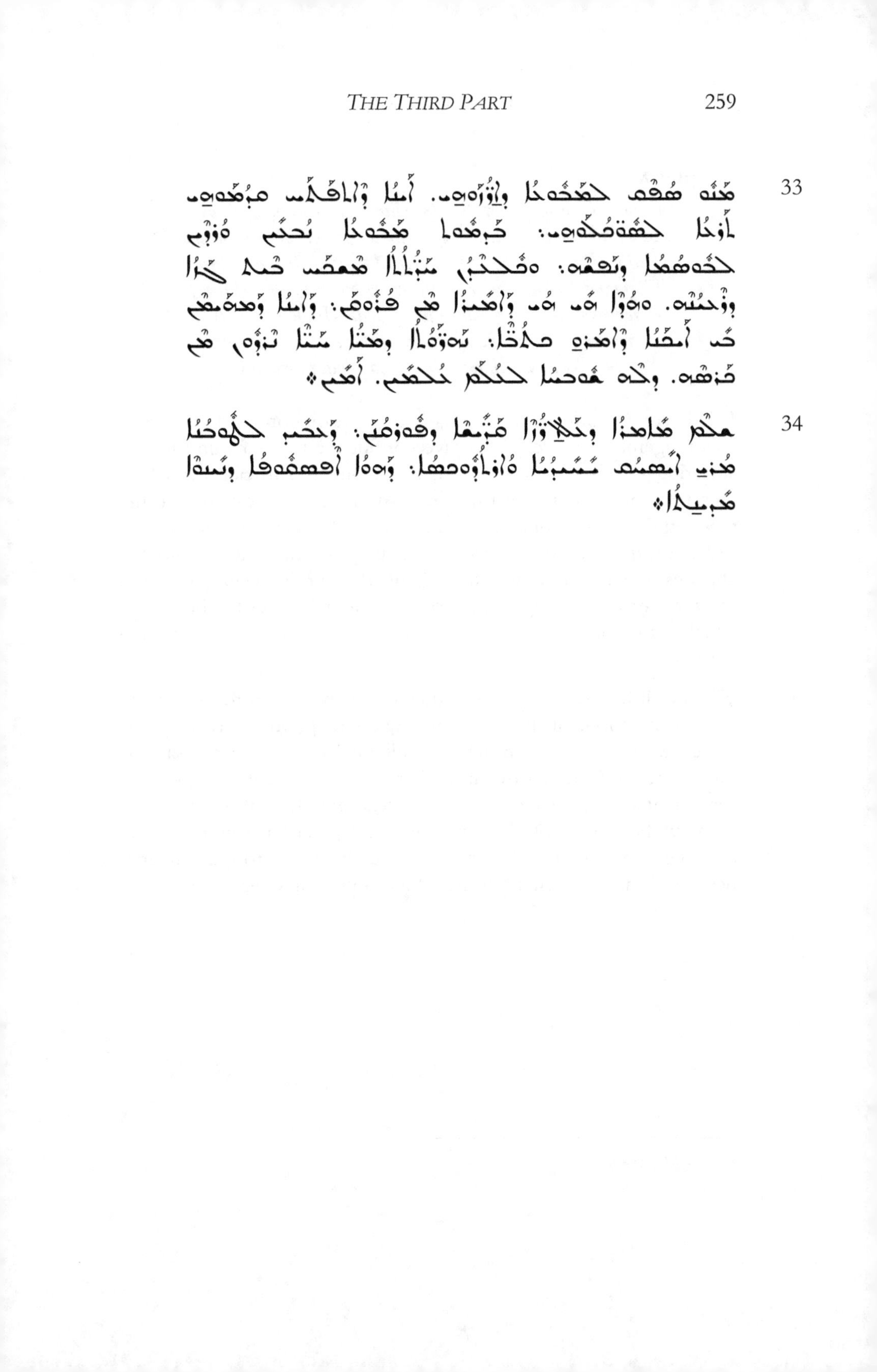

Chapter XII

Again, a letter of exhortation by Mar Isaac concerning <how> solitary life can be affected <when lived> in the midst of others, which was sent to a monk who desired to be assured about this. The monk had written him concerning his thoughts, asking if there was in them any blame from God. <Isaac> exhorts to surrender oneself to the afflictions of this life, with a prompt intelligence which examines God's hidden reasons.

1. I believe, O our brother, that for consolation and for your encouragement, as well as to give confidence to your mind in this suffering which has seized you, this alone is sufficient which is manifest and clear to all: that since antiquity and from before the many initial generations, there is this way of solitary life and of the migration from human company, for the peace of mind of whoever chooses it. This continues and is handed down in every generation by whoever wishes to give rest to the mind, whatever be the reason which summons and sets in motion one's exodus <from the world>.

2. Whether it be the adversities and evils which happen to humans in every generation, or an excellent request or good desire which is stirred within them by means of undivided faith – what is said by our Lord, the Christ, arises in their mind about what is impossible for humans but possible for God.[1] Because, indeed, it is certain for them, without a doubt, that by complete separation from the world and migration to God, they may receive liberation from all adversities and find the excellent desire which is in their souls.

---

[1] Mt. 19:26.

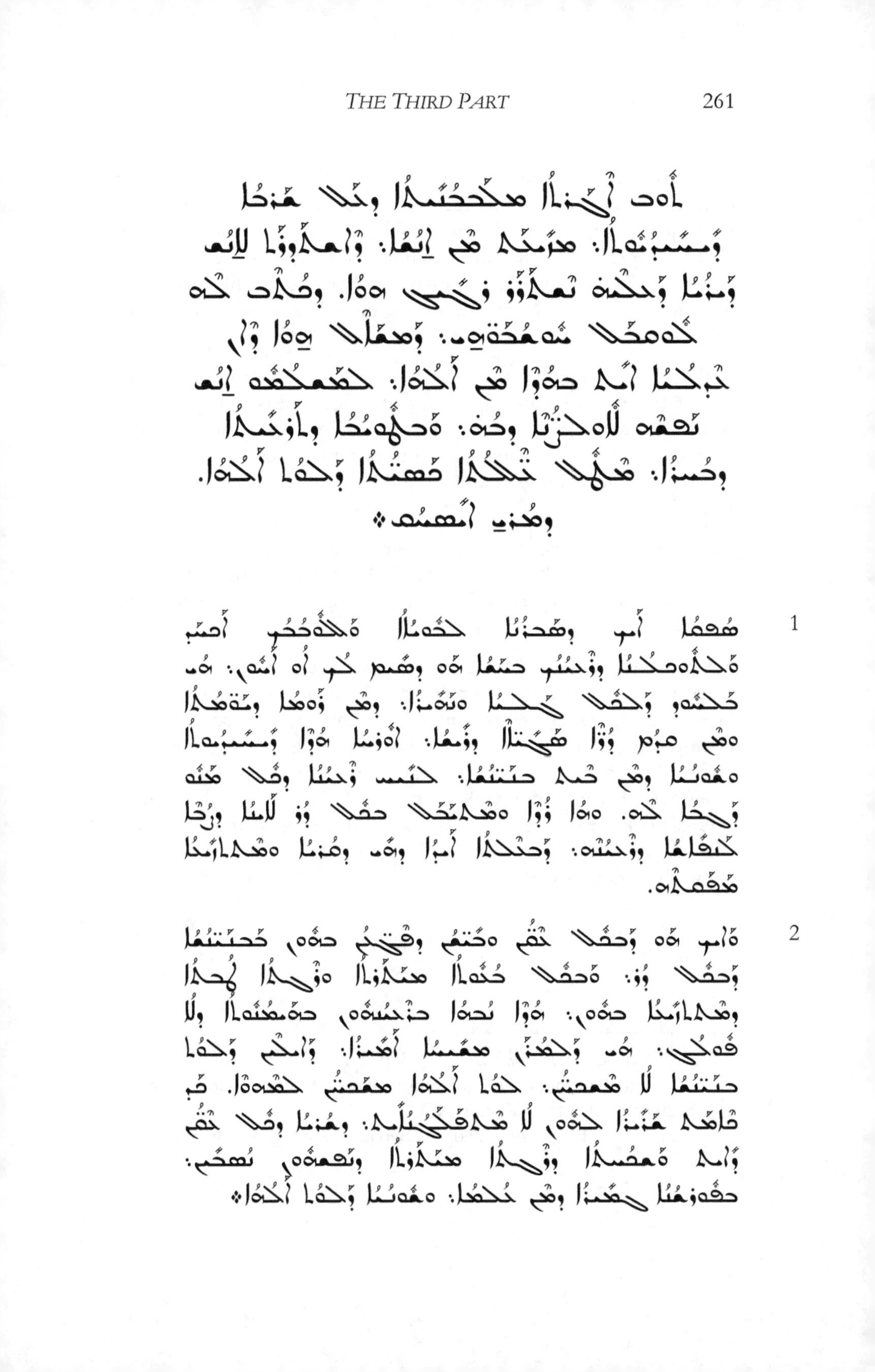

3   We also may see from the description of their accounts, how different and dissimilar was the exodus of each one of them. And the object of their thinking was not the same for all those holy ones in their migration from human habitation. Even the cause of exodus was not the same for all of them. Because of this, each one may find a model and a mirror among the things which occurred in the past in those who were called to this way of life.[2]

4   If the cause of migration be from sadness or adversities, or from joy, or from zeal, or love, or fear, or passion and compunction, or from afflictions brought on by others, etc.; or if migration occurs through a sense of righteousness or for repentance on account of sins. All of these things one may find in those who have gone before us.

5   For various causes, indeed, persons have abandoned human contact and have followed after God. They have surrendered their souls to death. They have been made worthy of the mercy and providence of God and have been received by grace.

6   Some have <followed after God> because of the distress of persecution for the faith, or fear of human wickedness, as the blessed Paul, first of the solitaries, who entrusted his soul to God and despising himself went out without clothing.[3] Some have acted out of fervor for God or by zealous thoughts, like the blessed Onesima. She went out with even less clothing, she did not take even a cloak for her body, but she went out stripped and barefoot.[4] Many others have been seen <to live> in this way, as the accounts about them demonstrate.

---

[2] Cf. Nilus, *Discorso sulle osservanze* 3, p. 78.

[3] Paul the Hermit, his life by Jerome may be found in Budge, *Paradise* I, 197–203. See also Is.I 560; Is.II XIV.21.

[4] Hermit in Egypt, recorded in a Syriac *Vita* edited by Bedjan, *AMS* V, 405–421.

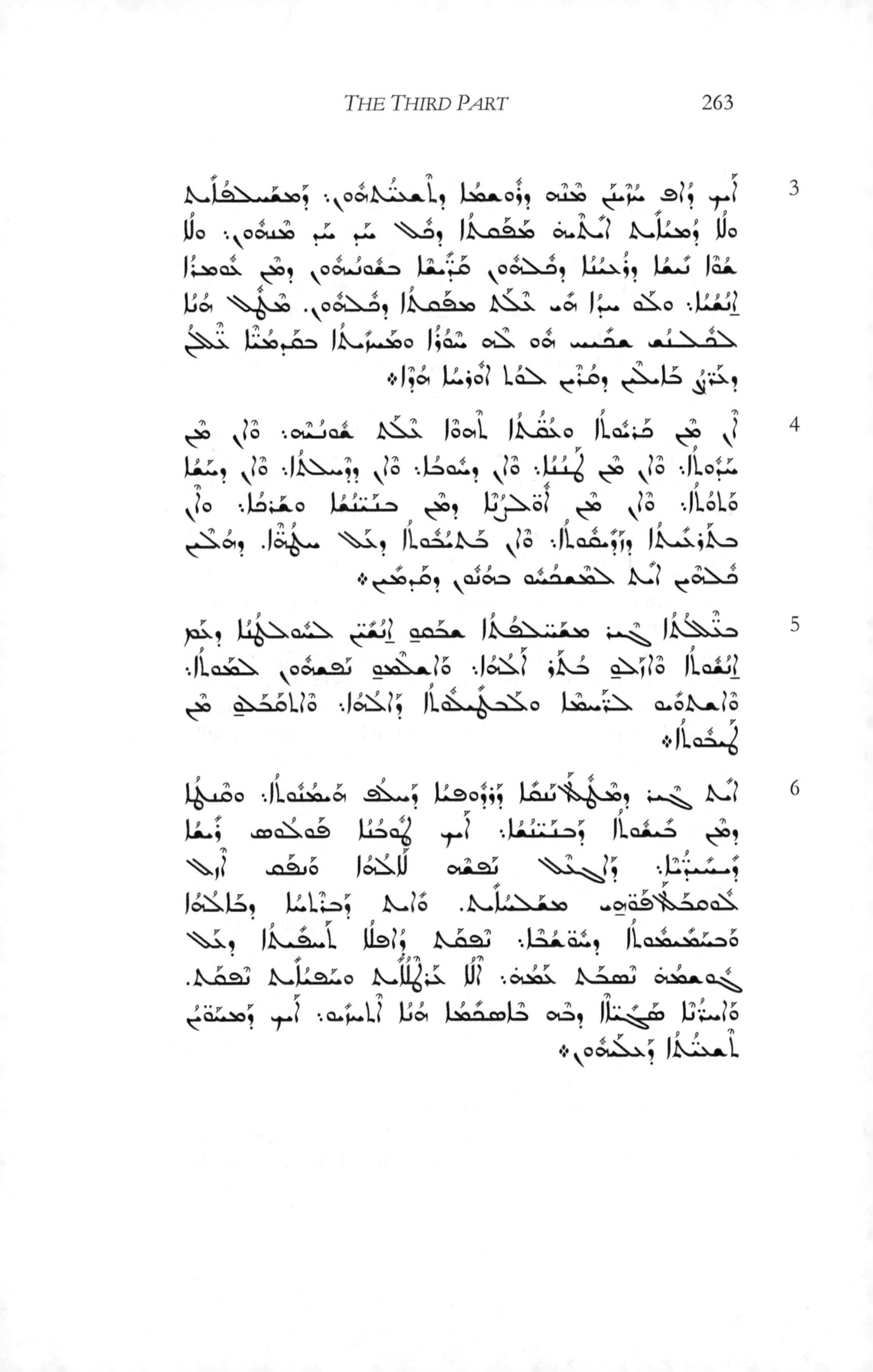

7   Again there are those who, weary of the world, because of the treachery and deceit they found in those who dwell there, have left it and moved on, such as those two brothers, sons of a governor, whom Serapion saw in the desert. When they were asked by him the reason for coming to this harsh place and for enduring for a long time near bitter waters, they said that their father had left them great riches when he died of which many friends and loved ones profited. But when the riches were spent, they all changed and became enemies instead of friends.

8   They added: "While seeing the deceitfulness and cunning of the world and that love there was not true nor desire for God enduring, only serving the times, and friendship there changed with the circumstances – in fact only one in a thousand, loves because of God – we have chosen to go out and to be with God: He who stands by His love for His friends and His love does not change."[5]

9   There are others who because of fear of falling, and the deceit of Satan's ways by means of a woman, have abandoned being near habitation and have gone out to a remote desert, so as not to lose the purity of their bodies. For example, holy Martinianus, having separated from the snare of a woman, burned his feet and departed to an island in the midst of the ocean where there was stillness and no humans at all.[6]

---

[5] Concerns Serapion, Bedjan, *AMS* V, 320–21. See also Is.I 554.
[6] On Martinianus, see Budge, *Paradise* II, 300–02. And see Is.I 554.

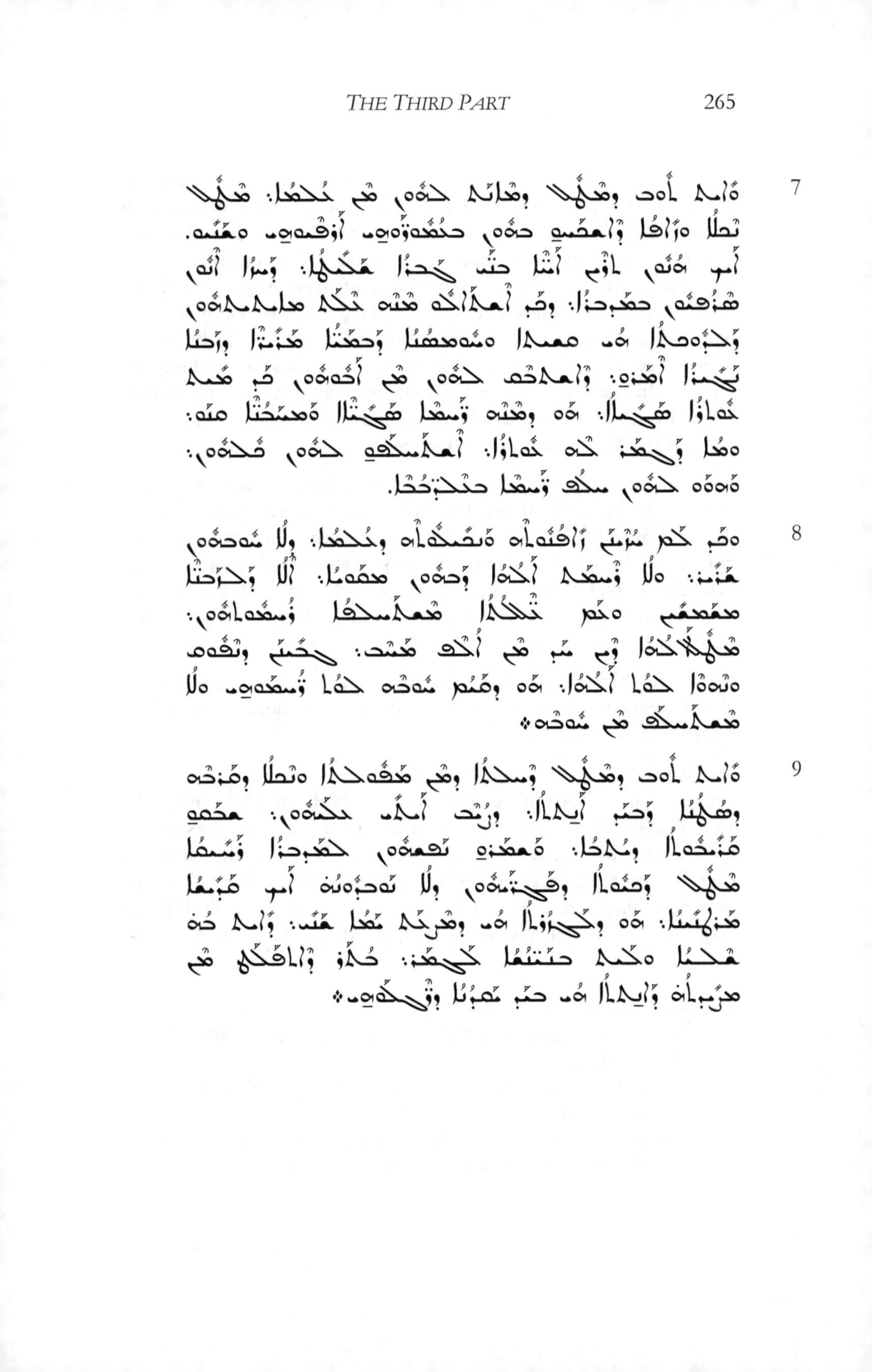

10   There is also <the story of> blessed Carpus, whom holy Serapion saw on the top of a mountain, in a remote desert with a little fenced celery garden. He was deceived by Satan by means of the wife of the governor, his friend, who frequently went up to his cell to see him. But one day, at the working of Satan, she gazed at him lustfully, etc. With these occasions, and again for other things with which Satan defiled his thought by an obscene vision in his imagination because of being near habitation, and lest something unpleasant happen to him, he left that place and moved to another. There he lacked most material necessities, befitting a meager existence, as the little celery garden indicates.[7]

11   Some have risen up from a life of ruin but because of great fear of future judgment, or on account of having repented <only> a few days before dying, they have gone forth with little hope of salvation. They thought it not even right to be shown salvation and they held themselves in contempt. Such was the case of that solitary who fell into sin with a virgin for six months, but his affliction was transformed by an angel.[8]

12   Or like the bishop who had apostatized and went out to the desert in repentance. These went out without any bodily provisions, thinking to be close to death.

13   Or like James the *gyrovague*[9] who fell into sin. He committed adultery, also killed and even threw the body into the river. But after all these things, he went out strengthened by a divine sign and dwelt in a tomb for ten years. Indeed, like Adam,[10] with a broken heart he went into that cave which became a tomb. All which happened to him is revealed in his account that also clearly informs how his nourishment was vegetarian, like for animals, twice a week.

---

[7] Chialà links Carpus with Polycarp in Bedjan, *AMS* V, 322–27.

[8] Cf. Is.I 553.

[9] James the *gyrovague*, information on his life available but unedited, see Is.III XII.13 (*CSCO*).

[10] Adam, used in an adverbial way perhaps to indicate human weakness, or in this case, nudity as alluded to in Is.III XII.6.

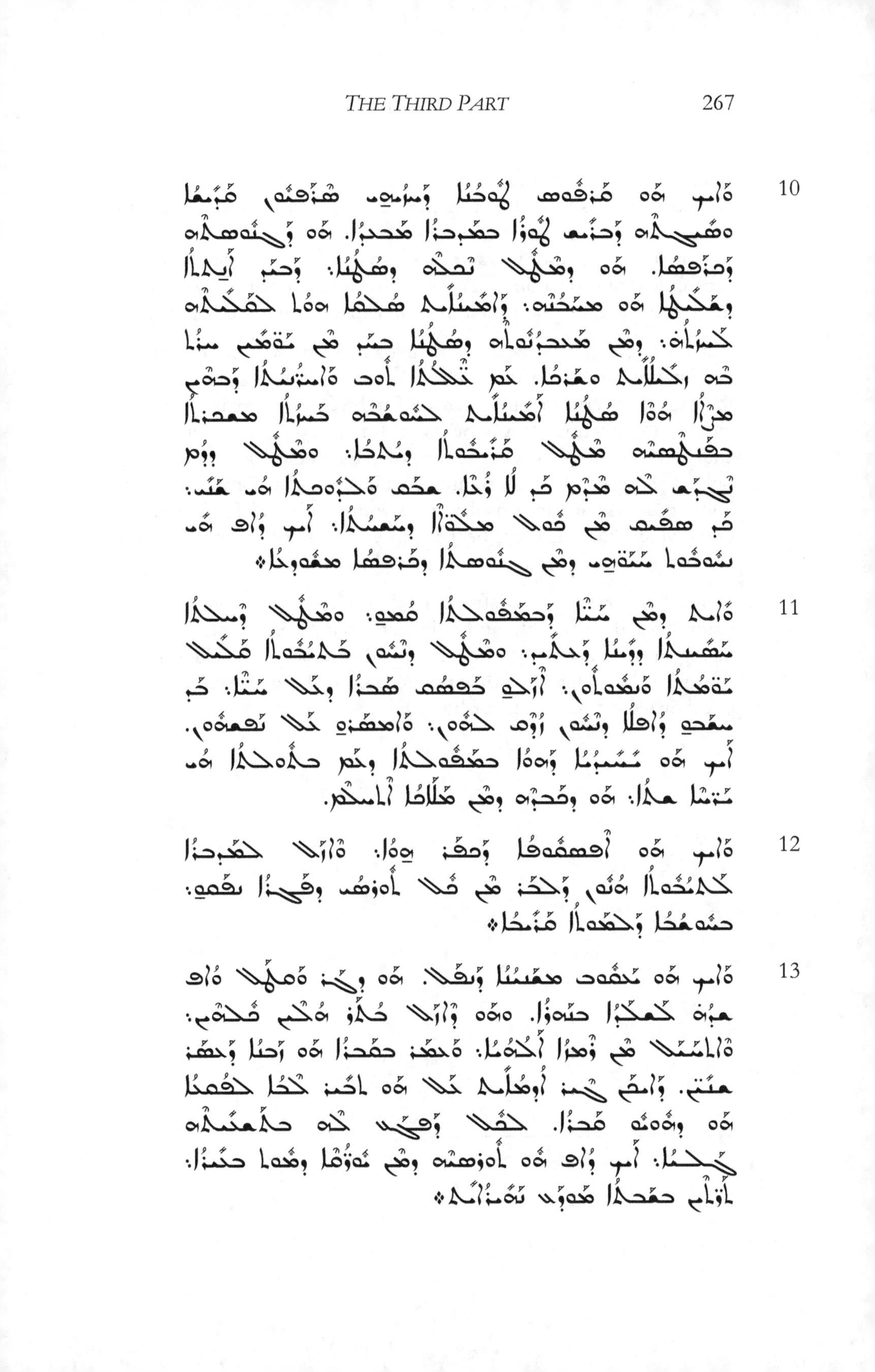

14   There are other causes such as these, for which many saints separated themselves from mankind and went to deserts and mountains without any provisions. And they gathered together in mountain caves, and in ravines or even in gorges of terrifying depth, without planning or being solicitous for life.[11] But they dwelt there and let go of their lives, in expectation of certain death.

15   If you wish, also you may become like one of these: follow the path in imitation and keep the cause of your exodus in your mind. If they acted in fervor or by a sense of righteousness; or if by suffering or compunction, or in repentance for sins; or if they were afraid and fled, mortified, lest the purity of their bodies be defiled: may one of these be your consolation, whichever is according to your intention. Take it for consolation at your death and for the afflictions which happen then, because in your way of life you are not alone among your kind.

16   I said these things to satisfy your mind. How for various reasons, many have despised life and delivered themselves to death, while taking on the thought <of death>, and choosing a dwelling place fit for his. Not only were they not accused by God on this account, but they were also made worthy of His great providence.

---

[11] Cf. Heb. 11:38.

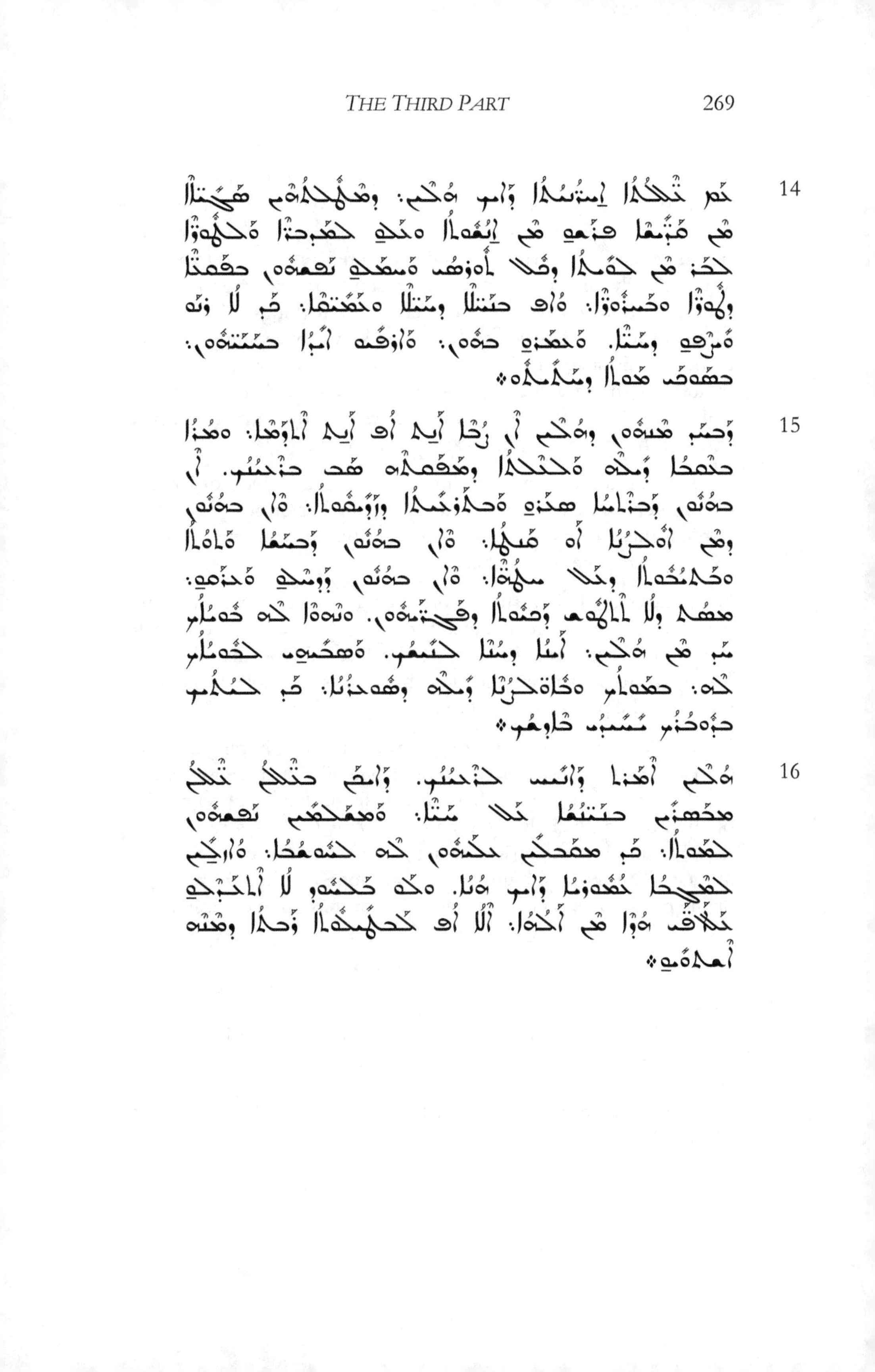

17 Remember that youth in a certain city, who had committed many sins and a great number of grievous evil deeds. He was mentioned by blessed John in his account or by its compiler: "This one, at a sign from God concerning his sins, repented and moved to a cemetery." Clearly, he was without provisions or whatever might be necessary, but was not preoccupied by such things. He remained like this for a whole week and persevered with weeping and lamentation for his sins, without any remembrance or concern for food. In addition, he received harsh torments from the demons for three nights, one after another, without any care or thought at all whether or not he would live, nor was he afraid of death.[12]

18 If you so desire, you may become like him in this. Do not let Satan cast you down in anxiety or care, as to whether or not you will die. Behold, these icons of all the types are before you: may you be a willing martyr like one of them.[13]

19 Nevertheless, this is assured: the word is true that whoever takes on the afflictions of repentance preparing his soul <to suffer> for what is excellent, and because of the fear of God introduces his soul to pains and temptations – this one is not able to be abandoned by the providence of God.

20 In faith, keep going forward on the way of virtue, hoping always in God's salvation, lest you be reproached like that people whose heart is blind. Because of their lack of faith, they were reproached by the Prophet, namely: *They did not believe in God nor hope in His salvation.*[14] Although seeing His wonders daily and His cares for them, in their mind they were utterly without hope in Him. Despairing of divine providence is clearly Satan's way of mastering the mind.

---

[12] This concerns John of Lycopolis (John of the Thebaid), late 4th cent. The episode is found in Budge, *Paradise* I, 327–28. See also Is.I 152, 568.

[13] On ascetical life as a martyrdom, see Is.I 31, 209, 242, 436, 456–57; *Keph.* I 53.

[14] Ps. 78:22.

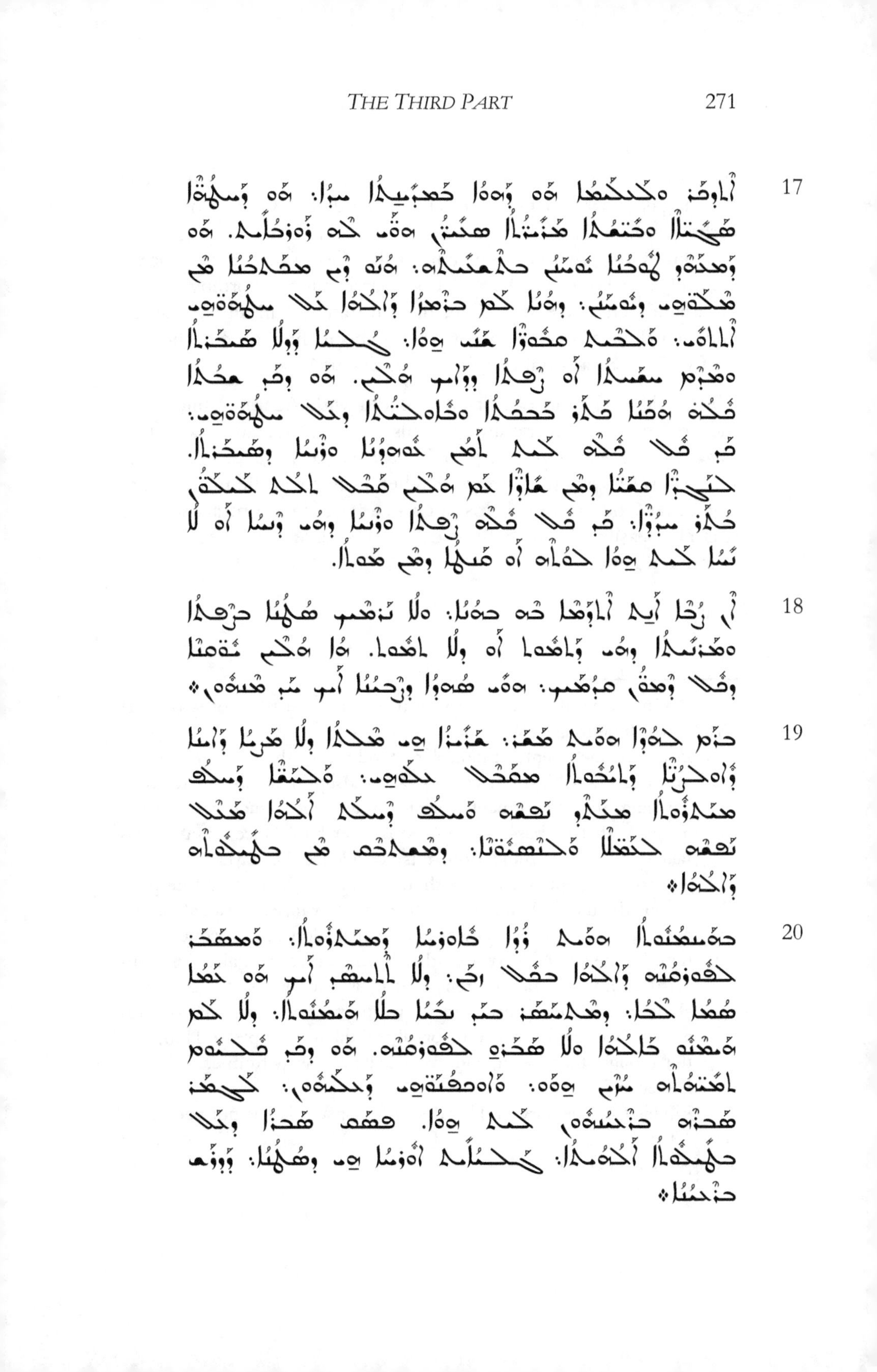

21 As also blessed Theodore says in his Commentary on Matthew: "Satan takes care to persuade all mankind that God is not concerned about them. Because he knows, indeed, that as long as we truly know this, that is to say, concerning God's providence for us, we will love Him and we will do what is right according to His commandments. We will, then, have no anxiety in all adversities, and we will be anxious only for virtue. This is the thought – he says – of which <Satan> takes pains to deprive us.[15]

22 Thus, said <Theodore>, Satan also did with Adam. While God, indeed, managed everything for his benefit, <Satan> said: *God knows that the day in which you eat of it, your eyes will be opened and you will be like God, knowing good and evil.*[16] When in this way, he made Adam think that God not only helps but also advises in a contrary way, he was able easily <to do> his work to dissuade from keeping the commandment.[17]

---

[15] On the work of Satan to destroy trust, see the words of Is.II VII.21, worth quoting:

> For someone to entrust himself to God means that, from that point onwards, he will no longer be swallowed up in anguish or fearover anything, (or) be tormented again by a thought such as when he imagines that he has no one to look after him. Once a person has fallen away in his mind from this confidence, he starts falling into myriads of temptations in his thoughts, just as the blessed Interpreter says in the Volume on Matthew the Evangelist: Satan's entire concern is this, to persuade a person that God has no concern for him. For he knows (very well) that as long as we recognize this (concern) clearly, and (an awareness of it) is fixed in us, our souls will abide in complete peace, and we will furthermore, acquire love towards (God) and a concern for all the things that please Him; it is this thought that (Satan) endeavors to snatch away from us.

[16] Gen. 3:5.

[17] This Commentary of Theodore of Mopsuestia has not been conserved. Chialà suggests a possible reference to Mt. 4.1–11, cf. Is.I 418; and see again Is.II VIII.21.

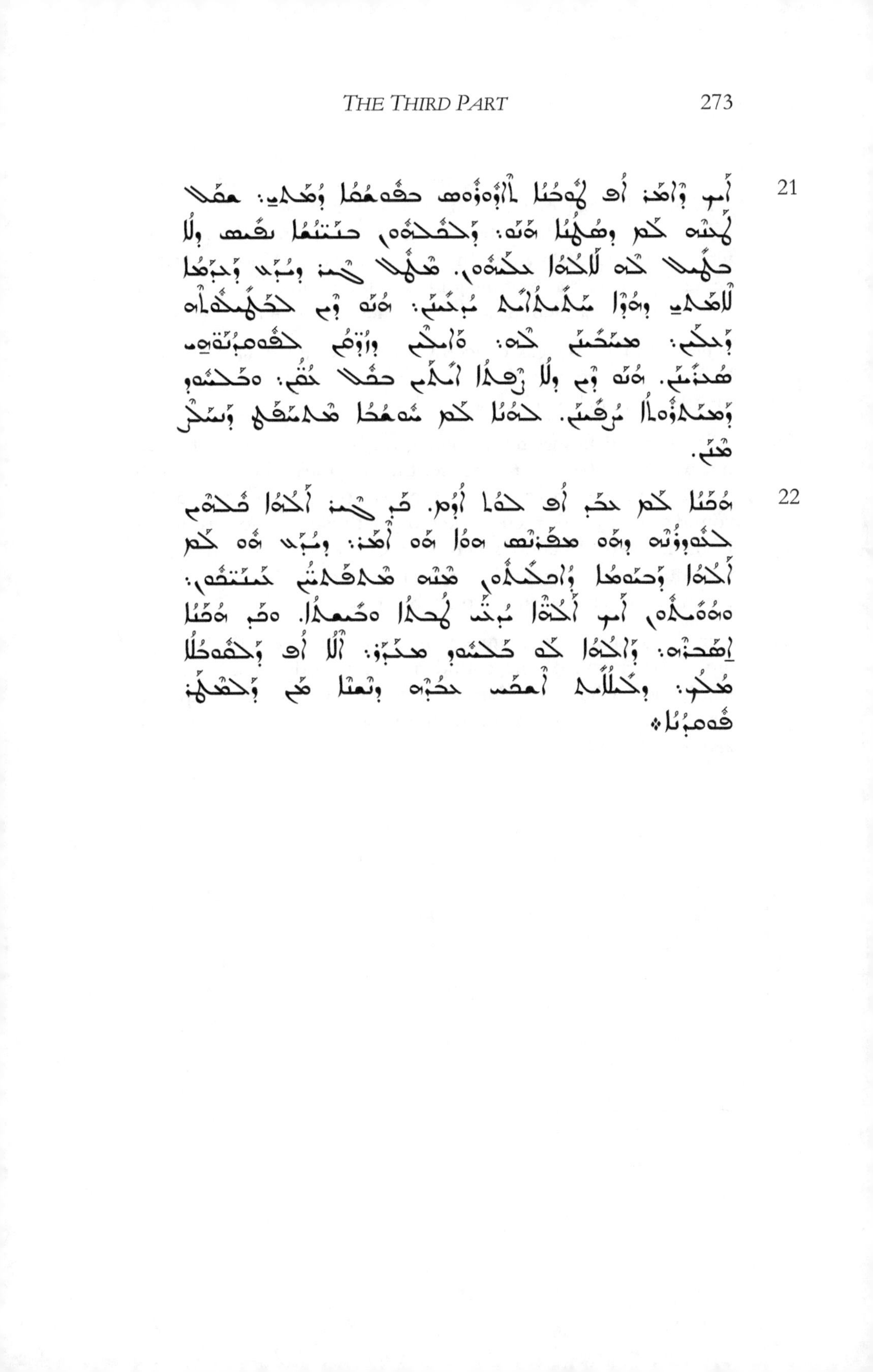

23 But you, therefore, do not be with God in a Jewish way of thinking, like that people, nor childishly like Adam. But let faith adhere to you, which on the way of virtue, generates hope in every temptation and affliction. In this way you will not be without strength, fearful and trembling in your mind, on the way of repentance and in the afflictions and adversities on account of virtue.

24 Whoever's faith is weak concerning God's care for him, will always be wretched and fearful in his mind. And this drives away from him the great riches of virtue.

25 It is right and fitting, remembering one's sins, to consider oneself not worthy of God's providence. But one must also, on the other hand, remember the mercy of God so as to be comforted. True confidence in God, then, makes one's thinking vigorous and not feeble in every affliction which occurs, and makes one strong so as to endure everything. Faith in the providence of God is the light of the mind, which rises in a person, by grace.

26 Encouragement accompanies temptations endured on the way of virtue, by reason of the confidence that God is near and treats kindly those who love Him, according to the word of the Apostle.[18] Also according to the word of the Prophet: *His salvation is always near to those who fear Him.*[19]

---

[18] Cf. Rom. 8:28.
[19] Ps. 85:10.

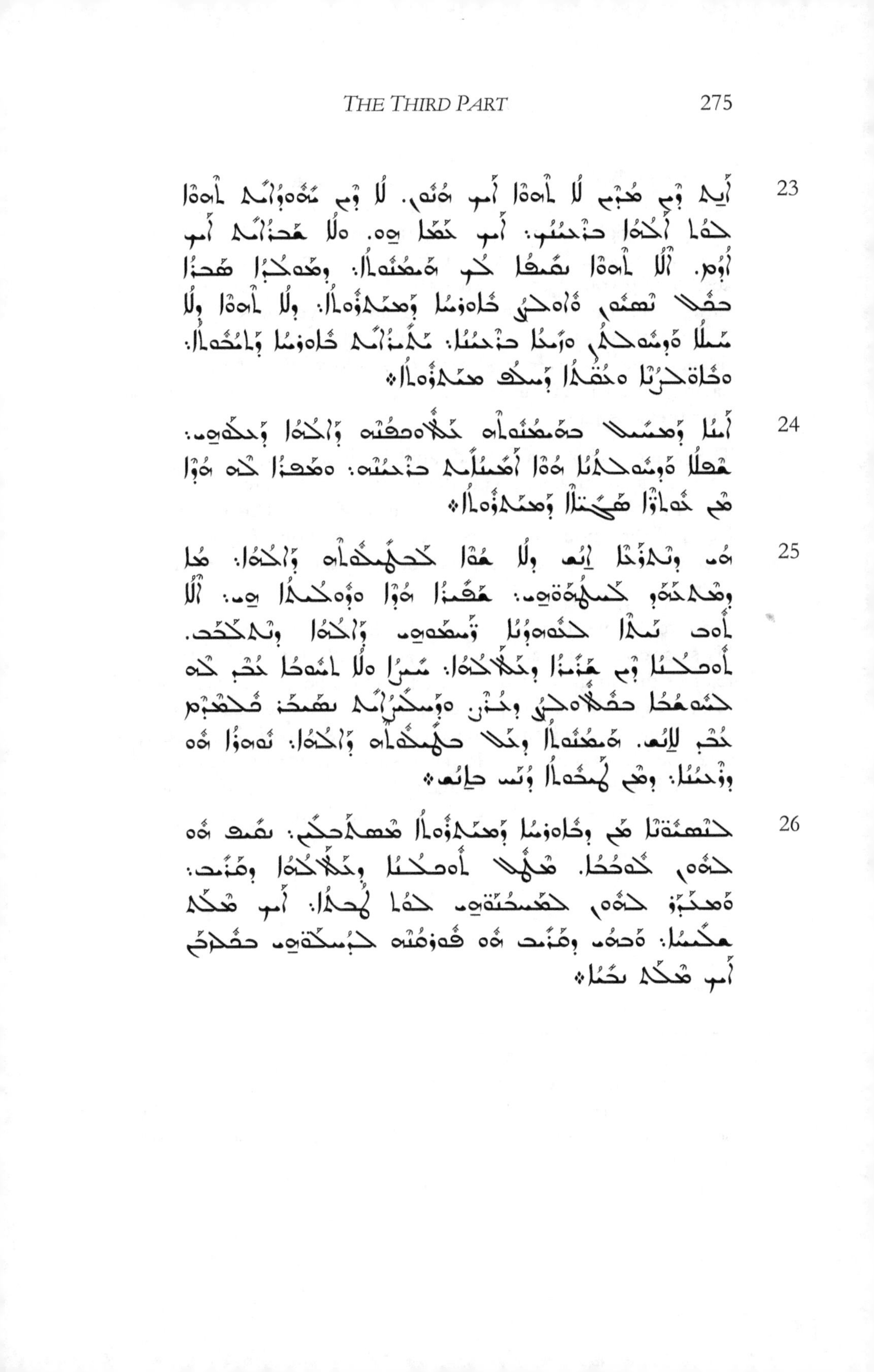

27   For even if before, you lived very much as an adversary,[20] now you adhere with your will to the afflictions of repentance. You are one who does righteousness because the grace of God accompanies you everywhere. It allows you to be severely afflicted, while not abandoning you as you receive proof of its aid, so that you might suffer affliction for the fear of God, and prove yourself, in the endurance of evils for its sake. In your mind there is a place for confidence now, not seeming to have walked wholly at rest without having experienced misfortunes in God's presence, according to your previous faults.

28   The sinner who has sinned and is defiled in his body, but afterwards is numbered with the company of penitents, is not afflicted in his will on account of the fear of God. This is not possible until that moment he becomes a companion of God, and has acquired confidence of heart and the trust that his former sins have been forgiven.

29   Whoever knows to be a sinner, and in his heart suffers the dread of his sins, does not fear afflictions and death. On the contrary, he rejoices that in the afflictions of repentance he may arrive at death, in that when the suffering of compunction subdues his heart, truly he reckons it as audacity to be alive. He agrees to die in the misfortunes he brings on himself in repentance for his sins. He considers it a sin, indeed, that one not have in his heart a sense of sorrow for his sins, for these thoughts would cast him down <again>.[21]

---

[20] Cf. Rom. 5:10; Tt. 3:3.

[21] This striking paragraph speaks of the importance of knowledge of one's sins. Elsewhere (Is.I 463), he says: "Better is he that has been deemed worthy of seeing himself, than he that has been deemed worthy of seeing the angels."

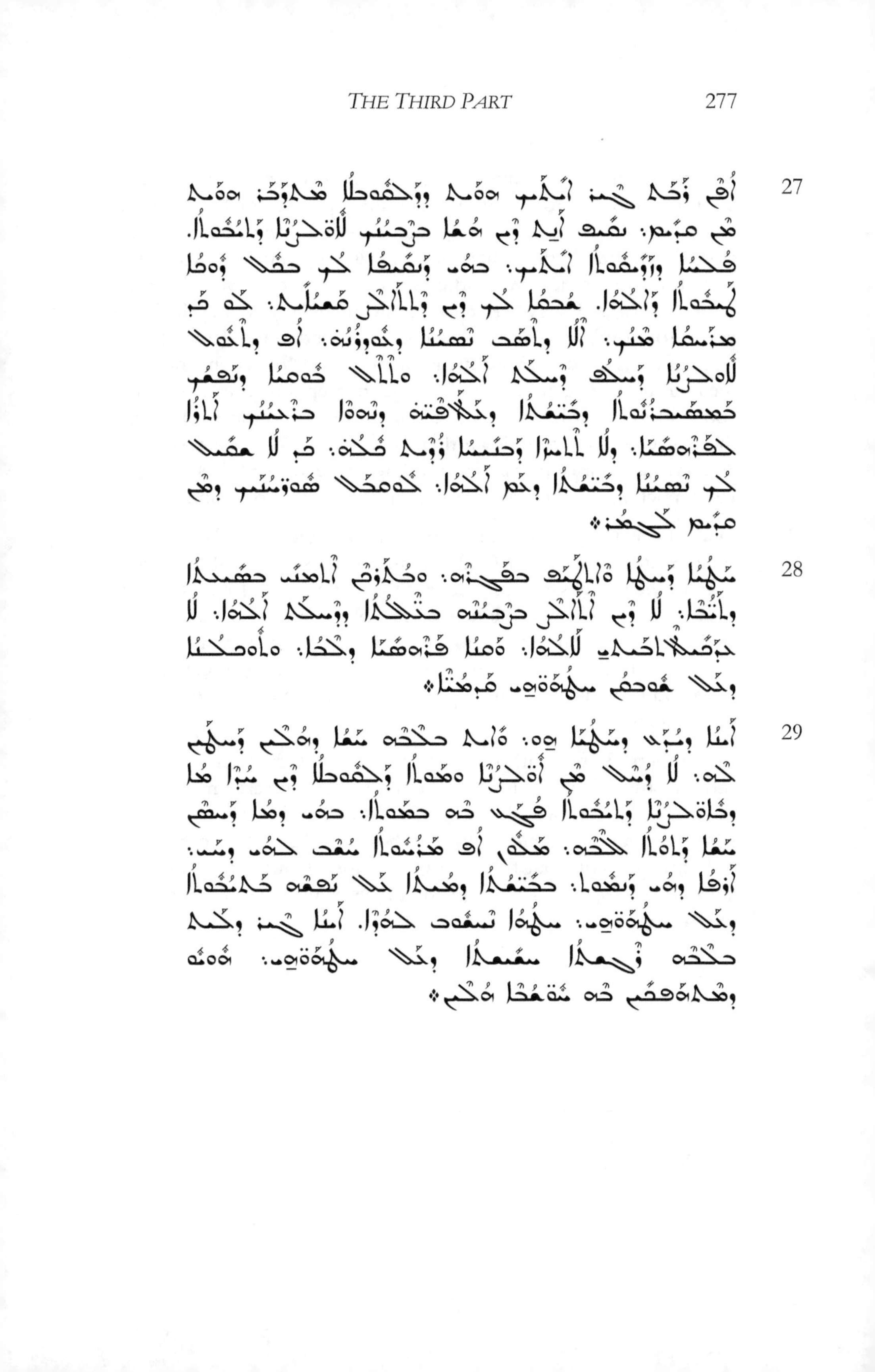

30   The holy fathers, while living in sublime righteousness, were taking upon themselves prolonged fasts and intercession, for four or five, even seven days. And suffering severe pain because of hunger, they wore down their bodies while they were in barren places. Also after their fast, they <ate> very little and not to satiety, even this was poor quality and very wretched. How many times they had no bread for food, but <only> steeped pot herbs and fruit of the trees. So it is written about many of the saints for whom this was their nourishment, in that they could not endure bread nor any cooked food after having fasted all their lives. With these torments, they tortured and wore down their bodies every day. They considered it as a sacrifice pleasing to God, to be dead to all these things. How much more, then, are these things becoming for a sinner!

31   One who is just, however, afflicts himself rejoicing to die like this as an *acceptable sacrifice* to God.[22] Many of these were often found dead in their <cells>. And there are those who were found lying in their caves in distant and lonely places. No one was aware of them at the time of their illness, nor was <anyone> near them at their death, because of their remoteness and their being alone. Some were found while kneeling at prayer, as their souls were leaving their bodies.

32   And others, how many times they exhausted themselves in the snow in rugged places for many days. Others were tormented by thirst, yet they praised God while rejoicing. But if such as these, *of whom the world is not worthy*,[23] lived with these afflictions and because of them have gone out from the world, how right for the sinner to consider his soul and what profit to his soul from his life <offered> to God!

---

[22] Cf. Phil. 4:18.
[23] Heb. 11:38.

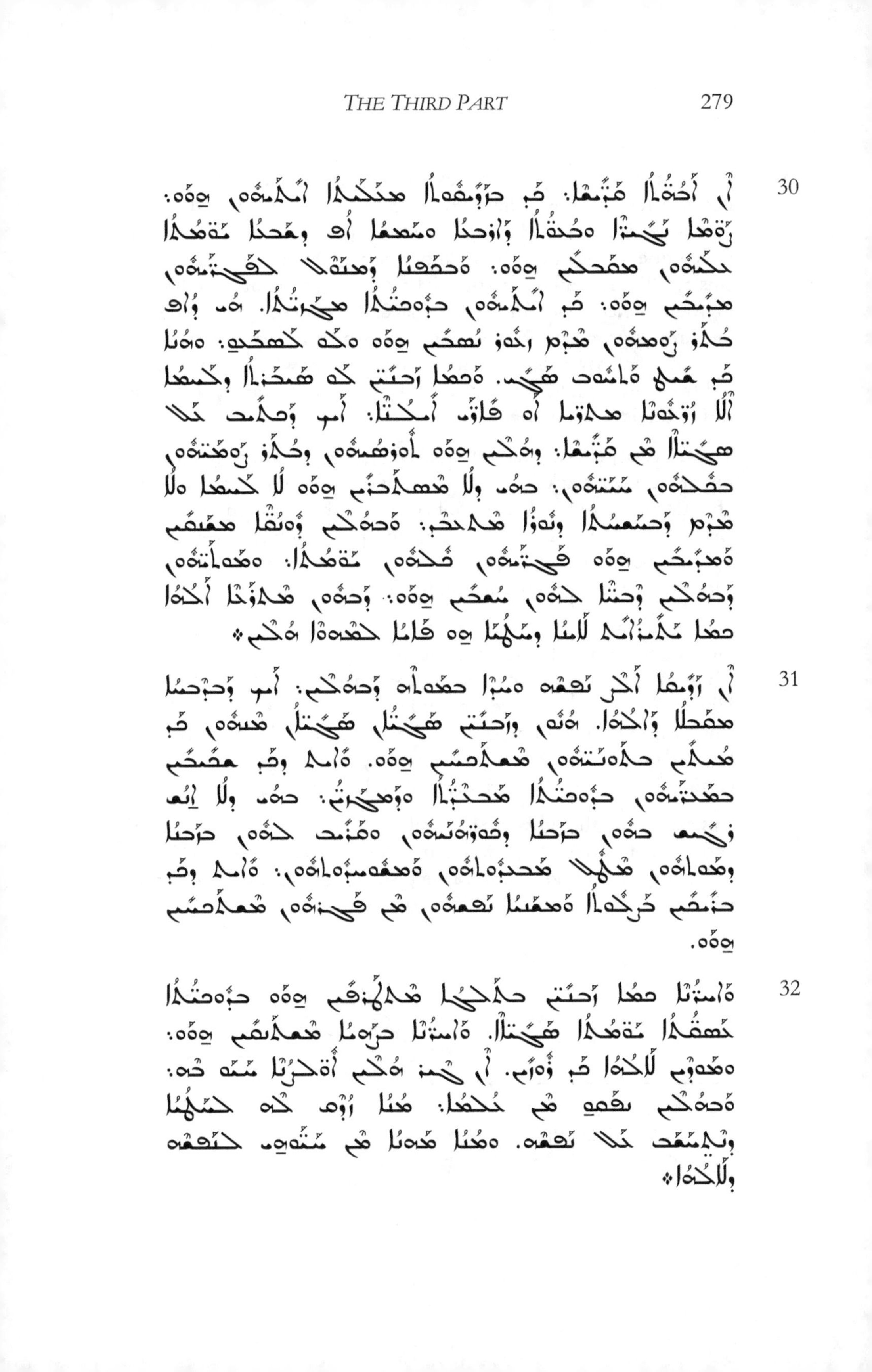

33 Remember your sins at all times so as to keep watch over yourself, because remembering them you may gladly endure the afflictions and adversities which happen to you in your zeal for those things which grieve your heart. Remember how great and numerous your sins are. Do not mention your righteousness, to your ruin, lest you be found twice guilty. In the first place, that you forget your debt to God for your great and numerous sins which He forgives you; and for His grace towards you, without doing away with you, when you did these great faults. Even after all this, He draws you near to Him through His compassion.

34 The other aspect of guilt is that if you think you are righteous, you might become slack in virtuous labors and shrink back from the afflictions you ought to endure because of them, as long as you are alive. You will fall into murmuring and pusillanimity. Even if lifted up, you will fall to the judgment reserved for Satan[24] for having forgotten your former things, so hateful and disgraceful.

35 Whoever forgets the measure of his sins, forgets the measure of God's grace towards him. He forgets how much he owes God in labor and recompense, on account of what he has <done> against Him *and His might.*[25] Whoever truly remembers his faults and his sins, considers as insignificant all the troubles and afflictions which he encounters, whether by choice or by necessities. And after becoming humble, he endures them with thanksgiving.

36 Appease your thoughts by remembering the *just judgment of God*,[26] and suddenly consolation will come to you in secret. You will have rest from all your adversities. If evil surrounds you, do not forsake what is good, and you will be victorious!

---

[24] Cf. Is. 14:12–15.
[25] Cf. Ps. 78:4; Eph. 6:10.
[26] 2 Macc. 9:18; Rm. 2:5; 2 Thess. 1:5.

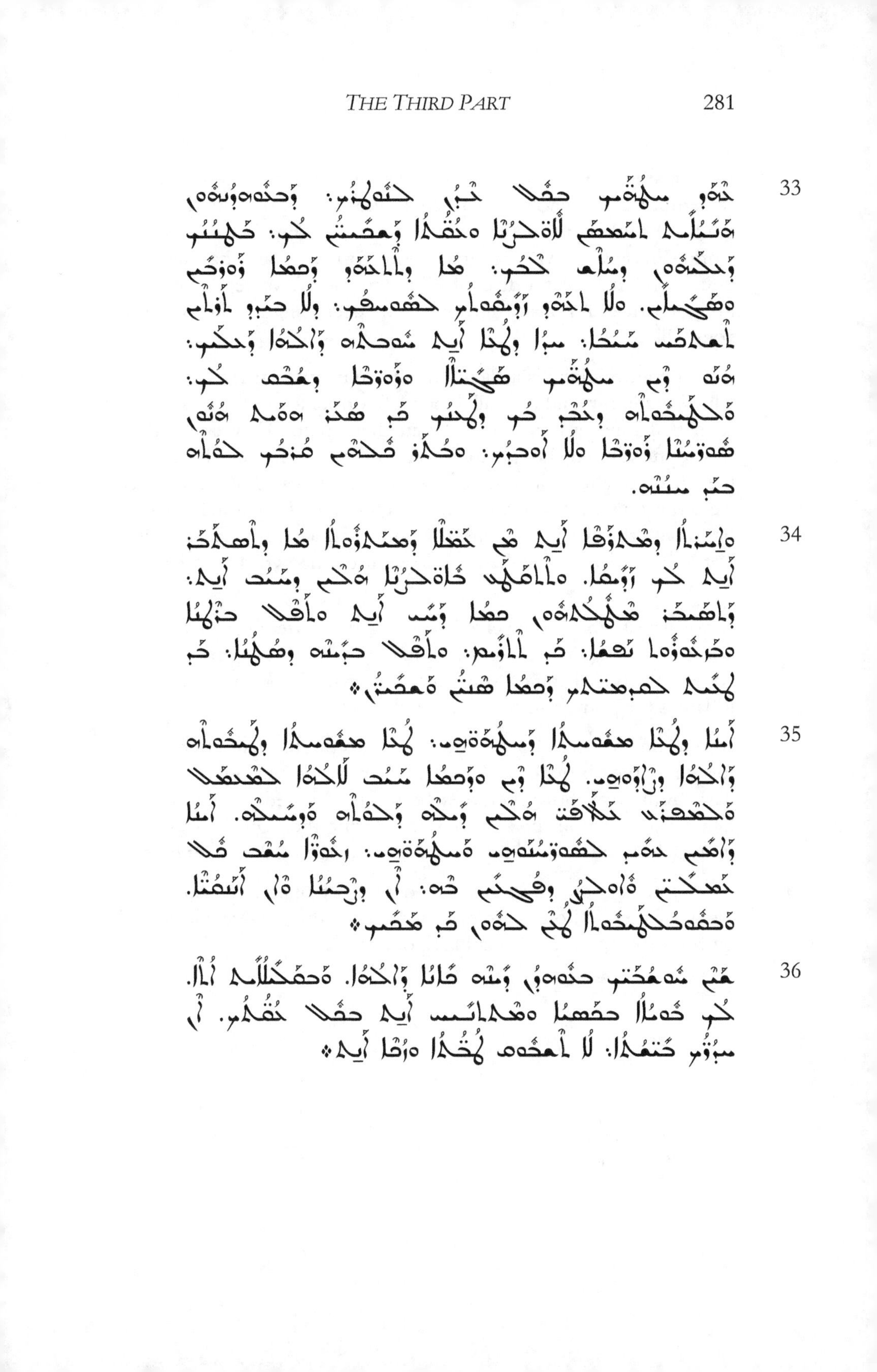

37 If you are weary, afflicted and tormented in the way of virtue, remember those who were afflicted, weary and prostrate under all kinds of violent torments, not of their will, but because of the world. Praise God who has made you worthy to be exhausted voluntarily because of the fear of Him and the life of repentance, by love of virtue and out of terror for sin, according to the choice of your will.

38 And if your thinking is afflicted by this, remember the holy martyrs who voluntarily endured all kinds of torments for love of faith, such that there was nothing else in their mind. They endured all this joyfully, even though they were able to turn aside from it, if they had sought to live at rest without love for God. And these were not only men, but women and children who naturally have a bond with this world and with the body, and what is peculiar to it.[27] Yet, they also were touched by all the torments which you have in mind.

39 If you speak about hunger or thirst or the suffering <involved>, also the persecutors torment the martyrs with these things. And if you speak about lying on scorching hot ground, the force of which inflames the body, also they have endured this.

40 About one of the holy martyrs it is written, that after many torments, they brought a skin and laid it in the sun on very warm days, until it was hot. Then they bound the blessed one and placed him on that skin in the sun. Besides, during the night he was continually lying on dry and hot ground, <as part> of their torments.

41 So if you say you suffer from cold or frost or ice, <know that> many of these <holy martyrs>, without clothing, were tormented by very stormy weather in cold regions.

---

[27] Cf. Sahdona I 3, 64.

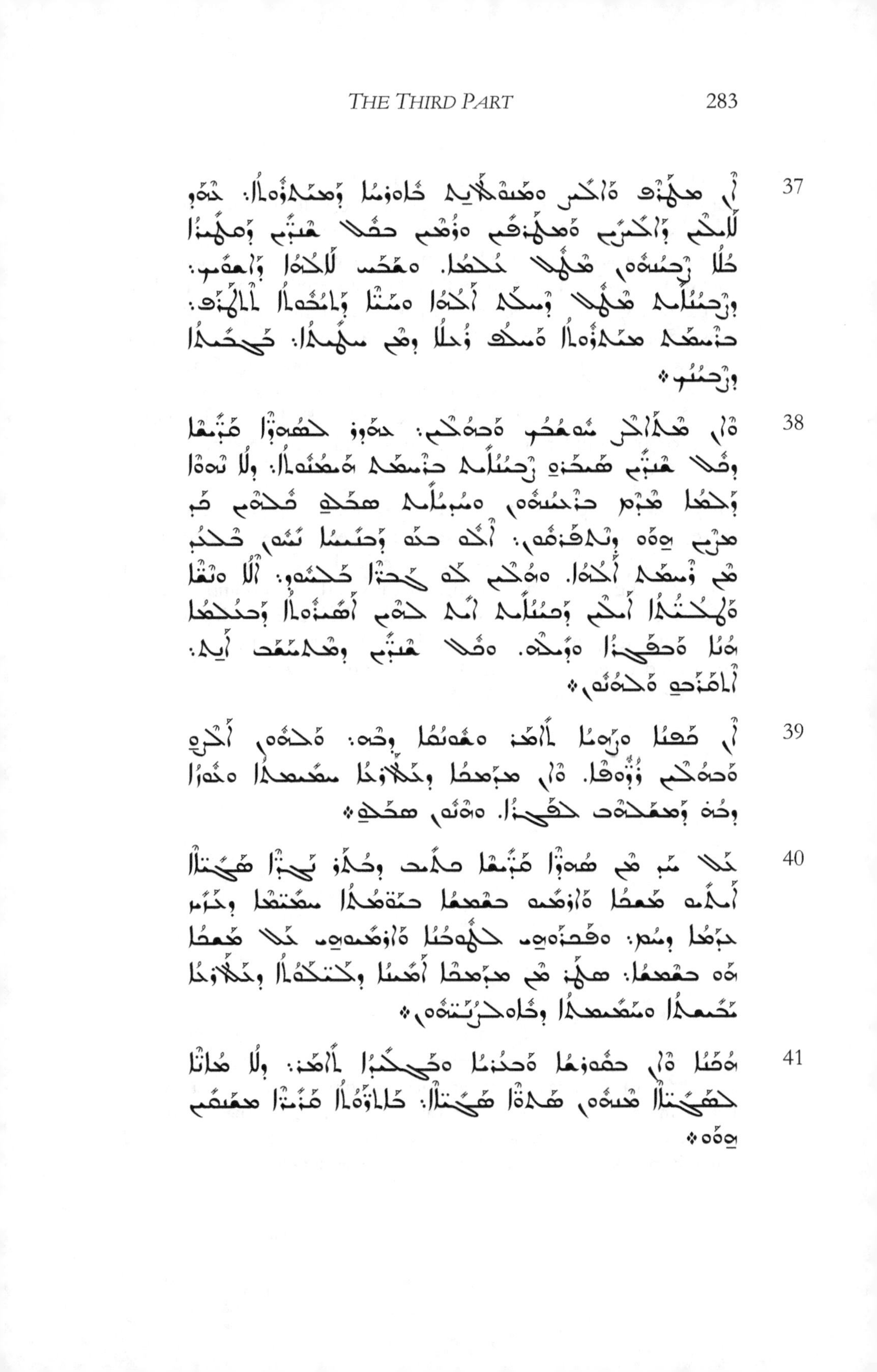

42   If separation from loved ones and friends concerns you, or being cut off in remote places from acquaintances: all of these things the martyrs suffered. There were also the straits of confinement, or prison for a long time while being deprived of any acquaintance, friend or comforter — such as this they suffered; without speaking of torments, or wounds, or mutilation of limbs and death on a cross. Some were strangled and were suspended in the sun head downwards, on the walls, on the doors and on trees. They were harassed and died a miserable death. Some were stoned <to death>. For some, their soul departed from the hard suffering because of the mutilation of their limbs which overpowered them, and they died.

43   They did not weaken in thought nor in word, <persevering> in these afflictions until the end of their lives. It is written that the greater part of these things were received and endured by your women and girls, having a nature that loves the world and is tied to love of the body with its pleasures. Yet they endured bravely and were valiant, giving proof of their soul's virtue when they were compelled to endure for the love of God, as even one of the authors writes in the account of their lives.[28]

---

[28] Chialà suggests various examples of women who were martyred in Persia: martyrdom of Martha, of Tarbo, of Thekla, of Anahid; and the martyrs of Karka d-Beth Slokh; as well as others. These accounts may be found in Brock – Ashbrook Harvey, *Holy Women*, 63–99.

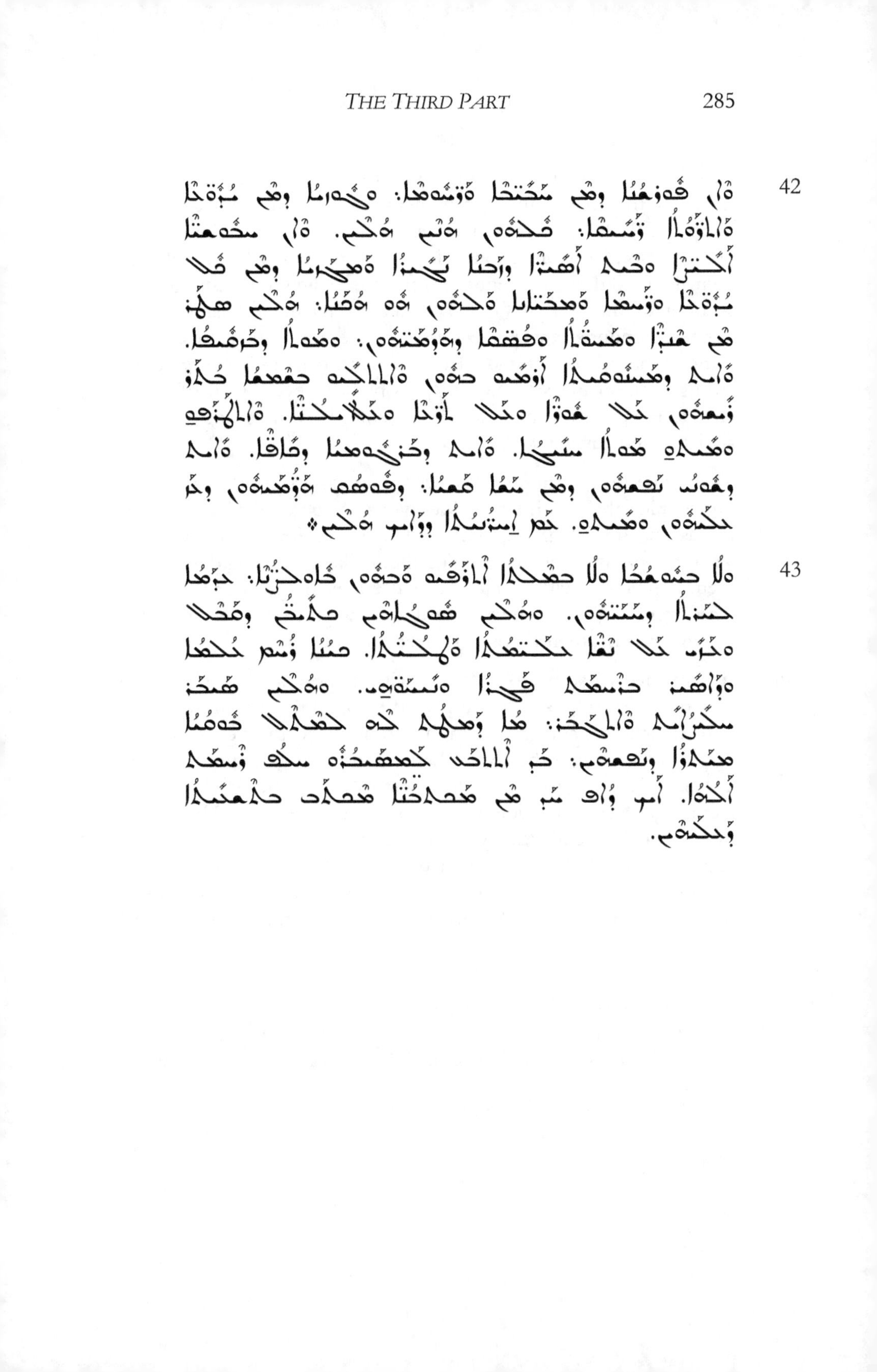

44   At this time, the author wrote, wicked pagans inflicted injuries on those of the Covenant,[29] even many women were seized: some from the Pact, some from lay-life; some of them were free-born, but even some servants; some rich and some poor. The fragility of their nature did not prevent them from excelling in the struggle on account of the fear of God. But like strong men, valiantly <the women> endured the persecutions: those bitter sufferings which came upon them, wounds from violent persons, scourging by strong arms, being strangled in prisons, the severe pain of heavy chains, hunger and thirst, heat and cold, weariness and sadness, anxieties and adversities.

45   They considered these <persecutions> as comforts and joys, proclaiming their faith with a loud voice in the eyes of all: "One is for us and we suffer for Him, as He suffers for our salvation."[30] Then the pagans who surrounded them, like destroying devils, slew them mercilessly with all kinds of sufferings. Some after being tortured were exposed to intense heat and they died. Some were beaten with swords, their limbs destroyed and they died.

46   It happened to some to be stuck with a spear in their sides, and they died. For others, a sword passed through them from their belly to their loins, and they died. Yet others had their eyes plucked out, and they died; others were battered with stones, and they died. Others had their noses and lips destroyed and by breaking their teeth, blood flowed inside their mouths, and they died. There were those who had children by natural partnership and because they had also raised them in the true faith, the persecutors angrily slaughtered them before their eyes, and mercilessly poured the blood of their children into their mouths, killing them at the end.[31]

---

[29] Covenant / Pact: refers to an early Syriac form of religious life, "sons and daughters of the Covenant." See Brock, "Early Syrian Asceticism"; Nedungatt, "Covenanters."

[30] Cf. the martyr Maḥya in Brock – Harvey, *Holy Women*, 109–11.

[31] The fate of martyrs at Najran, see Brock – Harvey, *Holy Women*, 114.

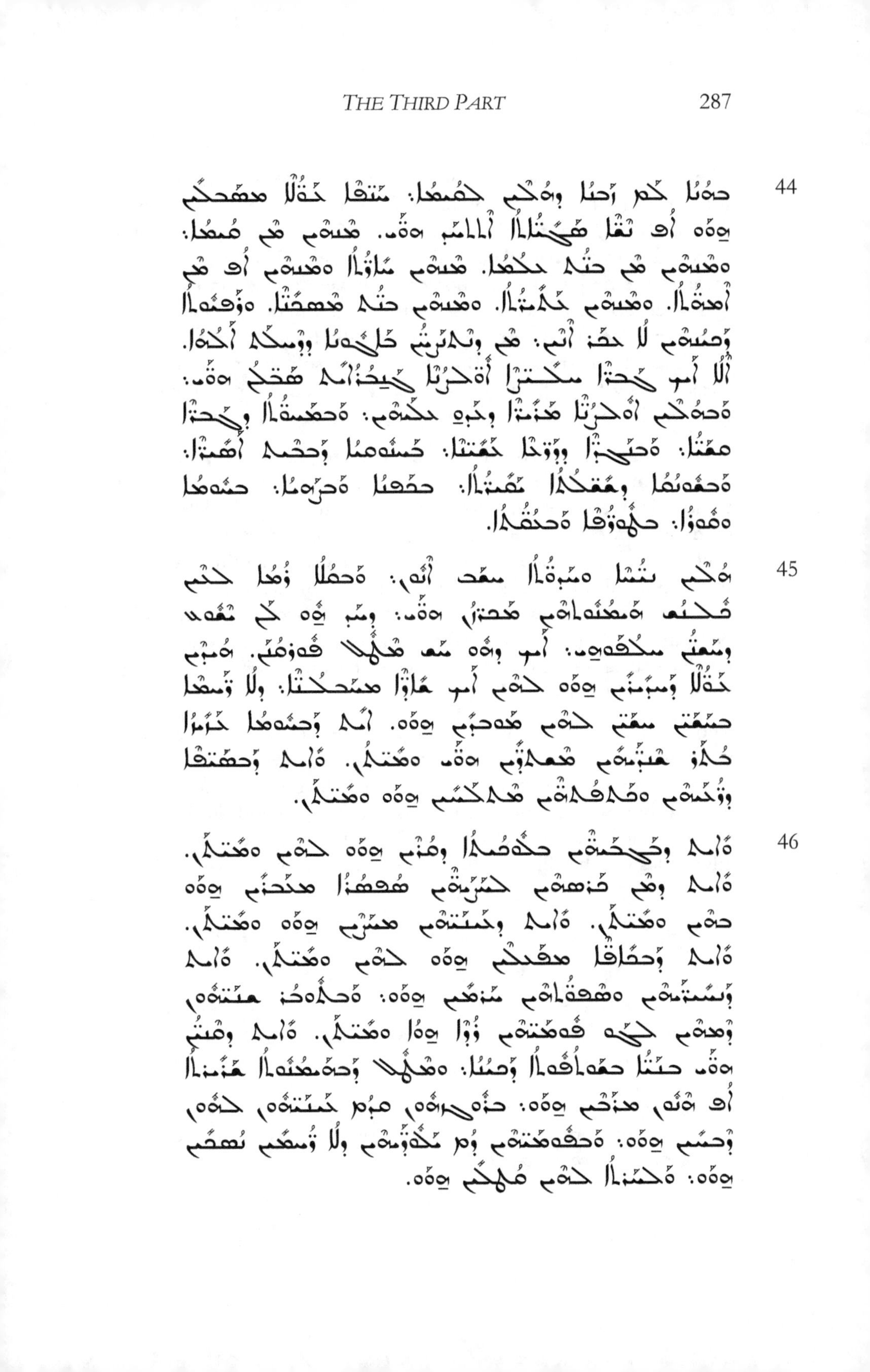

47 The love of the world did not weaken their intelligence, nor love for children, nor remembrance of their loved ones and their friends. Not desire for their riches or their houses, neither allurements nor threats, weakened their will. Yet others, saws passed through the middle of their bodies; they were divided in two parts and lifted up on the two sides of the road where the king's army passed between them, etc.[32] What things the fragile nature of women endured and resisted! But you, weary solitary, your mind is weakened by fear of hunger and thirst; by even the <thought> of lying on dry ground; by heat and cold; by the fear of demons.

48 Such things happened to <these women and men>, yet they laughed much and were not weakened. While just the <thought of these things terrifies this <solitary>, and for very little labor he glorifies himself not remembering the members of the Church, both women and men – how they acted very mightily and were received at all times near Christ. But this <solitary> is weak from an affliction of his own choosing. And while occupied with his labors and freely having left <the world>, he becomes weak in his intelligence, and at the remembrance of death is fearful of offering <his> blood to God.

49 Those who were tied to the world and the pleasures of the body, when it was required <of them>, they renounced the world and left the body in order not to deny God nor be guilty, even in word. Yet the one who is supposed to have left the world already, and was considered as dead to the body, is afraid of hunger and the adversities which afflict the body, for <fear> of dying.

---

[32] Cf. the martyrdom of Tarbo, her sister and her servant: see Brock – Harvey, *Holy Women*, 73–76.

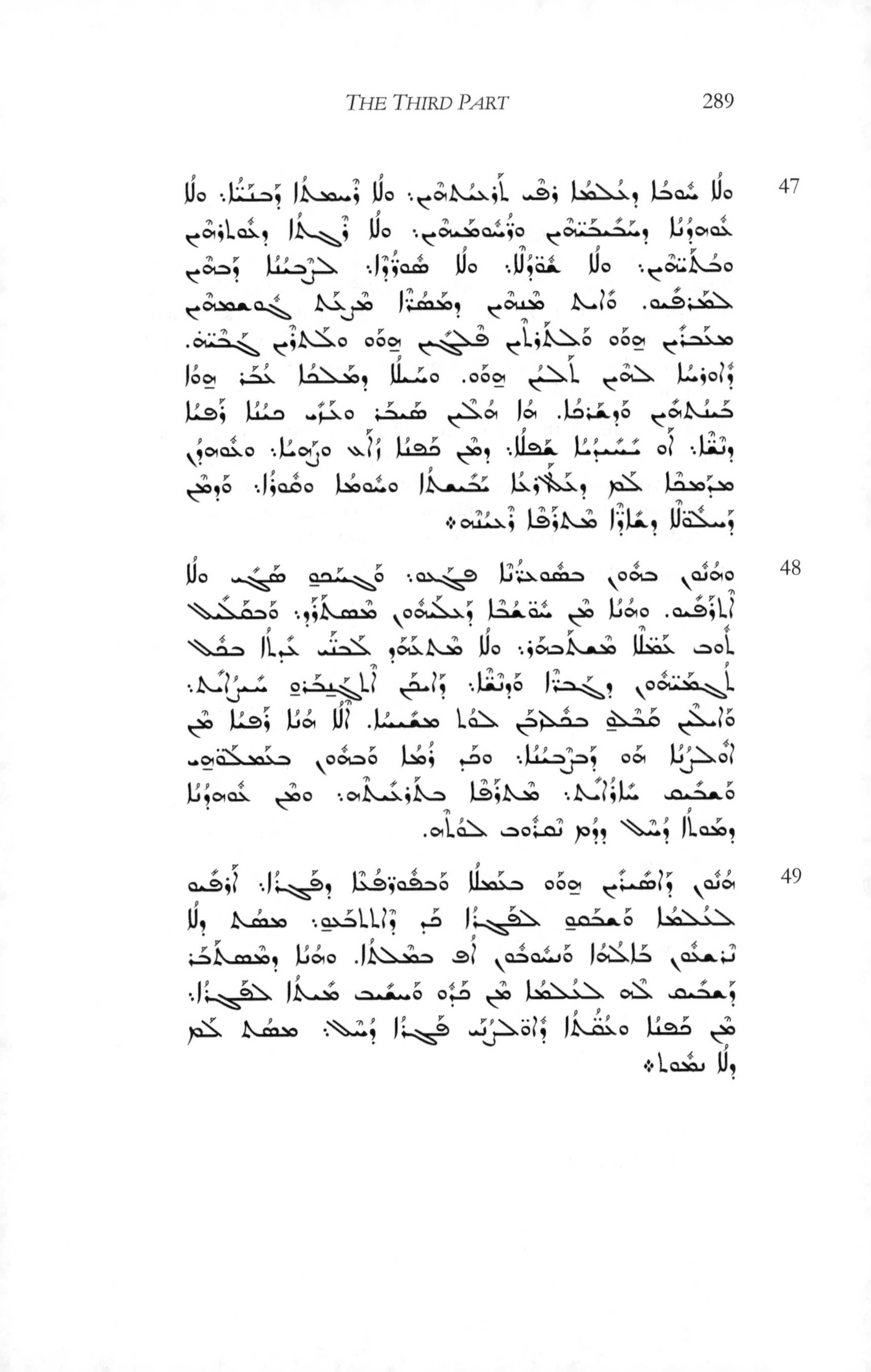

50   The heavens are amazed at how much the love of this life has ruled us, on account of the love of the pleasures that have laid hold of us. Consider, then, our brother, the things which I have written you, examine them in the crucible of your mind. See if there is assurance in them, giving rest to your mind on account of a word of righteousness. But if, indeed, you are frightened by these afflictions and you turn back to remain in what defiles life, you will be like those who have feared afflictions and renounced true life, on account of temporal life.

51   Therefore, one of the saints says: "All the afflictions and troubles which happen to you on this way of virtue, reckon them as jailers, leading you with the commands of cruel kings and harsh rulers. Endure and ask help, remembering the crowns reserved[33] for the blessed martyrs, and you will share their inheritance."

The letter of Mar Isaac is finished.

---

[33] Cf. 2 Tm. 4:8.

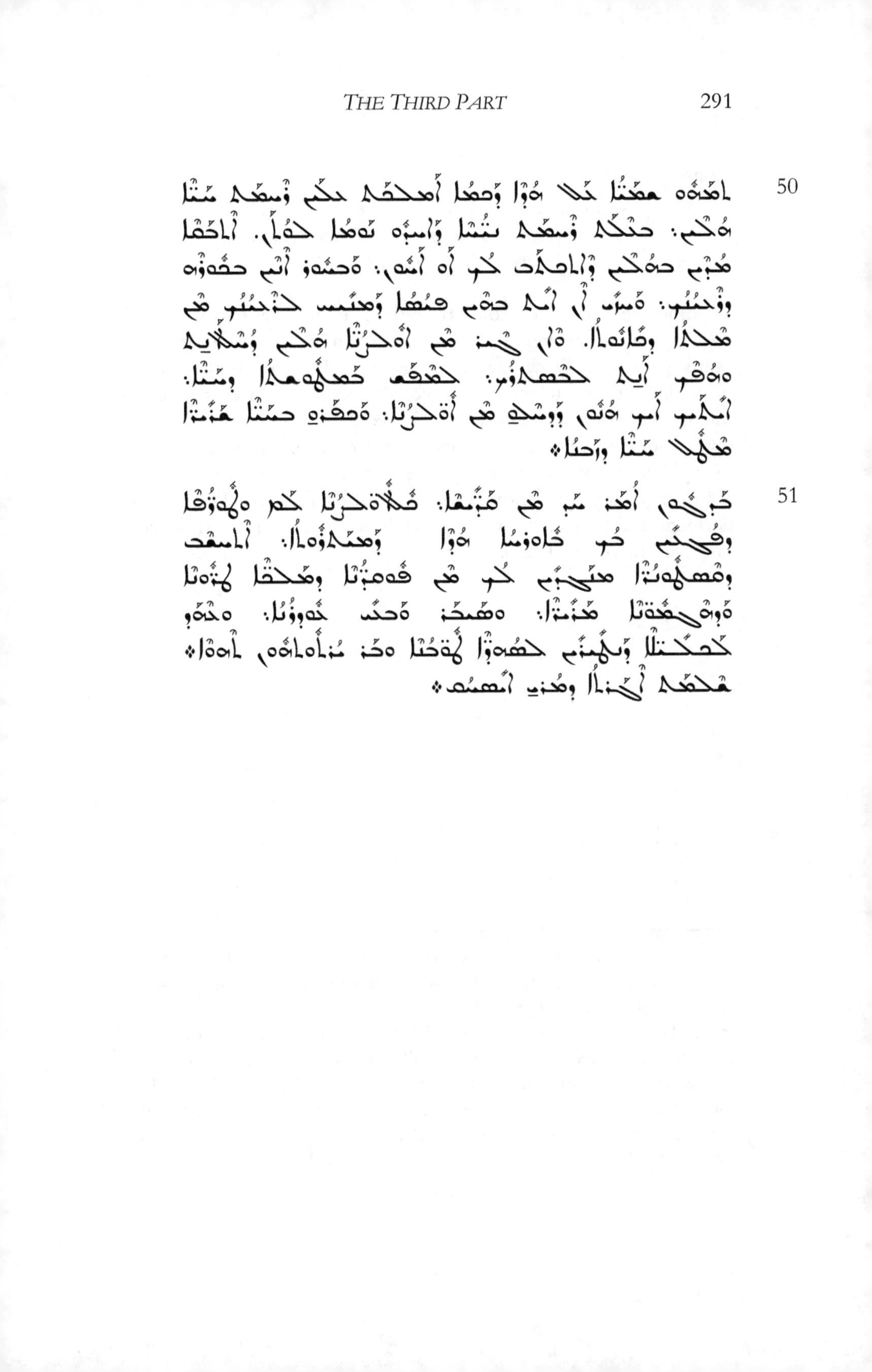

Chapter XIII

Again, a letter on the abodes in which holy men enter by the stirrings existing in the mind, in the journey on the way to the house of God.

1   Together with what I wrote you before, now I want to make this known to you, our venerable brother: from where is the joy of the saints generated, how far is it transmitted, into which dwelling place does it go into when it leaves them and by what is it substituted. This you must know our beloved: everywhere that there is joy in God,[1] it is from fervor and in every place, fervor is the cause of joy; because where there is no fervor, nor is there joy. However the place of joy is inferior to the place of perfection.[2] The place of perfection is in fact knowledge, while joy is not from knowledge but from fervor, as I said.

---

[1] Joy in God (*ḥadûtâ db-alâhâ*): Is.I 368, 431; Is.II VIII.11, XX.15.

[2] In the *Letters* of John of Dalyatha two Letters are included, which are probably by Joseph Hazzaya. In Letter 48 the author refers to the three places (*atrâwâtê*): Purity *dakyûtâ*; Limpidity *šapyûtâ*; Perfection *gmîrûtâ* (not spiritual perfection, more like a fullness / *šumlâyâ* of the mystical life). These places are connected to the three levels (*taksê*) inherited from John the Solitary. The level of the body leads to Purity; the level of the soul to Limpidity; the level of the spirit to Perfection. See Beulay, *Lumière*, 97–124; Harb, "Doctrine Spirituel," 225–60; and Hansbury, *Letters*.

THE THIRD PART

2   Fervor, then, is between an excellent way of life and excellence of the mind. Beneath excellence of the way of life, there is neither fervor nor joy; even above an excellent mind there is, therefore, neither fervor nor joy. In fact, beneath an excellent way of life coldness[3] prevails. But above excellence of the mind is the place of stillness of the mysteries.[4] Truly great, indeed, is the joy in God, yet it is inferior to the stirrings and impulses in the Spirit.

3   So then, from when a person begins <to do> excellent deeds before God, fervor begins to stir in him, even joy. And one proceeds in this way of joy until arriving at excellence of the mind which is the light of the mind and the revelation of hidden things. And when one has come near to this place, the stirring of joy[5] begins to lessen and be tranquil in him, because from this time he comes near to a certain calm.

---

[3] Coldness: lack of fervor, in Evag. Cent. VI. 25 it indicates demonic action. See also *Letter to Melania*, p.12 (Vitestam).

[4] Place of stillness of the mysteries (*atrâ...šelyâ d-râzê*): place (*atrâ*) and place of (*atrâ d-*) occur in John Sol. and in East Syrian writers such as John of Dalyatha, in his *Letters* and very often in his *Homélies*. These occurrences of *atrâ* may be due to an Evagrian influence. Evagrius saw the purified mind as the "place of God" from Exodus 24.10–11 (LXX). Shifting from Sinai to the human mind, he also speaks of "the place of prayer," internalizing the "place of God" within the person. See Columba Stewart, "Imageless Prayer," 173–204. Golitzin analyzes another perspective: the occurrence of *atrâ* in Aphrahat, also giving its linguistic history including *maqom* in the Hebrew Bible as the place of divine manifestation and as a "stand-in for God himself." In the Hekhalot literature *maqom* is used as a divine name. See Golitzin, "The Place of the Presence of God," 1–31. On *atrâ* see also his "The Image and Glory of God," esp. 338, 352–59. On *maqom* in Jewish sources see Urbach, *The Sages*, ch. IV.

[5] Stirring of joy (*zaw'â d-ḥadûtâ*): Is.II IX.8 (plur.); *Keph*.III 30.

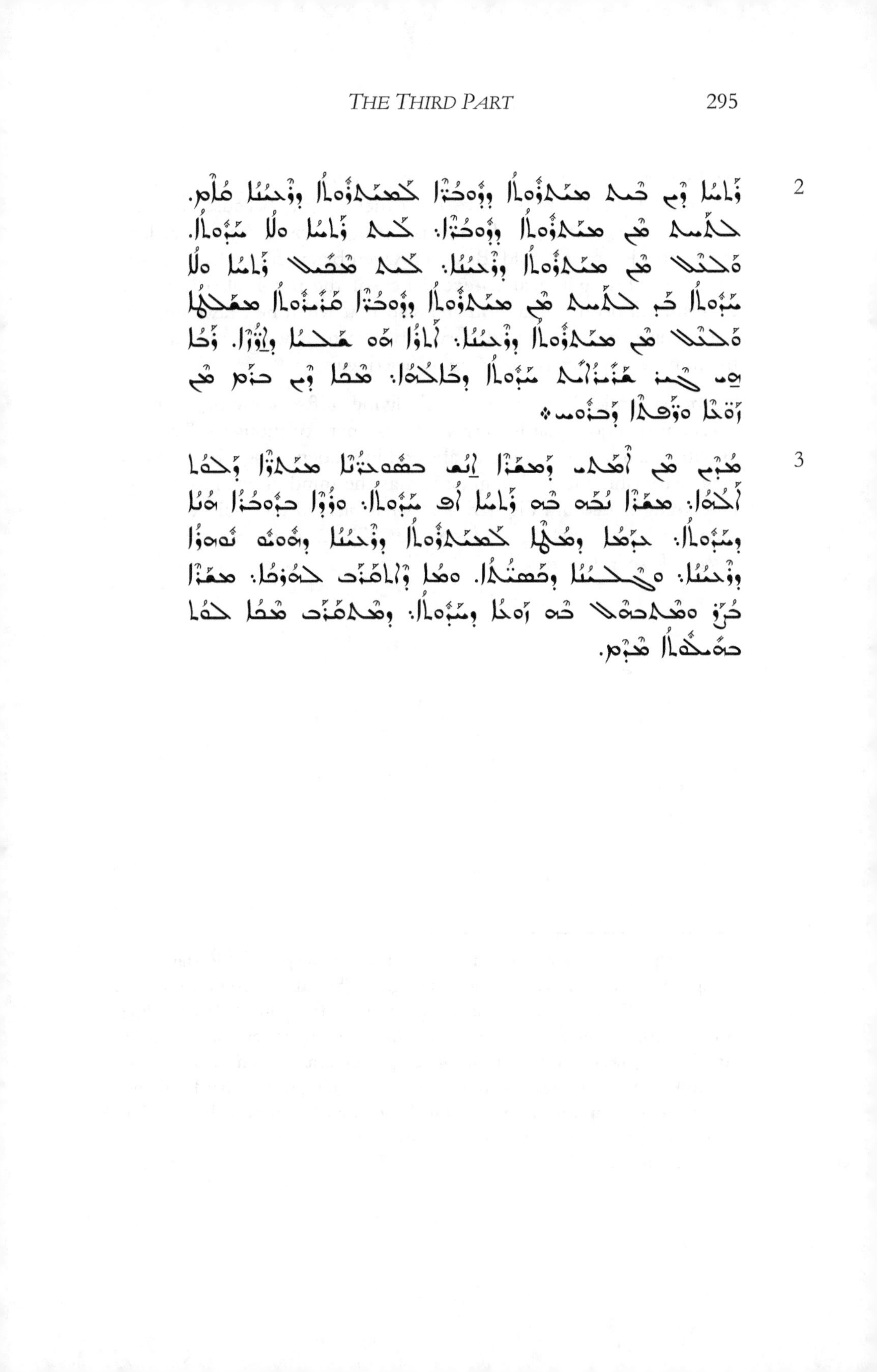

4   And when he enters here, then fervor has possession and continual joy, though he is lifted above the order of joy, because he feels what is better than joy. If one is brought down from excellent deeds, this joy grows cold. But even when by excellent deeds, gradually he is brought near to excellence of the mind, also here joy ceases. And do not marvel that I said that when he draws near to the excellence of the mind, fervor begins to have possession and the mind is at peace from being diffused with joy.[6]

5   There is, indeed, among these divine gifts something more excellent than joy, that is to say, astonishment of thoughts. Together with the mind beginning to abound in hidden things, it begins to have astonishment of thoughts; and as the mind grows in this way it is strengthened until it arrives at what blessed Paul said when he recounted the ravishing of his mind: *Whether in the body or whether without the body, I do not know.*[7]

---

[6] There are many references in Is.I which help to understand the complexity of joy (*ḥadûtâ*). It is a sign of grace (58). It may come without a cause (177, 471). Joy in God is stronger than earthly life (431). Healing occurs through spiritual joy (484). Joy which no tongue can express (486). And in (550) Isaac allows that one give up occasionally even the recitation of the Psalms because of the power of joy, seeming to be what he allows for divine interruptions in prayer. Finally joy may be unspeakable, leading to inebriation in God / *rawwîyûtâ db-alâhâ* (555).

[7] 2 Cor. 12:2–3.

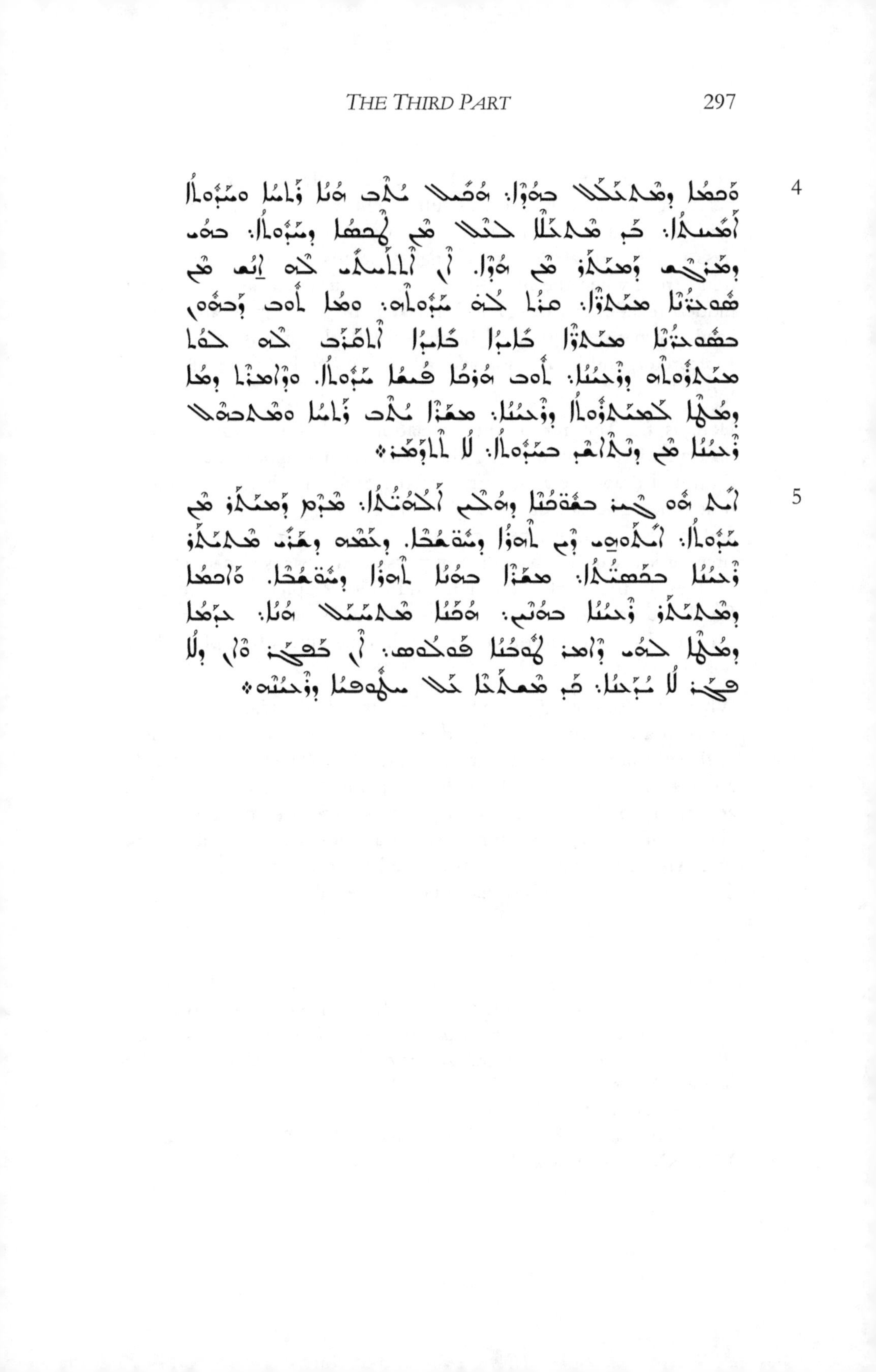

6   For one may not immediately nor suddenly draw near to this perfection directly, nor to this fulfillment; but at the beginning the soul is illumined[8] in the mysteries which are beneath this <fullness>. This amazement of thoughts begins to show itself in the mind from when the mind begins to be illumined[9] and to grow in hidden realities. So this partial amazement grows in it, and it proceeds to that perfection of the mind of Paul which is called by the Interpreter, and by the solitary fathers, an "authentic revelation of God."[10]

7   Here is the summit of the revelations about God; before this, however, is the mystery. To these particular realities, the force of the mind draws near by virtue of the Spirit, in that from time to time grace dwells in it. Its way of life is strengthened by the Spirit and every time it attains a certain calm, it remains above the stirrings of joy. But because it is not possible to always remain in these realities, in that such a constant and uninterrupted gift is reserved for the future world,[11] one who is of God is never completely deprived of joy and fervor, but every time he enters that place, he is raised up from the realities of nature.

8   When one goes out from there and returns to the realities of nature – which are reflection, thoughts, work, prayer and the rest – he is in these realities and also in fervor and in joy. They are, indeed, the abodes which he passes through and in which he stays: in each one according to the measure of his way of life;[12] sometimes in the abodes of nature, other times in the abodes which are above nature. Thus he is free, by means of the Economy of the grace of the Spirit, from all which is of nature or of the will.

---

[8] Illumination of the soul (*nahhîrûtâ d-napšâ*) Is.I 485; *Keph*. III 13.

[9] Illumination of the mind (*nahhîrûtâ d-re'yânâ*) Is.I 448; Is.II VI.2,4.

[10] Authentic revelation (*gelyânâ ḥattîtâ*): possibly attributable to Theodore of Mopsuestia.

[11] Cf. Heb. 2:5; 6:5.

[12] Measure of his way of life (*mšuḥtâ d-dubbârê*): Is.I 19, 492; Is.II XX.5, XXI.17; Evag. *Gnostique*, 40 (Guillaumont).

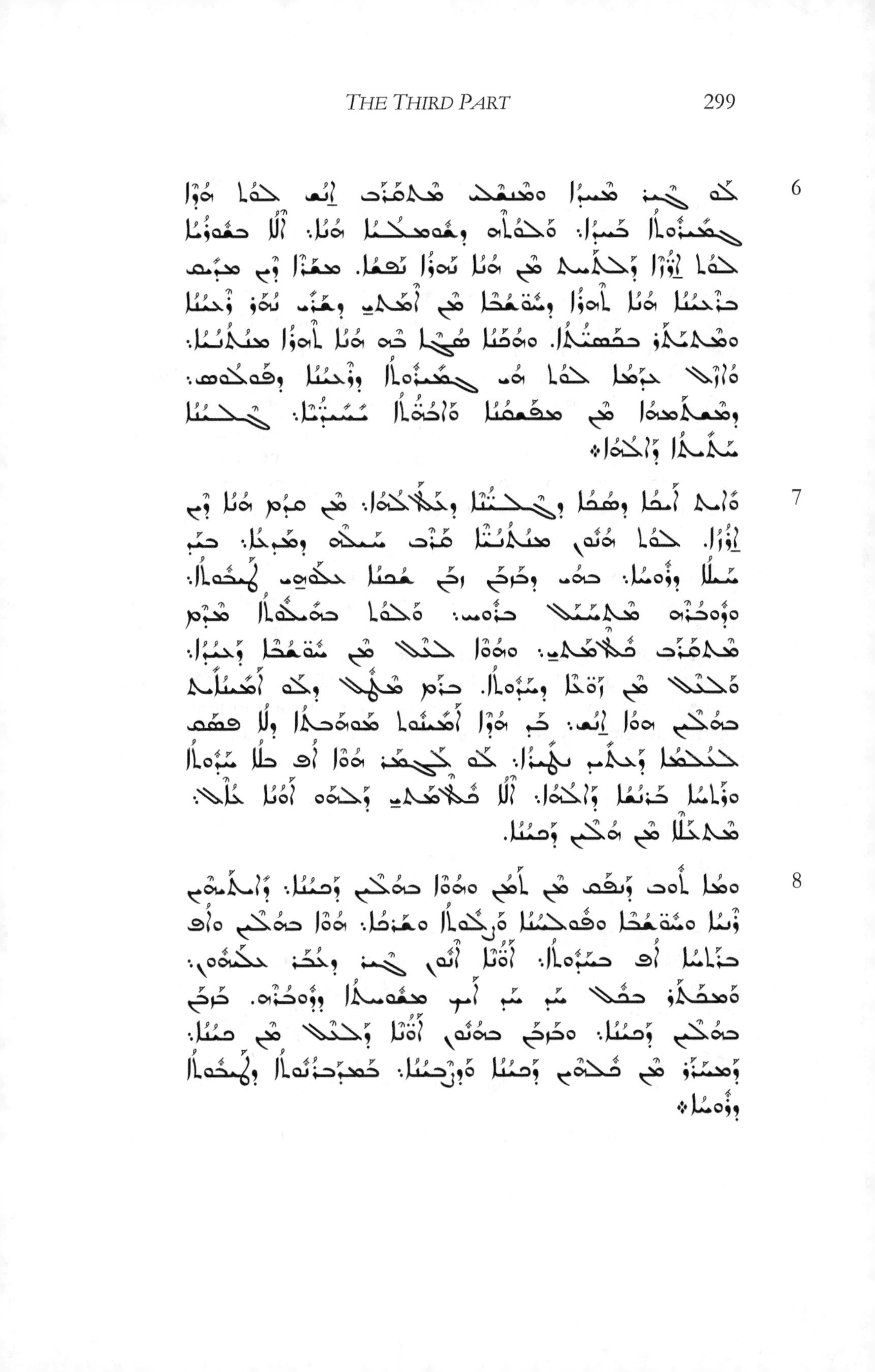

9   There are three places conceivable by the mind, according to the word of the fathers, which the intellect passes through in its transformation: nature; <what is> outside of nature, <what is> above nature.[13]

10 When, therefore, the <intellect> proceeds in the realities of nature, that is to say, in work and in excellent deeds, as I said above, it exists in joy and in fervor; also battles, gloom, temptations and the passions which assail, because all of these are part of nature. When, however, <the intellect> penetrates what is outside of nature, through negligence in a virtuous way of life and giving in to passions and sin, it remains in coldness and hopelessness. These, then, follow from negligence of good works and giving in to passions. And as the thoughts grow cold and <there is> hopelessness, there is neither fervor nor joy there.

11 When, however, the <intellect> penetrates what is above nature, by means of the excellence of those realities on which the soul rests, the mind is lifted from the passions and the battles, likewise from labor, by means of that sublime recollection in God which sees by wonder which is elevated above all stirrings. This takes place in freedom from all the things of this life and in limpidity of the intelligence,[14] which is more exalted than the world.

---

[13] In his 3rd homily, Isaac comments at length on what is natural to the soul (an understanding of all created things), what is outside of its nature (passions /ḥaššē) and what is above its nature (an impulse from divine contemplation). Khalifé-Hachem sees a dependence in this of Isaac on John Sol. The text may be found in Hansbury, *Ascetical Life*, 43–61. For an analysis of the text, see Khalifé-Hachem, "L'âme et les passions." See also his "La prière pure." And see Hansbury, *On the Soul*, Introd.

[14] Limpidity of the intelligence (*šapyûtâ d-tarʿîtâ*): Is.I 526; *Keph.* II 38, IV 33.

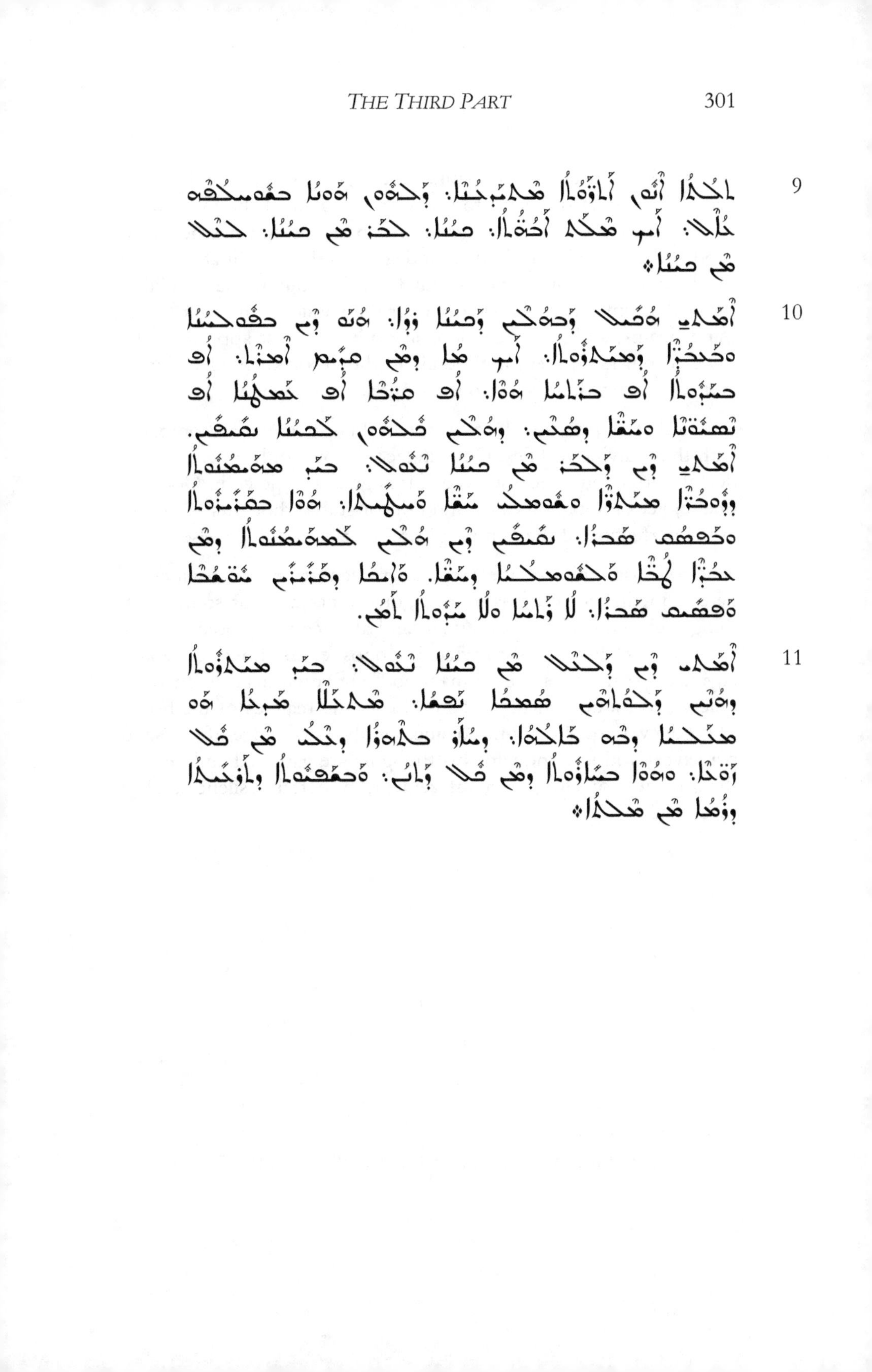

12   All of these realities are within the light of the mind.[15] The <intellect>, indeed, begins to arrive at this light of the mind from when it begins the conflict against the passions and has begun to subdue them. And as it subdues and silences them, so it abounds in the light of the mind and is enlightened about hidden realities. From that time, after the victory over the passions, the light of the mind begins; and as the passions are subdued, rest appears in the mind. From here, then, it abounds in the vision of hidden things, and continually draws near to the wonder of thoughts.

13   The order of joy, therefore, is yet a childish measure compared with these divine realities. How, indeed, is joy <only> near the order of perfection? Because even if it is great to rejoice in God – if one rejoices for a good cause and not for stupid thoughts – however the perfection of the mind is greater than everything <else>.

14   This <is something> one may learn even from the realities of nature: joy in the young is more vigorous, because for some small thing their temperament is fervent and at once they rejoice; but as easily they change back to what is opposite. As, however, youth advances to the measure of manhood, above all it takes on tranquility and modest stirrings. Thus also in the realities of the house of God: every time that one advances in the knowledge of God and perceives God in tranquility, his thoughts are gathered and he sees the greatness of God, as in amazement, in ineffable silence and in reverence.

---

[15] Light of the mind (*nuhrâ d-re'yânâ*): Is.I 482; *Keph.* IV 57–58, 69.

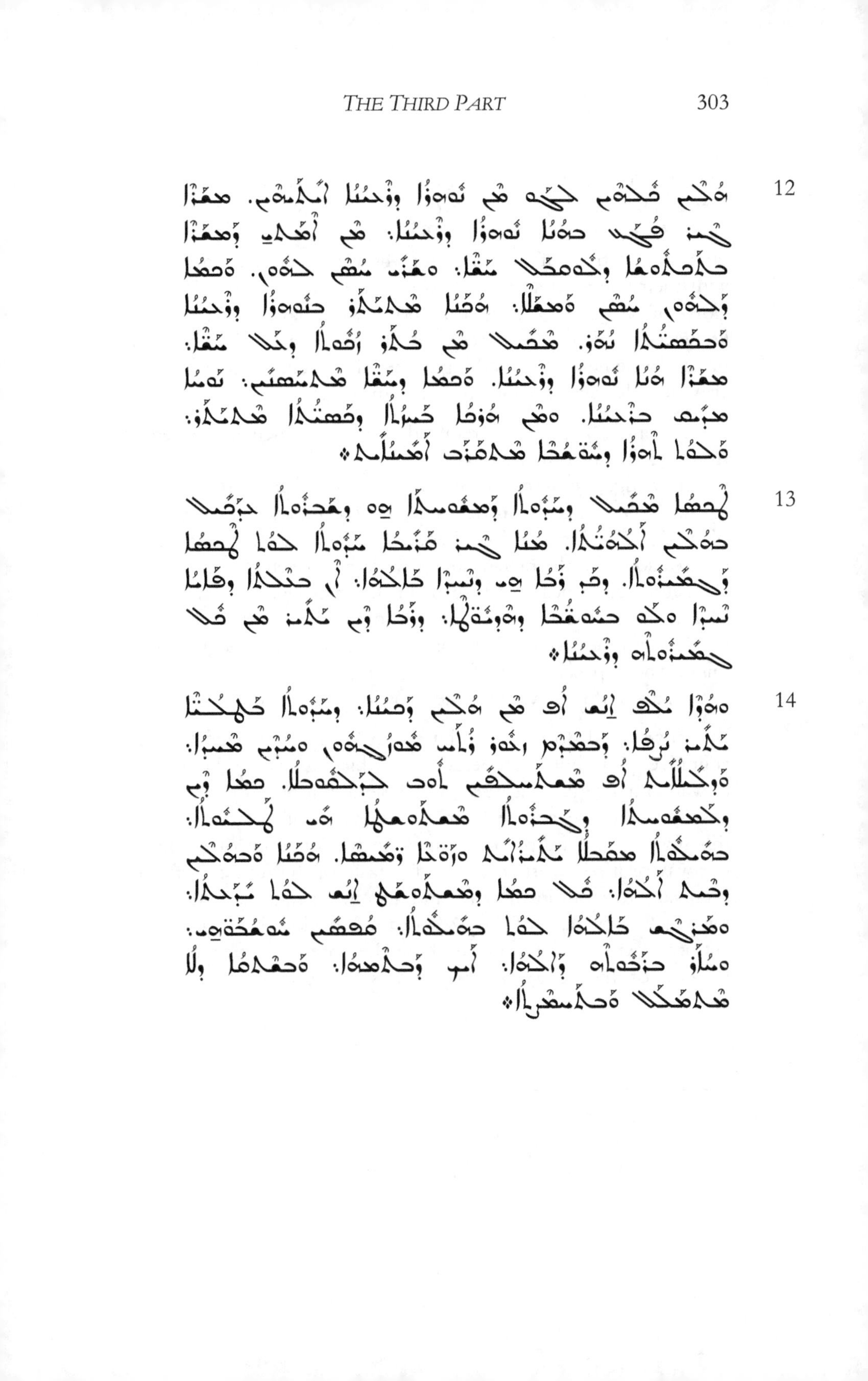

15 Then modesty descends on him to the point that he does not even dare to raise his thought to <God>, nor observe the throne of His glory. As the revelation of the Prophet teaches us about the seraphim at the time of the Trisagion, how they covered their faces with their wings so as not to observe freely the brightness of the glory of God.[16] So it is for those who have arrived at the knowledge which is the perception of what is in God, which looks on in amazement at something higher than human intelligence, as also the holy John the Solitary of Apamea says.

16 For he says: "The soul is reduced to silence when it is lifted up from the stirrings of the passions, has seen the hidden things and its knowledge has remained in the realities of the Spirit." He says again: "That which is unspeakable, it perceives when it dwells in silence."[17] The order of joy, then, is yet the measure of infancy, in comparison with the delight in which is the movement in the Spirit <which dwells> near God, through the knowledge of His nature. That is to say, this concerns His wisdom and the rest of the riches of His mysteries which from time to time appear suddenly in the mind, when speech ceases from the natural course of its stirrings, in the haven of rest, which is the knowledge of Him.

17 By knowledge I do not intend a rational motion or what is of the cognitive part, but that perception which assuages the rational power with a certain pleasure of wonder and it brings to the sweetness of stillness, <away> from the course of all thought. And by this mystery, we are prepared to be in the kingdom of heaven, if our way of life is worthy. This is the taste of the future perfection mystically foretold in this life, and also in a mystic way about the joy which is the taste of the *pledge* of the Kingdom;[18] for those who are not <yet> capable to hear about the order of perfection, from the taste of this pledge they may understand about things which are above their measure.

---

[16] Cf. Is. 6:2.
[17] Cf. John Sol.: Rignell, *Briefe*, 118–19
[18] Cf. 2 Cor. 1:21–22; 5:5; Eph. 1:13–14.

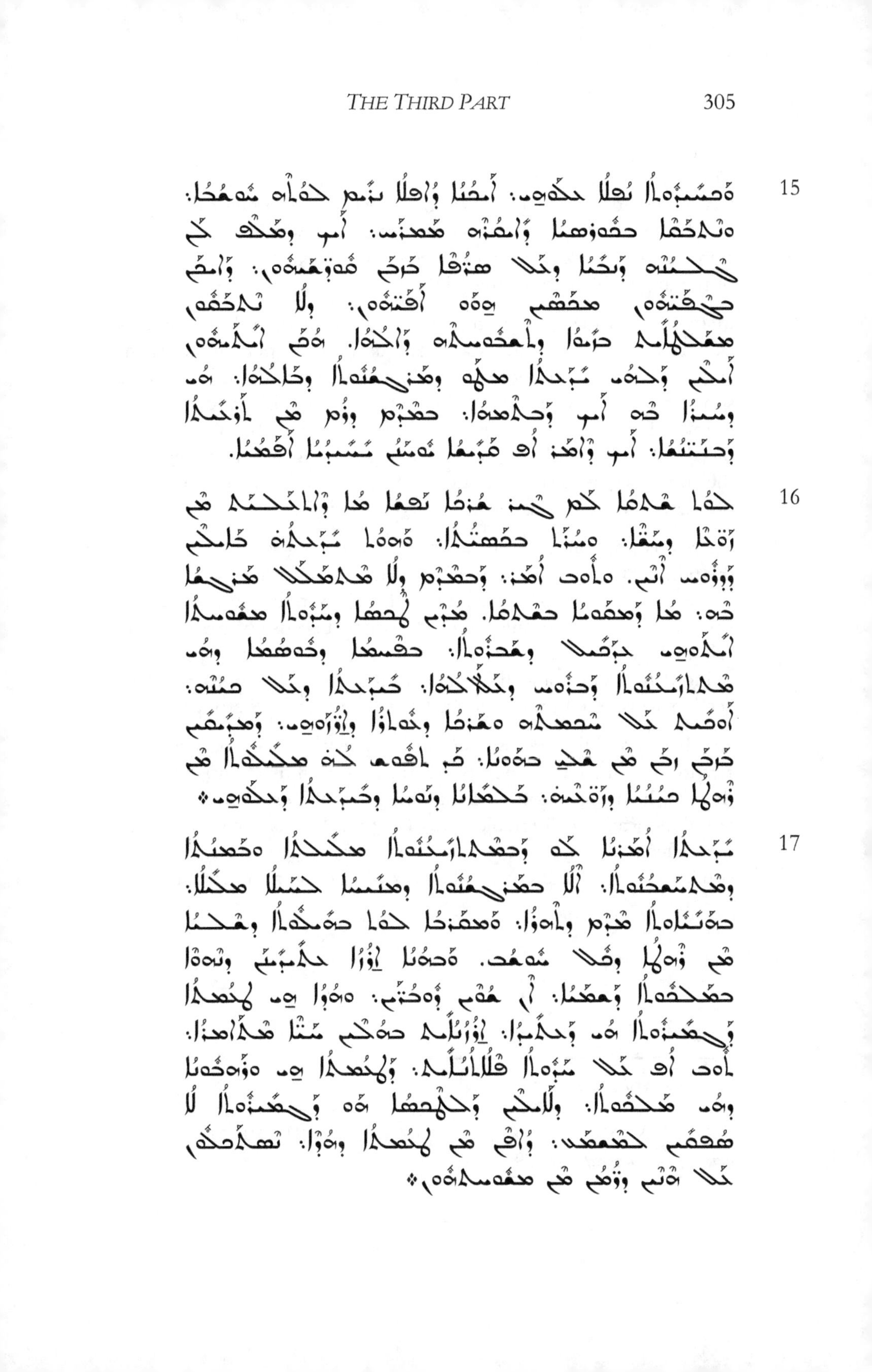

18   Therefore, from when the mind begins to be enlightened, after it has settled and rested a little from the battle, the tumult of the passions, and the distraction of empty intentions which disturb its vision – this wonder of thoughts begins to appear upon it, by means of the intelligible light of the mind.

19   Many times a day, wonderful stirrings arise in it, and the mind is gathered within itself and stays tranquil and the person sits silent and astonished. This occurs sometimes at moments of prayer or sometimes at the office. How pleasant, then, is this silence and this calm! Who knows this, except those who have been overshadowed![19] But this gathering together of the mind, when the light of the mind begins, lasts an hour, then again the mind returns to its order, until other similar <occasions> arise in it.

20   There <is possibility> of delay in this, according to the measure of the mind. The mind, then does not reach these realities whenever it wishes, or as often as it asks, omitting the recitation of the psalms. For sometimes when one begins the office, because of the wonderful stirrings which appear in the mind, the tongue is stopped and reduced to silence; and the verse is interrupted and does not proceed, because the mind is reduced to stillness and has stopped.

21   At this time, the Psalms are no longer allowed because the attention of his mind is removed from the Psalms to those hidden things which arise from within. These are not usual thoughts but are wonderful and ineffable.[20] If one, then, of his own will ceases the office and prayer, while not <yet> perceiving these realities, he is filled with bad thoughts, and empty distraction dominates him.

---

[19] *Overshadowed*, see Is.III I.4.

[20] On interruptions in prayer, see Is.I 53, 490; Is.II IV.4–5, VI.3, XXXII.2, XXXV.1, 4–5; *Keph.* II 78, IV 25. See Is.III XVI. And see Beulay, *L'Enseignement*, 215–39.

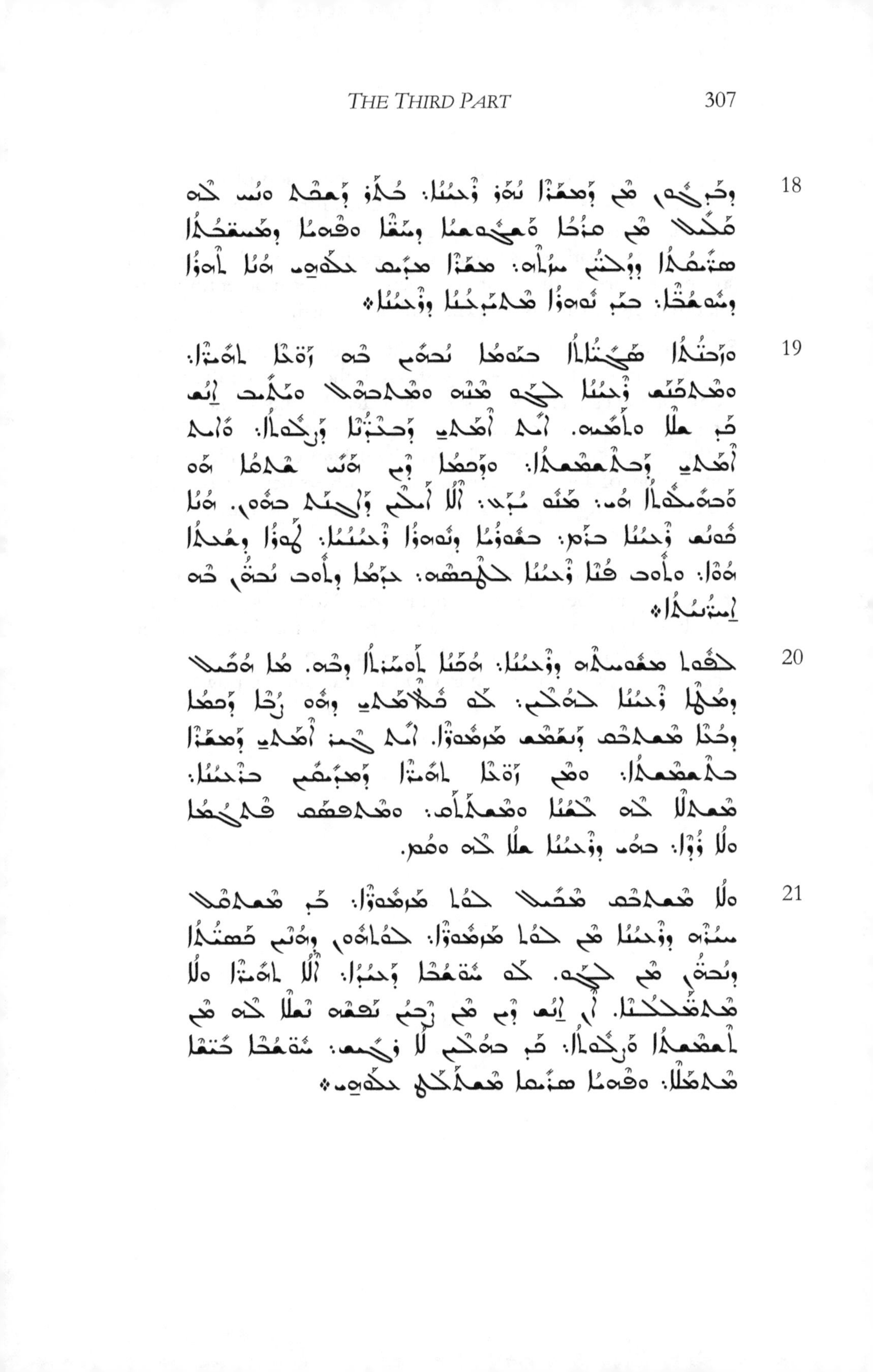

22 This gathering together of the mind and the vision of the intellect is fruit of great separation from others, from prudence <concerning> thoughts and the fight against passions. And as I said, every time that this gathering together of the mind and the marvelous stirrings occurs, at the beginning there is a brief moment; then the mind returns to what is its own, until other stirrings happen again.

23 So when the solitary has arrived at this order, and this sweetness is mingled with his hidden work with God, then he is uplifted a little from listlessness. His soul is not afflicted by the stillness or the long separation from others, nor by the afflictions or the infirmities of the body, as at one time. In that the delight of his mind and the consolation of his heart remove these adversities far from him. Until the solitary receives hidden consolation, the burden of listlessness in him does not diminish.

24 But when by this he is a little refreshed, then the difficult way of the solitary life becomes easy in his eyes. Now this which I have already said, I repeat, as a reminder especially for those who long for these realities: that these delights and apperceptions happen when grace rests upon the mind and it takes on the power of the Spirit.

ܗܳܢܰܘ ܕܶܝܢ ܫܽܘܒܚܳܐ ܕ݁ܚܰܝ̈ܶܐ ܐ̱ܚܪ̈ܳܢܶܐ ܘܗܳܘܢܳܐ: ܡܶܢ ܡܚܰܡܣܢܳܢܽܘܬ݂ܳܐ 22
ܗܰܝܡܳܢܽܘܬ݂ܳܐ ܘܡܶܢ ܚܰܣܺܝܢܽܘܬ݂ܳܐ. ܘܡܶܢ ܪܰܒ݁ܽܘܬ݂ܳܐ ܘܫܽܘܬ݂ܦܽܘܬ݂ܳܐ: ܘܳܐܚܝܕ݂ܘܬ݂ܳܐ
ܘܰܠܚܽܘܡܠܳܐ ܡܶܛܽܠ ܗܳܕ݂ܶܐ. ܘܳܐܦ ܩܢܳܐ ܘܰܐܚܺܝܕ݂. ܫܠܳܐ ܬܶܚܕ݂ܰܝ ܘܗܳܘܶܐ ܗܳܢܳܐ
ܫܽܘܒܚܳܐ ܕ݁ܚܰܝ̈ܶܐ ܡܰܐܨܡܳܢܳܐ ܩܶܢܛܳܐ. ܐܶܠܳܐ ܪܰܒܽܘܬ݂ܳܐ ܗܳܘܳܐ ܚܣܺܝܡܽܘܬ݂ܳܐ. ܘܶܐܠܳܐ
ܘ̇ܚܢܳܐ ܚܒܺܝܫܬ݁ܶܗ: ܒ݁ܰܪܥܰܐ ܘܰܐܘܕ݂ ܦܽܘܝܳܬ݂ܳ ܗܽܘ ܝ̣ܣܰܛܣܕ݂ܳܐ.

ܗܐ ܘܡܶܛܽܠ ܗܳܠܶܝܢ ܬܶܫܒܽܘܚܬܳܐ ܕ݁ܚܰܝܳܐ ܕ݁ܪܽܘܚܳܐ. ܘܳܐܳܐ ܐܶܡܰܪ ܕ݁ܝܼ ܕ݁ܶܝܢ 23
ܗܘܳܐ ܣܰܟ݂ܠܽܘܬ݂ܳܐ ܘܚܰܫܽܘܫ̣ܬܳܐ ܪܶܡܳܢܳܐ ܘܶܐܚܳܐ ܐܰܟ݂ܣܳܐ. ܗܽܘ ܕ݁ܶܝܢ
ܫܽܘܠܳܡܶܗ ܡܶܢܶܗ ܦܽܘܠܚܳܐ ܕ݁ܰܥܰܝܢ ܡܶܢ ܡܶܟ݁ܺܝܠ. ܘܠܳܐ ܚܣܺܝܓ݁ܳܐ
ܘܰܠܡܰܡܣܺܢܽܘܬ݂ܳܐ ܘܡܶܢ ܚܰܣܺܝܢܽܘܬ݂ܳܐ ܘܬܽܘܩܺܝܦܳܐ ܐܳܠܳܐ ܐ̱ܚܪܺܢܳܐ ܘܰܫܳܢܳܐ ܐ̱ܚܪܺܢܳܐ
ܢܶܗܘܶܐ. ܘܠܳܐ ܕ݁ܐܚܰܕܪܺܝܢܳܐ ܐܳܘ ܚܣܽܘܩܽܘܬ݂ܳܐ ܘܰܩܺܝܢܳܐ. ܐܰܝܟ݂ ܕ݁ܰܪܰܓ݂.
ܚܶܫܶܡ ܘܚܽܘܣܦܳܐ ܘܙܳܚ̣ܢܶܗ ܘܚܽܘܡܳܐ ܘܰܠܚܕ݂ܶܗ ܘܫܳܘܶܐ ܚܽܘܩܠܳܐ ܡܶܢܶܗ
ܫܢܺܝܩܳܐ ܗܳܘܺܟ݂. ܒ݁ܰܪܥܰܐ ܘܰܡܟ݂ܰܫܠܳܐ ܬܶܫܒܽܘܚܬܳܐ ܕ݁ܚܰܝܳܐ ܚܰܫܳܢܳܐ. ܠܳܐ
ܡܶܠܶܐ ܡܶܢܶܗ ܬܽܘܗ̈ܡܶܐ ܘܬܽܘܡܠܳܐ.

ܗܳܐ ܕ݁ܶܝܢ ܘܳܐܠܳܩܦܳܐ ܡܶܢ ܗܳܢܳܐ ܡܶܟ݁ܺܝܠ ܡܶܢ ܗܳܠܶܝܟ݂. ܗܽܘܒܰܝ 24
ܫܽܘܠܳܩܳܦܰܡ ܚܺܝܣܶܟܬܳܘܺܢ ܘܳܐܘܚܳܕ݂ܳܐ ܝܰܨܺܝܦܳܐ ܘܣܰܣܒܪܽܘܬ݂ܳܐ. ܗܽܘ ܘܽܘܨܰܠܳܐ
ܘܡܶܢ ܟ݁ܒܰܪ ܐܶܡܰܪܢܳܐ. ܐܽܘ ܗܳܘܕ݂ܳܐ ܐܽܘܟܺܢܳܐ. ܐܰܝܟ݂ ܕ݁ܰܒܕ݂ܶܗܘܳܘܳܢܳܐ ܬܰܟ݁ܠܺܙܳܐ
ܘܳܐܠܟ݂ܰܝ ܘܫܰܠܡܳܐܟ݁ܰܝ ܠܕ݂ܽܘܟ݁ܰܝ. ܘܗܳܟ݁ܰܝ ܬܽܘܩܶܡܦܳܐ ܘܡܶܢܙܺܓܡܶܢܬ݂ܳܐ
ܗܳܘܶܡ: ܐܶܬ݁ܚܕ݂ܰܝ ܘܗܰܨܢܳܐ ܠܡܶܫܘܳܐܠܳܐ ܢܶܓ݁ܠܳܐ ܕ݁ܚܰܝܳܐ. ܘܰܟ݁ܬ݂ܶܒ ܣܰܠܶܠ
ܘܳܐܘ̇ܗܡܳܐ.

25 This force, indeed, is of the Spirit[21] and is not a force <gained through> exercise or simple thoughts that a solitary possesses, by correcting the passions which are in him,[22] or abandoning the world and staying in stillness <away> from others.

26 May the Lord grant you this, that it not only be from simple reading that you know these things, but that in the experience of your person you may know, feel and taste these things, by means of the grace of the holy Spirit which rests upon your intellect. Amen.

---

[21] Variant of ms A: 'of the Spirit'. The ms of Teheran has "hidden."

[22] Elsewhere (Is.I 25) Isaac says: "All existing passions are given for the support of each of the natures to which they belong naturally and for whose growth they were given by God (for support and growth of body and soul)." This approach to the passions is transformative rather than a work of extirpation not unlike the approach in John Sol. where the Evagrian *apatheia* never occurs. In fact regarding this positive approach Beulay comments concerning John of Dalyatha who was also influenced by John Sol. Beulay notes that he had only found one usage of the term *lâ-ḥāšôšûtâ* for impassibility in all the writings of John of Dalyatha. For East Syrian writers, impassibility is not necessarily a complete absence of all sensation of the passions, rather they are altered in their root and redirected: not simply a denial of human beauty or intimacy but exchanging them for an even greater reality. See the recently edited text of John Sol.: "We have forsaken beauty on account of His beauty and pleasure for His pleasure and the sweetness of all our restful desires for His sweetness." See Maroki, "Quatre lettres inédites," 3.2. On the passions in John Sol. see Hansbury, *Soul*, Introd. For the comments on John of Dalyatha see Beulay, *L'Enseignement*, 285–86; *Lumière*, 21–3.

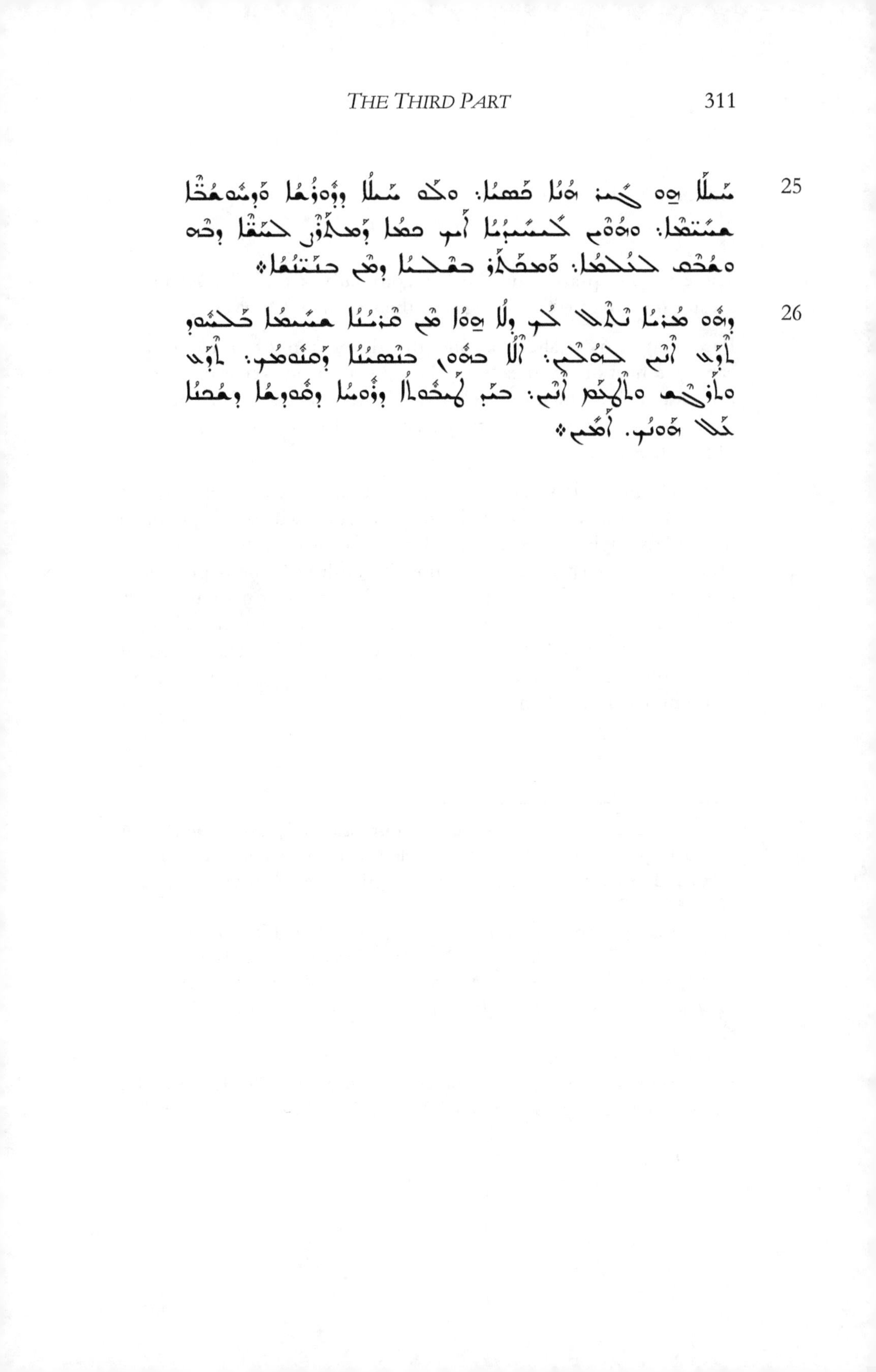

Chapter XVI

Of the same.

1. There is pure prayer and there is spiritual prayer.[1] The second is greater than the first as the light of the sun than its rays.

2. Pure prayer[2] is exalted beyond the distraction of thoughts and earthly reflection by means of the reflection on <celestial> good things and the remembrance of the future world.[3] <Pure prayer> has in it a petition for fine things and it is free from the confusion of transient things.

3. Spiritual prayer[4] is what is stirred in the intellect by the action of the Holy Spirit, with an impulse of perception which is superior to the understanding of creatures. There is no place in it for requests, not even for what is excellent, nor the desire of things promised, nor for the Kingdom of heaven. But by the action of the Holy Spirit, nature goes out from what is its own, outside of the will, and the soul remains only in that amazing divine glory, in the order of those holy hosts in ineffable praises: the hosts which Paul indicates further concerning them.[5]

---

[1] See Is.I 164–75 for a systematic discussion of prayer. The chapter is actually part of Isaac III as ch.14. Included are fathers on prayer: Theodore of Mopsuestia, Ps.Dionysius and Evagrius. See also Khalifé-Hachem, "Prière Pure."

[2] Pure prayer (*ṣlôtâ dakyûtâ*): Is.I 165, 167, 168, 175, 354, 447, 453. Is.II IV.5; VI.7; XV title 2, 3, 7; XXXII.4. *Keph.* I 63, 97; III 11, 13, 14, 41–43, 46; IV 35, 63, 65, 66. See also Aphrahat I, 4; IV 1, 4, 18,19. Evag. *Thoughts* 16; Mark the Monk, *Justified by Works* 162–63, p.182; Sahdona, II 8, 44.

[3] Cf. Heb. 3:5; 6:5.

[4] Spiritual prayer (*ṣlôtâ ruḥânâytâ*): Is.I 168, 170, 175 519; Evag. *On Prayer* 28 (Bamberger). See John Sol. *Soul* 90; Bettiolo, "Sulla preghiera," 2, p. 79.

[5] Cf. Eph. 1:21; Col. 1:16.

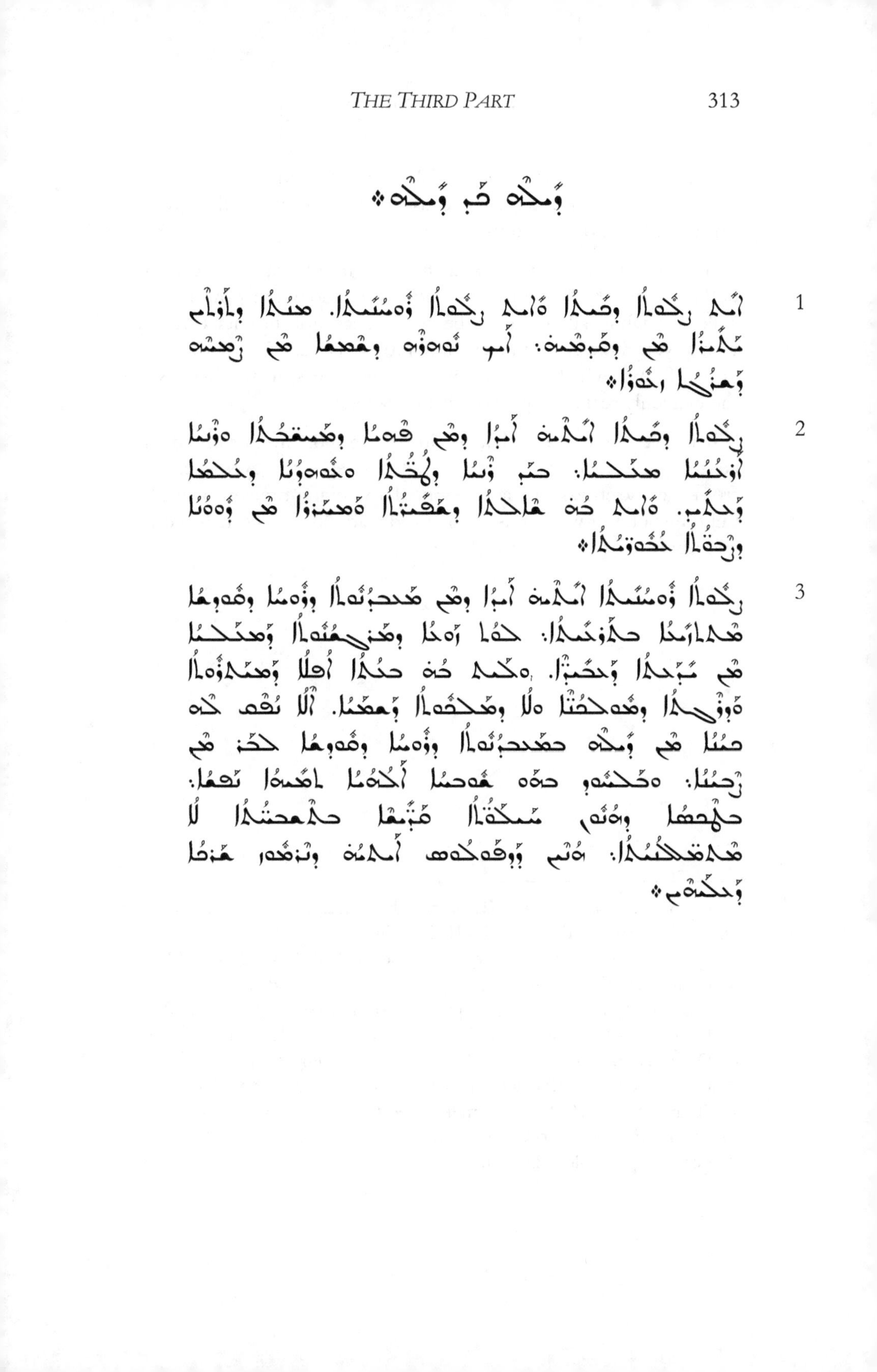

4   In the first prayer, then, there is labor and it is under the power of the will. Its stirrings are set because it is the soul which prays together with the body and the mind.

5   In the second, neither the soul nor the mind pray, not even the bodily senses. <The prayer> is not even under the power of the will. But while all is quiet, the Spirit accomplishes its own will, when even there is no prayer, only rather silence. This is the incorporeal liturgy which is performed by the saints, in the likeness of the heavenly realities, on earth as in heaven.[6]

6   When the soul sees what is in the mind, by means of the contemplation of what is in these <realities>, the eyes shed tears from the sweetness of their vision.[7] How many times thoughts assail the soul, but when it is in the Godhead <there is only> wonder and not one of these <thoughts>.

---

[6] See the *Book of Steps* XII on the three liturgies in heaven, on earth and in the heart. And see Is.III VIII.5; X.84.

[7] On tears at an advanced stage, see Is.I 49, 93, 125–26, 144–46. Tears and weeping occur frequently in Is.II, see the Indexes (*CSCO* 225). John Sol. dedicates three pages to a discussion of tears, *Soul* 16–18. Beulay looks at tears of repentance, and tears of joy and wonder, comparing John of Dalyatha and John Sol. and how tears come during the stage of Limpidity, see Beulay, *L'Enseignement*, 201–05. See *Book of Steps* XVIII, 18: "On the Tears of Prayer." Tears are mentioned throughout the *Ascetic Discourses* of Abba Isaiah. See also G. Panicker, "Prayer with Tears." And see Harb, "Doctrine Spirituelle," 251–54.

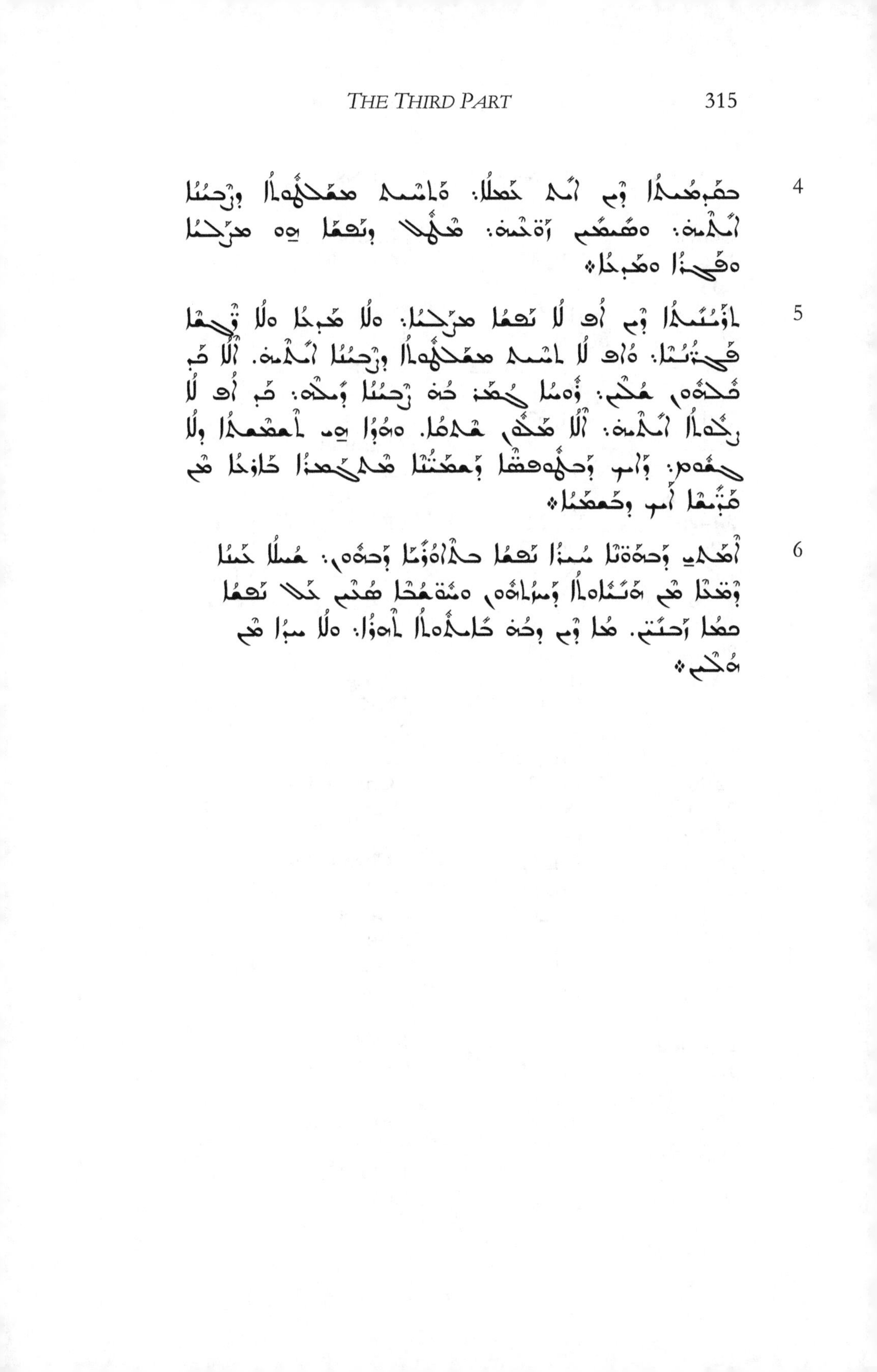

BIBLICAL CITATIONS AND ALLUSIONS

Genesis
1.16:	VII, 47
2:13:	VII, 12
2.21:	III, 33
3:	VII, 35
3.5:	V, 9; XII. 22
3.7–21:	VI, 28
15.12:	III, 33
28.12:	IX, 12, 13

Exodus
3.1–2:	IX, 22
3.2:	VII, 20
13.21–22:	IX, 25
19.16:	IX, 30
19.18:	IX, 25
20.20–21:	IX, 30
20.21:	III, 23; VII. 5,7; IX, 25; XI, 31
20.24:	VIII, 15
22.26:	VI, 32
23.20–21:	IX, 24
23.21:	IX, 25
25.17:	VII, 11
25.21–22:	VII, 11
32.1–14:	VI, 26
34.7:	XI, 4
39.3:	VII, 11
40.34:	VIII,7

Leviticus
16.2:	VII, 11
16.13–15:	VII, 11
19.2:	III, 16
26.11–12:	VIII,7

Numbers
16.38–39:	VII, 11

Deuteronomy
5.22:	IX, 28
27.26:	VI, 9, 10, 12
34.1–4:	X, 52

2 Samuel
12.13:	VI, 26

1 Kings
1.33:	VII, 12
8.27:	VIII, 7
8.39:	IV, 18
21:	VI, 27

2 Kings
19.34:	I, 4; VI, 26
20.6:	I, 4; VI, 26

1 Chronicles
28.2:	VII, 4

2 Chronicles
5.13:	VIII, 7
5.13–14:	VIII, 8
5.14:	VII, 4
7.1–2:	VIII, 4, 8
24.14:	I, 12

Judith
9.8 (Peshitta 9.11):	VII, 4

2 Maccabees
9:18:	XII, 36
12.43–45:	XI, 6
14.35:	VII, 4

Job		56.7:	VIII, 1, 18
33.30:	VI, 55	**Jeremiah**	
Psalms		3.12:	VI, 32
9:5:	VII, 18; X, 61	31.34:	VIII, 1, 18
14.3:	VI, 10		
50.23:	IX, 15	**Ezechiel**	
51.5:	VII, 22	2.4:	XII, 20
71.15:	VII, 14	10.3–4:	VIII, 12
74.16:	X, 48	10.4:	VIII, 12
78.4:	XII, 35	11.19:	X, 66
78.22:	XII, 20	40.1–2:	VIII, 10
84.3:	VII, 13	40.4:	VII, 10
85.3–7:	VII, 18	43.1:	VIII, 10
85.10:	VII, 26	43.1–2:	VIII, 11
103.1:	VII, 13; VIII, 16	43.2:	VIII, 17
		43.2–4:	VIII. 12
104.33:	VII, 13	43.5:	VIII, 9
110.1:	X, 104		
112.4:	X, 1	**Jonah**	
116.7:	VII, 3	4.11:	V, 9
131.1:	II, 8		
142.4:	VII, 44	**Matthew**	
143.2:	VII, 3	4.1–11:	XII, 21–22
145.1:	VIII, 16	5.8:	XIII, 6
145.17:	VI, 19	5.17–6.8:	III.3
146.1:	VII, 13	5.45:	III, 31, 39
		5.48:	IV, 11
Wisdom		6.7:	III, 4
5.16:	V, 9	6.8:	III, 9
		6.9:	III, 14, 15
Ecclesiasticus		6.10:	III, 17, 18
36.15:	VII, 4	6.11:	III, 20
		6.12:	III, 21
Isaiah		6.13:	III, 22
6.2:	XIII, 15	6.25–34:	III, 4
6.3:	III, 34	6.31:	III, 9
14.12–15:	XII, 34	6.32:	III, 9
37.35:	I, 4; VI, 26	6.33:	III, 9
55.8:	VI, 32	12.29	VIII, 6

13.15:	IX, 20	5.37:	IX, 28
13.17:	VII, 12; VIII, 19	7.38:	XI, 33
		8.12:	VII, 47
13.44:	X, 20	9:	VII, 34
13.52:	XI, 33	11.42:	IV, 12
14.24–31	X, 60	17.5:	IV, 14
19.26:	XII, 2		
19.28:	I, 8; IX, 31; XI, 2	**Acts**	
		1.24:	IV, 18
		2:	IX, 27
21.13:	VIII, 1, 18	2.1–2:	X, 47
22.14:	X, 66	2.23:	VII, 8
22.30:	I, 1	2.38:	IV, 21, 22
24.30:	X, 93	7.35–36	IX, 23
25.1–13:	X, 37, 40	10.9:	IX, 13, 17
26.36–46:	IV, 12	10.11:	IX, 13
26.39:	X, 45	10.45:	IV, 21, 22
		15.8:	IV, 18
Mark		17.29:	X, 95
9.26:	VIII, 4	21:13:	III, 31
Luke		**Romans**	
2.25–32:	VII, 13	1.20:	I, 17
7.41–42:	VI, 29	2.5:	XII, 36
7.47:	VI, 62	3.12:	VI, 10
10.24:	VII, 12	3.20:	VI, 6,7
10.42:	X, 107	3.22:	VI, 6
11.9–13:	VI, 50	3.25:	XI, 30
15.10:	VII, 4	4.5:	VI, 12
15.11–32:	VI, 35	4.13:	VI, 6
15.17:	VII, 48	5.8:	VI, 41
16.24:	X, 76	5.10:	VI, 41; XII, 27
18.3:	X, 58	5.17–19:	V, 10
18.9–14:	VI, 35	5.20:	VI, 35
19.12–15:	X, 93	6.2–11:	I, 18
22.41–44:	X, 46	6.3:	XI, 31
23.39–43:	VI, 37	6.6:	VIII, 3
		7.14:	X, 54
John		7.22:	X, 7
1.14:	IX, 29	7.23:	X, 53, 54
3.16:	VI, 41		

8.1–12:	IV, 30	3.18:	I, 13; II, 5; III, 13
8.15:	III, 16		
8.17:	III, 31	4.6:	VII, 21, 47
8.28:	XII, 26	4.16:	X, 7
8.32:	VII, 18	5.5:	VII, 36; X, 45, 94; XIII, 17
8.35:	III, 31		
9.20–21:	I, 2	5.7:	V, 17
9.29:	X, 103	6.10:	VI, 39
12.1:	VI, 60; VII, 10	10.17:	VI, 5
12.2:	XI, 1	12.2–3:	IX, 20; XIII, 5, 6
12.5:	V.10; X, 92		
14.17:	VI, 58	12.9:	VII, 26
16.25–26:	VII, 18		
16.27:	III, 39	**Galatians**	
		2.16:	VI, 6, 7, 12
1 Corinthians		3.10:	VI, 9, 10, 12
1.31:	VI, 5	3.27:	XI, 31
2.6:	IV, 11; IX, 31	4.1–2:	XIII, 13
2.9:	III, 36; V, 4	4.4:	VII, 47
2.10:	IX, 20	4.24–25:	III, 16
2.10–11:	IX, 31	5.16–17:	IV, 30
2.15:	X, 24	6.14:	III, 31
3.16:	VIII, 1		
3.16–17:	VIII, 14, 18	**Ephesians**	
11.17–34:	XI, 14	1.13–14:	VII, 36; X, 45, 94; XIII, 17
11.27–29:	XI, 11, 12, 15		
11.33–34:	XI, 15	1.18:	I, 11
12.12:	V, 10; X, 92	1.21:	XVI, 3
13.12:	II, 5; V, 17; IX, 9	1.22–23:	V, 10; X, 92
		2.4:	V, 18; VI, 43
14.1:	IV, 29	2.6:	XI, title, 1, 31
14.12:	IV, 29	2.9:	VI, 6
15.28:	V, 10; VI, 62	2.15:	III, 16
15.50:	VI, 53	3.10:	VI, 44
		3.16:	X, 7
2 Corinthians		4.13:	IV, 11
1.21–22:	VII, 36; X, 45, 94; XIII, 17	4.23:	XI, 1, 4
		5.30:	V, 10; X, 92, 106
3.3:	IV, 22		
3.14:	XII, 20	5.32:	V, 16

6.10:	XII, 35	3.5:	IV, 26; XI, 1

Philippians   **Hebrews**
2.7:	V, 15	2.2:	IX, 23, 26
3.15:	IV, 11; IX, 31	2.2–3:	IX, 28
4.10:	VI, 58	2.4:	IX, 29
4.18:	IX, 15; XII, 31	2.5:	I, 1; IV, 14, 22; VI, 18, 57; VIII, 19; IX, 27, 30, X, 12; XI, 31; XIII, 7; XVI, 2

Colossians
1.16:	XVI, 3
1.18:	V, 10; X, 92
2.12:	XI, title, 1
3.1:	XI, title, 1
3.1–3:	VI, 51
4.6:	III, 4
4.12:	IV, 11

		5.9:	IX, 15
		9.13–14:	VII, 10
		9.14:	VI, 15
		9.22–23:	VI, 9
		10.1–18:	IX, 15

1 Thessalonians
1.6:	VI, 58	10.10:	XI, 29
2.12:	VII, 19	10.26:	XI, 32
3.13:	VIII, 19	11.38:	XII, 14, 32
		12.22:	VII, 16, 17
		13.15:	IX, 15; X, 64

2 Thessalonians
1.5:	XII, 36

James
1.17:	X, 39

1 Timothy
1.1:	VIII, 19	2.7:	VIII, 14
2.4:	XI, 29, 32	2.10:	VI, 9, 10, 12
4.4–5:	VIII, 14	2.17:	VI, 6
6.19:	XI, 27	4.8:	VI, 42

1 Peter
1.2:	VII, 8

2 Timothy
2.21:	I, 12	3.3–4:	IV, 32; VI, 55
3.7:	XI, 32	4.8:	XI, 5, 29
4.8:	VII, 26; XII, 51		

2 Peter
1.4:	III, 15
1.19:	VII, 21, 47

Titus
2.12:	III, 7
3.3:	XII, 27

1 John
1.1:	V, 13

2.1:	XI, 28	5.4:	VII, 21
2.13:	III, 39		
2.27:	I, 10	**Revelation**	
3.2:	IV, 11; V,17	21.5: VII, 20, 33	

Some Key Concepts

In order of appearance:

Chapter I

way of life after the resurrection: title
solitary: 1
world to come: 1
zeal: 2
Lord of all: 3
overshadow: 4
converse with God: 5
stillness: 5
limpidity: 6
Divine Economy: 7
wonder (*tehrâ*): 8
New World: 8
migration: 8
intellect (*hawnâ*): 9
eyes of the soul: 11
stirrings: 11
meditation: 14
converse with hope: 16
searching / investigation: 16

Chapter II

excellency of the mind: 1
passion: 2
mirror: 5
contemplation: 7

Chapter III

continual meditation on God: 1
providence of God: 4
divine Nature: 15
cloud of thick darkness: 23
converse of prayer: 32
stupor (*temhâ*): 33
true vision: 33

Chapter IV

authentic prayer: 1
fervent love: 6
silence of the spirit: 7
divine insights: 8
future world: 14
spiritual knowledge: 17
recollected mind: 20
knowledge of the Spirit: 21
revelation of insights: 21
impassibility of the soul: 28
labor of the body: 32
action of the Holy Spirit: 32

Chapter V

spiritual realities: 2
divinization: 4
divine love: 6
divine power: 9
other world: 17

Chapter VI

salvation by grace: 6
eschatology: 18
compassion for sinners: 24
continual remembrance: 45
divine intelligence: 46
inebriation: 56
tears: 58

Chapter VII

Shekinah: 4
cloud of thick darkness: 5
divine contemplation: 17
silence of the soul: 33
interior eye: 33
word of silence: 34
accidents (*gdêšê*): 44
spiritual light: 46

Chapter VIII

constant prayer: 1
activity of the Holy Spirit: 1
crucifixion of the intellect: 3
heart as altar: 5
divine revelation: 9
mediation of the angels: 11
divine vision: 11

Chapter IX

contemplation of the soul: 2
reading: 3, 5, 7, 9, 10, 11, 12, 15
vision of the mind: 5
future hope: 9
way of the spirit: 19
revelation of the intellect: 20

Chapter X

inner person: 7
harbor: 10
future world: 12
spiritual person: 24
spiritual world: 25

Chapter XI

renewal: 1
transformation: 2
renewal of the mind: 3
Messalians: 9
wonder at God: 25
hope of the future world: 31

Chapter XII

ascetical life as martyrdom: 18
Covenant: 44

Chapter XIII

joy in God: 1
place of stillness: 2
stirring of joy: 3
illumination of the soul: 6
illumination of the mind: 6
authentic revelation: 6
measure of his way of life: 8
limpidity of the intelligence: 11
light of the mind: 15

Chapter XVI

pure prayer: 2
spiritual prayer: 3
tears: 6

ABBREVIATIONS

AMS	Acta Martyrum et Sanctorum.
ASR	Annali di Scienze Religiose (Milan).
ASE	Annali di Storia dell' Esegesi (Bologna).
CO	Cahiers d'Orientalisme.
ChrOR	Christian Orient (Kottayam).
CPE	Connaissance des Pères de l'Église (Montrouge).
CSCO	Corpus Scriptorum Christianorum Orientalium (Louvain).
DSpir	Dictionnaire de Spiritualité (Paris).
Harp	The Harp: a Review of Syriac and Oriental Studies (Kottayam).
JCSSS	Journal of the Canadian Society for Syriac Studies (Toronto).
JECS	Journal of Early Christian Studies (Baltimore).
JECS	Journal of Eastern Christian Studies (Nijmegen).
JSS	Journal of Semitic Studies (Oxford/Manchester).
JTS	Journal of Theological Studies (Oxford).
LM	Le Muséon (Louvain la Neuve).
MKS	Mémorial Mgr. Gabriel Khouri-Sarkis, ed. F. Graffin (Louvain,1969).
OCA	Orientalia Christiana Analecta (Rome).
OCP	Orientalia Christiana Periodica (Rome).
OS	L'Orient Syrien (Vernon).
PdO	Parole de l'Orient (Kaslik, Lebanon).
PG	Patrologia Graeca (Migne).
PO	Patrologia Orientalis (Turnhout).
POC	Proche-Orient Chrétien (Jerusalem).
SEERI	St Ephrem Ecumenical Research Institute (Kottayam).
SC	Sources Chrétiennes (Paris).
SympSyr	Symposium Syriacum (OCA).
StPatr	Studia Patristica (Kalamazoo/Leuven/Berlin/Oxford).
SVTQ	St. Vladimir's Theological Quarterly (New York).
TS	Theological Studies (Baltimore).
WS	Woodbrooke Studies (Cambridge).
ZAC	Zeitschrift für Antikes Christentum (De Gruyter).
ZNW	Zeitschrift für die neutestamentliche Wissenschaft und die Kunde des alten Christentum (Berlin).

Bibliography of Works Cited

Ancient Authors and Translations
Abba Isaiah

R. Draguet, *Les Cinqs recensions de l'Asceticon syriaque d'Abba Isaïe*, CSCO SS 120–23 (Louvain, 1968); cited by Discourse and section number.

Acts of the Martyrs

P. Bedjan (ed.), *Acta Martyrum et Sanctorum* I-VII, (Paris – Leipzig, 1890–97).

Acts of Thomas

W. Wright, *The Apocryphal Acts of the Apostles*, Vol.1 *Syriac Texts* (London, 1871); cited by page.

Ammonius

M. Kmosko, *Ammonii Eremitae Epistolae* (PO 10, 6; 1914).

Aphrahat

A. Lehto (tr.), *The Demonstrations of Aphrahat the Persian Sage* (Piscataway: Gorgias Press 2010).

K. Valavalonickal, *Aphrahat, Demonstrations*, I-II (Moran Etho 23–24; Kottayam, 2005).

Babai

Babai the Great, *Commentary on Evagrius' Centuries* in W. Frankenberg, *Evagrius Ponticus* (AKGWG, 1912), 8–471.

Basil

M. Forlin Patrucco (ed.), *Basilio di Cesarea. Le lettere I* (Turin, 1983).

Book of Steps

R. Kitchen and M. Parmentier, *The Book of Steps: The Syriac Liber Graduum* (Kalamazoo: Cistercian Publications, 2004).

M. Kmosko, *Liber Graduum, Patrologia Syriaca* 3 (1926).

Dadisho Qaṭraya

R. Draguet, *Commentaire du livre d'Abba Isaie (logoi I-XV) par Dadisho Qatraya (VII e s.)*, CSCO SS 144–5 (Louvain, 1972); cited by Discourse and section number.

Ephrem

E. Beck, CSCO *SS*: *Hymns on Faith* 73–4; *Hymns against Heresies* 76–

7; *Hymns on Paradise* 78–9; *Hymns on Nisibis* 92–3, 102–3; *Hymns on Unleavened Bread* 108–109.

S. Brock (tr.), *The Paradise Hymns* (New York: St. Vladimir's Seminary Press, 1990).

M. Hansbury (tr.), *The Hymns of St.Ephrem the Syrian* (Oxford: SLG Press, 2006).

L. Leloir (ed.), *Commentaire de l'Évangile Concordant, Texte syriaque*, Chester Beatty Monographs 8 (Dublin, 1963; french trans., SC 121 Paris 1966).

J.B. Morris (tr.), *Selected Works of St.Ephrem the Syrian* (Piscataway: Gorgias Press, 2008).

E. Mathews and J.P. Amar (tr.), *St. Ephrem the Syrian Selected Prose Works* (Washington: CUA Press, 1994): *The Homily of Our Lord*.

C. Mc Carthy, *St. Ephrem's Commentary on Tatian's Diatessaron* (*JSS* Supplement 2, 1993).

Evagrius

J-E. Bamberger (tr.), *Evagrius Ponticus The Pratikos Chapters on Prayer* ((Kalamazoo MI: Cistercian Publications, 1981).

A. M. Casiday (tr.) *Evagrius Ponticus*, The Early Church Fathers (London: Routledge, 2006): *The great letter* (Letter to Melania); *On Thoughts*; *Notes on Ecclesiastes*.

W. Frankenberg, *Evagrius Ponticus*, Berlin 1912.

P. Gehin (ed.), *Évagre le Pontique. Scholie aux Proverbes* SC 340 (Paris, 1987).

A. Guillaumont and C. Guillaumont, *Le Gnostique* SC 356, 1989.

A. Guillaumont (ed.), *Les six Centuries des "Kephalia Gnostica" d'Évagre le Pontique* (PO 28, I; 1958); cited by Century and number.

W. Harmless and R. Fitzgerald (tr.), "The Sapphire Light of the Mind: The Skemmata of Evagrius Ponticus," *TS* 62 (2001), 498–529.

J. Muyldermans (ed.), *Evagriana Syriaca* (Louvain, 1952). *Admonitio paraenetica*; *Paraenesis*; *La foi de Mar Évagre*; *Les justes et les parfaits*.

M. Parmentier, *Evagrius of Pontus* "Letter to Melania," Bijdragen 46 (1985) 2–38; repr. E. Ferguson, *Forms of Devotion* (New York: Garland, 1999).

G. Vitestam (ed.), *Seconde partie du traité qui passe sous le nom de "La grande lettre d'Évagre le Pontique a Melania l'ancienne" publiée et traduite d'après le manuscrit du British Museum Add. 17192*, Lund 1963.

Gregory of Cyprus

I. Hausherr (ed.), "Gregorii Monachi Cyprii De Theoria," OCA 110, 1937.

Hierotheos

F.S. Marsh, *The Book of the Holy Hierotheos* (London/Oxford, 1927).

Holy Women

S. Brock – S. Ashbrook Harvey (tr.), *Holy Women of the Syrian Orient* (Berkeley: Univ. of California Press, 1987).

Isho'dad of Merv

M. Gibson (ed.), *The Commentaries of Isho'dad of Merv on the New Testament*, The Acts & Epistles in Syriac and English Vol.IV (Cambridge: University Press, 1913).

Isaac the Syrian

P. Bedjan (ed.), *Mar Isaacus Ninivita, de Perfectione Religiosa* (Paris/Leipzig, 1909).

P. Bettiolo (tr.), *Isacco di Nineve. Discorsi Spirituali* (Magnano, IT: Edizioni Qiqajon, 1985; 2nd ed., 1990). (Kephalia gnostica/ *Keph.*)

S. Brock (ed.), *Isaac of Nineveh 'The Second Part' Chapters IV – XVI*, CSCO SS 224–25 (Louvain: 1995). (Part II)

S. Chialà (ed.), *Isacco di Ninive.Terza Collezione*, CSCO SS 246–47 (Louvain: 2011). (Part III)

M. Hansbury (tr.), *Isaac of Nineveh, On Ascetical Life* (New York: St.Vladimir's Seminary Press, 1989).

A. Louf, *Isaac le Syrien, Oeuvres Spirituelles – III* , Spiritualité Orientale 88 (Bellefontaine, 2009).

D. Miller (tr.) *The Ascetical Homilies of Saint Isaac the Syrian* (Boston, 1984).

A. J. Wensinck (tr.), *Mystic Treatises by Isaac of Nineveh* (Amsterdam, 1923; repr. Wiesbaden, 1969). (Part I)

Jacob of Serug

P. Bedjan (ed.), *Homiliae Selectae Mar-Jacobi Sarugensis* I-V (Paris/Leipzig, 1905–10).

H. Connolly (tr.), "A Homily of Mar Jacob of Serugh on the Memorial of the Departed and on the Eucharistic Loaf," Bedjan, *Homiliae Selectae*, V 615–27; trans. in *The Downside Review* 29 NS 10 (2010), 260–70.

A. Golitzin (tr.), *On that Chariot that Ezekiel the Prophet Saw* (forthcoming, Gorgias Press).

"A Homily on the Ten Virgins Described in our Saviour's Gospel," Bedjan, *Homiliae Selectae*, II 375–401; trans. in *The True Vine* 4 (1992), 39–62.

John of Dalyatha

R. Beulay, o.c.d. (ed.) *La Collection des Lettres de Jean de Dalyatha* PO 180 (Belgium: Brepols, 1978).

B. Colless (ed.), *The Mysticism of John Saba*. Syriac text and English trans. of the *Discourses*, reprint of Ph.D. thesis submitted in 1969 to the University of Melbourne.

M.Hansbury (tr.), *The Letters of John of Dalyatha* (Piscataway: Gorgias Press, 2008).

N. Khayyat (ed.), *Jean de Dalyatha, Les Homélies I-XV* Sources Syriaques (Lebanon: CERO/UPA, 2007).

John the Solitary

P. Bettiolo, "Sulla Preghiera: Filosseno o Giovanni?," *LM* 94 (1981), 74–89.

S.P. Brock (ed.), "John the Solitary, On Prayer," *JTS* ns 30 (1979), 84–101.

_____(ed.), "Letter to Hesychius" in *The Syriac Fathers on Prayer and the Spiritual Life* (Kalamazoo: Cistercian Publications, 1987), 78–100.

M. Hansbury (tr.), *John the Solitary on the Soul* (Piscataway: Gorgias Press, 2013).

R. Lavenant (tr.), *Jean d'Apamée, Dialogues et Traités*, SC 311 (Paris: Éditions du Cerf, 1984).

S. Maroki (ed.), "Jean le Solitaire 'Quatre lettres inédites' Textes syriaques et traduction française," *PdO* 35 (2010), 477–506.

D. Miller (tr.), Mar John the Solitary, "An Epistle on Stillness" in *The Ascetical Homilies of Saint Isaac the Syrian* (Boston, 1984).

L. Rignell (ed.), *Briefe von Johannes dem Einsiedler* (Lund, 1941); cited by page.

_____ (ed.), *Drei Traktate von Johannes dem Einsiedler* (Lund, 1960); cited by page.

W. Strothmann (ed.), *Johannes von Apamea Sechs Gesprache mit Thomasios, der Briefwechsel zwischen Thomasios und Johannes und drei an Thomasios gerichtete Abhandlungen* Patristiche Texte und Studien 11 (Berlin: Walter de Gruyter, 1972).

Joseph Hazzaya

P. Harb, F.Graffin (ed.), *Joseph Hazzaya, Lettre sur les trois étapes de la vie monastique*, PO 45, 2 (Brepols, 1992).

Macarius

W. Strothmann, *Die syrische Uberlieferung der Schriften des Makarios*, Teil 1, Syrischer Text (GOFS 21, 1981).

Mark the Monk

T. Vivian and A. Casiday (tr.), *Counsels on the Spiritual Life* (Mark the Monk) 2 vols. (Crestwood, NY: St.Vladimir's Press, 2009): *On Baptism*; *Concerning Those Who Imagine That They Are Justified by Works*; *On the Spiritual Law*.

Narsai

J. Frishman (ed.), *The Ways and Means of the Divine Economy*. An Edition, Translation and Study of Six Biblical Homilies by Narsai (Diss. Leiden, 1992): V, *Homily on the Tabernacle*.

Nilus

P. Bettiolo (ed.), *Gli scritti siriaci di Nilo il Solitario* (Louvain-la-Neuve, 1983): *Discorso di ammonimento*; *Discorso sulle osservanze*; *Lettera per gli uomini virtuosi*; *Perle*; *Sulla virtû e sull'uscita da mondo*; *Sulla virtû e sulle passioni*.

Odes of Solomon

J.H. Charlesworth (tr.), *The Odes of Solomon* (California, 1977).

J.A. Emerton (tr.), *The Odes of Solomon* in *The Apocryphal Old Testament* ed. H.F.D. Sparks (Oxford, 1984).

Paradise of the Fathers

E.A.W. Budge (tr.), *Paradise of the Holy Fathers*, 2 vols. (London: 1907; repr. Blanco, Texas: New Sarov Press, 1994).

Philoxenus

E.A.W. Budge, *The Discourses of Philoxenus* I (London 1894); cited by page.

Pseudo-Dionysius

Colm Luibheid (tr.), *Pseudo-Dionysius, the Complete Works* (New York: Paulist Press, 1987).

Rabbinics

P. Alexander (tr.), *3 (Hebrew Apocalypse of) Enoch* in The Old Testament Pseudepigrapha ed. J.H. Charlesworth, 2 vols. (New York: Doubleday, 1983), vol.1.

W. Braude (tr.), *The Midrash on Psalms*, 2 vols. (New Haven: Yale Univ. Press, 1959).

S. Buber (ed.), *Midrasch Tehillim*, 2 vols. (Trier, 1892–93).

A. Cohen (ed.), *Minor Tractates of the Talmud*, 2 vols. (London: Soncino Press, 1965).

I. Epstein (ed.), *The Babylonian Talmud* (London: Soncino Press 1935–52).

Sahdona

A. de Halleux (ed.), *Martyrius (Sahdona). Oeuvres spirituelles*, CSCO SS 86–7, 90–91, 110–113 (Louvain, 1960–65); cited by text volume and page.

Sergius of Resh'aina

P. Sherwood, "Mimro de Serge de Reshayna sur la vie spirituelle," *OS* 5 (1960), 433–59; 6 (1961), 95–115, 121–56; cited by section number.

Shem'on d-Taybuteh

P. Bettiolo (tr.), *Simone di taibuteh. Violenza e Grazia. la coltura del cuore* (Rome, 1993).

A. Mingana, *Early Christian Mystics* (WS VII,1934) 282–320; cited by page and column.

Shubhalmaran

D. Lane (tr.), *Šubḥalmaran The Book of Gifts*, CSCO SS 236–37 (Louvain, 2004).

Synodicon Orientale

J.B. Chabot (ed.), *Synodicon orientale ou recueil des synodes nestoriens* (Paris, 1902).

Theodore of Mopsuestia

R. Greer, *Theodore of Mopsuestia. Commentaries on the minor Epistles of Paul* (Atlanta, Ga: Society of Biblical Literature, 2010).

R. Hill (tr.), *Theodore of Mopsuestia: Commentary on the Twelve Prophets* (Washington: CUA Press, 2004).

F. McLeod (tr.) *Theodore of Mopsuestia*, <u>The Early Church Fathers</u> (London: Routledge, 2009).

J.-P. Migne, *Patrologia Graeca* (1856–66) Vol. 66.

A. Mingana, *Commentary of Theodore of Mopsuestia on the Nicene Creed WS* V (Cambridge, 1932); cited by page.

_____ *Commentary of Theodore of Mopsuestia on the Lord's Prayer and on the Sacraments of Baptism and the Eucharist WS* VI (Cambridge, 1933); cited by page.

H.B. Swete, *Theodori Episcopi Mopsuesteni in Epistolas B. Pauli Commentarii* 2 vols. (Cambridge, 1880 and 1882).

R. Tonneau and R. Devreese, *Les Homélies Catéchétiques de Théodore de Mopsueste* (Rome, 1949).

J. Vadakkal (ed.), *The East Syrian Anaphora of Mar Theodore of Mopsuestia. Critical Edition, English Translation and Study,* (Kottayam: Vadavathoor, 1989).

J-M Vosté, *Theodori Mopsuesteni Commentarius in Evangelium Iohannis Apostoli*, CSCO SS 62–3 (Louvain, 1940); cited by page of text volume.

Modern Works

L. Abramowski, "The Theolgy of Theodore of Mopsuestia," *Formula and Context: Studies in Early Christian Thought* (Variorum, 1992), 1–36.

H. Alfeyev, *The Spiritual World of Isaac the Syrian* (Kalamazoo: Cistercian Publications, 2000).

I. de Andia, "Hesychia et contemplation chez Isaac le Syrien," in *Collectanea Cisterciensia* 53 (1991), 20–48.

I.A. Barsoum, *The Scattered Pearls* A History of Syriac Literature and Sciences, 2nd rev.ed. tr. Matti Moosa (Piscataway: Gorgias Press, 2003).

A. Becker, "The Dynamic Reception of Theodore of Mopsuestia in the Sixth Century," in *Greek Literature in Late Antiquity*, ed. S.F. Johnson (Aldershot, Hampshire: Ashgate, 2006), 29–47.

_____ *Fear of God and the Beginnng of Wisdom* (Philadelphia PA: University of Penna. Press, 2006).

P. Bettiolo, " 'Avec la charité comme but': Dieu et création dans la méditation d'Isaac de Ninive," in *Irénikon* 3 (1990), 323–45.

_____ "Esegesi e purezza di cuore. La testimonianza di Dadišo' Qatraya (VII sec.), nestoriano e solitario," ASE 3 (1986), 201–13.

_____ "Lineamenti di Patrologia Siriaca" in *Complementi interdisciplinari di patrologia*, ed. A. Quacquarelli (Rome: Citta Nuova, 1989), 503–603.

_____ "Povertà e conoscenza. Appunti sulle Centurie gnostiche della tradizione evagriana in Siria," *PdO* XV (1989), 107–25.

_____ " ' Prigioneri dello Spirito'. Libertà creaturale ed *eschaton* in Isacco di Ninive e nelle sue fonti," *ASR* 4 (1999), 343–63.

R. Beulay, *L'Enseignement Spirituel de Jean de Dalyatha* (Paris: Beauchesne, 1990).

_____. *La Lumière sans forme. Introduction a l'étude de la mystique chrétienne syro-orientale* (Belgium: Éditions de Chevetogne, 1987).

B. Bitton-Ashkelony, "The Limit of the Mind (ΝΟΥΣ): Pure prayer according to Evagrius Ponticus and Isaac of Nineveh ," *ZAC* 15 (2011), 291–321.

G. G. Blum, *Mysticism in the Syriac Tradition* (Kerala: SEERI, vol.7).

T. Bou Mansour, "La distinction des écrits des Isaac d'Antioche," in *JECS* 57 (2005), 1–46.

_____ *La pensée symbolique de saint Ephrem le Syrien* (Lebanon: Kaslik, 1988).

_____ *La Théologie de Jacques de Saroug*, 2 vols. (Lebanon: Kaslik, 1993).

B. Bradley, "Jean le Solitaire," *DSpir* VIII (1974), 764–772.

S.P. Brock, "Dieu Amour et Amour de Dieu chez Jacques de Serug," Actes du Colloque VIII, *Patrimoine Syriaque* (Lebanon: CERO, 2003), 175–182.

_____ "Discerning the Evagrian in the Writings of Isaac of Nineveh: A Preliminary Investigation," in *Adamantius* 15 2009), 60–72.

_____ "An Early Interpretation of *pasah* : *'aggen* in the Palestinian Targum," in *Interpreting the Hebrew Bible*, ed. J.A. Emerton and S.C. Reif (Cambridge University Press, 1982), 27–34.

_____ "Early Syrian Asceticism," in *Numen* 20 (1973), 1–19.

_____ "Humanity and the natural world in the Syriac tradition," *Sobornost* 13 (1991), 131–42.

_____ "The Imagery of the Spiritual Mirror in Syriac Literature," *JCSSS* 5 (2005), 3–17.

_____ "Jewish Traditions in Syriac Sources," *JJS* 30 (1979), 212–32.

_____ *The Luminous Eye* (Kalamazoo, MI: Cistercian Publications, 1992).

_____ "Maggnânûtâ: A Technical Term in East Syrian Spirituality and its Background," in *MG* (Geneva, 1988) 121–29.

_____ "Passover, Annunciation and Epiclesis: some remarks on the term *aggen* in the Syriac versions of Luke 1:35," *Novum Testamentum* 24 (1982), 222–33.

_____ "Some Paths to Perfection in the Syriac Fathers," *StPatr* 51 (2011), 79–94.

_____ "Some Prominent Themes in the Writings of the Syriac Mystics of the 7th/8th Century AD (1st/2nd cent. H)" M. Tamcke (ed.) *Gotteserlebnis und Gotteslehre* vol. 38 (Wiesbaden, 2010), 49–59.

_____ "Some Uses of the Term *theoria* in the Writings of Isaac of Nineveh," *PdO* 22 (1996), 407–19.

_____ "The Spirituality of the Heart in Syrian Tradition," *Harp* I (1988), 93–115.

_____*Spirituality in Syriac Tradition* (Kottayam, 1989).

_____ "Three Syriac Fathers on Reading the Bible," *Sobornost* 33:1 (2001), 6–21.

_____ "Traduzioni siriache degli scritti di Basilio," in Comunità di Bose (ed.) *Basilio il Grande e il monachesimo orientale* (Bose, 2001), 165–80.

_____ "World and Sacrament in the Writings of the Syrian Fathers," *Sobornost* 6:10 (1974) 685–96; repr. in *Studies in Syriac*

Spirituality (Kottayam,1988), 1–12.

T. Buchan, "Paradise as the Landscape of Salvation in Ephrem the Syrian," in *Partakers of the Divine Nature*, ed. M.J. Christensen and J.A.Wittung (Madison NJ: Fairleigh Dickenson University Press, 2007), 146–59.

G. Bunge, "Le 'lieu de la limpidité': a propos d'un apophthegme énigmatique: Budge II, 494," *Irénikon* 55 (1982), 7–18.

A. Casiday, "Universal Restoration in Evagrius Ponticus' 'Great Letter'," *StPatr* 47 (2010), 223–28.

D. Cerbelaud, "Aspects de la Shekinah chez les auteurs chretiens syriens," *LM* 123 (2010), 91–125.

S. Chialà, *Dall' ascesi eremitica alla misericordia infinita. Ricerche su Isacco di Ninive e la sua fortuna.* (Florence, 2002).

_____ "Evagrio il Pontico negli scritti di Isacco di Ninive," *Adamantius* 15 (2009), 73–84.

_____ "L'importance du corps dans la prière, selon l'enseignement d'Isaac de Ninive," *CDP* 119 (2010), 30–39.

_____ "Une nouvelle collection d'écrits d'Isaac de Ninive," *POC* 46 (2004), 290–304. (Part III)

_____ "L'umiltà nel pensiero di Isacco di Ninive: via di umanizzazione e di divinizzazione," in E. Vergani and S. Chialà (eds.), *Le ricchezze spirituali delle Chiese sire* (Milan, 2003), 105–20.

R.H. Connolly, "The Early Syriac Creed," *Zeitschrift fur die Neutestamentliche Wissenschaft und die Kunde des Urchristentums* 7 (1906), 202–23.

S. Daccache, "Figures Remarquables dans la Mystique Syriaque du VII-VIII Siècle," *POC* 60 (2010), 245–56.

J. Frishman, "Type and Reality in the Exegetical Homilies of Mar Narsai," *StPatr* 20 (1989), 169–75.

P. Gehin, "La dette d'Isaac de Ninive envers Evagre le Pontique," *CPE* 119 (2010), 40–52.

A. Golitzin, "The Image and Glory of God in Jacob of Serug's Homily On that Chariot that Ezekiel the Prophet Saw," *SVTQ* 43:3–4 (2003), 323–64.

_____ "The Place of the Presence of God: Aphrahat of Persia's Portrait of the Holy Man," http://www.marquette.edu/maqom/aimilianus

S.Griffith, "Asceticism in the Church of Syria: the Hermeneutics of Early Syrian Monasticism," *Asceticism* ed. V. Wimbush & R. Valantasis (New York: Oxford University Press, 1995), 220–45.

P. Hagman, *The Asceticism of Isaac of Nineveh* (Oxford: University Press, 2010).

_____"St. Isaac of Nineveh and the Messalians," in M. Tamcke (ed.), *Mystik – Metapher – Bild. Beiträage des VII. Makarios- Symposiums* (Göttingen 2007), 55–66.

A. de Halleux, "La Christologie de Jean le Solitaire," *LM* 94 (1981), 5–36.

_____"Le milieu historique de Jean le Solitaire," III *SympSyr*, ed. R.Lavenant OCA 221 (Rome, 1983), 299–305.

M. Hansbury, " 'Insight without Sight': Wonder as an Aspect of Revelation in the Discourses of Isaac the Syrian," *JCSSS* 8 (2008), 60–73.

_____ "Love as an Exegetical Principle in Jacob of Serug," *Harp* XXVII (2012), 353–68.

P. Harb, "Doctrine spirituelle de Jean le Solitaire," *PdO* 2 (1971), 225–60.

I. Hausherr, *Études de spiritualité orientale*, OCA 183 (Rome, 1969).

_____"Par delà l'oraison pure, grace à une coquille: à propos d'un texte d'Évagre," *Revue d'Ascéetique et Mystique 13* (1932), 184–8.

_____ " Un précurseur de la théorie scotiste sur la fin de l'incarnation," *Recherches de Sciences Religieuses* 22 (1932), 316–20.

H. Hunt, " 'Praying the Body': Isaac of Nineveh and John of Apamea on Anthropological Integrity," *Harp* XI-XII (1998–99), 153–58.

N. Kavvadas, "On the Relations between the Eschatological Doctrine of Isaac of Nineveh and Theodore of Mopsuestia," *StPatr* XLV (2010), 245–50.

_____ "Theodore of Mopsuestia as a Source of Isaac of Nineveh's Pneumatology," *PdO* 35 (2010), 393–405.

G. Kessel, Review of Sabino Chiala', *Isacco di Ninive Terza Collezione* (Leuven: Peeters, 2011) in *Studia Patristica* vol. LXIV, 374–81.

E. Khalifé-Hachem, "L'Âme et les Passions des Hommes d'après un texte d'Isaac de Ninive," *PdO* 12 (1984), 201–18.

_____ "La Prière Pure selon Isaac de Ninive," *MKS*, ed. F. Graffin (Louvain, 1969), 157–73.

J-M. Lera, "Theodore of Mopsuestia," *DSpir* XV (1991), 385–400.

A. Louf, "L'homme dans l'histoire du salut selon Isaac le Syrien," *CPE* 88 (2002), 49–54.

_____ "Pourquoi Dieu se manifesta, selon Isaac le Syrien," *CPE* 80 (2000), 37–56.

_____ "*Temha*-stupore e *tahra*-meraviglia negli scritti di Isacco il Siro," *La grande stagione della mistica Siro-orientale (VI-VIII secolo)*, ed. E. Vergani and S. Chialà (Milan: Biblioteca Ambrosiana, 2009), 93–119.

S. Maroki o.p., JEAN LE SOLITAIRE (D'APAMÉE) (5th Cent.): Quattre lettres inédites, Textes syriaques et traduction française," *PdO* 35 (2010), 477–506.

G. Nedungatt, "The Covenanters of the Early Syriac Speaking Church," *OCP* 39 (1973), 191–215; 419–44.

M. Nin, "La sintesi monastica di Giovanni il Solitario," *Le Chiese sire tra IV e VI secolo. Dibattito dottrinale e ricerca spirituale*, ed. E. Vergani and S. Chialo (Milan: Centro Ambrosiano, 2005), 95–117.

G. Panicker, "Prayer with Tears: A Great Feast of Repentance," *Harp* (1991), 111–33.

C. Pasquet, "Le Notre Père, une règle de vie pour le chrétien? L'enseignement de Théodore de Mopsueste," *CPE* 116 (2009), 50–61.

N. Russell, *The Doctrine of Deification in the Greek Patristic Tradition* (Oxford: University Press, 2004).

N. Sed, "La Shekhinta et ses amis 'araméens'," in *Mélanges A. Guillaumont. Contributions à l'étude des christianismes orientaux*, Geneva 1988 (CO 20), 233–42.

S. Seppälä, "In Speechless ecstasy: expression and interpretation of mystical experience in classical Syriac and Sufi literature," *Studia Orientalia* 98 (2007).

_____ "The Idea of Knowledge in East Syrian Mysticism," *Studia Orientale* 101 (2007), 265–77.

A. Shemunkasho, *Healing in the Theology of St. Ephrem* (Piscataway, NJ: Gorgias Press, 2002).

C. Stewart, "Imageless Prayer in Evagrius Ponticus," *JECS* 9 (2001), 173–204.

E. Urbach, *The Sages* (Jerusalem: Magnes Press, 1979).

E. Vergani, "Isaia 6 nella letteratura siriaca. Due autori del V secolo: Balai e Giovanni il Solitario," *ASR* 7 (2002), 169–92.

S. Vethanath, "St. Ephrem's Understanding of Church as New Paradise and *Locus* of Divinization," *ChrOr* XXIX/1 (2008), 12–22.

TWO DISCOURSES OF THE *FIFTH PART* OF ISAAC THE SYRIAN'S WRITINGS

INTRODUCTION

Born in Beth Qaṭraye in the seventh century, Isaac the Syrian has left a large collection of writings:

First part

P. Bedjan (ed.) *The Ascetical Homilies of Mar Isaac of Nineveh* (Piscataway NJ: Gorgias Press, 2007).

A.J. Wensinck (tr.) *Mystic Treatises of Isaac of Nineveh* (Amsterdam, 1923; repr. Wiesbaden, 1969).

Second part

S. Brock (ed.) *Isaac of Nineveh 'The Second Part' Chapters IV – XVI*, CSCO SS 224–25 (Louvain: 1995).

P. Bettiolo (ed.) *Discorsi spirituali e altri opusculi* (Magnano, IT: Edizioni Qiqajon, 1985, repr.1990).

Third part

S. Chialà (ed.) *Isacco di Ninive Terza Collezione*, CSCO SS 246–47 (Louvain: 2011).

And now there is the *Fifth Part*.[1] How the tradition attests to it has been amply demonstrated by Sabino Chialà.[2]

---

[1] For the critical edition, see Sabino Chialà, "Due discorsi ritrovati della *Quinta parte* di Isacco di Ninive?," *Orientalia Christiana Periodica* 79 (2013), 61–112.

[2] See also Chialà's article: "Two Discourses."

Available manuscripts of the *Fifth Part* have been found:
- Sharfet: Rahmani 80
- Baghdad: Dawra sir. 694
- Dawra sir. 938
- Vatican: sir. 592

Manuscripts where the *Fifth Part* is either cited or mentioned:
- Seert, Episcopio caldeo 109
- Mosul, Patriarcato caldeo 100
- Alqosh, Nostra Signora delle Sementi

And there are two lost manuscripts:
- Mosul, Patriarcato caldeo 97
- Diyarbakir, Episcopio caldeo 25

Until more of the *Fifth Part* is found, it cannot be ruled out that Isaac intended to amplify his thoughts on a final recapitulation. And that the "theological character" of what is included here: infinite mercy for creation and the design of universal salvation are of Isaac. The style is very different from Isaac I, II and III but I would tend to agree that it is by Isaac.

According to Chialà in one of his articles, Isaac is a "witness to God's mercy."[3] And mercy appears prominently in Isaac's schema of the mystic way: in repentance, in purity and in perfection.[4] This is not a linear development. Even at the state of perfection, one may return to repentance or to purity.

> "And what is the sum of purity?"
> "A heart full of mercy unto the whole created nature…"
> "And what is a merciful heart?"
> "It is the heart's burning for the sake of the entire creation, for men, for birds, for animals, for demons and for every created thing; and at the recollection and the sight of them the eyes of

---

[3] "Witness to God's Mercy," unpublished article of Sabino Chialà (available online).

[4] See the discussion of this by Wensinck in his Mystic Treatises, xxiv.

the merciful man pour forth abundant tears. From the strong and vehement mercy that grips his heart and from his great compassion, his heart is humbled and he cannot bear to hear or to see any injury or slight sorrow in creation. For this reason he offers up prayers with tears continually even for irrational beasts, for the enemies of truth and for those who harm him, that they be protected and receive mercy. And in like manner he even prays for the family of reptiles, because of the great compassion that burns without measure in his heart in the likeness of God."[5]

At the conclusion of his article, Chialà suggests that it is out of Isaac's own experience of mercy, as described above, that he developed his theories of Apocatastasis and how they do not contain anything contrary to the Gospel. And that Isaac was informed and motivated more by his own insight and experience than by the controversy surrounding the issue.

"Apocatastasis is the teaching that everyone will, in the end, be saved: an ultimate reconciliation of good and evil; all creatures endowed with reason, angels and humans, will eventually come to a harmony in God's kingdom (Acts 3.21; 1 Timothy 2.4)."[6] It had appeared in Origen, Gregory of Nyssa and Maximus the Confessor.[7] But also in Theodore of Mopsuestia[8] and Diodorus whom Isaac quotes directly in Isaac II. XXXIX.

First from Isaac:

> I am of the opinion that He is going to manifest some wonderful outcome, a matter of immense and ineffable compassion on the part of the glorious Creator, with respect to the order-

---

[5] Miller, *Ascetical Homilies*, Homily 71.

[6] See Apocatastasis in OrthodoxWiki, a definition used here for its precision and brevity.

[7] Chialà comments briefly on each of these authors and their possible influence on Isaac. See *Dall' Ascesi*, 269–76.

[8] Kavvadas says that in his opinion: "…Isaac not only studied Theodore's tract (*Contra defensores peccati originalis*), but he was deeply influenced by this reading while developing his own eschatological doctrine." See Kavvadas, "Eschatological Doctrine," 248–49.

ing of this difficult matter of (Gehenna's) torment: out of it the wealth of His love and power and wisdom will become known all the more – and so will the insistent might of the waves of His goodness. (Isaac II. XXXIX.6)[9]

Then from Theodore:

In the world to come, those who have chosen here what is good, will receive the felicity of good things along with praise; whereas the wicked, who all their life have turned aside to evil deeds, once they have been set in order in their minds by punishments and fear of them, choose the good, having come to learn how much they have sinned, and that they have persevered in doing evil things and not good; by means of all of this they receive a knowledge of religion's excellent teaching, and are educated so as to hold on to it with a good will, (and so eventually) they are held worthy of the divine munificence. For (Christ) would never have said "Until you pay the last farthing" unless it had been possible for us to be freed from our sins once we had recompensed for them through punishments. Nor would He have said "He will be beaten with many stripes" if it were not (the case) that the punishments, measured out in correspondence to the sins, were finally going to have an end. (Isaac II XXXIX.8)[10]

Finally from Diodore of Tarsus:

If the reward for labors is so great, how much greater is the time of immortality than the time of contests, that is, than this world; whereas the punishments are (far) less than the magnitude and number of sins. The resurrection from the dead should not be considered as belonging only to the good, but it also takes place for the wicked (as well). For God's goodness is

---

[9] For an analysis of the eschatological themes in Isaac II XXXIX–XI, see Alfyev, *Spiritual World*, 269–97.

[10] This passage is found in Solomon of Bosra (thirteenth century), *Book of the Bee*, ch. 60. According to Brock, Solomon quotes from Isaac. See Isaac II XXXIX.8, note 8.

greatly to be held in honor: it chastises sparingly. Isaac II XXXIX.11.[11]

I conclude with a ninth century witness to Isaac's tradition: Ibn as-Salt. He has written three letters which include extracts from the writings of Isaac.[12] What drew him to Isaac was apparently his teaching on mercy. To paraphrase:

> He preached insistently the love of mercy, which is the foundation of adoration, and humility which is the rampart of virtues... (13)
>
> Having recognized that the precepts of this Saint are in conformity with those of Jesus and his Apostles, I adhered to his doctrine. (14)

Of interest also is how Ibn as-Salt raises the question of Isaac's orthodoxy. Daniel Bar Tubanita, bishop of Tahal (seventh century), had written a work which is now lost: *Solutions to the questions on the fifth theological volume of Mar Isaac of Nineveh,* in which he refutes Isaac because of issues of Apocatastasis. Ibn as-Salt, in his third letter, asks of a visiting Church official if he prefers the teaching of Isaac or the refutation of Daniel. The response:

> Mar Isaac speaks the language of heaven and Daniel that of earth. Isaac's teaching is only suitable to advanced monks and to those living in solitude in their cells and who are dedicated to prayer. (75)

Since the work of Daniel is lost, it is helpful to read further comments of Ibn as-Salt regarding questions raised about Isaac's writings: that the actions of creatures do not cause a change in God; that he is merciful and that His immutable clemency is above punishment; that in the other world the mercy of God embraces all

---

[11] From Diodore's Discourse V on Providence; this passage is also quoted by Solomon of Bosra, *Book of the Bee,* ch.60. Solomon may have quoted this from a source other than Isaac, see Isaac II XXXIX.13, note 1.

[12] See Sbath, *Traités religieux.*

human beings.[13] The infinite mercy of God and Isaac's eschatology are outlined here.[14] This is what was so unacceptable to Daniel and even to a modern interpreter of Isaac.[15]

Actually now there is another witness available to the *Fifth Part* of Isaac: Shebadnaya, a fifteenth century priest from Northern Iraq. In his "Poem on God's Government from 'In the beginning' until Eternity," he has ten citations concerning ideas and opinions of Isaac's *Fifth Part*. Of particular interest: "Thus wrote Mar Isaac in that *Fifth Part* of his: The suffering which sinners undergo from the torments in Gehenna has a likeness to the suffering of the Son, that which he endures for our sins." This may suggest a redemptive quality, in addition to the punitive aspect of suffering in Gehenna, towards a final redemption.[16]

As startling as this may seem, it is best understood in the context of God's love for mankind. One of the most moving statements about this may be found in Isaac's Discourses (Bettiolo):

> The aim of the death of Our Lord was not to redeem us from our sins, nor for any other reason, but exclusively that the world might become aware of the love of God for creation. If all this had been aimed solely at the remission of sins, it would have been enough to redeem us in some other way.[17]

---

[13] See the six questions and answers in the 1st letter (16–20) in Sbath, 77–78. See also Chialà, *Dall'Ascesi*, 62–63.

[14] In these questions and answers, Chialà notes the theology of Theodore of Mopsuestia concerning God's immutability: that human sin cannot change God's project, see Dall' Ascesi, 63. For other comments of Chialà concerning Theodore's influence on Isaac, see his *Dall'Ascesi*, 92–101.

[15] Bedjan finds God's mercy and compassion for sinners and demons, as expressed in Isaac, to be unacceptable. See Bedjan, *Ascetical Homilies*, xi–xiii.

[16] For the quote and the context, see T. Carlson, "The Future of the Past," 185.

[17] Discourse 4.78, translation as found in Ramelli, *Apokatastasis*, 761; see also the context, 758–66.

Conclusion

As to the actual translation, I am grateful to S. Chialà for the numbered paragraph divisions which he has devised that are not in the manuscripts. Also given the difficulties in translation, particularly of section II, I have often needed to consult with his translation. In addition to being difficult, the *Fifth Part* has a very different style which anyone who has read Isaac's other works will notice immediately. Basically, section I is a collection of Biblical passages in support of what will be affirmed in section II. Most of the quotations are from the Old Testament with few explanations given.[18] But the author concludes section I with an insightful paragraph:

> In fact, He is not the one who puts in motion actions of correction or of punishment, nor does He work in those who do the actions but He consents, only allowing that they occur where He wills that they occur. He does not even make good and bad actions happen by means of those with inclinations such as these. Nor does He set in motion the manner of the chastising and distressing action. (34)[19]

Chialà sums up the very difficult section II: "…nothing of what happens can be said to be outside God's plan, outside his economy (*mdabbrânûtâ*). God, then, takes care of creation, as the author hastens to affirm at the end of the second discourse."[20] And since Apocatastasis is never mentioned explicitly in this translation, Chialà attempts to link it to what is said in these two sections how: "…God will find a way to reintegrate every fragment of creation into his design of salvation, hence the sufferings of sinners in hell do not have a definitive character, but only cathartic."[21] Chialà thus sees a tie between the statement that "nothing happens without

---

[18] As noted by Chialà, Isaac uses predominately the Peshitta; citations from it are italicized throughout the translation.

[19] Perhaps realizing the possible difficulty of this passage, elsewhere Isaac assures that he speaks "according to what I have understood from both the divine vision of the Scriptures and from true mouths, and a little from experience itself…" See Miller, *Ascetical Homilies*, Homily 14.

[20] Chialà, "Two Discourses," 7.

[21] Ibid., 7.

God willing it and the idea of a final recapitulation in which God finds a way to bring back to himself every fragment of creation, without violating its liberty…"[22] And though this may not seem obvious, Chialâ reminds that sections I and II of the *Fifth Part* are only part of a larger document that when found may contain more explicit statements to substantiate this.

Thanks are due to Sabino Chiala' for making the Syriac text of Isaac V available.

---

[22] Ibid., 8.

Bibliography

H. Alfeyev, *The Spiritual World of Isaac the Syrian* (Kalamazoo MI: Cistercian Publications, 2000).

W. Braude (tr.), *The Midrash on Psalms*, 2 vols. (New Haven: Yale Univ. Press, 1959).

T. Carlson, "The Future of the Past: The Reception of Syriac Qaṭraye Authors in Late Medieval Iraq," in Kozah, M., Abu-Husayn, A., Al-Murikhi, S. S., Al Thani, H., (eds.), *The Syriac Writers of Qatar in the Seventh Century* (Piscataway: Gorgias Press, 2014), 169–193.

S. Chialà, *Dall'ascesi eremitica alla misericordia infinita. Ricerche su Isacco di Ninive e la sua fortuna* (Florence, 2002).

——— "Two Discourses of the "Fifth Part" of Isaac the Syrian's Writngs: Prolegomena for Apokatastasis?," in Kozah, M., Abu-Husayn, A., Al-Murikhi, S. S., Al Thani, H., (eds.), *The Syriac Writers of Qatar in the Seventh Century* (Piscataway: Gorgias Press, 2014), 123–131.

——— "Witness to God's Mercy: Conference of Br. Sabino Chialà on Isaac of Nineveh," delivered at a colloquium in Ghent in 2006; posted on the internet 14 June 2008.

R.H. Connolly, "The Early Syriac Creed," *Zetschrift fur die Neutestamentliche Wissenschaft und die Kunde des Urchristentums* 7 (1906), 202–23.

M. Hansbury (tr.), *Isaac the Syrian, Third Part* (in this volume).

N. Kavvadas, "On the Relations between the Escahatological Doctrine of Isaac of Nineveh and Theodore of Mopsuetia," *Studia Patristica* 45 (2010), 245–50.

R. Lavenant (tr.), *Jean d'Apamée, Dialogues et Traités*, Sources Chrétiennes 311 (Paris: Éditions du Cerf, 1984)

A. Louf (tr.), *Isaac le Syrien Oeuvres Spirituelles – III* (Éditions de Bellefontaine, 2009).

D. Miller (tr.), *The Ascetical Homilies of Saint Isaac the Syrian* (Boston: Holy Transfiguration Monastery, 1984; repr. 2011).

I. Ramelli, *The Christian doctrine of Apokatastasis*: A Critical Assessment from the New Testament to Eriugena (Leiden; Boston: Brill, 2013).

P. Sbath (ed.), *Traités religieux philosophiques et moraux, extraits des oeuvres d'Isaac de Ninive (VII siècle) par Ibn as-Salt (IX siècle)*, (Cairo, 1934).

Solomon of Akhlat, *The Book of the Bee*, ed. by E.A.W. Budge (Piscataway: Gorgias Press, 2006).

Text and Translation –
From the *Fifth Part* of Mar Isaac, bishop of Nineveh

I

Examples of confirmation from the Scriptures, against those who say that the world proceeds by chance, without a guide.

1. That a country or a city, or human beings individually even the whole universe, be guarded by God or with His gesture be handed over to misfortune, we learn this from divine Scriptures.

2. We learn this first of all from what is said: *On your walls, O Jerusalem, I have placed watchmen by night and by day, continuously.*[1] And this, Zion has said: "*The Lord has forsaken me and the Lord has forgotten me.*" <*Can*> *a woman forget her newborn babe and not have compassion on the child of her womb? Even if these forget I will not forget you. Behold, on the palms of my hands I have graven you and your walls are continually before me.*[2]

3. And again <God says>: *I will deliver this city into the hand of the king of Babylonia.*[3] And: *I will deliver you into the hand of those whom you have feared.*[4] And this: *Behold I make you a stranger, you and all your friends. They will fall by the sword of their enemies <while you look on>. I will deliver all of Judah into the hand of the king of Babylonia and he will kill them with the sword. I will deliver all of the fortresses of this city and all the fruit of its labor and all its magnificence; and all the treasures of the king of Judah I will deliver into the hand of their enemies; and they will lead them away captive and they will plunder them.*[5]

---

[1] Isaiah 62.6.
[2] Ibid., 49.14–16.
[3] Jeremiah 34.2.
[4] Ezekiel 23.28; Jeremiah 22.25.
[5] Jeremiah 20.4–5.

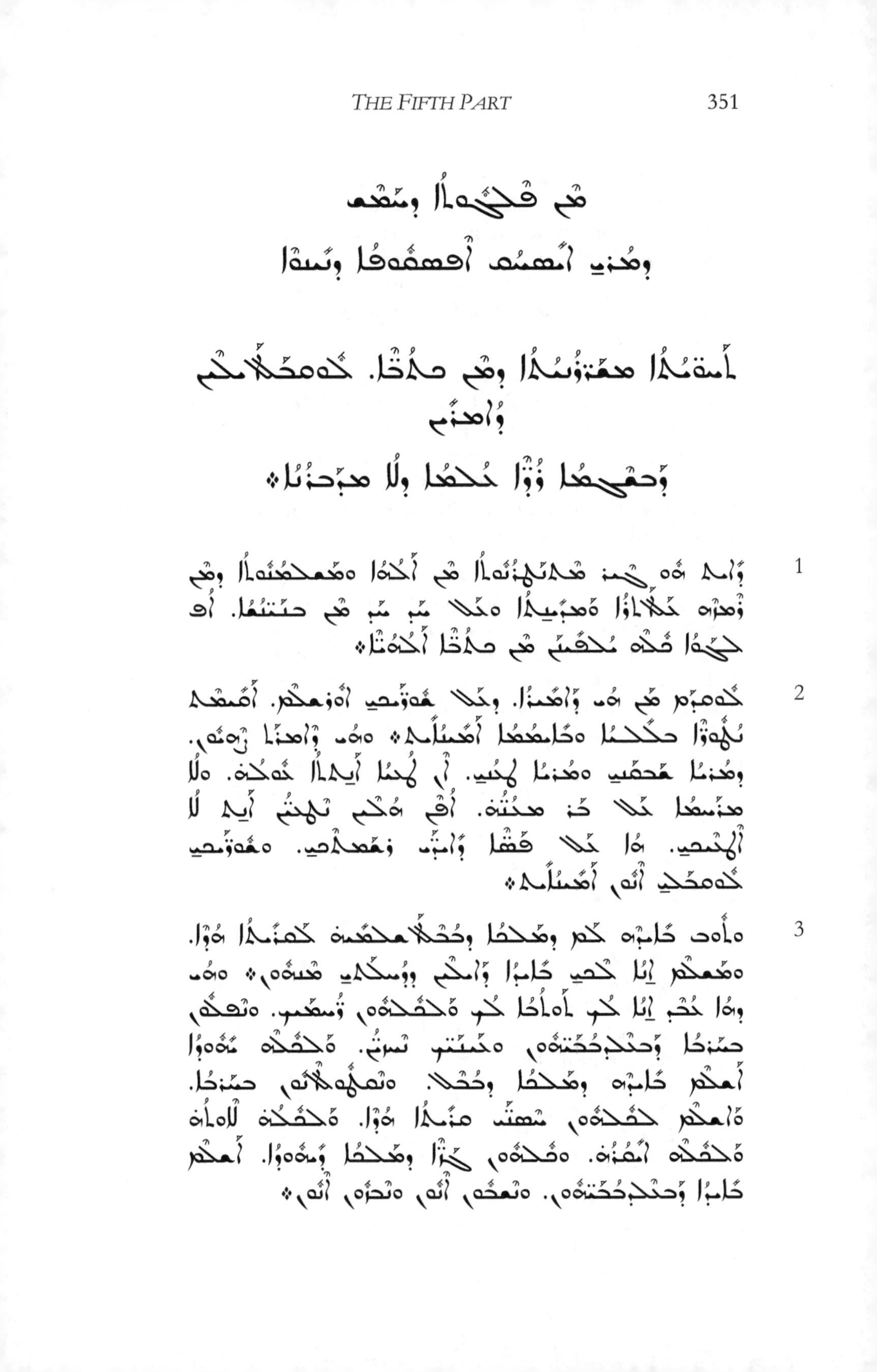

4   You see that it is God who delivers humans, each one into the hands of his neighbor, with their riches and their land; and then one is subject to his neighbor. Are you still in doubt? <God> says: *Raise the javelin which is in your hand against Ai, because I have delivered <the city> into your hands.* [6] And to Baruch, <Jeremiah> said: *I make evil to come upon all flesh, says the Lord, but for you I will preserve your life in all the places where you will go.*[7]

5   And it is said: *Saul was seeking David everyday but God did not give him into his hands.* And it is said: *David inquired of God and said: "Shall I go up against the Philistines? Will you give them into my hands?"*[8] And the Lord said to him: *Go up because I will give all of them into your hands.*[9] And in Zechariah <God> said: *Behold I will deliver all men, each into the hands of his neighbor and into the hands of the king. They will divide the land and I will not rescue it from their hands.*[10]

6   And <God said>: *It is I who incite men, each one against his neighbor.*[11] And again <God said>: *Do not fear him (Og the king of Basan) because I have given him into your hands, he and all his people, and all of his land.*[12] And again it says: *Do not harass the Moabites or contend with them in battle because I will not give you any of their land as a possession.*[13] And again: *See that I have delivered into your hands Sihon king of Heshbon, the Amorite, and his land: begin his destruction and contend with him in battle.*[14]

---

[6] Joshua 8.18.
[7] Jeremiah 45.5.
[8] 1 Samuel 23.14.
[9] 2 Samuel 5.19
[10] Cf. Zechariah 11.6.
[11] Isaiah 19.2.
[12] Deuteronomy 3.2.
[13] Ibid., 2.9.
[14] Ibid., 2.24; 31.

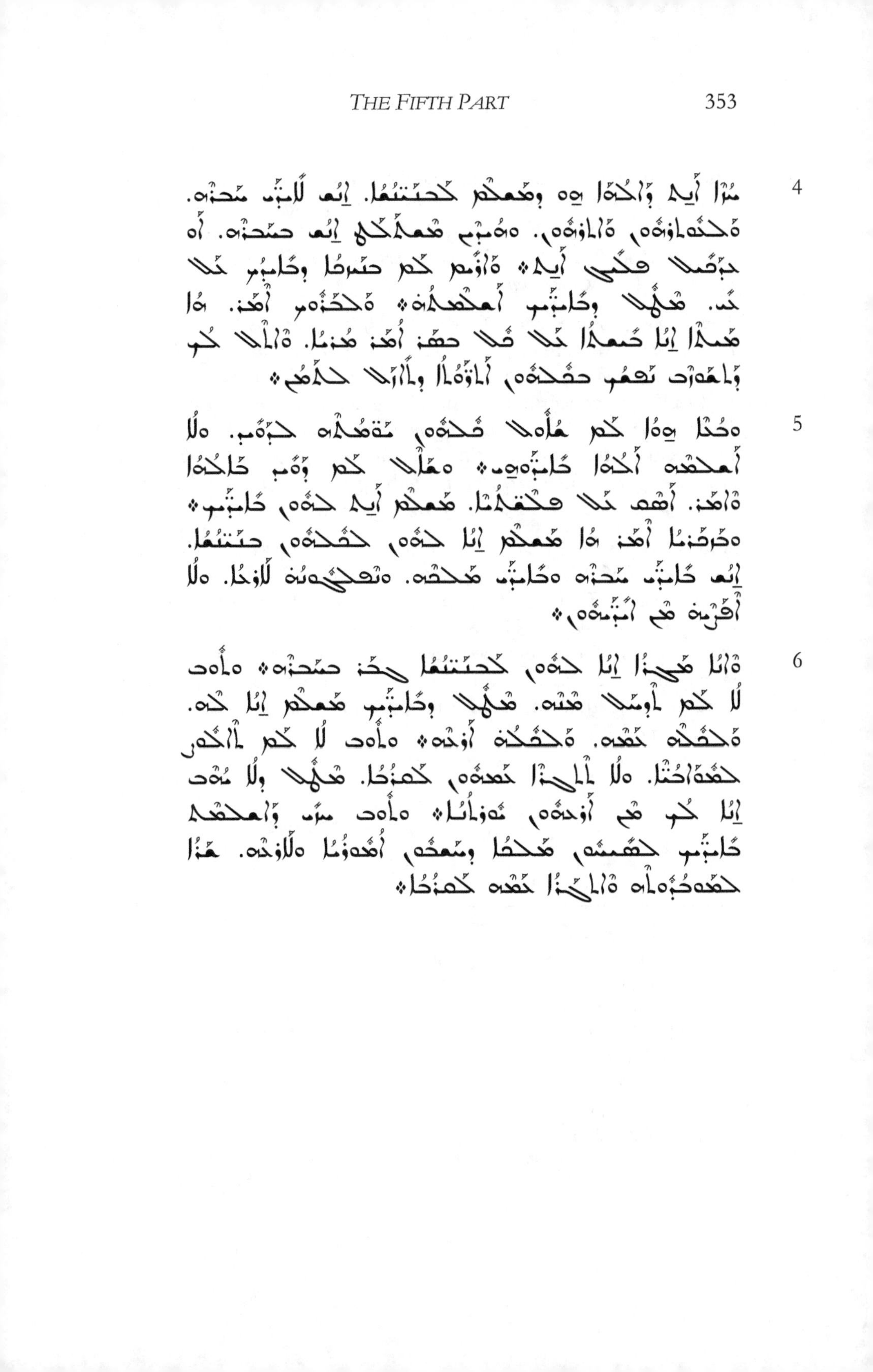

7   And again David said to Abiathar the priest: *Remain with me and do not fear because the one who seeks my life also seeks your life <but> with me there is a guard.*[15] He did not say "guards" but "guard", *that is to say an angel.* And, *Let <this> Benjamite curse, because it is the Lord himself who said to him: "Curse David!"*[16]

8   This is the passage where God says, *My Spirit remains in your midst: Do not fear!*[17] And He says: *Behold I will put a spirit upon him and he will hear a rumor and return to his land; and I will make him fall by the sword in his land.*[18] And concerning Egypt it is said: *The Lord has mingled within her an erring spirit and has made Egypt err in all their deeds.*[19] And <the Lord said to Joshua>: *See that I have delivered Jericho into your hands, and his king and all his army.*[20] And <the passage>: *The Lord thwarted them before the sons of Israel and they struck them with a great blow.*[21]

9   And <this passage>: *Do not fear them because tomorrow at this time I will cause that all of them be slain before the sons of Israel.*[22] And to Ahab, a prophet said: *"Thus says the Lord, Have you seen all this army? I will deliver it into your hands."*[23] He would not have said that he would hand them over if they were not guarded by His providence.[24] Nor would He have said "I hand over" and "I do not hand over," if it were possible that someone rule over his neighbor unless God hand him over.

---

[15] 1 Samuel 22.23.
[16] 2 Samuel 16.10–11.
[17] Haggai 2.5.
[18] 2 Kings 19.7.
[19] Isaiah 19.14.
[20] Joshua 6.2.
[21] Ibid., 10.10.
[22] Ibid., 11.6.
[23] 1 Kings 20.13.
[24] Providence (*bṭîlûtâ*).

THE FIFTH PART

10 And according to what is said in the book of Numbers, *The sons of Israel made a vow to the Lord and said: If indeed you will give this people into our hands, we will utterly destroy their cities. The Lord listened to the voice of Israel and gave the Canaanites into their hands and they destroyed them.*[25] Now is it because they were preserved by God that it is said that the handing over was His work? Or is this referred to in Scripture with a word of irony?

11 And <this passage>: *The anger of the Lord was kindled against Israel. He delivered them into the hand of spoilers and they plundered them. And he delivered them into the hand of their enemies round about them and they were no longer able to rise up before their enemies. Wherever they went the hand of the Lord was against them for evil.*[26] And <where Debra> says: *The glory will not be yours, Barak, in the way you are going, for the Lord will deliver Sisera into the hand of a woman.*[27]

12 And <where the Lord said to Gideon>: *I will be with you and you will lay waste the Midianites as a man.*[28] And where he said: *This people is too numerous that I deliver the Midianites into your hands.*[29] And <the passage>: *The Lord set the sword of each one against his neighbor in all the encampment.* And <again>: *All slept because a deep sleep from the Lord fell on them, on those of the house of Saul.*[30]

---

[25] Numbers 21.2–3.
[26] Judges 2.14–15.
[27] Judges 4.9.
[28] Ibid., 6.16.
[29] Ibid., Judges 7.2.
[30] 1 Samuel 26.12.

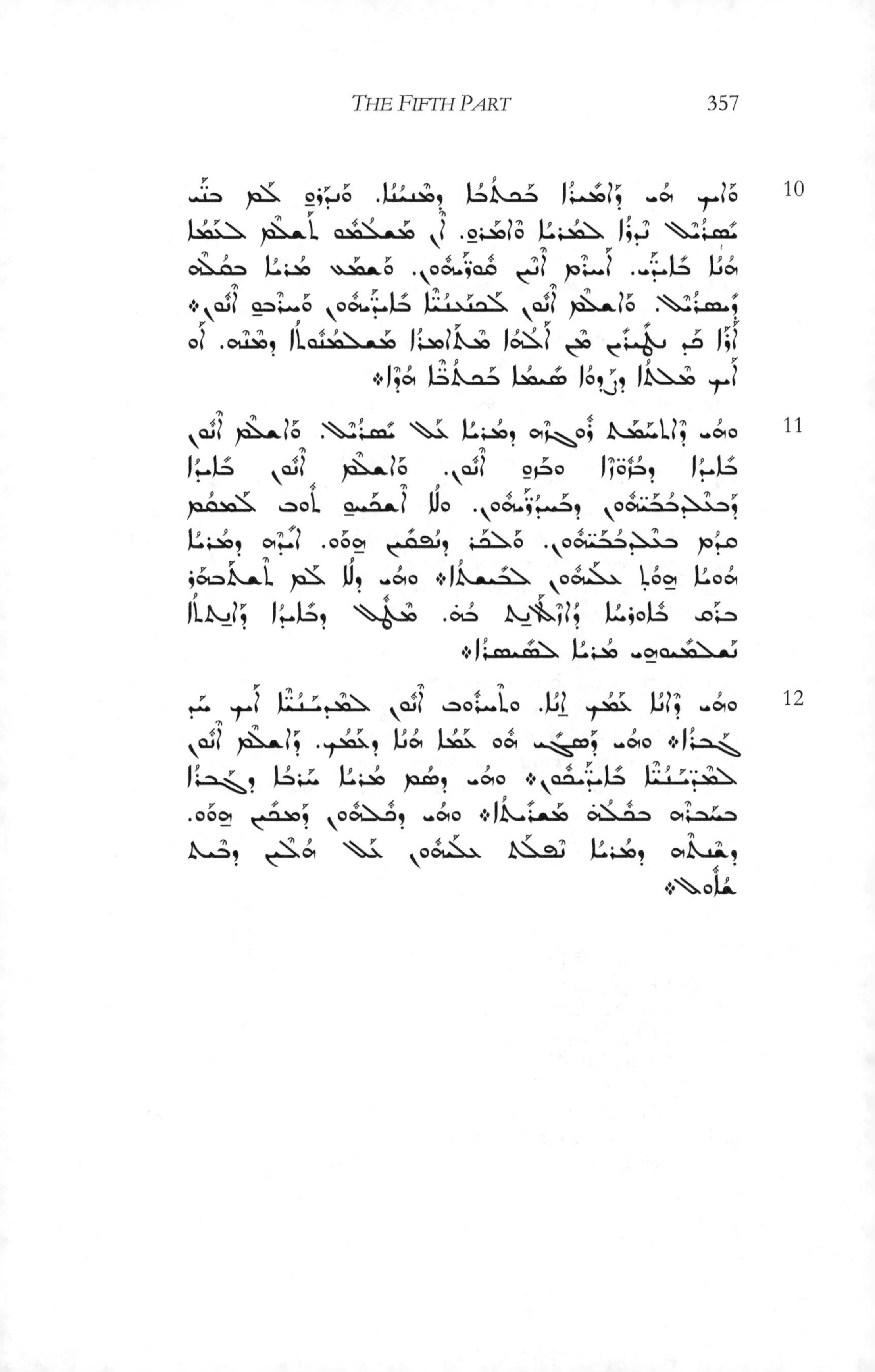

13 And <it says>: *The Lord commanded to defeat the good counsel of Ahithophel, <so as> to bring evil upon Absalom.*[31] And of Rehoboam is said: *He did not listen to the counsel of the people because the stirring of strife was from the Lord.*[32] And the <passage>: *The Lord has put a spirit of lies in the mouth of all these your prophets and the Lord has spoken evil in your regard.*[33] And <the passage>: *Do not fear them, because those who are with us are more numerous than those who are with them.*[34]

14 And <the passage where God says>: *Behold I have created the smith who blows air on the fire and produces an instrument for his work; and I have created the ravager to destroy. No weapon that is fashioned against you shall be successful; and every tongue that shall rise against you in judgment, you shall vanquish.*[35] And again: *Behold, I am bringing upon you a nation from afar, says the Lord. A nation whose language you do not know nor can you understand what they say. They shall eat up your harvest and your bread; they shall eat up your sons and your daughters; they shall eat up your flocks and your herds; they shall eat up your vines and your fig trees; your fortified cities which you rely on, they shall destroy with the sword.*[36]

15 And to show again that situations, of both good and of evil are from Him, in Isaiah is found also this other <passage>, *The Lord has sworn by his right hand and his mighty arm: I will no longer give your inhabitants*[37] *in food to your enemies, and foreigners shall not drink the wine for which you have labored. But those who have gathered it shall eat it and praise the Lord, and those who have gathered it will drink it in the courts of my sanctuary.*[38]

---

[31] 2 Samuel 17.14.
[32] 1 Kings 12.15.
[33] Ibid., 22.23.
[34] 2 Kings 6.16.
[35] Isaiah 54.16–17.
[36] Jeremiah 5.15–17.
[37] While the four manuscripts have this reading, both the Peshitta and the Hebrew texts say "your grain."
[38] Isaiah 62.8–9.

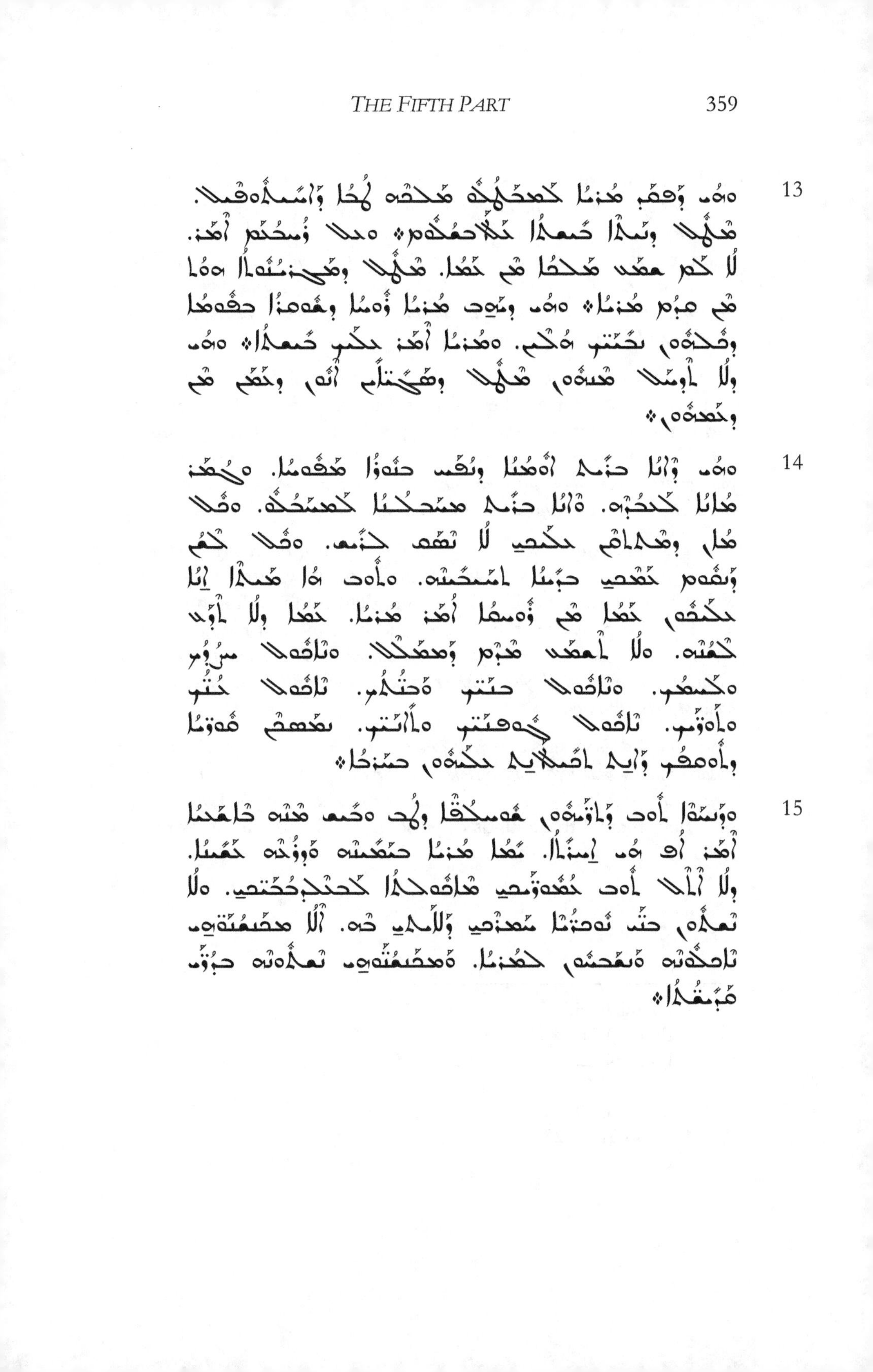

16 And again in Jeremiah it says: *Behold I will send and take the tribes of the kingdoms of the north, says the Lord, and Nebuchadnezzar my servant, and I will bring them against this land and its inhabitants to destroy them.*[39] And again it says: *I will give them into the hand of the army of the king of Babylon who are rising against them.*[40] *And again: Behold, I will command, says the Lord, and cause them to return to this city, they shall fight against it and take it and burn it with fire,* etc.[41]

17 And hear what is more wonderful and grievous! To explain that it is not possible that all these things happen without His approval and without the working of His sign, <God> says: *I will do with you something which I have never done, nor will I do again anything similar: in your midst fathers shall eat their sons and sons shall eat their fathers; and I will scatter to all the winds whoever remains in your midst.*[42]

18 And again: *Everyone shall eat the flesh of his neighbor in the siege and in the distress which I will bring on them.*[43] And again, wanting to show – when it says that the evils will end and deliverance will come – that it is He who provokes the distress and by Him that it ceases, *Thus says the Lord, your Lord: Behold, I have taken from your hands the cup of terror, and no more shall you drink from the cup of wrath. I will put it in the hand of those who afflict you.*[44]

19 And again <God says>: *I will judge those who judge you and save your children; I will make your oppressors eat their own flesh and become drunk on their blood as with wine; and all flesh will know that I am the Lord.*[45] You see, then, that all these kinds of good and evil come to us from the Lord.

---

[39] Jeremiah 25.9.
[40] Ibid., 34.21.
[41] Ibid., 34.22.
[42] Ezekiel 5.9–10.
[43] Jeremiah 19.9.
[44] Isaiah 51.22–23.
[45] Ibid., 49.25–26.

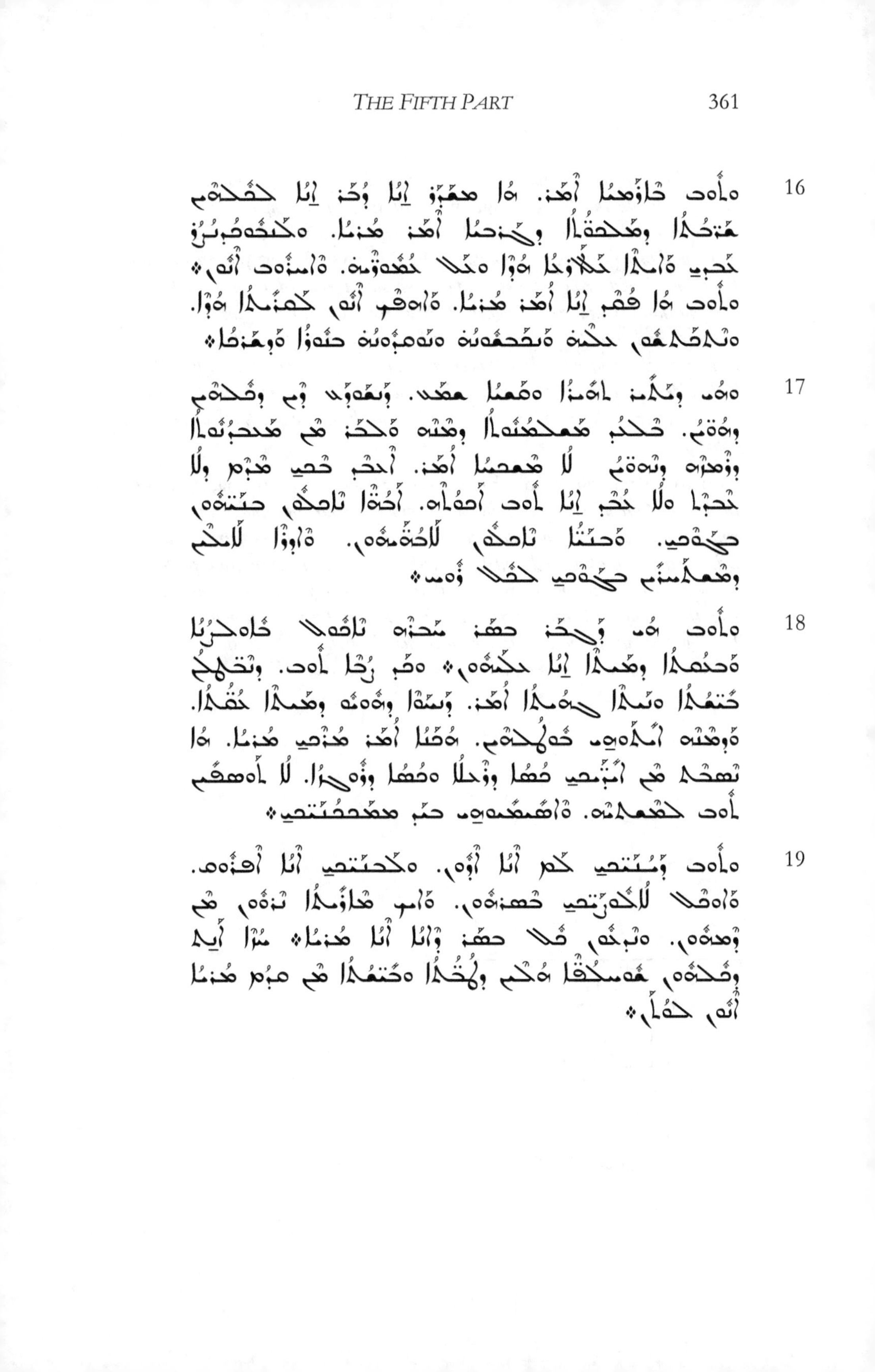

20 And where it says: *From my hands this will happen to you so that you will lie down in distress.*[46] And again: *I will send famine upon you and cruel beasts and they will destroy you. Pestilence and blood will pass in your midst, and I will bring the sword upon you.*[47] And it says: *Because you are afraid of the sword, I will bring the sword upon you, says the Lord of lords, and I will give you into the hands of foreigners.*[48] And the verse: *I will give their women to others and their property as plunder.*[49] And the verse: *Whoever is found will be pierced and whoever is taken will fall by the sword; and their children will be destroyed before their eyes, their houses will be plundered and their women dishonored.*[50] And: *Will there be an evil in the city which the Lord has not done?*[51]

21 And this <passage> in which Amos <said> to Amasia, *Thus says the Lord: Your wife shall be a harlot in your city, your sons and your daughters will fall by the sword, your land will be parceled out by a measuring-line, you will die in a polluted land and Israel will be deported in exile from its land." Thus the Lord has shown me.*[52] And the <passage> of Zechariah: *Behold the day of the Lord is coming and in your midst your spoil will be divided. I will gather all the nations to Jerusalem for the battle, the city shall be taken, the houses will be plundered and the women will be abused.*[53]

---

[46] Ibid., 50.11.
[47] Ezekiel 5.17.
[48] Ezekiel 11.8–9.
[49] Jeremiah 8.10.
[50] Isaiah 13.15–16.
[51] Amos 3.6.
[52] Amos 7.17–8.1.
[53] Zechariah 14.1–2.

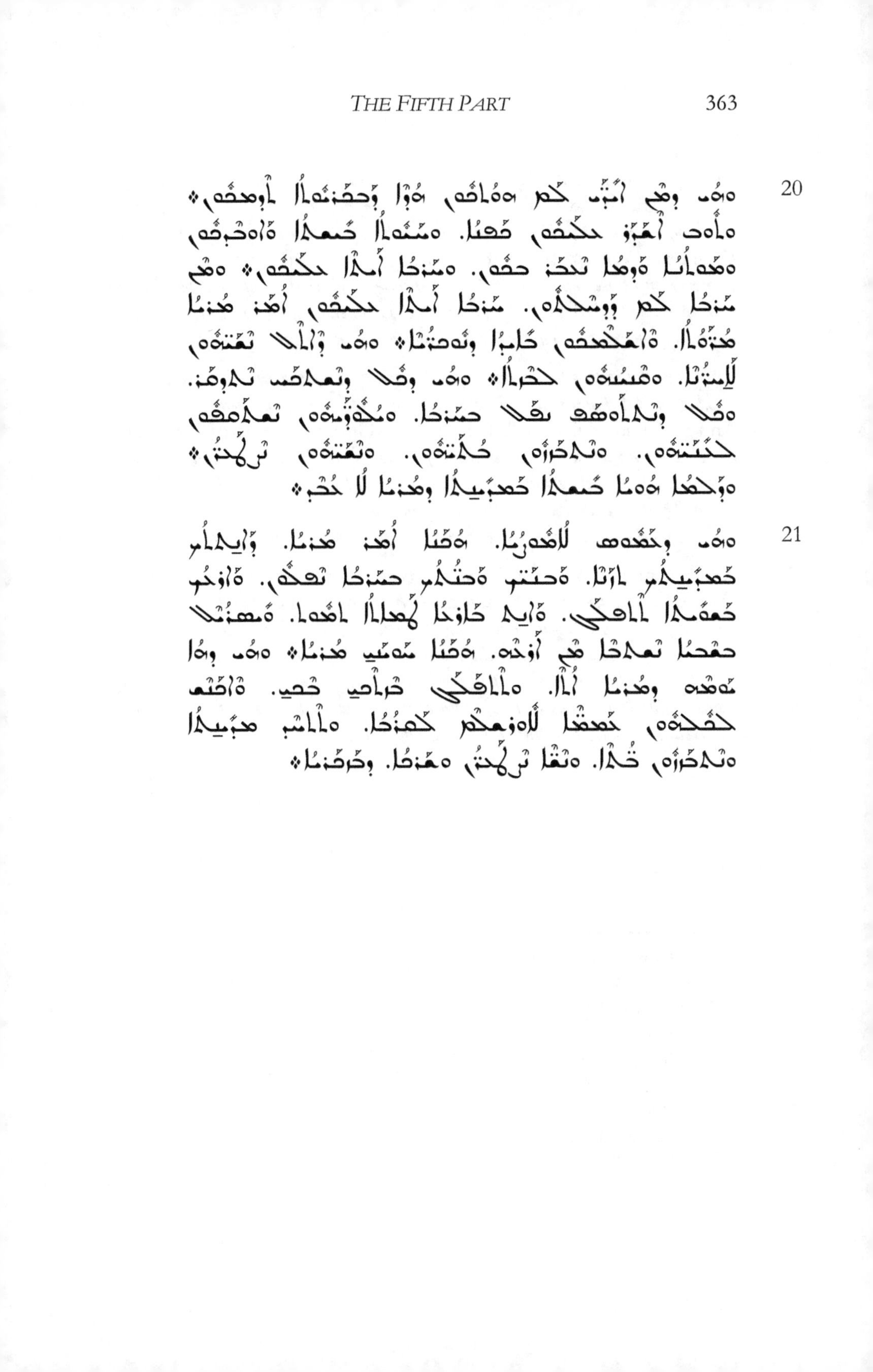

22   And again it says: *Women in Zion bore disgrace and virgins in the towns of Judea.*[54] And it says: *Who has ever spoken and this happened unless the Lord had commanded it? From the mouth of the Most High proceed good things and evil things.*[55] And the <passage where God says>: *I will lead your women before your eyes and give <them> to your neighbor, and he will lie with them.*[56] And it says: *I gave you the daughters of your masters and these women of your master, I have made lie down at your bosom.*[57]

23   And this: *I brought plunderers against the mother and against her children at midday, and I have made confusion and fear to fall upon them suddenly.*[58] And to Ebed-Melech the Ethiopian, <God by means of Jeremiah> said: *I send words for evil and not for good upon this city; in that day they will come to pass before you. But in that day I will save you, says the Lord, and you will not be delivered into the hands of those you fear. I will save you and you will not fall by the sword, because you trusted in me, says the Lord.*[59]

24   And again: *Behold I send ferocious serpents against you, which <cannot be charmed>, and they will bite you, says the Lord.*[60] And the <passage>: *From before me messengers will go out in haste to destroy Ethiopia which dwells in tranquility; and in their midst there will be confusion <as> in the day of Egypt; and behold it has come.*[61] And the <passage> which says: *I, the Lord, delivered the sons of Israel into captivity among the nations; and I have gathered them back into their land and have not left anyone there.*[62]

---

[54] Lamentation 5.11.
[55] Ibid., 3.37–38.
[56] 2 Samuel 12.11.
[57] Ibid., 12.8.
[58] Jeremiah 15.8.
[59] Ibid., 39.16–18.
[60] Ibid., 8.17.
[61] Ezekiel 30.9.
[62] Ibid., 39.28.

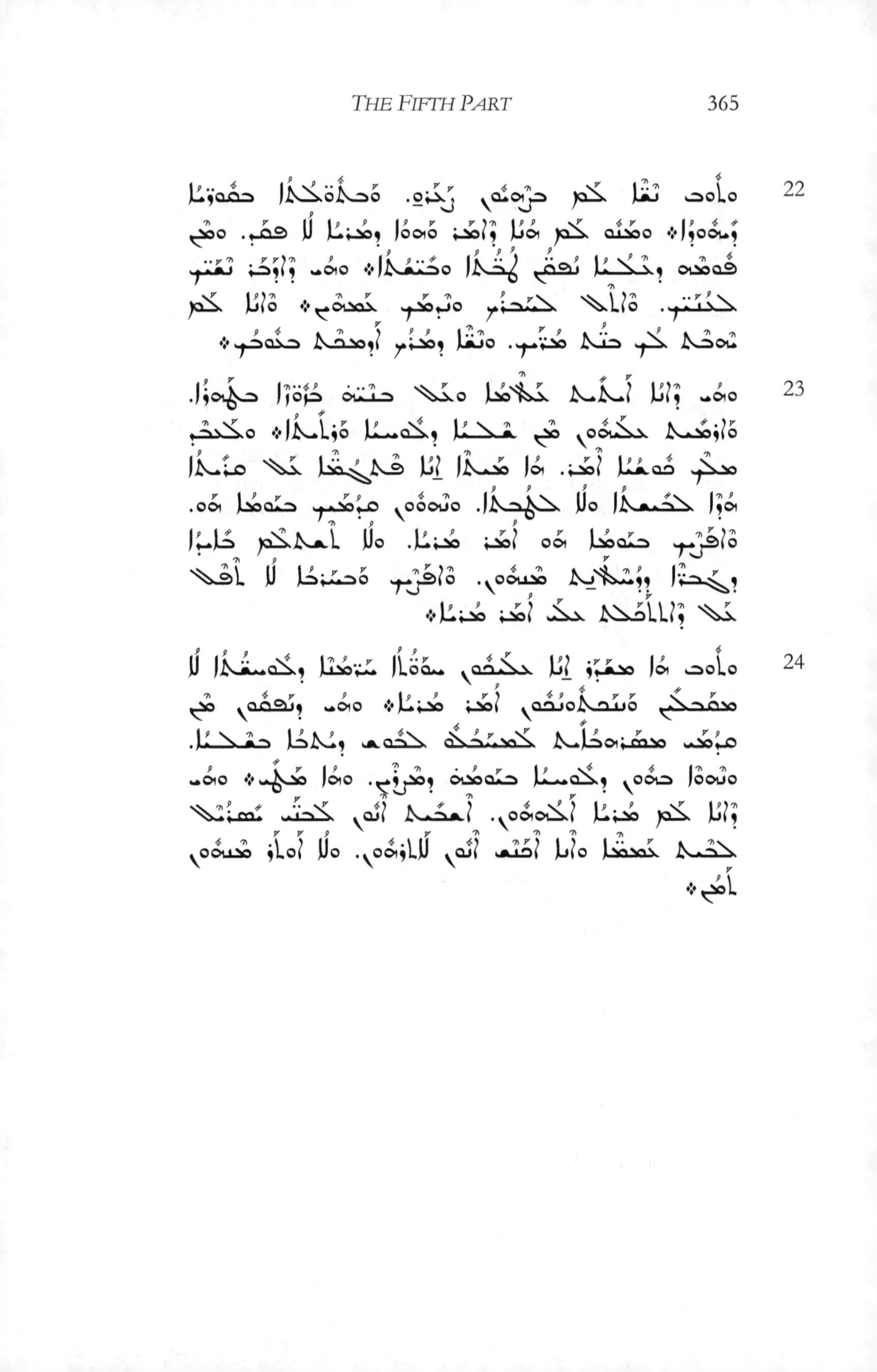

25 And this: *He will command his angels concerning you to guard you in all your ways; they will carry you in their arms that your foot not stumble.*[63] And this <passage>: *If he falls he will not be hurt, because the Lord holds him by the hand.*[64] And the <passage>: *He caused them to be pitied by all who carried them captive.*[65] And again: *And he gave them into the hand of the Gentiles and their adversaries had dominion over them.*[66] And: *In his anger he brought evil to come <upon them>.*[67]

26 And <Jesus said>: *Two sparrows are sold for a penny yet not one of them will fall to the ground without your Father's <will>.*[68] And <also in the Gospel> it says: Herod *sent to cut off the head of John in prison.*[69] And the angel made Peter come out by the iron gates, while he was tied with two chains and slept between two soldiers; and <the text> says: *The chains fell from his hands and the iron door opened by itself.*[70]

27 And: *Even the hairs of your head are numbered* for him.[71] And it is said: Herod *killed James the brother of John with a sword.*[72] And, *The Lord said to Paul in a vision: "Do not fear, but speak and do not be silent, because I am with you and no one can hurt you."*[73]

---

[63] Psalm 91.11–12.
[64] Ibid., 37.24.
[65] Psalm 106.46.
[66] Ibid., 106.41.
[67] Cf. Jeremiah 49.37.
[68] Matthew 10.29.
[69] Ibid., 14.10.
[70] Acts 12.6–10.
[71] Luke 12.7.
[72] Acts 12.2.
[73] Ibid., 18.9–10.

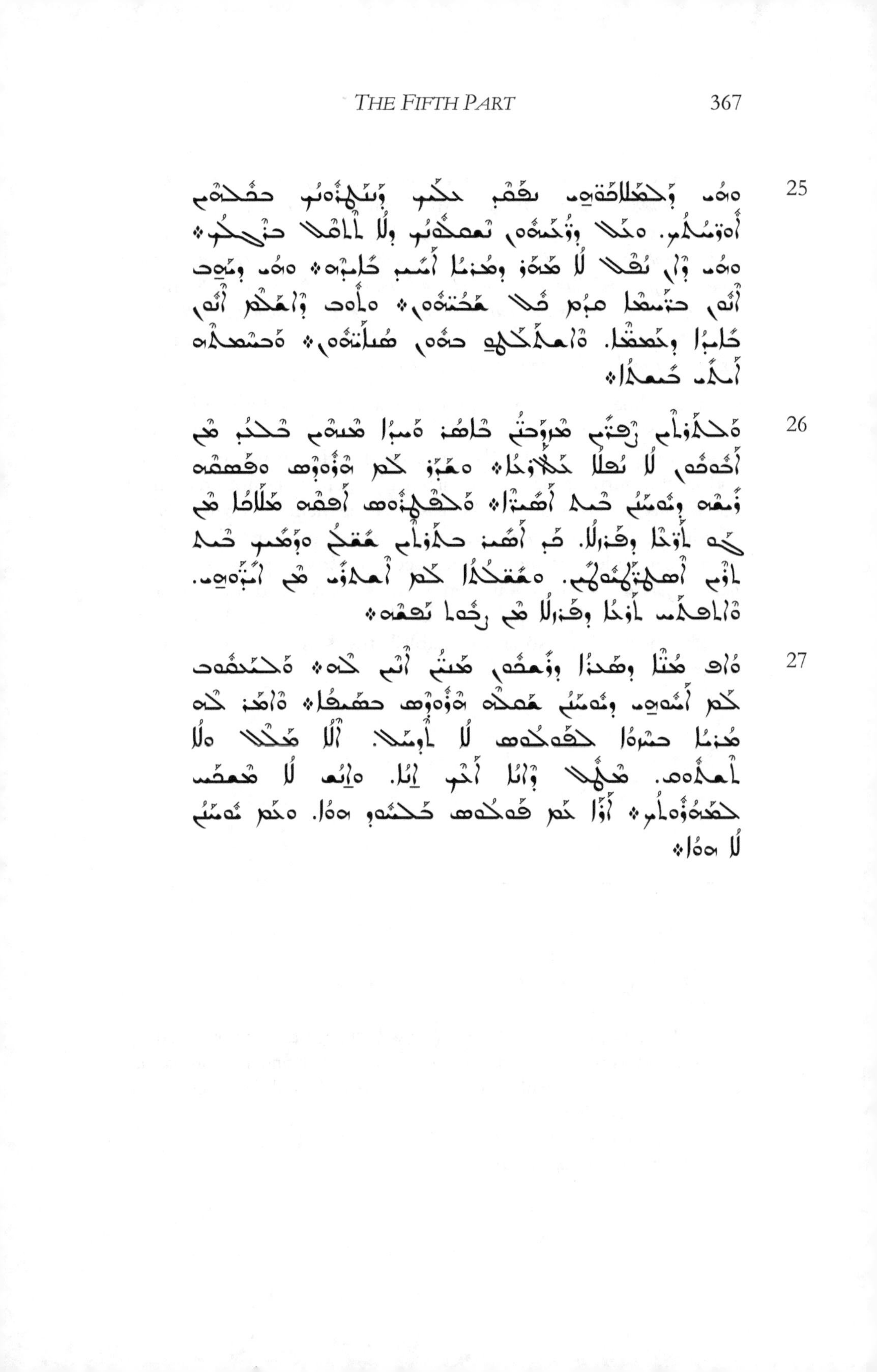

28 And <Jesus said to Pilate>: *You would have no power over me if it had not been given to you from above.*[74] And it says: *Truly in this city were gathered together against your holy Son, Jesus whom you have anointed, Herod and Pilate, together with the Gentiles and the peoples of Israel, to do whatever your hand and your will had foreordained would happen.*[75] And <the Psalmist> says: *The Lord brings the counsel*[76] *of the Gentiles to nought and the Lord causes the projects of the peoples to cease; but the intelligence*[77] *of the Lord subsists forever and the intention of his heart for generations.*[78]

29 Complete liberty, in humans, consists and may be known in these two things: in the counsel which <comes> from the mouth, that is to say a sound of a voice[79] expressing the hidden will in the soul; and in the purpose of the intelligence which is the foundation of the faculty of speech and the essential element of liberty. Now, <Scripture> says that *the Lord brings to nought* the authority of both of these realities among people, because *the intelligence of the Lord stands* <*forever*>.[80] How is it then, some say that God does not hinder the deeds of rational beings, while many times bringing to nought their power, so as to establish the <works> of his providence.[81]

---

[74] John 19.11.
[75] Acts 4.27–28.
[76] Counsel (*malkâ*).
[77] Intelligence (*tarʿîteh*).
[78] Psalm 33.10–11.
[79] Sound of a voice: *ba(r)t qâlâ* (*bat kol*), "daughter of a voice," sound or resonance as found in Syriac and in some Midrash and Talmud passages; an echo of a heavenly voice which revealed God's will, choice or judgment to mankind.
[80] Psalm 33.10–11.
[81] Providence (*mparnsânûtâ*).

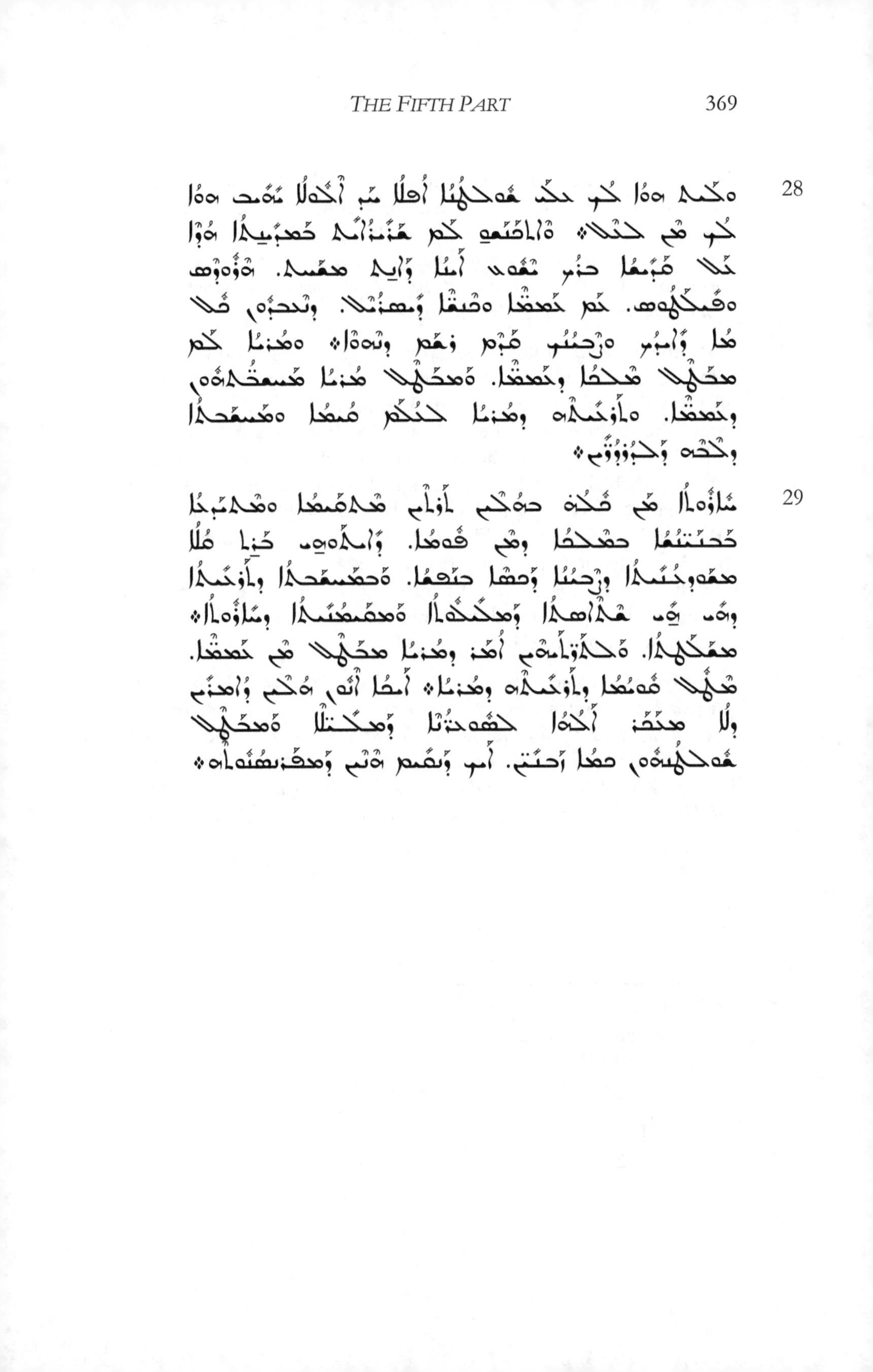

30 And again where Solomon says: *Many are the thoughts in one's heart but it is the intelligence of the Lord that confirms them.*[82] And again another sage says: *The Lord hardened the heart of Pharaoh, that his works be seen on earth.*[83] And in Isaiah: *Shall perhaps the axe vaunt itself over the one who hews with it? Or shall the saw exalt itself over the one who saws with it? Or shall a rod prevail over him who lifts it up?*[84]

31 Now there is an enlightened word, which shows how rational beings are placed before the will of God as instruments in the hand of the Artificer for the acts of the Economy of God,[85] that He accomplishes by means of them. As it were, it is the same God who with His hands holds the hand of the one who acts, at the time of correction which is in His hands; and He lifts up or brings down that <hand>, according to His will, because it is not possible that <rational beings> do anything outside of what is granted by His will. And thus, it is possible that one exercise some power upon oneself or one's possessions, or upon all which is one's own; each one upon his neighbor and upon his companion, according to how much power is given to him.

32 And of Job it is said, *The Lord said to Satan: "Behold, I deliver <him> into your hands." Satan went out from the presence of the Lord and struck Job with a malignant ulcer, from the sole of his foot to his brain.*[86] And where it says: *The Lord gave and the Lord has taken; may the name of the Lord be blessed.*[87] And: *We have received good things of God, shall we not receive his evil things?*[88] It says both of these are of a just God.

---

[82] Proverbs 19.21.
[83] Exodus 9.12 *passim*.
[84] Isaiah 10.15.
[85] Economy of God (*mdabbrânûtâ d-alâhâ*).
[86] Job 2.6–7.
[87] Ibid., 1.21.
[88] Ibid., 2.10.

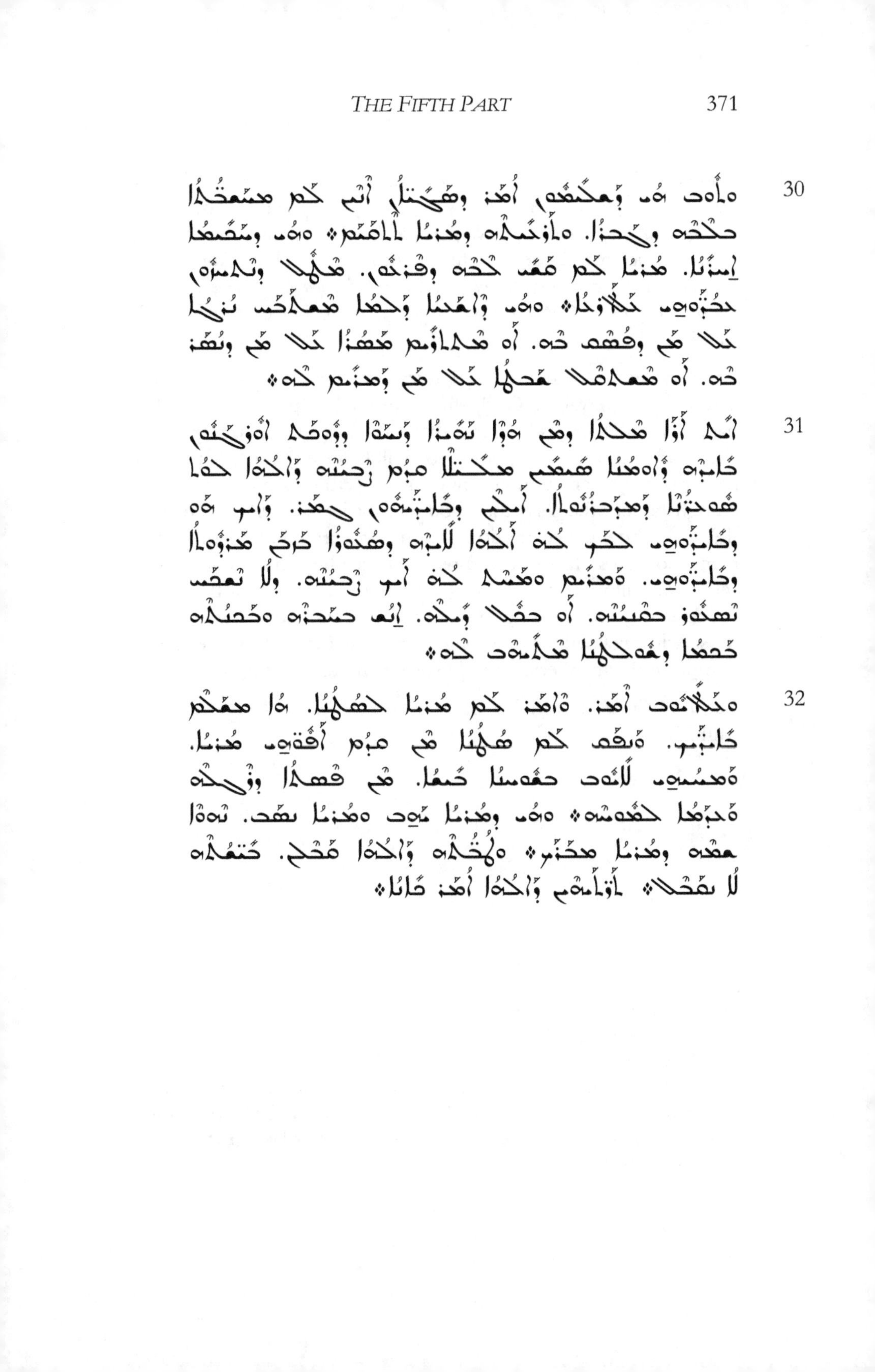

33   And <God says>: *I cause to die and I make alive; I wound and I heal; and there is nothing that escapes from my hands.*[89] Understand this: *There is nothing that escapes my hands!* Which means there is nothing in all the entire world, mainly death, life, sickness and healing. And the demons said to our Lord: *If you grant it, we will enter these swine. And <Jesus> said to them: Go!*[90] And there are many other examples similar to these.

34   At this point, do you confess that in all of this there is an action of care or of betrayal by God, that without His permission nothing happens and there is nothing that may distress or satisfy on account of man or by man; or do you still believe that the happenings and stirrings of creation are by chance; <either way> it would not be right to let others say that God wills or lets go. In fact, He is not the one who puts in motion actions of correction or of punishment, nor does He work in those who do the actions but He consents, only allowing that they occur where He wills that they occur. He does not even make good and bad actions happen by means of those with inclinations or thoughts such as these. Nor does He set in motion the manner of the chastising and distressing action.

But how little knowledge there is of this and <far> from the truth![91]

---

[89] Deuteronomy 32.39.

[90] Matthew 8.31–32.

[91] This seems to reflect a humble awareness on the part of the author concerning how precarious these assertions may be. Chialà notes a certain resemblance with the authentic Discourses of Isaac (Bettiolo, Discorsi): I, 51; II, 102.

THE FIFTH PART

II

Other examples with another intention

1. We will show now that the divine Scriptures do not even lack examples which clearly indicate how the impulse of the will, and the thoughts relative to the things which then happen – under the forms of a corrective action or favorable events – and also the total number of such actions, occur <on their own>.[1] But since, according to the divine dispensation and by divine Economy, <on their own> the thought and the will develop within <specific> beings, then what happens – which brings rest, or adversity, or affliction – happens by means of them.

2. Not that this is from them. But they are impelled by God to bring about what will annoy a person, or be good, or destroy, or save, or afflict, as the prophet says clearly: *The Lord has stirred up the spirit of the king of the Medes because his purpose concerning Babylon is to destroy it.*[2] And <Isaiah> says: *Behold, I am stirring up the Medes against you who have no regard for silver and do not delight in gold.*[3]

3. And it says: *The Lord will whistle for the flies of the rivers of Egypt, and for the bees which are in the land of Assyria. And they will all come and settle in the valley of Jathoth and in the hollows of the rock and in all the caves.*[4] And again it says: *The Lord will bring up the waters of the rivers against you, many and strong, even the king of Assyria and all his army. He will rise over all their brooks and walk upon all their fortified walls.*[5]

---

[1] The translation "on their own" (Syr. *mene*), suggested by Chialà, is to resolve the contrast implied here between human initiative and God's action.

[2] Jeremiah 51.11.
[3] Isaiah 13.17.
[4] Ibid., 7.18–19.
[5] Ibid., 8.7.

THE FIFTH PART

4   And the <passage>: *The Lord will strengthen the oppressors of Rezin against him and stir up his enemies.*[6] And <where God> says: *It is I who have spoken and I have called, I have brought him and made his way prosperous.* And <the passage>: *I will raise up evil against you, from your house;*[7] He did not say "will rise against you," but "I will raise up against you."

5   And the <passage>: *I will provoke Egyptians against Egyptians, and brother will fight against his brother, a man against his neighbor, city against city and kingdom against kingdom.*[8] And the <passage>: *I am summoning the sword against all the inhabitants of the earth, says the Lord of hosts.*[9] And the <passage>: *Behold, I will rouse against you all your lovers whom your soul rejected, and I will bring them against you.*[10] And the <passage>: *Against Tyre I will bring Nebuchadnezzar, king of Babylonia.*[11]

6   And this: *Behold, I will bring strangers against you, the most powerful among the nations; they will draw their swords against the beauty of your wisdom, they will defile your glory and cast you down to destruction.*[12] And to Egypt He said: *Behold I will throw my net over you with a host of many peoples, and they will haul you up in their nets. I will cast you upon the ground and all the bright lights of heaven I will make dark over you.*[13]

---

[6] Isaiah 9.10.
[7] 2 Samuel 12.11.
[8] Isaiah 19.2.
[9] Jeremiah 25.29.
[10] Ezekiel 23.22.
[11] Ibid., 26.7.
[12] Ibid., 28.7–8.
[13] Ibid., 32.3–4, 8.

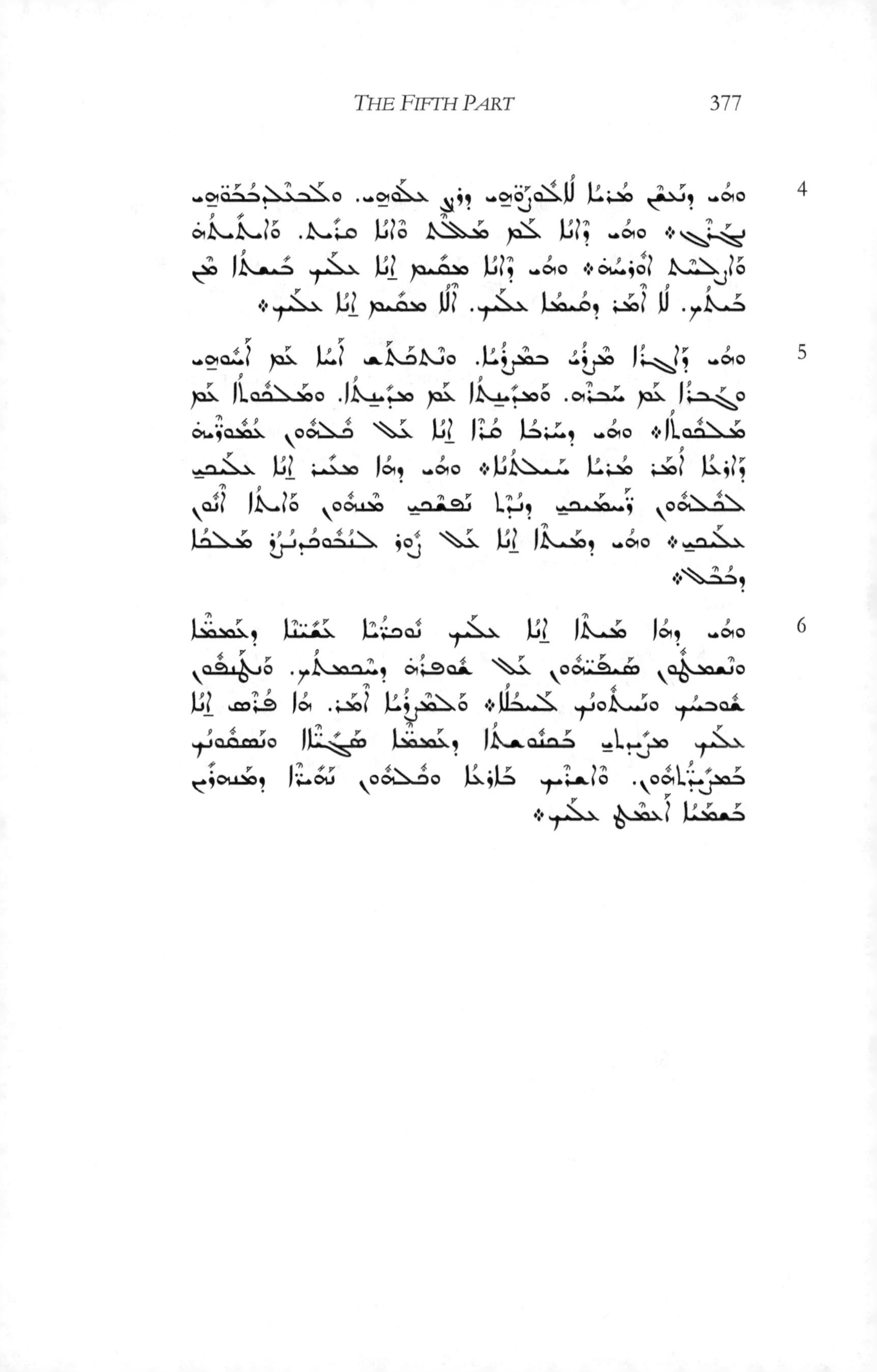

7   And this: *I will embitter the heart of numerous peoples, when I bring about your ruin among the nations and in cities which you do not know.*[14] And the <passage>: *You betrayed the Israelites to the sword at the time of their distresses and at the time of their extreme iniquity.*[15] And the <passage>: *Behold I am sending many hunters, says the Lord, and they will hunt them on every mountain and on every hill, and out of the holes in the rocks. For my eyes are on all their ways, and they are not concealed from me.*[16]

8   Moreover, since this occurs also because of these advantages and it is according to His will that the projects are set in motion, at His time, by means of those who are placed as intermediaries for their realization, <God> says: *Behold, I will lift up my hand to the nations, and raise a sign to the peoples; they shall bring your sons in their hands, and your daughters they shall carry on their shoulders. Kings shall be your foster-fathers and their princesses, your wet-nurses. With their faces to the ground they shall bow down to you, and wipe the dust of your feet.*[17]

9   And <where> it says: *The sons of Judah and the sons of Jerusalem whom you sold to the sons of the Greeks, removing them far from their border, behold, I will stir them up from the place where you have sold them, while I will bring your retribution on your heads. I will give your sons and your daughters into the hands of the sons of Judah and they will sell them to Saba, a distant people, because the Lord has spoken.*[18] And the <passage> which says: *The Lord was with Joseph and he showed him kindness and gave him favor in the eyes of the head of the prison.*[19]

---

[14] Ibid., 32.9.
[15] Ibid., 35.5.
[16] Jeremiah 16.16–17.
[17] Isaiah 49.22–23.
[18] Joel 4.6–8.
[19] Genesis 39.21.

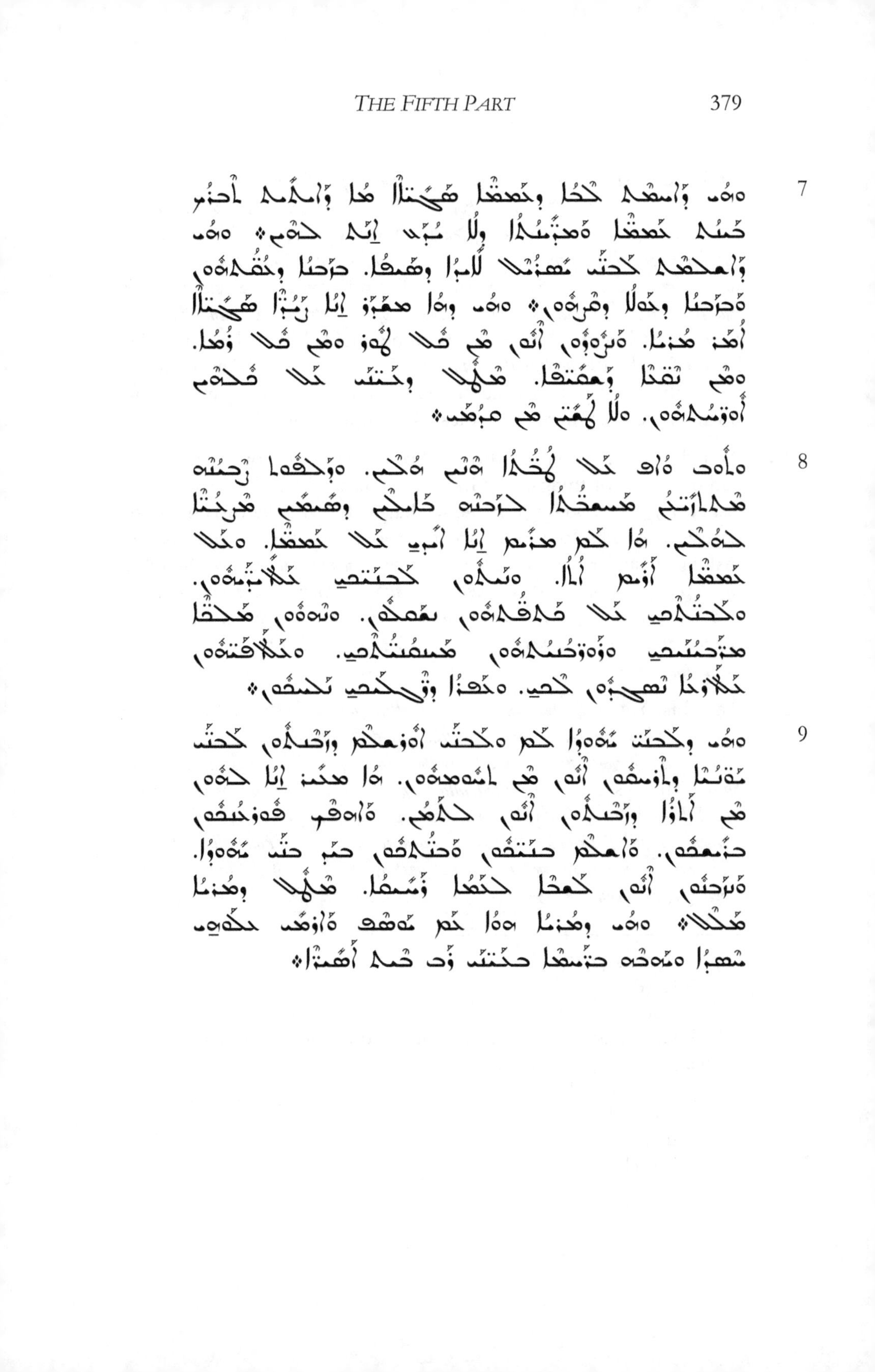

10 And the <passage>: *The Lord gave the people favor in the eyes of the Egyptians <concerning> what they had asked for, and they despoiled the Egyptians.*[20] And the <passage>: *I will send my strength before you, and will lay waste all the peoples against whom you shall come, and I will make all your enemies turn their backs before you.*[21] And <where> it says: *For it was from the Lord that the heart of these people be strengthened and that they go out to battle against Israel in order that* he might deliver them into the hand of Joshua *to destroy them and they be without recourse;*[22] and <there are> other passages on which I will not linger longer because in the divine Scriptures there are endless <examples> like these.

11 And thus it happens for those who are without words or reason and make use of things.[23] <God> says: *Surely, I will begin to strike you and destroy you because of your sins*; in that <He> usually ordains these occasions of His Economy, for the most part, for the purpose of making to suffer. And it says <again>: *You will eat but you will not be satisfied, <you will be afflicted with> dysentery; you will seize but not save, and what you do save, I will deliver to the sword; you will sow and not harvest; you will tread olives but not anoint with oil; and you will crush grapes and not drink the wine.*[24]

12 And this: *You sow much and you reap little; you eat but never have enough; you drink but you never have your fill; you dress but do not feel warm; and whoever among you earns wages, earns them in a purse with holes in it.*[25] And again <it says>: *You expected much and there is little; you bring it home and I blow it away.*[26] And again this: *I will open for you the windows of heaven and will pour out blessings on you until you say: "Enough"!; and I will rebuke the devourer so that it will not destroy the fruits of the land, and not ravage for you even one vine in the land, says the Lord of hosts.*[27]

---

[20] Exodus 12.36.
[21] Exodus 23.27.
[22] Joshua 11.10.
[23] Here Isaac refers to examples where divine intervention makes use of animals or inanimate objects.
[24] Micah 6.13–15.
[25] Haggai 1.6.
[26] Ibid., 1.9.
[27] Malachi 3.10–11.

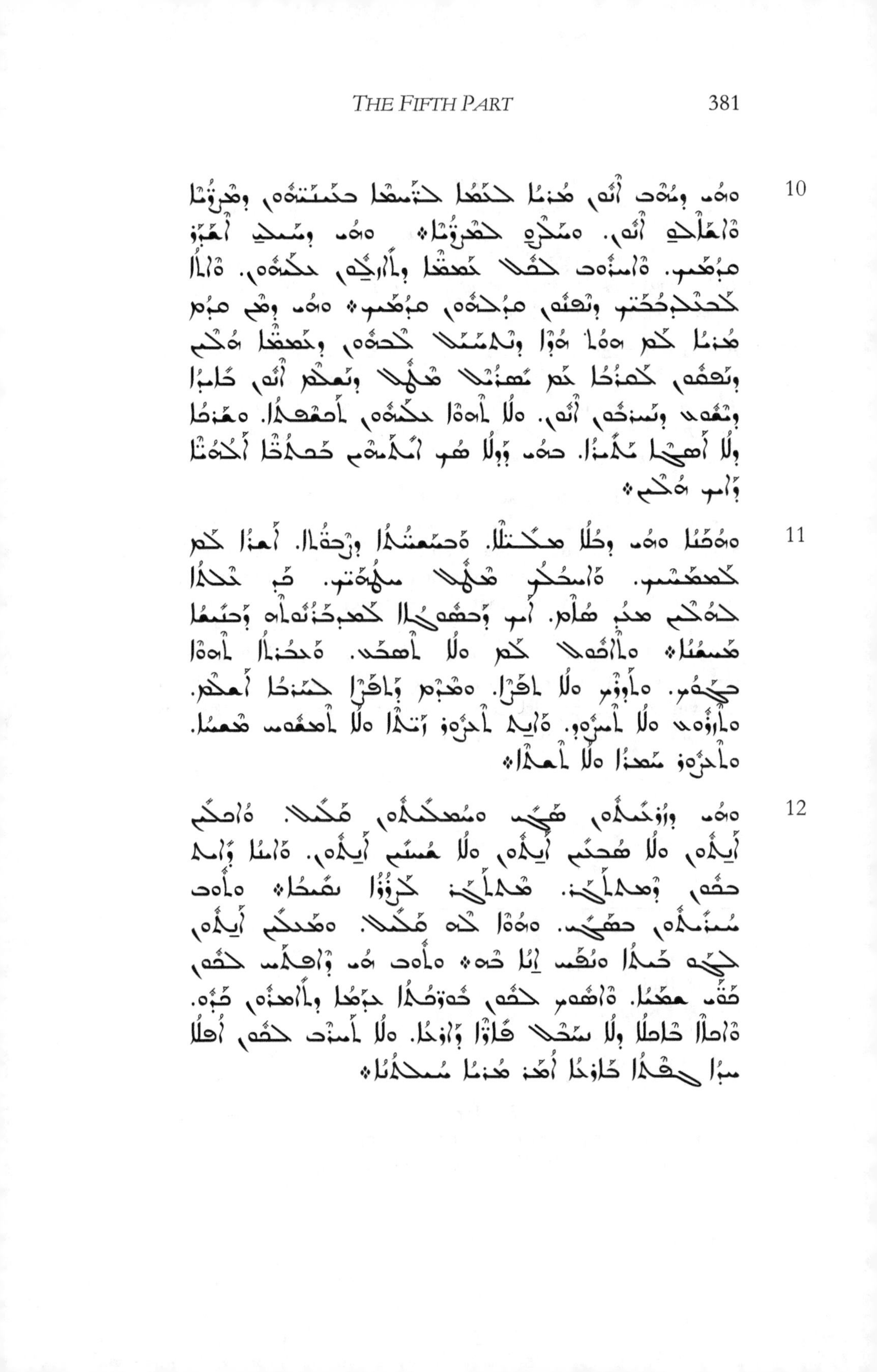

13 And again this: *The Lord prepared a great fish and it swallowed Jonah.*[28] And: *The Lord commanded the fish and it vomited Jonah upon dry land.*[29] And: *The Lord ordered that a young gourd plant grow and it sprouted and went up on Jonah's head. But the Lord God, as dawn arose, appointed a worm and it nibbled on the gourd and cut it off; then the Lord God ordered a parching wind and it dried up the gourd.*[30]

14 And again <this passage>: *I have commanded the ravens to feed you.*[31] And it <also> says: *I have commanded a widow to feed you.*[32] And this: *The Lord visited Anna and she conceived and gave birth to three sons and two daughters.*[33] And the <passage>: *The Lord commanded to bring to naught the good counsel of Ahithophel.*[34]

15 And in a thousand places, so to say, <it> is written in the Scriptures that the Lord commanded this or that, as the above <passages> indicate, making it sufficiently clear. And behold, these are shown to declare clearly the fact that the Lord has commanded such and such and also that these happen without delay. This is true as it is also true that he has said to me,[35] "How did He command?" He said to me: "Did He indeed command all these things by means of the sound of the voice?[36] Or is what God willed only the will and the impulse corresponding to these and <that> is set in motion in those <who have acted>?"

---

[28] Jonah 2.1.
[29] Ibid., 2.11.
[30] Ibid., 4.6–8.
[31] 1 Kings 17.4.
[32] Ibid., 17.9.
[33] 1 Samuel 2.21.
[34] 2 Samuel 17.14.
[35] Chialà resolves a difficult passage by suggesting that here Isaac refers and responds to someone specific who opposed his thinking.
[36] Sound of a voice (*ba(r)t qâlâ*), see Isaac V/I, note 79.

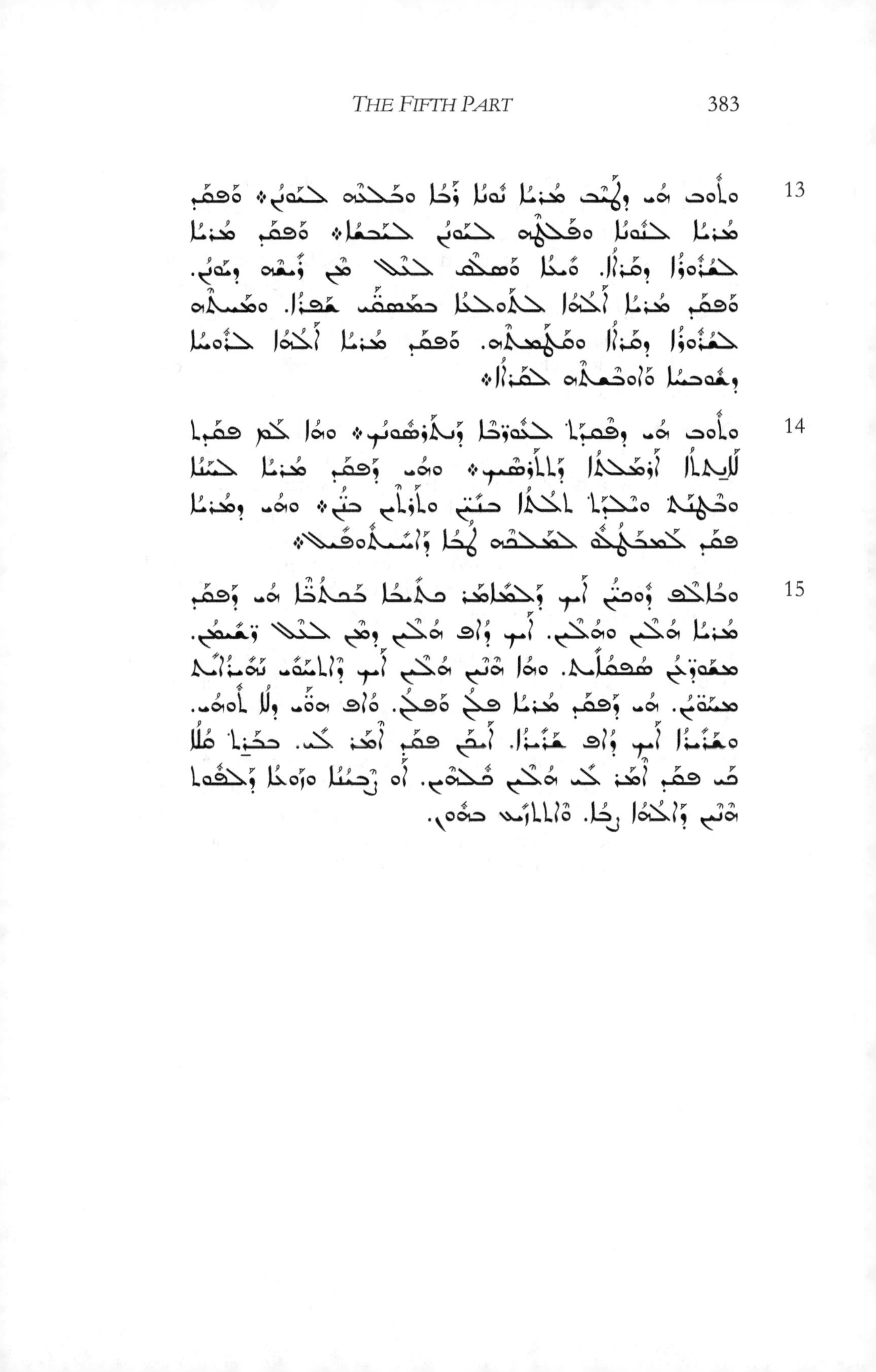

16 If in fact this occurred by a sound of the voice, with the fish or with the worm or with the young gourd plant or with the scorching wind or with the ravens, how did God speak and command voiceless creatures not even endowed with senses, by means of a sound of a voice? Or rather, where it is written that <He> spoke with the widow or that <He> commanded her, by a sound of a voice, to feed the prophet – which clearly refers to the action which <God> fulfilled providentially by means of her – Scripture also calls a "command" the will that <God> put in her to fulfill the action.

17 Or rather: how is it that <God> truly ordered Anna to conceive and give birth to sons and daughters, in that this was not of her will but of divine action? Or again: perhaps it is with a sound of the voice that <God> commanded Absalom and the people that were with him to not accept the counsel of Ahithophel, given that Scripture says that the Lord ordered to bring to nought <the counsel>; or according to what seemed to God, was the thought and the will to nullify the thing put in motion in them?

18 You see that by means of rational creatures and voiceless ones, God moves and works so that what He wills be accomplished without delay. It is, however, according to His will that the impulses of rational and voiceless creatures be transformed and confirmed for those things that God had willed that they might be. How then is it possible that it not be God who does or moves, according to His will, those things which actually happen in the manner of corrections or favorable things, by means of an action? On the contrary, it is surely He who truly wills and truly allows that they happen.

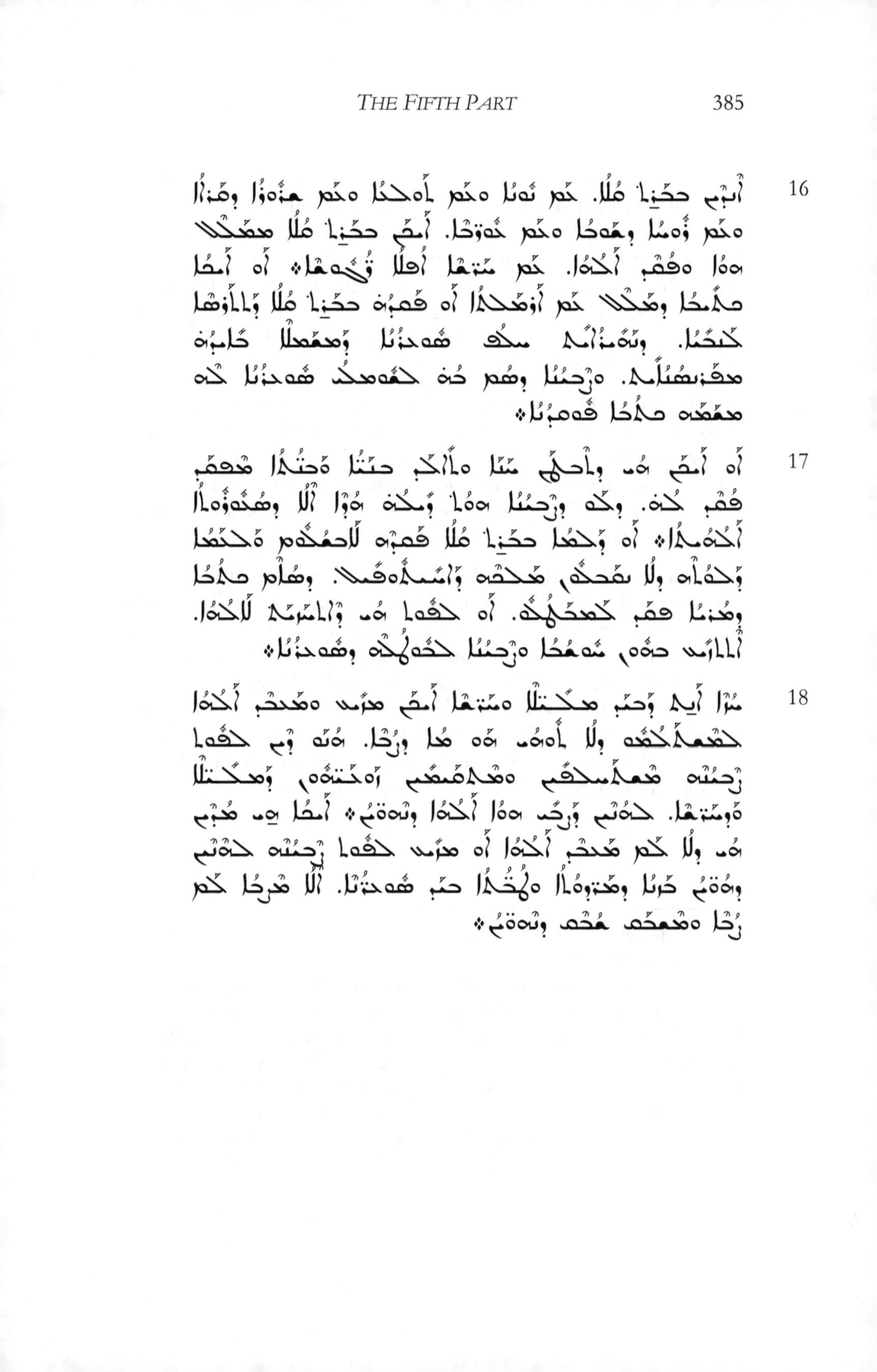

19   Not that, in such a way, also the preparation and impulse of the things which happen proceed – as if indeed only God can desire and permit, simply and without distinction – nor that from His interventions come <their> sequence and their quantity. But the "why," the "when" and the "how" are given to chance.[37] He in fact did not establish by Himself the limit[38] in which these things <will happen>, rather this has been given by Him to the will and the thought of those who bring it about.

20   If this happens by means of rational beings or irrational ones, and as to how one will be punished and why, and who will be punished is not determined; not even concerning glad events. Chance also serves the divine will about these things. Therefore to examine this word to see "how" < it occurs comes> from a supposition full of absurdity concerning the wonderful Wise One of the universe.[39]

21   What then? All the things which are, how they are and when they are, God wills according to what has been said? Or is it <only> those favorable events or those actions for correction that God wills, as He wills, when He wills, and by means of whom He wills? In the first case, then, God is guided in what and how He wills following the actions which are done; and not that the actions are stirred according to the will of God. Even if in the second case, it is clear that these actions, in their variety, are administered by the will of God, concerning time, limit and number.

---

[37] Chance (*suqbâlâ*).

[38] Limit (*thômâ*).

[39] This is a form of Lord of all (*mârê-kul*) or Lord of the universe. It is considered to be a trace of the early Syriac Creed. See Connolly, "Early Syriac Creed." It appears in Acts of Thomas, Aphrahat, Ephrem, *Book of Steps*. It also may be found in the Jewish liturgy and in rabbinic literature as *ribbon shel ʿolam*. In *Midrash on Psalms*, practically every Psalm's commentary includes the invocation, see Braude. And in the Jewish prayer book, in the morning service, "King of the universe" (*melekh ha ʿolam*) occurs 27 times.

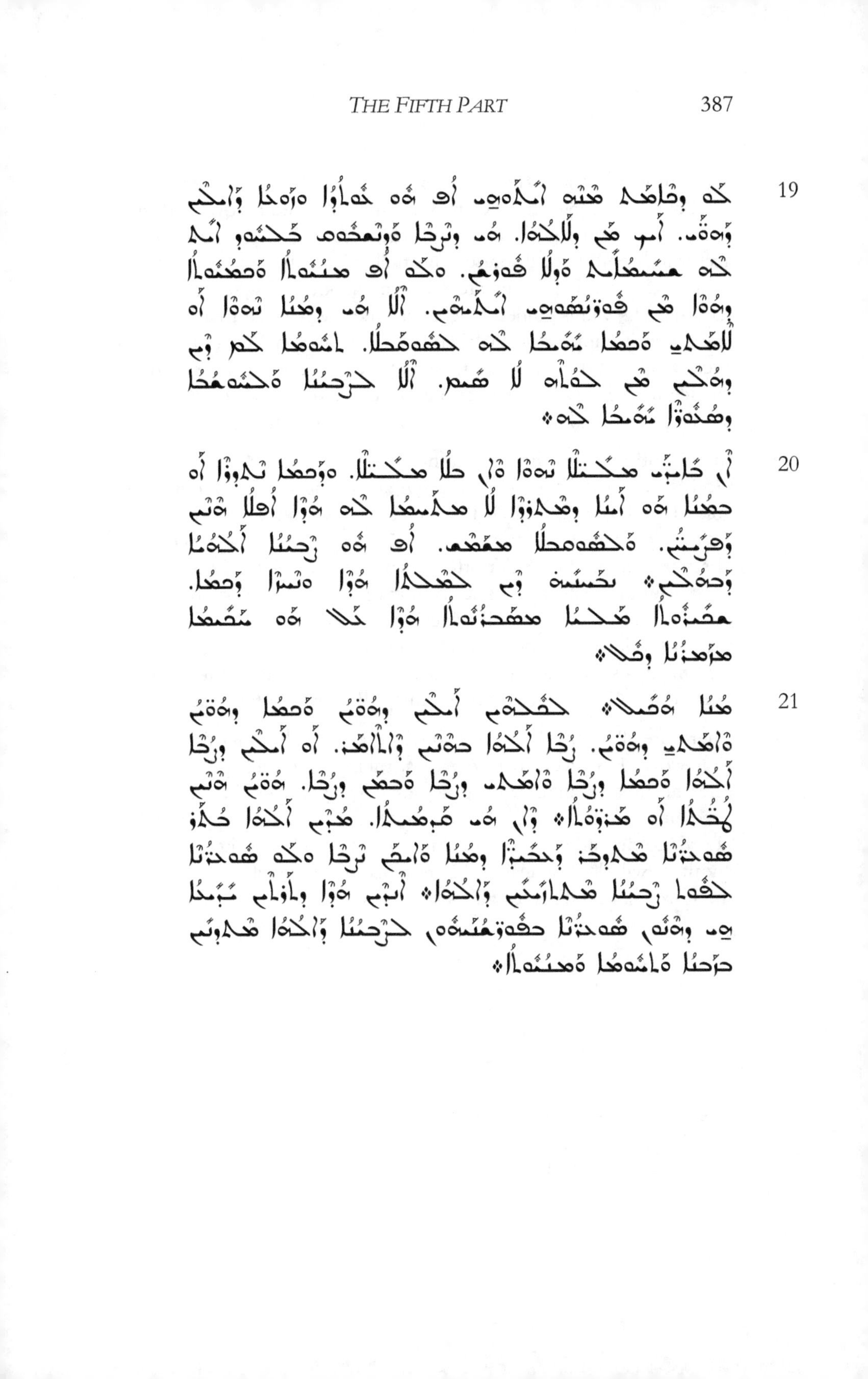

22 What more? Already knowing ahead of time the things which are, God consented that they occur? Or, He had willed beforehand that these occur and the actions conformed to His will, one by one, according to all their impulses and their plans? In the first case, all which are provided for us are not even actions of wisdom, by the fact that His will is guided by chance; and He wills all that happens and when it happens – this then is not of wisdom. Wisdom, however, in all that it does keeps its own precept[40] and is not guided by chance in the doing of its actions. Every action is determined according to its will: this is said <to be> the beginning of wisdom.

23 In this other case, then, all things move in the limit defined by God, and in their timing they begin according to His will and are guided by His will; and all the <realities> which God ordains by means of rational beings or irrational ones keep to the precept of His wisdom. In fact <Scripture> says: *All which the Lord wills he does*.[41] But also this is still said in human terms. The Lord does not do everything He wills. All which He willed, not only recently as they come into existence, but eternally He willed the things which He willed – such that there is nothing that He willed only recently – nor does <He> desist from anything of all which He willed.

24 Therefore all which the Lord had willed exists. The will of the Lord is at work. However, instead <of speaking> of will, in the Scriptures all these realities whose names correspond to the variety of necessities are laid down. There is a <place> where it says that the "Lord commanded," another "the Lord said," another "acted," another "will do," or again "the sentence of the Lord," or "word of the Lord," and the rest of all these things.

---

[40] Precept (*thômâ*).
[41] Psalm 135.6; cf. 115.3.

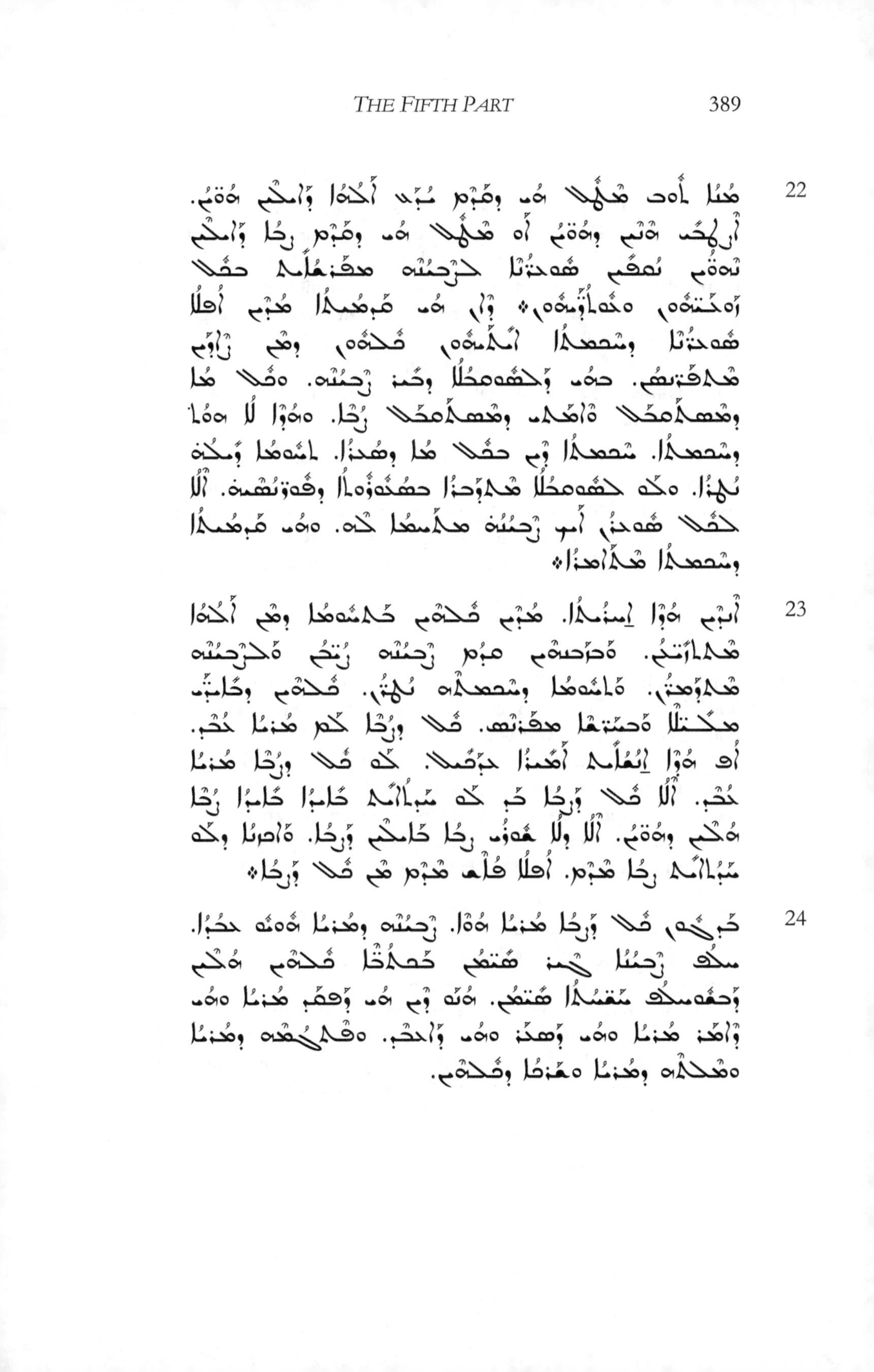

25 Instead of saying that <God> had always willed and that things happened in their time, Scripture says all these things <noted above>. For God to do anything at all, willing alone is sufficient. For creatures, however, their will alone is not sufficient for the completion of their actions; but with the will they have need of assistance, a movement with regard to the actions – a going towards and a substantive motion regarding these matters. Then comes the perfection of the deed which they willed. I speak of spiritual realities – even if a small action – but still we humans struggle with corporal <realities>.

26 As to God, however, it is not possible that for the fulfillment of His will a natural impulse be joined, or someone's personal manner for the doing <of it> and so the action be completed. This, in fact, is of composed[42] and created beings or of those who need to make use of the word. Whereas God, whose will alone sufficed for Him to bring forth these primary elements, in the beginning, in silence, from nothing in existence – is said <of Him>: "You willed, and all exists before You."[43]

27 Such is His will: the fulfillment of every action of rational beings and the transformation of their thoughts, even concerning the course of creation. And what He willed that it be, He does not do, but it is! As if He wanted to say, that if there is a flood, and the natural elements immediately be obedient to His will: at the time in which this appeared, the elements received a transformation beyond what is usual and inundated creation, as it is written.[44] And for God it sufficed only that He will it.

---

[42] Composed: though here a different Syriac word is used this may very well refer to the concept of composite <*mrâkâbtâ*> which concerns the discussion of human nature created with a composite structure having elements for its subsistence and being subject to growth in simplicity. Only in the world to come after the resurrection will humans have the complete simplicity of the angelic life. John the Solitary discusses this in detail, see Lavenant *Dialogues V*.

[43] Cf. Judith 9.5; Psalm 33.9; Genesis 1.14.

[44] Cf. Genesis 7.17–20.

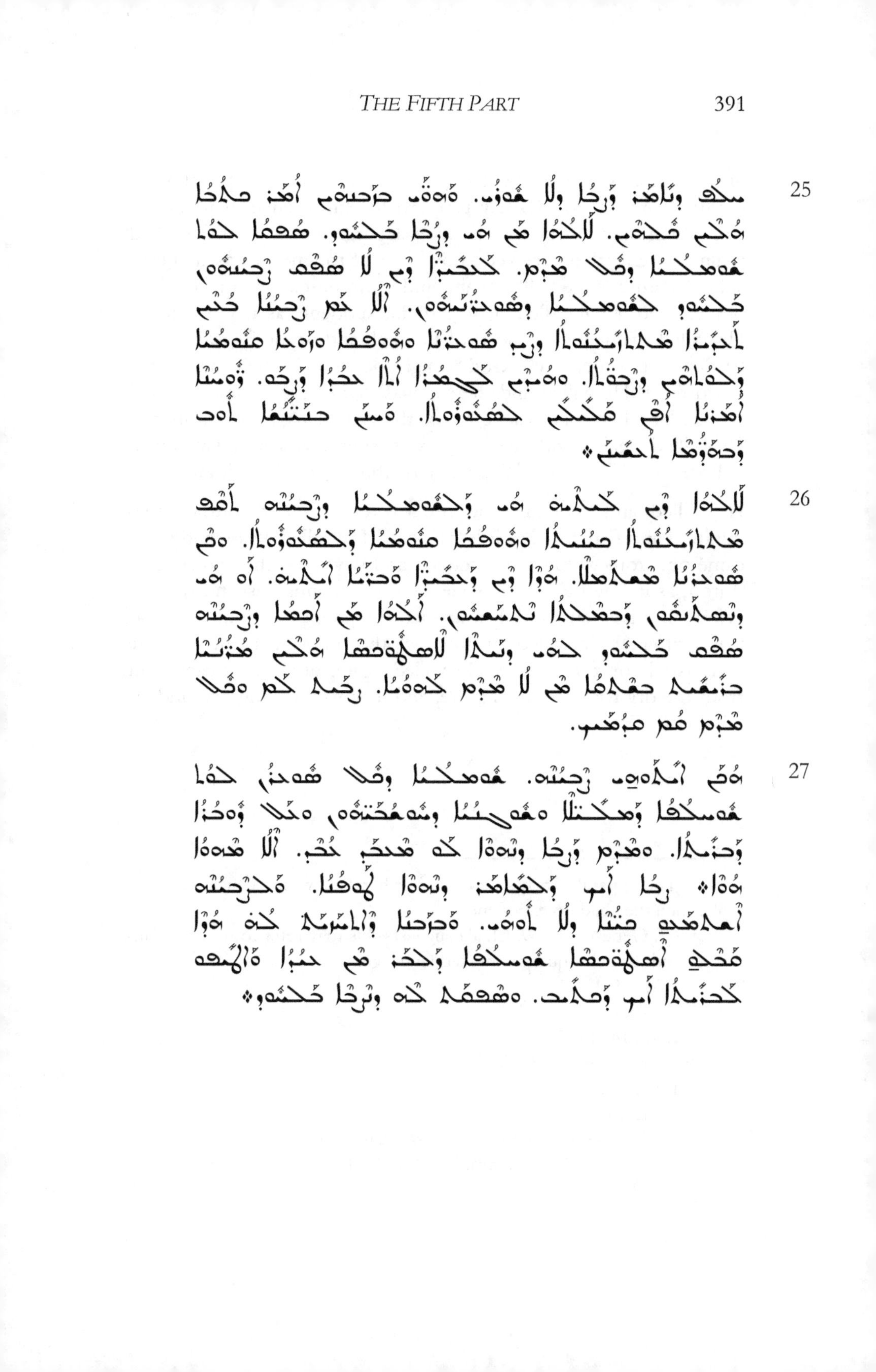

28 He willed again, and the tongues at the tower of Babel were confused. But suddenly they received the knowledge of tongues[45] <of which they had no experience> according as it is written. And again suddenly they received knowledge of tongues, translated outside of nature.[46] He willed again, and a fire descended on the Sodomites, and it enkindled against them, suddenly as it is written.[47] He willed again, and the heart of Pharaoh and of the Egyptians was hardened, in order that <God> might do signs in their midst, as it is written.[48] He willed and the sea was divided, and Israel crossed the dry land but <the sea> covered the Egyptians, as it is written.[49] He willed again, and the earth was split apart and swallowed <those> of the house of Dathan and Abiram, as it is written.[50]

29 He willed and suddenly the fire of their censors burned two hundred and fifty men, as it is written.[51] He willed again, and a fire came out from within the sanctuary and devoured the two sons of Aaron, as it is written.[52] He willed and the manna descended, marvelous nourishment, and it nourished the people without effort, as it is written.[53] He willed and their clothes grew with their stature and lasted for forty years. He willed again, and water came out from the dry rock, against nature, and it flowed on the dry land, as it is written.[54]

---

[45] The apparatus notes an omission here for which Chialà supplies: <of which they had no experience>.

[46] Cf. Genesis 11.1–9. Chialà suggests this may refer to the "one language" and the subsequent confused language.

[47] Ibid., 19.23–25.

[48] Cf. Exodus 7–14.

[49] Ibid., 14.15–31.

[50] Cf. Numbers 16.31–32.

[51] Ibid., 16.35.

[52] Cf. Leviticus 10.1–2.

[53] Cf. Exodus 16; Numbers 11.4–9; Deuteronomy 8.3, 16.

[54] Cf. Exodus 17.1–7; Numbers 20.1–11; Deuteronomy 8.15.

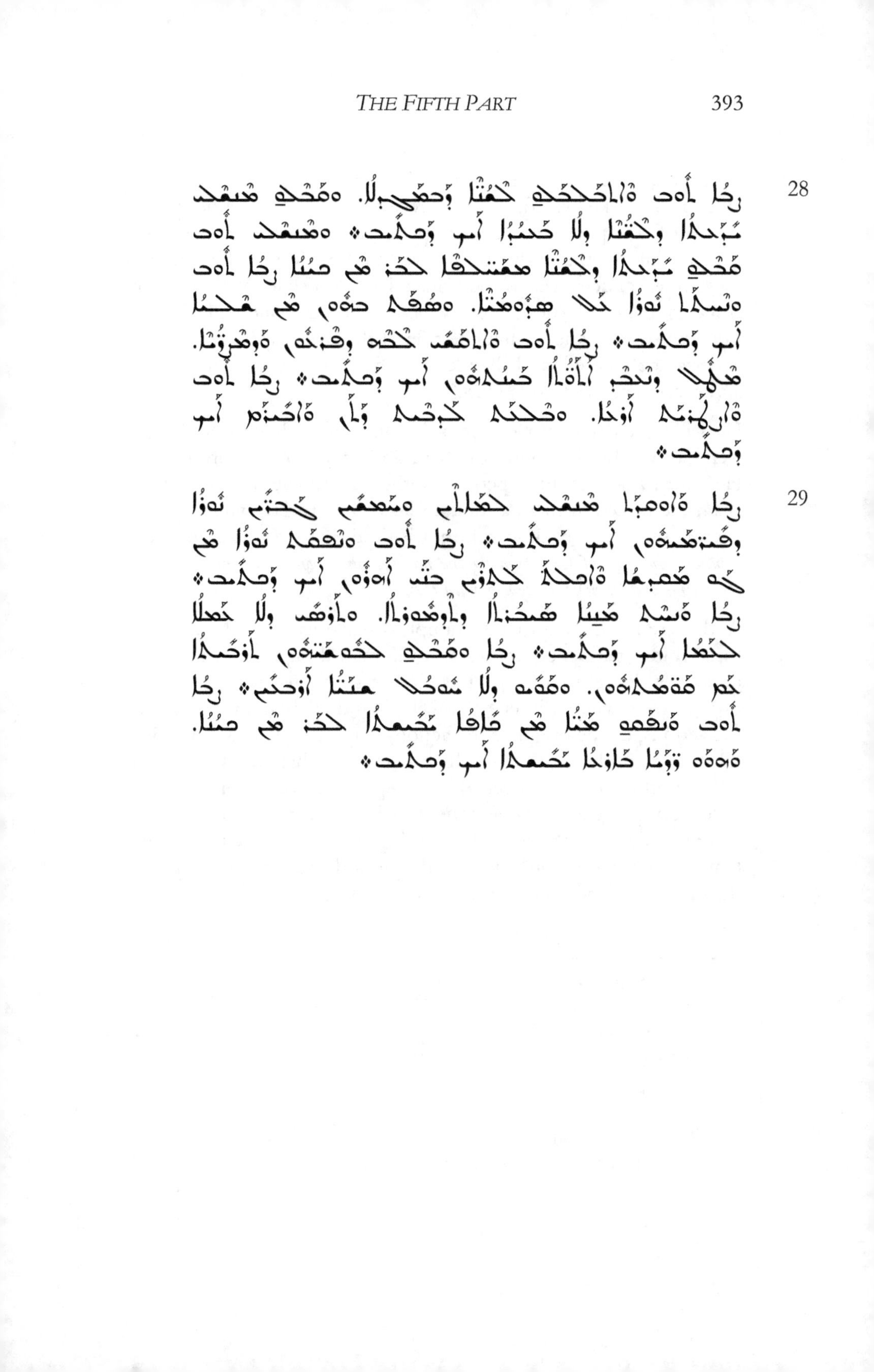

30 Again He willed, and serpents broke out among them, and they killed many.[55] He willed, and they received the power of healing by means of a serpent made of inanimate material, and the sight of it gave healing to the body and to the mind.[56] He willed again, and they were handed over to the Canaanites who slew many of them, showing their weakness.[57] He willed again, and suddenly Israel's side was strengthened, while the side of the adversary became weak and was conquered, and they learned by this that all is from Him and everything is towards Him.[58]

31 He willed, and the fear of them fell on famous heroes, and these were shaken by the sound of them and they knelt before them.[59] He willed again, and the peoples gathered and captured them; but again He placed in them a thought according to His will, and their captors sent them back with honor. <God> said: *I have delivered into captivity the sons of Israel among the nations and then I gathered them into their land and let none of them remain there.*[60]

32 And there are many other <examples> such as these. Not one of these things happened according to human thought, alas these actions were impelled and completed corresponding to the precept[61] of the divine will. <Either> the will of God adapts to the origin of the actions, or the origin of the actions is by the will of God. If it is the first case, therefore that which is ready to happen, God willed it, but nothing that God willed is a preparation for actions in a planification of <concrete> actions. But if this last possibility would be unseemly to be thought of regarding God, therefore it is known that the other <option> is true, that it is divine precept[62] guiding the impulse of the actions in those doing them.

---

[55] Cf. Numbers 21.6.
[56] Cf. Numbers 21.9.
[57] Cf. Numbers 14.44–45.
[58] Exodus 17.11.
[59] Cf. Joshua 10.1–2.
[60] Ezekiel 39.28.
[61] Precept (*thômâ*).
[62] Divine precept (*thômâ alâhâyâ*).

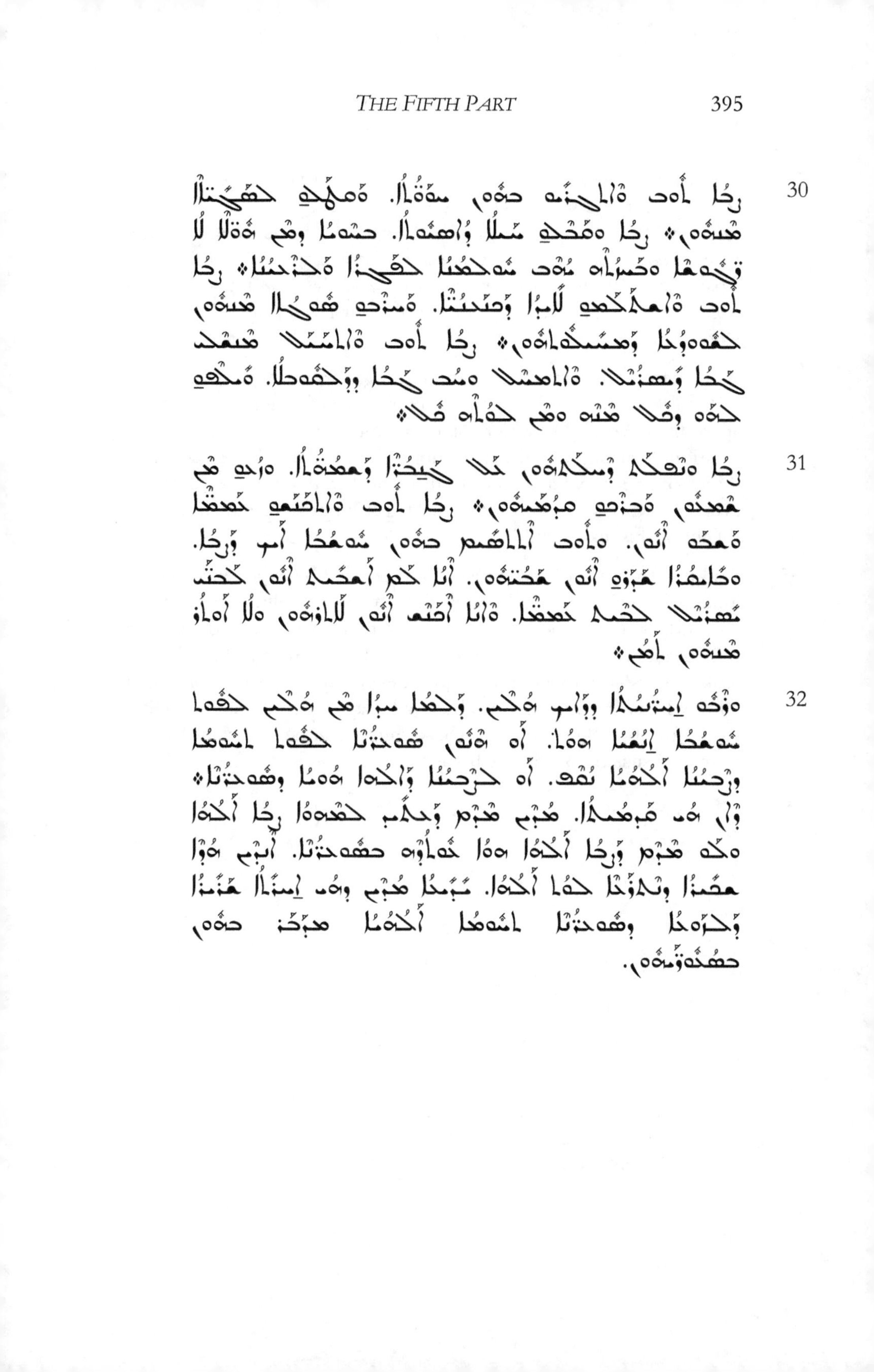

33 It is said: *I command says the Lord, and they will return and fight* against you.[63] And there where <it says>: *You have feared this or that, and I will make this or that to come upon you.*[64] And the <passage>: *Do not fear them because I am with you and no one is able to do you harm.*[65] And the <passage>: *I begin to place the fear of you and the terror of you on all the peoples who are under heaven;*[66] but for the rest I will not add anymore <now>.

34 Who then is childish of heart and lacking in knowledge about all of this, so as to say that the distress or the benefits come to humans apart from God? Or which of even only one of the motions of creation is lacking in <divine> support? Not that I have said these things of myself, what a childish thought! I think, however, that not even one who is very insolent is willing to oppose or remain doubtful about this, like a child.

35 And this from well-known testimony, learned by experience and by inquiry, showing clearly how all these various realities are verified by God: that by God our being is <either> preserved or handed over to all evils. <Only> then may something which afflicts dare to strike a person. However one cannot even say that being consigned <to evil> is from God, but above all may the care that <comes> from Him be acknowledged. These things will be sufficient for the useful persuasion of those who ask.

---

[63] Jeremiah 34.22.
[64] Cf. Deuteronomy 28.60; Ezekiel 11.8.
[65] Acts 18.9–10.
[66] Deuteronomy 2.25.

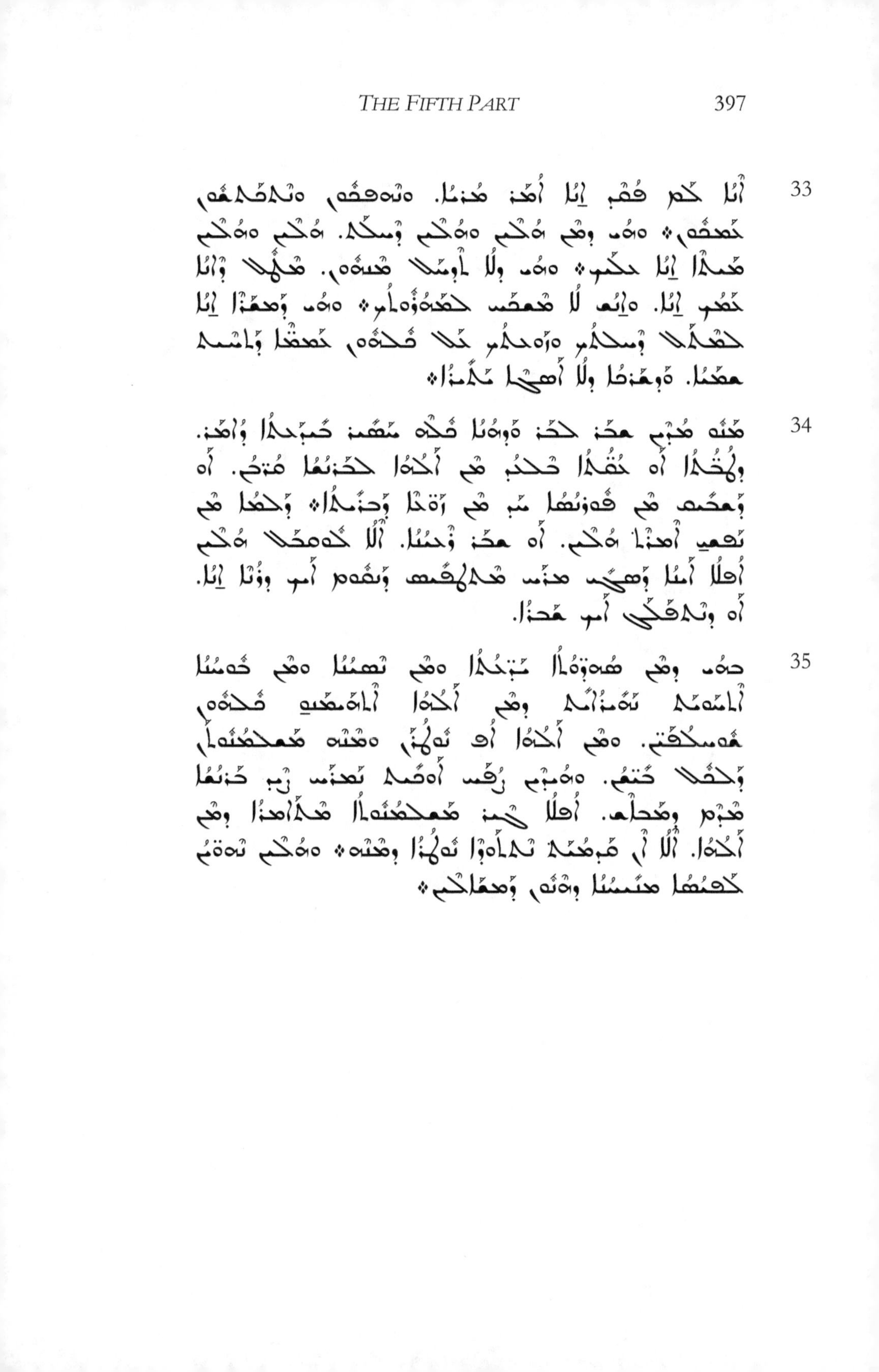

www.ingramcontent.com/pod-product-compliance
Lightning Source LLC
Chambersburg PA
CBHW071437300426
44114CB00013B/1476